STUDIES ON THE LEGEND OF
THE HOLY GRAIL.

STUDIES

ON THE

LEGEND OF THE HOLY GRAIL

WITH ESPECIAL REFERENCE TO THE HYPOTHESIS

OF ITS

CELTIC ORIGIN.

BY

ALFRED NUTT.

"Welchem Volke das Märchen (von Parzival's Jugendgeschichte) angehörte, welches die schriftliche oder mündliche Ueberlieferung mit der Gralsage in Verbindung brachte, ist schwer zu bestimmen, doch würde dasjenige Volk den meisten Anspruch darauf haben, bei welchem sich dies Märchen ausserhalb jenes Zusammenhangs nachweisen liesse."—K. SIMROCK.

"The Celtic hero who in the twelfth century became Perceval le Chercheur du basin . . . in the end became possessed of that sacred basin le Saint Graal, and the holy lance which, though Christian in the story, are the same as the talismans which appear so often in Gaelic tales . . . the glittering weapon which destroys, and the sacred medicinal cup which cures."—J. F. CAMPBELL.

"In all the Fenian stories mention is made of Fionn's healing cup . . . it is the same as the Holy Grail of course."—J. F. CAMPBELL.

A MARANDELL BOOK

COOPER SQUARE PUBLISHERS, INC.
NEW YORK
1965

Published 1965 by
Cooper Square Publishers, Inc.
59 Fourth Avenue, New York, N.Y. 10003

Library of Congress Catalog Card Number: 65-23219

PRINTED IN THE UNITED STATES OF AMERICA
by SENTRY PRESS, NEW YORK, N. Y. 10019

DEDICATION.

————◆————

To the Memory

OF

J. F. CAMPBELL,

FROM WHOM

I FIRST LEARNT TO LOVE CELTIC TRADITION.

CONTENTS.

CHAPTER V.

CHAPTER VI.

CHAPTER VII.

CHAPTER VIII.

CHAPTER IX.

CHAPTER X.

INTRODUCTION.

———◆———

THE present work is, as its title states, a collection of " Studies."
It does not profess to give an exhaustive or orderly account of
the Grail romance cycle ; it deals with particular aspects of the
legend, and makes no pretence of exhausting even these.

It may be urged that as this is the case the basis of the work
is too broad for the superstructure, and that there was no need to
give full summaries of the leading forms of the legend, or to discuss at such length their relation one to another, when it was only
intended to follow up one of the many problems which this romance
cycle presents.   Had there existed any work in English which did
in any measure what the writer has here attempted to do, he would
only too gladly have given more space and more time to the
elaboration of the special subject of these studies.   But the only
work of the kind is in German, *Birch-Hirschfeld's Die Gralsage*.
Many interested in the Arthurian romances do not know German ;
and some who profess an interest in them, and who do know
Germàn, are not, to judge by their writings, acquainted with Birch-
Hirschfeld's work.   It seemed worth while, therefore, to present
the facts about the cycle with greater fulness than would have
been necessary had those facts been generally accessible.   The
writer felt, too, that whatever judgment might be passed upon
his own speculations, his statements of fact might give his book
some value in the eyes of students.   He also wished to give all who
felt an interest in the line of investigation he opened up the
opportunity of pursuing it further, or the means of checking his
assertions and conjectures.

The writer has taken his texts as he found them.   He has

studied the subject matter of the romances, not the words in which they have been handed down. Those who seek for philological disquisitions are, therefore, warned that they will find nothing to interest them; and those scholars who are well acquainted with the printed texts, but who are on the search for fresh MS. evidence, must not look here for such. On the other hand, as the printed texts are for the most of such rarity and price as to be practically inaccessible to anyone not within reach of a large library, the writer trusts that his abstract of them will be welcome to many. He has striven to take note of all works of real value bearing upon the subject. He endeavoured, though unsuccessfully, to obtain a copy of M. Gaston Paris' account of the Arthurian romances which, though it has been for some months in print, is not yet published.

The writer has done his best to separate the certain from the conjectural. Like M. Renan, in a similar case, he begs the reader to supply the " perhaps " and the " possibly's " that may sometimes have dropt out. The whole subject is fraught with difficulty, and there are special reasons why all results must for some time to come be looked upon as conjectural. These are glanced at here and there in the course of these studies, but it may be well to put them together in this place. Firstly, whatever opinions be held as to which are the older forms of the legend, it is certain that in no one case do we possess a primary form. All the versions that have come down to us presuppose, even where they do not actually testify to, a model. Two of the forms which there is substantial agreement in reckoning among the oldest, the poems of Chrestien de Troyes and Robert de Borron, were never finished by the authors; sequels exist to both, of a later date and obviously affected by other forms of the legend. A reconstruction of the original story is under these circumstances a task of great uncertainty. So much for the difficulty inherent in the nature of the evidence, a difficulty which it is to be feared will always beset the student of this literature, as no new texts are likely to be found. Secondly, this evidence, such as it is, is not accessible in a form of which the most can be made. The most important member of the group, the Conte du Graal, only exists in one text, and that from a late and poor MS. It is certain that a critical edition, based upon a survey of the entire MS. evidence, will throw great light upon all the questions here treated of. The Mabinogi of Peredur has not yet been critically edited, nor have the MSS. of the other romances yielded up all that can be learnt from them. Thirdly, whatever opinion be held respecting the connection of the North French romances and Celtic tradition, connection of some kind must be admitted. Now the study of Celtic tradition is only beginning to be placed upon a firm basis, and the stores of Celtic myth and legend are only beginning to be thrown open to the non-Celtic scholar. Were there in existence a Celtic parallel to Grimm's great work on German Mythology, the views for which the writer contends would have been, in all likelihood, admitted ere now, and there would have been no necessity for this work at all.

Whilst some of the reasons which render the study of the Grail legends so fascinating, because so problematic, will probably always remain in force, others will vanish before the increase of know-ledge. When the diplomatic evidence is accessible in a trustworthy form; when the romances have received all the light that can be shed upon them from Celtic history, philology, and mythology, the future student will have a comparatively easy task. One of the writer's chief objects has been to excite an interest in these romances among those who are able to examine the Celtic elements in them far more efficiently than he could do. Welsh philologists can do much to explain the *Onomasticon Arthurianum*; Cymric history generally may elucidate the subject matter. But as a whole Welsh literature is late, meagre, and has kept little that is archaic. The study of Irish promises far better results. Of all the races of modern Europe the Irish have the most considerable and the most archaic mass of pre-Christian traditions. By the side of their heroic traditional literature that of Cymry or Teuton (High and Low), or Slav is recent, scanty, and unoriginal.

A few words must be said in defence of the free use made of conjecture in the course of these studies. This is well nigh unavoidable from the way in which the texts we have to deal with have come down to us. What M. Renan has said about the Hebrew historical scriptures is excellently exemplified in the Grail

romances. There was no fixed text, no definite or rounded
sequence of incidents, of which scribes respected the integrity.
On the contrary, each successive transcriber was only anxious
to add some fresh adventure to the interminable tale, and those
MSS. were most thought of which contained the greatest number
of lines. The earlier MSS. have, therefore, almost entirely disappeared, and we are dealing with works which we know to have
been composed in the twelfth century, but of which we have only
thirteenth or fourteenth century transcripts. Inconsistencies in
the conduct of the story are the inevitable consequence in most
cases, but sometimes the latest arranger had an eye for unity
of effect, and attained this by the simple process of altering the
old account so as to make it fit with the new. In dealing with the
text of an *individual* author, whether ancient or modern, it would
be in the last degree uncritical to explain difficulties by such
hypotheses as the loss of an earlier draft, or the foisting into the
work of later and incongruous incidents and conceptions. Not so in
the case of the romances; this method of explanation is natural
and legitimate, but none the less is it largely conjectural.

The writer may be blamed for not having presented his subject
in a more engaging and more lucid form. He would plead in
excuse the circumstances under which his work has been carried
on. When the only hours of study are those which remain after
the claims, neither few nor light, of business and other duties
have been met, it is hard to give an appearance of unity to a
number of minute detail studies, and to weld them together into
one harmonious whole. The fact that the work has been written,
and printed, at considerable intervals of time may, it is hoped, be
accepted as some excuse for inconsistency in the terminology.

The writer has many acknowledgments to make. First and
chief to Dr. Birch-Hirschfeld, but for whose labours, covering well
nigh the whole field of the Grail cycle, he would not have been
able to take in hand his work at all; then to Dr. Furnivall, to
whose enthusiasm and spirit the publication of some of the most
important texts are due. In these two cases the writer acknowledges his gratitude with the more readiness that he has felt
compelled to come to an opposite conclusion from that arrived at

by Dr. Birch-Hirschfeld respecting the genesis and growth of the legend, and because he has had to differ from Dr. Furnivall's estimate of the moral value of the Galahad romances. To M. Hucher, to Mons. Ch. Potvin, the editor, single-handed, of the Conte du Graal, to M. d'Arbois de Jubainville, to Professor Ernst Martin, to the veteran San-Marte, to Herr Otto Küpp, and to Herr Paul Steinbach, these studies owe much. Professor Rhys' Hibbert Lectures came into the writer's hands as he was preparing the latter portion of the book for the press ; they were of great service to him, and he was especially gratified to find opinions at which he had arrived confirmed on altogether independent grounds by Professor Rhys' high authority. The writer is also indebted to him, to Mr. H. L. D. Ward, of the British Museum, and to his friend Mr. Egerton Phillimore for help given while the sheets were passing through the press. Lastly, the writer desires to pay an especial tribute of gratitude and respect to that admirable scholar, J. F. Campbell. Of all the masters in folk-lore, Jacob Grimm not excepted, none had a keener eye or surer, more instinctively right judgment.

Although the writer admits, nay, insists upon the conjectural character of his results, he believes he is on the right track, and that if the Grail romances be worked out from any other point of view than the one here taken, the same goal will be reached. It should be said that some of the conclusions, which he can claim as his own by right of first mention, were stated by him in a paper he read before the Folk-Lore Society in 1880 (afterwards reprinted, Celtic Magazine, 1887, August–October) ; and in a paper he read before the Honourable Society of Cymmrodorion, in 1884.

These studies have been a delight and a solace to the writer; had it been otherwise, he would still feel himself amply repaid for his work by the thought that he had made a contribution, however slight, to the criticism of the Legend of the Holy Grail.

ERRATA.

Page 22, line 12, *for* Corbièrc *read* Corbière.

,,   25, line 37, *insert* Passion *before* Week.

,,   30, 7 lines from bottom, *for* Avallon *read* Avalon.

,,   85, line 24, *for* Percival *read* Perceval.

,,   86, line 12, *for* Percival *read* Perceval.

,,   90, 5 lines from bottom, *for* Pelleur *read* Pelleans.

,, 102, line 22 *for* seems *read* seem.

,, 120, line 3, *for* 1180 *read* 1189.

,, 124, line 29, *for* Bron *read* Brons.

,, 156, line 11, *insert* comma *after* specially.

,, 159, line 11, *for* Henessey *read* Hennessy.

,, 163, note, *i.e., for* Graal *read* Gaal.

,, 183, line 23, *insert* comma *after* more.

,, 188, line 5, *for* euphemerised *read* euhemerised.

,, 188, line 5, *for* invasion *read* invasions.

,, 188, line 17, *for* mystic *read* mythic.

,, 189, line 1, *for* LXXVII *read* LXXXII.

,, 197, note, *for* Carl the Great *read* Karl the Great.

,, 200, line 12, *insert* comma *after* plight; *dele* comma *after* love

,, 201, 1 line from bottom, *insert* late *before* mediæval.

,, 204, note, *for* Percival *read* Perceval.

,, 217, line 23, *for* mystic *read* mythic.

STUDIES ON THE LEGEND OF THE HOLY GRAIL.

CHAPTER I.

Description of the leading forms of the Romance : Conte del Graal—
Joseph d'Arimathie—Didot-Perceval—Queste del Saint Graal—Grand
Saint Graal—Parzival—Perceval le Gallois—Mabinogi of Peredur—
Sir Perceval—Diu Crône—Information respecting date and authorship
of these works in the MSS.

THE following are the forms in which the Legend of the Holy
Grail has come down to us :—

A.—**Le Conte del Graal,** a poem of over 60,000 verses, the
major part of which (45,379 verses) was printed for the first time by
Potvin : Le Conte del Graal, six volumes, 8vo. (vols. ii.-vi. containing our poem), Mons, 1866-71, from a MS. preserved in the Mons
Library.*   The portion of the poem which is not printed in full is
summarised by Potvin in the sixth volume of his edition.   The
poem, so far as at present known, is the work of four men :

> A I. Chrestien de Troyes, who carried the work down to
> verse 10,601.
> A II. Gautier de Doulens, who continued it to verse 34,934.
> A III. Manessier, who finished it in 45,379 verses.
> A IV. Gerbert, to whom are due over 15,000 verses, mostly
> found interpolated between Gautier de Doulens and
> Manessier.

---

* Fully described by Potvin, VI, lxix, etc.

A MS. preserved in the Library of Montpellier* differs in important respects from the Mons one as far as Gautier de Doulens and Manessier are concerned. It intercalates 228 verses between verses 20,294 and 20,296 of the Mons MS., and gives a different redaction of verses 34,996–35,128 in agreement with the aforesaid intercalation. It likewise mentions two visits of Gawain to the Grail Castle. The intercalation in Gautier may be called A II*a*, and the variant in Manessier A III*a*.

B.—**Joseph d'Arimathie, Merlin,** exists in two forms: (1) a fragmentary metrical version entitled in the sole existing MS. (Bibliothèque Nationale, No. 20,047. Fonds St. Germain, No. 1,987) Li R(o)manz de l'est (o)ire dou Graal, and consisting of 4,018 verses, 3,514 for the Joseph, the remainder, for about one-fifth of the Merlin. First printed by Francisque Michel: Le Roman du St. Graal. Bordeaux, 1841. Secondly by Furnivall: Seynt Graal or the Sank Ryal. Printed for the Roxburghe Club, two volumes, 4to., London, 1861–63, where it is found in an appendix at the end of vol i. (2) A prose version of which several MSS. exist, all of which are fully described by E. Hucher: Le Saint-Graal, ou le Joseph d'Arimathie, three volumes, 12mo., Le Mans, 1875–78, vol. i., pp. 1–28. The chief are: the Cangé MS. (*circa* 1250) of which Hucher prints the Joseph, vol. i., pp. 209–276, and the Didot MS., written in 1301, of which Hucher prints the Joseph, vol. i., pp. 277–333. Hucher likewise gives, vol. i., pp. 335–365, variants from the Huth MS. (*circa* 1280).

These different versions may be numbered as follows:—

> B I. The metrical version, which I shall always quote as Metr. Jos., from Furnivall's edition.
>
> B II. The prose versions: B II*a*, Cangé Jos.; B II*b*, Didot Jos.; B II*c*, Huth Jos., all quoted from Hucher, vol. i.

C.--**Perceval,** prose romance found in the already-mentioned Didot MS. at the end of the Merlin, printed by Hucher, vol. i., pp. 415–505, from which it will be quoted as Didot-Perceval.

D.—**Queste del Saint Graal,** prose romance commonly found in the MSS. in combination with Lancelot and the Mort Artur.

---

* Potvin, VI, lxxv, etc.

Edited by Furnivall: La Queste del St. Graal. Printed for the Roxburghe Club, 4to., London, 1864. The introduction contains a full account of the existing MSS. A different redaction from that of any of the known French MSS. is preserved in a Welsh translation, printed, with a modern English version by the editor, from a fifteenth century Hengwrt MS., by the Rev. Robert Williams: Y Seint Graal, London, 8vo., 1876. I shall quote—

D I. Queste, from Furnivall's edition.

D II. Welsh Quest, from Williams' edition.

E.—The so-called **Grand Saint Graal,** prose romance found in the MSS., both preceding the Merlin and the Queste, and preceding the Queste and the Mort Artur. Printed by Furnivall from Cambridge and Brit. Mus. MSS., together with a metrical English adaptation by Henry Lonelich, of about the time of Henry the VIth, in the already-mentioned Seynt Graal; and by Hucher, vols. ii. and iii., from a Le Mans MS.; will be quoted as Grand St. Graal, from Furnivall's edition.

F.—**Parzival,** by Wolfram von Eschenbach, German metrical romance, critically edited from the MSS. by Karl Lachmann, Wolfram von Eschenbach, Vierte Ausgabe, 8vo., Berlin, 1879, from which it will be quoted as Wolfram.

G.—**Perceval le Gallois,** prose romance, first printed by Potvin, vol. i. of his Conte del Graal, from a Mons MS., with variants from a fragmentary Berne MS. (as to both of which see pp. 353, etc.). A Welsh translation, with modern English version by the editor, made from a MS. closely allied to the Berne fragments, and representing a superior text to that printed by Potvin, in Williams' already-mentioned Y Seint Graal.

Besides these works there exist two versions of the Perceval legend in which the Holy Grail, as such, does not appear. These are:—

H.—**The Mabinogi of Peredur, the son of Evrawc,** Welsh prose romance found in the Red Book of Hergest, a MS. of the end of the fourteenth century, and in MSS. a hundred years older. I shall quote it as Peredur, from Lady Guest's English translation of the Mabinogion, 8vo., London, 1877.

I.—**Sir Perceval of Galles,** English metrical romance, printed for the first time from the Thornton MS., of *circa* 1440, by Halliwell: The Thornton Romances, printed for the Camden Society, small 4to., London, 1884; from which I shall quote it as Sir Perceval.

Finally there exists an independent German version of certain adventures, the hero of which in the Conte du Graal, in Wolfram, and in the Mabinogi, is Gawain. This is—

K.—**Heinrich von dem Türlin.** Diu Crône. Edited by G. H. F. Scholl. Bibliothek des Litterarischen Vereins, vol. xxvii., Stuttgart, 1852.

The positive information which the different MSS. of the above mentioned works afford respecting their authors, date of composition, sources, etc., is as follows:—In the prologue to his poem, Chrestien (Potvin i., pp. 307–308) dedicates his work to " Li quens Felippes de Flandres," who as he states (verse 67), " li bailla le livre," which served him as model, and whom he praises at great length as surpassing Alexander. We know that Count Philip of Flanders took the cross in 1188, set out for the Holy Land in 1190, and died on the 1st of June, 1191, before Akkon.* As Chrestien says not a word about the crusading intentions of Philip, it may be inferred that he wrote his prologue before 1188, and began the poem in 1189 at the latest. Gautier de Doulens (probably of that ilk, in Picardy, some miles from Amiens)† has only left his name, verse 33,755, Gautiers de Dons qui l'estore, etc. Manessier the next continuator has been more explicit; he describes himself as completing the work at the command of . . .

> Jehanne la Comtesse
> Qu'est de Flandre dame et mestresse.
> (Potvin, vi., p. 157.)

This Joan, daughter of Baldwin the VIth, ruled Flanders *alone* during the imprisonment of her husband after the battle of Bouvines (1214–1227), and Manessier's words can only apply to her during this period, so that his continuation must have been

---

* Birch-Hirschfeld: Die Sage vom Gral, 8vo., Leipzig, 1877, p. 81.
† Birch-Hirschfeld, p. 89.

written between 1214–1227.* The third continuator, Gerbers, only mentions his name (Potvin, vi., p. 212).

The author of version B, names himself, B 1, verse 3,461, Messires Roberz de Beron; verses 3,488–94 state that no mortal man had told the story, until he had it from

> Mon seigneur Gautier en peis
> Qui de Mont Belyal estoit.

Verse 3,155 gives the name somewhat differently, Meistres Robers dist de Bouron. The prose versions follow the poem with additions, thus Cangé Jos. (p. 275); Messires Roberz de Borron lou restrait à mon seigneur Gautier, lou preu conte de Mobéliart.

Walter of Montbeliard, brother to Count Richard of Montbeliard, went to the Holy Land in 1199, became Constable of Jerusalem, Regent of Cyprus, and died in 1212. The date of his birth is uncertain, but as his elder brother died in 1137, Walter could hardly have been born before 1150. His father, Amadeus, died in 1183, in which year he received the countship of Montfaucon. It may only have been after he thus became independent that Robert entered his service. In any case Robert could not have spoken of him as "mon seigneur," before 1170. That year may, therefore, be taken as a *terminus a quo*, and the year 1212 as a *terminus ad quem* for dating these versions.

The Grand St. Graal is likewise ascribed in the MSS. to Robert de Borron, and it is further stated that he translated from Latin into French—Et ensi le temoigne me sires robiers de borron qui a translatee de latin en franchois cheste estoire (ii. p. 78).

The Queste ascribed in the MSS. to Walter Mapes, is said to have been compiled by him for the love of his lord, King Henry—maistre Gautiers Map les extrait pour l'amor del roy Henri son seignor, qui fist l'estore translater du latin en francois†—Walter Mapes, born before 1143 (he presided at the assizes of Gloucester in 1173), died in 1210. If we may believe the MSS., the Queste

---

* Birch-Hirschfeld, p. 110.

† Birch-Hirschfeld, p. 232, quoting the colophon of a Paris MS., after Paulin Paris, Cat. des MSS. français, vol. ii, pp. 361, etc.

would probably fall within the last twenty-five years of the twelfth century.

The author of Perceval le Gallois describes himself (Potvin, i., 348) as writing the book for the "Seignor de Neele," whose Christian name, "Johan," is given four lines lower down, at the command of the "Seingnor de Cambresis," *i.e.*, the Bishop of Cambray. This John of Nesle is probably the one who in the year 1225 sold the lordship of Bruges to Countess Joan of Flanders.*

Wolfram von Eschenbach, of that ilk, in North Bavaria, born in the last thirty years of the twelfth century, died about 1220. He knew Chrestien's poem well, and repeatedly refers to it, but with great contempt, as being the wrong version of the story, whereas he holds the true version from Kyot, the singer, a "Provenzal," who found the tale of Parzival written in heathen tongue at Dôlet (Toledo), by Flegetanis, a heathen who first taught concerning the Grail, put it into French, and after searching the chronicles of Britain, France, and Ireland in vain, at length found information in the chronicles of Anjou (pp. 202 and 219).

Nothing is stated in the works themselves respecting the authors of the Mabinogi and the Thornton Sir Perceval.

Heinrich von dem Türlin frequently quotes Chrestien as his authority, *e.g.*, verses 16,941, 23,046, 23,982.

If these various statements are to be accepted, it follows that in the course of fifty years (1170–1220) a great body of romance came into existence, partly in France, Chrestien, his continuators, and Robert de Borron; partly in England, Walter Mapes; and partly in Germany, Wolfram von Eschenbach, and Heinrich von dem Türlin. Of this body of romance only a portion has come down to us, the work of Kyot and the Latin originals of the Queste and the Grand St. Graal having disappeared. Furthermore, it is only possible to date with any accuracy three or four of the works, viz., Chrestien, Manessier, Wolfram (whose poem falls certainly within the first ten years of the thirteenth century), though it may also be taken as certain that R. de Borron wrote after 1170, and the anonymous author of Perceval le Gallois before 1225. Of the

---

* Birch-Hirschfeld, p. 143.

dated works Chrestien's is the oldest, 1188–90, and it postulates the existence of previous versions.

The object of the present investigation being to determine, as far as possible, the age and relationship to one another of the different versions which have come down to us, to exhibit the oldest form of the story as we have it, and to connect it with Celtic traditional belief and literature, it will be well, before proceeding to further discuss the various points left doubtful by the evidence gathered from the MSS., to give clear and detailed summaries of the most important versions.

CHAPTER II.

The Conte du Graal.—PSEUDO-CHRESTIEN.*—The story tells of the "Graal," whose mysteries, if Master Blihis lie not, none may reveal ; it falls into seven parts, and shows how the rich land of Logres was destroyed. (1) In the wells and springs of that land harboured damsels who fed the wayfarer with meat and pasties and bread. But King Amangons did wrong to one and carried off her golden cup, so that never more came damsels out of the springs to comfort the wanderer. And the men of King Amangons followed his evil example. Thereafter the springs dried up, and the grass withered, and the land became waste, and no more might be found the court of the Rich Fisher, which had filled the land with plenty and splendour. (2) The Knights of the Table Round, learning the ill done to the damsels, set forth to protect them ; they found them not, but fair damsels wandering in the woods, each with her knight ; with the latter they strove, and when they overcame them sent them to Arthur. Thus came Blihos Bliheris to Arthur's court conquered by Gauvain ; he knew goodly tales and he told how the wandering damsels were sprung from those ravished by King Amangons. So long would they wander till God gave them to find the court, whence joy and splendour would come to the land. (3) Arthur's knights resolved to seek the court of the Rich Fisher —much knew he of black art, more than an hundred times changed he his semblance, that no man seeing him again recognised him. Gauvain found it, and had great joy therefrom ; but before him a young knight, small of age, but none bolder of courage—Percevaus li Galois was he—he asked whereto the Grail served, but nought of the lance why it dripped blood, nor of the sword one half of which was away whilst the other lay in the bier. But he asked surely concerning the rich cross of silver. Now in the

---

* This prologue is certainly not Chrestien's work ; but there is no reason to doubt that it embodies a genuine tradition, and affords valuable hints for a reconstruction of the original form of the story. *Cf*. Otto Küpp in Zeitschrift für deutsche Philologie, vo.l xvii., No. 1.

room three times there arose such great sorrow that no man who heard it, so bold he might be but feared. Afterwards the room filled and the king came in, full richly dressed, so that he might hardly be known of them that had seen him the day before, fishing. And when all were sat down the Grail came in, and without serjeant nor seneschal served all present, and 'twas wonder what food it gave them. And then came the great marvel which has not its like. But Perceval will tell of this, so I must say no more ; it is a great shame to tell beforehand what is in a good tale. When the good knight shall come who found the court three times you shall hear me tell of Grail and lance, and of him who lay in the bier, of the sword, of the grief and swooning of all beholders. (4) Now the court was found seven times, and each time shall have a fresh tale :—

The seventh (the most pleasing) tells of the lance wherewith Longis pierced the side of the King of holy Majesty ;
The sixth of warlike feats ;
The fifth of the anger and loss of Huden ;
The fourth of heaven, for he was no coward, the knight Mors del Calan, who first came to Glamorgan ;
The third of the hawk whereof Castrars had such fear—Pecorins, the son of Amangons, bore all his days the wound on his forehead ;
The second has not yet been told ; it tells of the great sorrows Lancelot of the Lake had there where he lost his virtue ;
And the last is the adventure of the shield, never a better one was there.

(5) After this adventure the land was repeopled ; court and grail were found ; the streams ran again ; the meadows were green, the forests thick and leafy ; so that all folk marvelled. But there came back a folk, the same that came out of the springs (save they were not cooks), a caitiff set, and built for their damsels the rich Maidens' Castel, and the Bridge Perillous, and Castel Orguellous, and warred against the Table Round. In the castle were 376, each sire of 20 knights. And not till after four years did Arthur overcome them and was there peace.

(Here beginneth the Story of the Grail.)

(6) There were in the land of Wales twelve knights, of whom Bliocadrans alone survived, so eager were they in seeking tournament and combats. After living for two years with his wife, childless, Bliocadrans set forth to a tournament given by the King of Wales and Cornwall against them of the Waste Fountain. At first successful, he is at length slain. A few days after his departure his wife has borne a son. When at length she learns her husband's death, she takes counsel with her chamberlain, and pretending a pilgrimage to St. Brandan, in Scotland, withdraws to the Waste Forest far removed from all men. Here she brings up her son, and though she allows him to hunt in the forest, warns him against men covered with iron—they are devils. He promises to follow her counsel, and thenceforth he goes into the forest alone.

The Conte du Graal.—(*a*) CHRESTIEN.—(1) When as trees and meadows deck themselves with green, and birds sing, the son of the widow lady goes out into the wood. He meets five knights, and, as their weapons shine in the sun, takes them for angels, after having first thought them to be the devils his mother had warned him against. He prays to them as his mother has taught him. One of the knights asks if he has seen five knights and three maidens who had passed that way, but he can but reply with questions concerning the arms and trappings of the knights. He learns of Arthur the King who makes knights, and when he returns to his mother tells her he has beheld a more beautiful thing than God and His angels, knights namely, and he too will become one. In vain his mother tells him of his father's and his two elder brothers' fates, slain in battle. Nothing will serve, so the mother makes him a dress of coarse linen and leather, and before he leaves counsels him as follows : If dame or damsel seek his aid he is to give it, he is to do naught displeasing to them, but to kiss the maiden who is willing, and to take ring and girdle of her if he can ; to go for long with no fellow-traveller whose name he knows not, to speak with and consort with worthy men, to pray to our Lord when he comes to church or convent. She then tells him of Jesus Christ, the Holy Prophet. He departs clad and armed in Welsh fashion, and his mother swoons as though dead. (2) Perceval comes to a tent in the wood, and, taking it for a convent, goes in and finds sleeping on a bed a damsel, whom the neighing of his horse wakes. In pursuance of his mother's counsel he kisses her more than twenty times, takes her ring from her, and eats and drinks of her provisions. Thereafter he rides forth, and her lover returning and hearing what has taken place, swears to avenge himself upon the intruder, and until such time the damsel, whose tale he disbelieves, is to follow him barefoot and not to change her raiment. (3) Perceval learns the way to Carduel from a charcoal-burner ; arrived there, he sees a knight coming forth from the castle and bearing a golden cup in his hand, clad in red armour, who complains of Arthur as having robbed him of his land. Perceval rides into the castle hall and finds the court at meat. Arthur, lost in thought, pays no attention to the first two salutations of Perceval, who then turns his horse to depart, and in so doing knocks off the King's hat. Arthur then tells him how the Red Knight has carried off his cup, spilling its contents over the Queen. Perceval cares not a rap for all this, but asks to be made knight, whereat all laugh. Perceval insists, and claims the Red Knight's armour. Kex bids him fetch them, whereat the King is displeased. Perceval greets a damsel, who laughs and foretells he shall be the best knight in the world. For this saying Kex strikes her, and kicks into the fire a fool who had been wont to repeat that the damsel would not laugh till she beheld the best of knights. (4) Perceval tarries no longer, but follows the Red Knight, and bids him give up his arms and armour. They fight, and Perceval slays his adversary with a cast of his dart. Yonès, who has followed him, finds him put to it to remove the knight's armour—he will burn him out of it if need be—and shows him how to disarm the dead man and to arm himself. Perceval then mounts the knight's steed and rides off, leaving the cup to Yonés to be given to the King, with this message: he, Perceval, would come back to avenge the damsel of the blow Kex struck her. (5) Perceval comes to a castle, in front of which he finds an old knight, to whom he relates what has befallen him, and of whom he asks counsel as his mother bade him. The knight, Gonemans of Gelbort, takes him into his castle, teaches him the use of arms, and all knightly practices. In especial he is to avoid over-readiness in speaking and in asking questions, and to give over his habit of always quoting his mother's counsels. He then dubs him knight, and sends him forth to return to his mother. (6) After a day's journey Perceval comes to a town defended by a castle, and, being allowed entrance therein, finds all waste and deserted, even the very convents. The lady of the castle, a damsel of surpassing beauty, welcomes him and bids him to table. Mindful of Gonemans' counsels he remains silent, and she must speak to him first. She turns out to be Gonemans' niece. At night the young stranger is shown to his chamber, but the damsel cannot sleep for thought. Weeping she comes to Perceval's bedside, and in reply to his wondering questions tells him how the forces of King Clamadex encompass the castle, and how that on the morrow she must yield, but rather than be Clamadex's she will slay herself. He promises to help her, and bids her to him in the bed, which she does, and they pass the night in each other's arms, mouth to mouth. On the morrow he begs for her love in return for his promised aid, which she half refuses, the more to urge him on. He fights with and overcomes Aguigrenons, Clamadex's marshal, and sends him to Arthur's court. Clamadex hearing of this tries afresh to starve out the castle, but a storm luckily throws a passing ship ashore, and thereby reprovisions the besieged ones. Clamadex then challenges Perceval, is overcome, and sent to Arthur's court, where he arrives shortly after his marshal. They relate wonders concerning the Red Knight, and the King is more than ever displeased with Kex for having offended such a valiant warrior. After remaining for a while with Blanchefleur, Perceval takes leave of her, as he longs to see his mother again. (7) He comes to a river, upon which is a boat, and therein two men fishing. One of them, in reply to his questions, directs him for a night's shelter to his own castle hard by. Perceval starts for it, and at first unable to find it reproaches the fisher. Suddenly he perceives the castle before him, enters therein, is disarmed, clad in a scarlet mantle, and led into a great hall. Therein is a couch upon which lies an old man; near him is a fire, around which some four hundred men are sitting. Perceval tells his host he had come from Biau-Repaire. A squire enters, bearing a sword, and on it is written that it will never break save in one peril, and that known only to the maker of it. 'Tis a present from the host's niece to be bestowed where it will be well employed. The host gives it to Perceval, "to whom it was adjudged and destined." Hereupon enters another squire, bearing in his hand a lance, from the head of which a drop of blood runs down on the squire's hand. Perceval would have asked concerning this wonder, but he

minds him of Gonemans' counsel not to speak or inquire too much. Two
more squires enter, holding each a ten-branched candlestick, and with them
a damsel, a " graal " in her hands. The graal shines so that it puts out the
light of the candles as the sun does that of the stars. Thereafter follows
a damsel holding a (silver) plate. All defile past between the fire and the
couch, but Perceval does not venture to ask wherefore the graal is used.
Supper follows, and the graal is again brought, and Perceval, knowing not
its use, had fain asked, but always refrains when he thinks of Gonemans,
and finally puts off his questions till the morrow. After supper the guest
is led to his chamber, and on the morrow, awakening, finds the castle
deserted. No one answers his calls. Issuing forth he finds his horse
saddled and the drawbridge down. Thinking to find the castle dwellers
in the forest he rides forth, but the drawbridge closes so suddenly behind
him that had not the horse leapt quickly forward it had gone hard with steed
and rider. In vain Perceval calls : none answer. (8) He pricks on and
comes to an oak, beneath which sits a maid holding a dead knight in her
arms and lamenting over him. She asks him where he has passed the
night, and on learning it tells him the fisher who had directed him to the
castle and his host were one and the same ; wounded by a spear thrust
through both thighs his only solace is in fishing, whence he is called the
Fisher King. She asks, had Perceval seen the bleeding lance, the graal, and
the silver dish ? had he asked their meaning ? No ; then what is his name ?
He does not know it, but she guesses it : Perceval le Gallois ; but it should
be Perceval the Caitiff, for had he asked concerning what he saw, the good
king would have been made whole again, and great good have sprung
therefrom. He has also a heavy sin on his conscience in that his mother
died of grief when he left her. She herself is his cousin. Perceval asks
concerning the dead knight, and learning it is her lover offers to revenge
her upon his slayer. In return she tells him about the sword, how it will
fly in pieces if he have not care of it, and how it may be made whole
again by dipping it in a lake, near which dwells its maker, the smith
Trebucet. (9) Perceval leaves his cousin and meets, riding on a wretched
horse, a scantily and shabbily clad woman of miserable appearance,
lamenting her hard fate and unjust treatment. She is the lady of the
tent whose ring Perceval had carried off. She bids him fly her husband,
the Orgellous de la Lande. The latter appears, challenges Perceval, but is
overcome by him, convinced of his wife's innocence, compelled to take her
into favour again, and both must go to Arthur's court, relate the whole
story, and renew Perceval's promise to the damsel whom Kex had struck,
to avenge her. Arthur, when he hears of the deeds of the young hero,
sets forth with his whole court to seek him. (10) Snow has fallen, and
a flock of wild geese, blinded by the snow, has had one of its number
wounded by a falcon. Three blood drops have fallen on the snow, and
Perceval beholding them falls into deep thought on the red and white in
his love's face. Arthur and his knights come up with him. Saigremors
sees him first, bids him come, and, when he answers no word, tilts against

him, but is overthrown. Kex then trys his luck, but is unhorsed so rudely that arm and leg are broken. Gauvain declares that love must be mastering the strange knight's thoughts, approaches him courteously, tells his own name and learns Perceval's, and brings the latter to Arthur, by whom he is received with all honour. Perceval then learns it is Kex he has overthrown, thus fulfilling his promise to the damsel whom Kex had smitten, and whose knight he offers himself to be. (11) Perceval returns on the morrow with the court to Carlion, and the next day at noon there comes riding on a yellow mule a damsel more hideous than could be pictured outside hell. She curses Perceval for having omitted to ask concerning the lance and graal ; had he done so the King would have been healed of his wound and ruled his land in peace ; now maidens will be put to shame, orphans and widows made, and many knights slain. Turning to the King she tells of the adventures to be achieved at the Castel Orgellous, where dwell five hundred and seventy knights, each with his lady love. He, though, who would win the highest renown must to Montesclaire to free the damsel held captive there. She then departs. Gauvain will forth to the imprisoned damsel, Giflès to the Castel Orgellous, and Perceval swears to rest no two nights in the same place till he have learnt concerning graal and lance. (12) A knight, Guigambresil, enters and accuses Gauvain of having slain his lord. The latter sets forth at once to the King of Cavalon to clear himself of this accusation. (13) On his way he meets the host of Melians, who is preparing to take part in a tournament to approve himself worthy the love of the daughter of Tiebaut of Tingaguel, who had hitherto refused his suit. Gauvain rides on to Tingaguel to help its lord. On arriving at the castle the eldest daughter jeers at him, whilst the youngest takes his part, declaring him a better knight than Melians, whereat her sister is very indignant. On the first day of the tournament Melians shows himself the best knight, but the younger sister still declares her faith in Gauvain, and has her ears boxed in consequence. She appeals to Gauvain to be her knight and avenge the injury done her. He consents, overcomes Melians, whose horse he sends to his little lady, and all other knights ; then, after telling his name, rides forth. (14) He meets two knights, the younger of whom offers him hospitality, and sends him to his sister, bidding her welcome him. She receives him kindly, and when, struck with her beauty, he asks her favours, grants them at once. They are interrupted by a steward, who reproaches her with giving her love to her father's murderer, and calls upon the castle folk to attack Gauvain. The latter defends himself until the return of Guigambresil, who reproaches the lord of the castle for letting Gauvain be attacked, as he had expressed his readiness to do single combat. Gauvain is then allowed to go, and is excused the combat if within a year he can bring back the bleeding lance. He sets off in search of it. (15) The tale returns to Perceval, who has wandered about for five years without thinking of God, yet performing many feats. He meets three knights accompanied by ladies, all clad in penitents' dress. 'Twas a Good Friday, and the eldest knight rebukes Perceval for riding fully armed on such a day. He must confess him to a holy hermit who lives hard by. Perceval goes thither, accuses himself of having forgotten God through his great grief at not learning the use of the graal. The hermit reveals himself as his uncle, tells Perceval that he is in sin as having caused his mother's death, and for that reason he could not ask concerning lance and graal; but for her prayers he had not lived till now. Perceval remains two days with his uncle, receives absolution, and rides forth. (16) The story turns to Gauvain, who, after Escalavon, finds beneath an oak a damsel lamenting over a wounded knight ; the latter advises Gauvain to push on, which he does, and comes upon a damsel who receives him discourteously, and when at her bidding he has fetched her horse from a garden hard by, mocks at him and rides off. He follows, and culls on the way herbs with which he heals the wounded knight. A squire rides up very hideous of aspect, mounted on a wretched hack. Gauvain chastises him for discourteous answers ; meanwhile the wounded knight makes off with Gauvain's steed, making himself known as Griogoras, whom Gauvain had once punished for ill-doing. Gauvain has to follow the damsel upon the squire's hack, comes to a river, on the other side of which is a castle, overcomes a knight who attacks him, during which the damsel vanishes, is ferried across the stream, giving the vanquished knight to the ferryman as toll ; (17) comes on the morrow to the Magic Castle, wherein damsels are held fast, awaiting a knight full of all knightly virtues to restore their lands to the ladies, marry the damsels, and put an end to the enchantments of the palace. Upon entering, Gauvain sees a magnificent bed, seats himself therein, is assailed by magic art, over- comes a lion, and is then acclaimed lord of the castle. He would then leave the castle, but the ferryman says he may not, whereat Gauvain is moved to anger. On the morrow, looking forth, Gauvain beholds the (18) damsel who led him to the ford, accompanied by a knight. He hastens forth, overcomes the knight, seeks again the damsel's love, but is sent by her to the Ford Perillous. Here he meets Guiromelant, who loves Gauvain's sister, Clarissant, a dweller in the Magic Castle. A combat is arranged to take place after seven days. Upon his return to the damsel, named Orgellouse de Logres, he is now well received by her. She hates Guiro- melant for having slain her lover, and has long sought a good knight to avenge her. Guiromelant on his side hates Gauvain for having, as he says, treacherously killed his father. Gauvain and Orgellouse return to the Magic Castle. One of the queens who dwells there is mother to Arthur ; the second one, his daughter, mother to Gauvain. The latter gives his sister Clarissant a ring Guiromelant had begged him, unknowing who he was, to bring to her. He then sends a knight to Arthur to bid him and his whole train come witness the fight 'twixt him and Guiromelant. The messenger finds Arthur plunged in grief at Gauvain's absence. . . .

Here Chrestien's share breaks off abruptly in the middle of a sentence, and the poem is taken up by

(b) GAUTIER DE DOULENS.*—(1) Arthur and his court accept Gauvain's invitation and make for the Castle of Wonders, the Queen whereof has meantime made herself known to Gauvain as Ygène, Arthur's mother. The duel between Gauvain and Guiromelant is hindered, and the latter weds Gauvain's sister. (Montp. MS. here inserts a first visit of Gawain to Grail Castle, which is substantially the same as the one it repeats afterwards in the same place as the Mons MS.) Adventures of Arthur and Gauvain against Brun de Branlant follow, of Gauvain with a maiden in a tent and her brother Brandalis, of Carduel of Nantes, whose wife is beloved of the magician Garahiet, and of their son Carados, and the magic horn (verses 11,000–15,800). (2) (A fresh series of adventures begins) Arthur sets forth to seek Giflet, son of Dos ; Gauvain meets again with Brandalis, whose sister has meanwhile borne him a son ; Castel Orgellous, where Giflet is imprisoned, is captured ; Gauvain's son by Brandalis' sister is lost. (3) An unknown knight comes to Arthur's court; Keie, who demands his name, is unhorsed ; Gauvain brings the unknown to the court, but the latter is slain by a javelin cast by invisible hands. Gauvain equips himself in the unknown's armour and starts forth to learn the latter's name. After praying in a chapel, in which he beholds a light on the altar quenched by a black hand, he rides through Brittany and Normandy, and comes to a castle where, owing to his armour, he is at first hailed as lord. In one of the rooms stands a bier, whereon lies a knight, cross and broken sword upon his body, his left hand bleeding. A crowned knight enters and goes to battle with Gauvain ; canons and clerks come and perform the Vigil of the Dead ; whilst at table Gauvain sees the rich Grail serving out bread and wine to the knights. Gauvain remains alone after the meal ; he sees a lance which bleeds into a silver cup. The crowned knight again enters, bearing in his hand a broken sword which had belonged to the unknown knight, over whom he mourns. He hands the sword to Gauvain and asks him to put the pieces together. Gauvain cannot, whereupon the knight declares him unfit to fulfil the quest (li besoin) on which he came. Later he may try again. Gauvain asks concerning lance, sword, and bier. The lance, he is told, is the one wherewith the Son of God was pierced in the side, 'twill bleed till Doomsday. The tale of the broken sword which brought so much woe upon the kingdom of Logres will also be told, but here Gauvain falls fast asleep.† On the

---

* Potvin's text, from the Mons MS., is taken as basis.

† Several MSS. here intercalate the history of Joseph of Arimathea : Joseph of Barimacie had the dish made ; with it he caught the blood running from the Saviour's body as it hung on the Cross, he afterwards begged the body of Pilate ; for the devotion showed the Grail he was denounced to the Jews, thrown into prison, delivered thence by the Lord, exiled together with the sister of Nicodemus, who had an image of the Lord. Joseph and his companions came to the promised land, the White Isle, a part of England. There they warred against them of the land. When Joseph was short of food he prayed

morrow he wakes, and finds himself on the sea strand. He rides off, and
behold the country has burst into green leaf, and the reason thereof is his
having asked concerning the lance. The countryfolk both bless and curse
him for having so far delivered them and for not having completed the
deliverance by asking concerning the Grail. (4) He meets a young knight
who turns out to be his son. (5) (Adventures in which Carahiès, Gauvain's
brother, is chief actor.) (6) The story returns to Perceval, who, after
leaving the hermit, rides for three days and comes to a castle, over the
door of which hangs a horn. Perceval blows therein, overcomes the knight
who answers the challenge, and sends him to Arthur's court. (7) On his
way to the Castle of Mont Orgellous, to the pillar of which only an accomplished knight might tie his horse, he comes to the stream on whose banks
he had previously met the Fisher King. Seeking for a bridge he meets a
damsel on a mule, who, under pretence of showing a way across the river,
tries to drown him. He then comes to a castle, which entering he finds
untenanted. In the hall stands a chessboard. Perceval plays, is beaten,
seizes the board and makes as if to throw it in the moat. Hereupon a
damsel rises from the water to stay his hand, and coming into the room
reproaches him. Overcome by her beauty he asks her favours. She will
grant them if he bring the head of the stag which roams in the castle park.
Thereto she lends him her hound, bidding him be sure he return it. The
hunt follows; Perceval overtakes the stag, slays it, and cutting off its head
prepares to bring it back, when a maid of ill-chance (*pucelle de malaire*)
takes and carries it off. Perceval claiming it is reproached by her for
having slain her stag, but told he may win again the hound if he go to a
mound whereon a knight is painted and say, " Vassal, what doest thou
here ?" The combat with the Knight of the Tomb follows, during which
hound and stag's head are carried off by another knight, whom Perceval
can only follow when he has overcome the Knight of the Tomb and driven
him back therein. Now this knight, hight the Black Knight, had dwelt
there summer and winter five years, striving with all-comers for the sake
of his love. Perceval, following up the Robber Knight, meets the damsel
who had carried off the hound, but she only mocks him for answer to his
questions. (8) After an adventure with a discourteous knight, Perceval
meets at length a brother of the Red Knight whom he had formerly slain,

---

to the Creator to send him the Grail wherein he had gathered the holy blood,
after which to them that sat at table the Grail brought bread and wine and meat
in plenty. At his death, Joseph begged the Grail might remain with his seed,
and thus it was that no one, of however high condition, might see it save he was
of Joseph's blood. The Rich Fisher was of that kin, and so was Greloguevaus,
from whom came Perceval.

It is hardly necessary to point out that this must be an interpolation, as if
Gauvain had really learnt all there was to be told concerning the Grail, there
would have been no point in the reproaches addressed him by the countryfolk.
The gist of the episode is that he falls asleep before the tale is all told.

who tells him he had seen the daughter of the Fisher King, and she had told him of a knight who had carried off a hound and stag's head belonging to a good knight who had been at her court, and had omitted to ask concerning the grail, for which reason she had taken his hound and refused him help to follow the Robber Knight.   (9) Perceval is directed by the Red Knight's brother to the Fisher King's castle, but misses his way, and after an adventure at a castle, where he slays a lion, overcomes Abrioris and sends him to Arthur ; finds a damsel mourning over a knight slain by a giant, whom he kills, achieves the feat of the Ford Amorous, meets and fights with Gauvain's son until they learn who each other is, and at length comes to Belrepaire.   (10) At first unrecognised by Blanchefleur he makes himself known, stays with her three days, and then rides off, in spite of her entreaties.   (11) He meets Rosette (the loathly damsel) and Le Biaus Mauvais, laughs at the former, is challenged by the latter, whom he overcomes and sends to Arthur.   (12) He comes to his mother's house, enters without making himself known, learns from his sister that his mother died at his departure ten years before, tells her who he is, and both set forth to their uncle, the hermit.   On the way Perceval slays a knight who offers violence to his sister.   They come to their uncle, sleep there, and on the morrow Perceval reveals himself, confesses, is reproved for having slain the knight the day before.   Perceval, after mentioning his desire to learn more concerning lance, Grail, and sword, and receiving good advice from the hermit, leaves with his sister, with whom he stays three days and then quits her, despite her piteous entreaties.   (12a) Perceval comes to the Castle of Maidens, where he falls untimely asleep, and on the morrow finds himself in the forest, far from any castle.   (13) Perceval finds the damsel who had carried off the hound, fights with her knight, Garalas, overcomes him, learns that the Knight of the Tomb is his brother, who had lived for ten years with a fay in a magic invisible castle, and had met no one to overcome him until Perceval came.   Perceval sends both knight and damsel to Arthur.   (14) Perceval meets with a white mule led by a damsel ; he joins her, although she entreats him not to do so.   Suddenly struck by a great light in the forest, he turns to ask his companion what it might mean, but finds her gone.   A violent storm comes on.   The morrow he meets the damsel with the mule, who had felt no storm.   She tells him about the great light : it came from the "Gréaus," which was given by the King of kings as He hung on the Cross ; the devil may not lead astray any man on the same day he sees it, therefore the king has it carried about.   Perceval asks further, but is told only a holy man may speak of these mysteries.   Perceval relates his adventure with the lady of the chessboard, and the damsel gives him the white mule, which will lead to her castle, together with a ring giving the possessor power over the mule.   He is to give both back when he meets her.   (16) The mule brings Perceval across a river, over a glass bridge, on the other side of which he meets with Brios, who persuades him to join in a tournament held by Arthur at the Castel Orguellous, as he must win the prize of knighthood before coming to the castle of the Fisher King. Perceval leaves stag's head and hound at Brios' castle, carries off the prize at the tournament, remaining unknown. (17) Proceeding thence he frees a knight imprisoned beneath a tombstone, who, in return, shuts him up in the tomb, but, being unable to make the mule go forward, is obliged to release him, and returns to his prison, telling Perceval he knows him for the best knight in the world. (18) Perceval meets the damsel of the mule, to whom he returns ring and mule, and who asks him if he has been at the Fisher King's court ; on his saying, No, she hurries off. Perceval prays God to direct him to the Castle of the Chessboard. A voice tells him to follow the hound ; he does so, reaches the castle, is greeted by the maiden, to whom he gives stag's head and hound, and who in return tells him concerning the chessboard which *Morghe la fée* had had made at London, on the Thames, and grants him her favours as she had promised. On the morrow Perceval rides forth, accompanied awhile by the damsel, who will show him his onward way. (19) They come to a river, on which is a boat tied to an oak tree. Perceval is to enter it, cross the river, and on the other side he will find a road leading to the Fisher King. On his way Perceval releases a knight whom he finds hanging by his feet from a tree ; 'tis Bagommedes whom Keie had treated thus, and who returns to Arthur's court, challenges Keie, and is only hindered by Arthur from slaying him. All Arthur's knights then start forth for the Mont Dolorous and in search of Perceval. The adventures of Gauvain alone are related in detail until the tale returns to Perceval. (20) After freeing Bagommedes, Perceval, wandering in the woods, comes to a tree, in whose branches sits a child, who can tell nothing of the Fisher King, but tells Perceval he will come on the morrow to the Mont Dolorous. This he does, and binds his horse to the pillar. A damsel on a white mule tells him of Arthur's birth, and how Merlin had made castle and pillar to prove who should be the best of knights. She was Merlin's daughter. (21) Perceval rides on, and towards evening sees afar off a tree upon which burn many lights ; as he draws near he finds only a chapel, upon the altar of which lies a dead knight. A great and sudden light is followed by the appearance of a black hand, which puts out the candle on the altar. On the morrow he meets first a huntsman, who tells him he is near the castle, then a damsel, who explains the child in the tree, the chapel, and the black hand as having connection with the Holy Grail and the lance. (22) Perceval comes at last to the castle of the Fisher King, whom he finds on a couch as heretofore. He tells him his adventures, and asks concerning the child on the tree, the tree full of lights, and the chapel with the dead knight. Meanwhile a damsel enters a hall bearing the Grail, another follows with the bleeding lance, then comes a squire with a sword broken in two. Again Perceval puts his questions, and will not eat until they are answered. First, he is told of the child which would not speak to him on account of his many sins, and which climbed ever upwards to show man's thoughts should be raised to the Creator. Before learning aught further Perceval is to try and weld the broken sword together ; none but a true knight

lover of God, and of God's spouse, Holy Church, may accomplish it. Perceval succeeds, save that a little crack still remains. The Fisher King
embraces him and hails him as lord of his house.

Here the section which goes under the name of Gautier ends.

[A portion of Gautier's section of the Conte du Graal is found in the
Berne MS., partly edited, partly summarised, by Rochat in his work, *Ein
unbekannter Percheval li Gallois (vide infra* p. 101). This version offers some
remarkable peculiarities. It has a short introduction of thirteen lines; then
follows line 21,930 of Gautier in Potvin's text (Mons MS.). An incident
follows, omitted in the Mons MS., but found in Montpellier and in Paris,
794 : Perceval meets a huntsman who upbraids him for having been at
the Fisher King's court, and failed to ask about Grail and bleeding lance.
Then follow Incidents 6, 7 (8 is absent so far as one can judge from Rochat's
summary), 9 to 13 (in which Perceval does not apparently send Garalas and
his love to Arthur), and 14 to end, the following finish being then tacked
on : The Fisher King is father to Alain le Gros, husband to Enigeus, sister
to that Joseph who, when Christ's body was taken down from the Cross,
had it from Pilate as a reward for his services. Joseph had the vessel
prepared to catch in it the blood from the body ; it was the same Jesus
had made the Sacrament in on the Thursday before. The Fisher King
dies on the third day and Perceval reigns in his stead.]*

The Conte du Graal is continued by—

(c) MANESSIER.—(1) Perceval, full of joy, sits down to table ; after the
meal, lance, Grail, and a goodly silver dish pass before the royal table
away into the next room. Perceval, sighing, asks concerning these objects
and the maidens bearing them. (2) The King tells as follows : the lance is
that wherewith Longis pierced God's side that day he hung on the Cross
(Montpellier MS. : When Longis withdrew the spear the blood ran down
to feet, so that Joseph of Barimacie turned black from sorrow, and he collected the blood in the holy vessel). On Perceval's asking further, the
Grail is the vessel wherein the holy precious blood of our Lord was
received. Then Perceval asks how it came thither ; (3) Joseph brought it
when he departed from the prison whence he was freed by Vespasian. He
baptized forty of his friends, and wandered forth with them till they came
to Sarras, where, as the tale tells, they found the King in the Temple of

---

* The existence of this fragment shows the necessity of collating all the
MSS. of the Conte du Graal and the impossibility of arriving at definite
conclusions respecting the growth of the work before this is done. The writer
of this version evidently knew nothing of Queste or Grand St. Graal, whilst he
had knowledge of Borron's poem, a fact the more remarkable since none of the
other poets engaged upon the Conte du Graal knew of Borron, so far, at least,
as can be gathered from printed sources. It is hopeless in the present state of
knowledge to do more than map out approximately the leading sections of the
work.

the Sun. Joseph helped the King against his enemies by means of a red cross which he fixed on the King's shield. Evelac, such was the King's name, won the battle thereby, was baptized, and renamed Noodrans. It went so likewise with his brother-in-law, Salafrès, renamed Natiien. Joseph departed thence, ever bearing the Grail with him, till at length he came hither, converted the land, and I, of his seed, am keeping manor and Grail, the which shall never dwell elsewhere, God willing. (Montpellier MS. merely says, how Joseph was put into a dark prison, and kept there forty years, but the Lord sent him the sweetness of the Grail twice or thrice a day. Tiberius and Vespasian deliver him and bring him to Rome, whence he carries away the lance.) (4) To Perceval's questions concerning the damsels : the Grail-bearer is of royal blood, and pure maid, or God might not let her hold it, she is my child ; the dish-bearer is also of high lineage, daughter to King Goon Desert. (5) The King would then go to sleep, but Perceval would know about the broken sword : In Quiquagrant dwelt Goon Desert, the King's brother. Besieged by Espinogre he made a sally and slew him. Espinogre's nephew swore revenge ; donning the armour of a knight of Goon Desert, he slew him, but the sword broke when the traitrous blow was struck. Goon Desert's body was brought to his brother's castle, whither came, too, his daughter with the broken sword, foretelling that a knight should come, rejoin the pieces, and avenge the foul blow. The Fisher King taking up the fragments incautiously was pierced through the thigh, and the wound might not be healed until his brother's death was avenged. The murderer's name is Partiniaus, Lord of the Red Tower. Perceval vows to avenge this wrong, but first, despite the King's strong hints that it is bed-time, must learn (6) about the candles on the trees, how they are fay trees, and the lights deceiving ones, but they might not deceive Perceval, he being destined to achieve the wonders of the earth, and he has put an end to this illusion ; (7) how the black hand haunted a chapel wherein Pinogres had slain his mother, and over four thousand knights had been slain by it. (8) Perceval starting on the morrow in search of Partinal meets with Saigremors, and with him delivers a damsel from ten robber knights. Perceval, wounded, stays a month at the damsel's castle, and (9) the story tells for some fifteen hundred verses (36,100–37,400) of Saigremors ; how he pursues the robber knights, comes to the Castle of Maidens, delivers the dame thereof from a knight, Calides, who wars upon her, and afterwards delivers another maiden, to whom two knights were offering violence; (10) then, for over two thousand verses of Gauvain ; how he prepares to set forth again in search of the Fisher King ; how a maiden comes to him whose brother had been slain in his service, reproaches Gauvain for his conduct at the Fisher King's castle, and carries him off ; how he saves a maid going to be burnt ; how after other adventures he slays King Margon, returns to Arthur's court, fights with Kex to avenge the brother of the damsel, etc. (11) Meanwhile Perceval, leaving the damsel who has tended him right well, rides forth into a wood, where he is over-taken by a great storm of thunder and hail, after which he comes to the chapel where lies the body of the knight slain by the black hand. Perceval strives with the devil to whom this belongs, overcomes, and with the help of a hermit who tells him the tale of all the knights who had fallen there, buries the body. He then confesses to the hermit, who warns him not to think of acquiring fame, but rather to save his soul. (12) Perceval, riding forth on the morrow, is met by the devil, who throws him from his horse ; he finds another, mounts it, but coming to a stream luckily crosses himself, when it disappears ; it was the devil. (13) A damsel passes by with a bark, wherein Perceval mounts ; she minds him of Blanchefleur, and desire masters him, but again he crosses himself in time, and ship and damsel vanish. (14) A hermit comes who instructs him concerning all these things, brings him where he finds a fresh steed, and to a fair castle. Perceval overcomes a knight who would bar his passing, delivers the lady love of Dodinel from a felon knight ; is appealed to for help by a damsel of Blanchefleur's, oppressed by Arides of Cavalon. (15) Setting off to the succour of his lady love, his horse falls lame, he comes to a smith who tells him his name is Tribuet, the forger of the broken sword. Tribuet makes the sword whole, and bids Perceval guard it well, never had king or conqueror a better one. (16) Perceval reaches Bel Repaire, overcomes Arides, whom he sends to Arthur's court, bidding him announce his own arrival for Whitsuntide. He then quits Blanchefleur, and (17) meets with the Coward Knight, who will not fight even when he sees two damsels carried off by ten knights. Perceval attacks the ravishers, the Coward Knight is drawn into the struggle, and quits himself valiantly. The rescued damsels bring the knights to their castle, where Perceval, sore wounded, remains for two months. (18) Meanwhile Saigremors has announced Perceval's arrival at Camelot. Whitsuntide passing, all the knights set forth in search of him, and, amongst others, Boort ; he meets his brother Lyonel led, bound and naked, by six knights, who scourge him, and at the same moment he hears the plaint of a maid to whom a knight is doing violence. Her he succours, then hurries after his brother, whom, meanwhile, Gauvain has rescued. Lyonel bitterly reproaches his brother for abandoning him, and falls upon him, sword in hand ; Boort offers no defence, and would be slain but for a passing knight, Calogrinant, who pays for his interference with his life. Finally, heavenly intervention appeases Lyonel. Calogrinant is buried by a hermit. (19) Perceval, healed, leaves the castle together with the Coward Knight, is present with him at a tournament, at which he distinguishes himself above all others, leaves his companion, to whom he gives the name Le Hardis, and (20) meets Hector, who challenges him. The two fight, and well-nigh kill each other. To them, lying on the field of combat, appears an angel with the Grail, and makes them whole. (21) Perceval rides on to Partinal's castle, before which stands a fir tree whereon hangs a shield. Perceval throws this down, whereupon Partinal appears and a desperate combat ensues, ended by the overthrow of Partinal, and, as he will submit to no conditions, his death. Perceval cuts off his head and makes for the Grail Castle, but only after a summer's seeking,

lights upon it chancewise.   (22) As he nears the castle, the warders come
to the King, telling him a knight is coming with a head hanging at his
saddle-bow ; hereupon the King leaps to his feet and is straightway made
whole.   Partinal's head is stuck on a pike on the highest tower of the
castle.   After supper, at which the same mystic procession of talismans
takes place as heretofore, the King learns Perceval's name, and thereby
finds that he is his own sister's son.   He would hand him his crown, but
Perceval has vowed not to take it, his uncle living.   (23) He returns
to Arthur's court, overcoming on the way seven knights, and tells his
adventures, which Arthur has written down and kept in a box at Salisbury.   The Grail damsel appears and tells Perceval his uncle is dead.
Perceval goes to Corbièrc accompanied by all the court, who assist at his
crowning and remain with him a month, during which time the Grail feeds
all with the costliest foods.   He marries his cousins, the two Grail-bearers,
to two valiant kings, and reigns in peace for seven years.   (24) After which
time he follows a hermit into the wilderness, accompanied by Grail, lance,
and holy dish.   He serves the Lord for ten years, and, when he dies, Grail,
lance, and dish were doubtless carried up to heaven, for since that day no
man saw them.

(*d*) GERBERT.—(According to Birch Hirschfeld interpolated between
Gautier and Manessier, and joining on therefore to the last incident in
Gautier.)*

(1) Perceval's sin in having indirectly caused the death of his mother
disables him from making whole the broken sword, and he must set forth
again in search of the Grail.   In the night he dreams a danger threatens
his sister, and on the morrow he wakes up in open field, the Grail
Castle having vanished.   (2) He comes to a fair castle in the midst of a
meadow, and, finding the door shut, knocks at it with his sword till the
latter breaks.   An old man appears, and tells him the broken sword will
cost him seven years more wanderings until he come again to the Grail
Castle.   All he can do for Perceval is to give him a letter which heals the
wounded and makes the wearer invincible.   (3) Perceval riding thence
through country that the day before was waste and folkless, finds it now
well cultivated and peopled ; all press round him and bless him for the
change wrought by his asking concerning the Grail.   (4) He comes to a
castle wherein is a forge guarded by two serpents, and on it was a sword
forged for a year, and it might not be broken, save in a certain danger, or
mended save at the same forge.   Perceval, after resisting the devil in the
shape of a fair maid, attacks and overcomes the two serpents, and has his
sword mended by the blacksmith, who tells him how he broke it at the

---

* It is by no means clear to me that Gerbert's portion of the Conte du Graal
is an interpolation.   I am rather inclined to look upon it as an independent
finish.   As will be shown later on, it has several features in common with both
Mabinogi and Wolfram, features pointing to a common prototype.

gate of Paradise. (5) After making whole by his letter two knights of the Round Table who had lost their wits in Castle Dolorous, Perceval comes to Carlion, to Arthur's court, and accomplishes the adventure of the Perillous Seat which a fairy had sent to Arthur. Only the destined Grail-finder might sit in it. Six knights who had previously essayed the feat had been swallowed up by the earth ; they reappear when Perceval is successful. (6) Perceval is called away from the court by a forsaken damsel, whose false lover he compels to marry her ; then, after overcoming fresh temptation in damsel-shape, he comes to his sister's castle, overcomes her adversary, who turns out to be Mordret, and reaches the Castle of Maidens, where he is healed of his wounds by the lady of the castle, his cousin. She tells him of his mother, Philosofine, and how the Grail was taken from the ken of man owing to the sinfulness of the world. Perceval leaves his sister in this castle where dames are chaste and damsels maids. (7) Returning to court, whither Mordret had preceded him in sorry plight, Perceval is mocked at by Kex, whom he overcomes, and afterwards meets Gauvain and Tristan. (8) Leaving the court, he meets with four knights carrying their father, mortally wounded, accompanies them to their castle, recognises in the wounded knight, Gornumant, who had knighted him, swears to avenge him, tells all that has befallen himself, and learns that the cause of his successive failures is his forsaking his betrothed, Blanchefleur, whom he knows to be Gornumant's niece. He is told that if he listen heedfully to mass and marry the damsel all will be well, and he will learn the secrets of lance and Grail. But first Perceval overcomes a hideous hag, who by night brings to life Gornumant's enemies slain during the day. She has a potion, whereof Christ made use in the sepulchre, and with it she quickens the dead. She recognizes Perceval and acknowledges him as her conqueror, yet while she lives he shall know nought of the Grail ; she works by order of the King of the Waste City, who hates all Christian folk. Perceval tries the virtue of the potion on the most valiant of his enemies, with whom he engages in a fresh and desperate struggle, heals Gornumant with it, and sets off to marry Blanchefleur, as he is wishful to live cleanly and fly deadly sin. (9) She is overjoyed at his arrival ; preparations are made for the marriage ; the night before, she comes to his bedside in smock and mantle, and they pass the night side by side, but with the sheet between them. The wedding follows, and then, fearful of losing the heavenly joy for sake of carnal longing, they resolve to resist the devil and live virginwise, for virginity surpasseth aught else, even as the topaz does crystal. Perceval, in a dream, is assured that of his seed shall be the Swan Knight and the deliverer of the Holy Sepulchre. Meanwhile he is still to search after lance and Grail. (10) On the morrow he quits Blanchefleur, "maid she laid her to bed, maid she arose ;" frees a maiden pursued by a brutal knight ; (11) comes to a castle where the wayfarer must first fight against four knights and then against the lord of the castle ; does away with this custom ; (12) comes to cross roads, whereof one is safe and easy, the other adventurous and full of danger ; meets a knight all on fire ; sees two hermits, one kneeling at a cross, the other scourging it ; then a wonderful beast, a doe followed by fawns, which assail and devour her ; (13) is presented at a hermit's with a shield none but the Grail-winner may wear, after which the table heretofore meanly spread is covered with rich fare, and learns the meaning of the mystic scenes he has witnessed. (14) He is summoned by a damsel, who tells him of the Dragon King, lord of a heathen folk dwelling in mid-sea, possessor of a shield whereon is painted a dragon that belches forth flame. Perceval sets forth to attack him, resists the devil who dwells in the dragon head, thanks to his miraculous shield whereon the cross is painted, and forces him to flee ; continues the fight against the Dragon Knight without his shield, and slays him, but not till he has repented him of his sins. (15) Meanwhile a thief has made off with the shield, in pursuing whom Perceval comes to an abbey, where he learns the story of Joseph of Arimathea. Some forty years after the Crucifixion lived a heathen king, Evelac, in Sarras, wherefrom the Saracens have their name, sore pressed by Tholomes, King of Syria. But Joseph of Barimaschie, who had been five years in Pilate's service, comes to him, and with him his brother-in-law, Seraphe ; he promised the King victory if he would let himself be baptized. The King consented, and received the name of Mordrach Joseph then came to this land, and with him sixty folk and two fair ladies, whereof the one, Philosophine, bore a plate, the other an ever-bleeding lance, whilst Joseph had a vessel, never saw man a fairer one. But King Crudel flung Joseph and his companions into prison, where they dwelt forty days, but it harmed them not, as through the Holy Grail they were filled with great plenty and had every wish fulfilled. Now, Mordrains, learning this, brought together a great host, invaded King Crudel's lands, attacked and slew him. Mordrains, disarming, was found to be covered with wounds, none of which he had felt. On the morrow Joseph put up a table, altar-wise, and thereon laid the Grail, which Mordrains seeing, pressed near to. But an angel with a fiery sword kept him back, and a voice assured him he had laid such a burden on his shoulders as he might not pass away, nor would his wounds be healed until should come the true knight, loved of Christ, sinless, and in his arms he, Mordrains, should die. And till then the Host should be his only food. Since then three hundred years have passed, and the monks have heard that the knight is in the land who shall ask concerning lance and Grail, and thereby heal the king. (16) Perceval leaves on the morrow and comes to a castle wherein is a coffin, brought thereto in a boat drawn by a swan ; none save the best knight in the world may open it. All have tried, even Gauvain, and failed. Perceval succeeds, and finds in the coffin the body of a knight, former lord of the castle, and a letter setting forth that he who should open the coffin was his murderer. Perceval, attacked in consequence by the dead man's sons, defends himself by making a buttress of the youngest son's body. Afterwards he overcomes the folk of the castle, and delivers Gauvain, held prisoner therein. (17) Perceval, after confessing his sins to a hermit, has an adventure with the devil, who comes out of a tomb, but whom he forces back therein. (18) He then succours a maiden whom her jealous lover has thrown into a fountain ; (19) punishes a damsel who tempts him in traitrous-wise ; (20) meets with and is sore pressed by a giant, whom he overcomes ; (21) has a fresh and victorious encounter with Kex, and, finally, (22) arrives at crossways, is directed by the cross to the Fisher King's court, reaches it, asks straightway for the Grail, is questioned by the King and relates his allegorical adventures. At table the Grail appears, followed by lance and sword. Perceval pieces together the sword, and the King, full of joy, embraces him.

Wolfram von Eschenbach's Parzival.—Gahmuret, Parzival's father, goes to the East, takes service with Baruc, wins the love of the heathen queen Belakane, but after remaining with her a short time forsakes her, promising to return if she become Christian. She bears a son, and names him Feirefiz. Gahmuret by his prowess at a tournament wins the love of Herzeloyde, whom he marries on condition he may go a tourneying every month. Hearing his old lord Baruc is in danger, he hastens to his aid, and is slain. Herzeloyde on receipt of the news resolves to withdraw to the wilderness, and bring up her son in ignorance of knighthood.

[From this point up to and including the adventure with Orgeuilleuse, where Chrestien's share of the Conte du Graal breaks off, Wolfram agrees very closely with Chrestien. It has been much debated in Germany whether he really had any other model but Chrestien, and whether his alleged model Kyot be not a feigned source to justify his departure from the story as found in the Conte du Graal. A brief outline of the arguments for and against this view will be found in Appendix A. The chief points of difference in the portion common to the two poets are : the more important position in the narrative assigned to Perceval's cousin, whom Wolfram names Sigune, who is fed from the Grail by the Grail messenger, the loathly damsel, and about whose loves with Schianatulander Wolfram has left fragments of another poem, Titurel. Parzival meets her immediately after his adventure with the lady of the tent. Parzival's love is named Condwiramur. On the first night of their marriage he leaves her maid (as in Gerbert's version). But the most important peculiarity of Wolfram's poem is his account of the Grail itself, a stone which yields all manner of food and drink, the power of which is sustained by a dove, which every week lays a Host upon it, given, after the fall of the rebel angels, in charge to Titurel and his dynasty, by them preserved in the Grail castle, Montsalvatch, guarded by a sacred order of knighthood whom it chooses itself The knights are vowed to virginity, the king alone being allowed marriage. The cause of the maimed king's (Amfortas) hurt is his having taken up arms in the cause of worldly and unlawful love. When Parzival leaves the Grail castle after the first visit, he is mocked at by the inmates for having omitted the question. More stress is laid on the broken sword, connected with which is a magic spell Parzival must master before he can become lord of the

Grail castle. The "loathly damsel," Kundrie, is also a much more important person with Wolfram than with Chrestien, and she is brought into
contact with Parzival's cousin, Sigune. Parzival's love for his wife is
dwelt upon at length, and he is urged by the hermit rather to rejoin her
than to seek the Grail.]

After the adventure with Orgueilleuse, Wolfram continues as follows:—
The lord of the magic castle, wherein are kept prisoners Arthur's mother
and the other queens, is Clinschor, nephew of Virgilius of Naples, who took
to magic after his unmanning at the hands of King Ibert, whose wife,
Iblis, he loved. Gawain overcomes the magician, and, both unknowing,
fights with Parzival. The latter, after many lesser adventures, meets his
half-brother Feirefiz, and sustains with him the hardest of all his fights.
At length recognition is brought about, the two embrace, and repair to
Arthur's court. Cundrie nears once more, tells Parzival he has been
chosen Grail king, that his wife and twin sons, Loherangrin and Kardeiz,
have been summoned to the Grail castle, and that the question will now
free Amfortas and his land. With Cundrie and Feirefiz, Parzival rides to
the Grail castle, meets his wife, together they all behold the talismans,
save Feirefiz, to whom as a heathen the sight of the Grail is denied. But
he is baptised, weds Repanse de Schoie, the Grail damsel, the two return
to India, and from them is born Prester John. Parzival rules over his
Grail kingdom. Of his son Loherangrin it is told how he is led to the
aid of the Duchess of Brabant by a swan, how he marries her on condition
she inquire not as to his origin, and how, on her breaking the command,
the swan carries him away from her.

Heinrich von dem Türlin.—*The Gawain Episodes of Diu Crône.*
—The parallelism of Heinrich's poem with those of Wolfram and Chrestien
begins about verse 17,500 with an adventure of Gawain's corresponding to
Inc. 13 in Chrestien (Tournament for the hand of Tiebaut of Tingaguel's
daughter, episode of the two sisters, combat with Melians de Lis). In
Heinrich the father is named Leigamar, the eldest daughter Fursensephin,
(Fleur sans epine ?), the youngest Quebelepluz, where Heinrich has taken a
French phrase setting forth the greater fairness of the damsel for a proper
name. Inc. 14 in Chrestien then follows with these differences : the name
of the castle is Karamphi ; Gawain and the facile damsel are surprised by
the latter's brother, and it is her father who, to avenge the wrong done his
house, makes Gawain swear that within a year he will either seek out the
Grail or return as prisoner to Karamphi. Chrestien's Inc. 15 is of course
missing, the story going straight on to Inc. 16, meeting with the wounded
knight (here Lohenis) and his lady love Emblie, who by treachery deprive
Gawain of his steed ; then the arrival at the Castle of Wonders, and the night
passed in the enchanted bed, where the hero is overwhelmed with cross-
bolts shot at him by invisible foes. The plucking of the flower from the
enchanted garden at the bidding of a damsel (Orgueilleuse in Chrestien
and Wolfram, here Mancipicelle), and the meeting with and challenge by

Giremelanz follow. Arthur's court comes to the Castle of Wonders to witness the combat. Gawain and Giremelanz are reconciled, the latter marries Gawain's sister, and Gawain himself sets off to search for the Grail. [Adventures then follow which correspond to nothing in Chrestien or Wolfram, in which Gawain wins talismans destined to aid him in his search.] Gawain sets forth on his quest accompanied by Kay, Lancelot, and Calocreant. They part at crossways. Gawain comes to the sister of the magician (anonymous in Chrestien, Klinschor in Wolfram, here Gans-guoter) of the Castle of Wonders. She bids him take heed, if he wish to see the Grail, he be not overcome by sleep, and for this that he drink not overmuch ; as soon as he saw it and its accompanying damsels, he was to ask about it. If he neglected this, all his past and any future toil would be useless. On his way to the Grail castle, the hero meets with all sorts of dangers, and obstacles, and wonders ; amongst others, passing the night in a castle where he is tended by invisible hands. After month-long wanderings he meets with Lancelot and Calocreant, and learns that Kay, in a vain attempt to penetrate to the Grail, has been flung into prison. The three comrades then come to the Grail castle. They are led into a hall which passes in splendour aught earthly eye ever saw. The floor is strewn with roses, on a bed lies an old man in gold-embroidered garments, and watches two youths playing at chess. Towards night the hall fills with knights and dames, a youth enters bearing a sword which he lays before the old man. Gawain is pressed to drink ; but refuses, not so his two companions, who straightway fall asleep. Then enter two damsels bearing lights, followed by two knights with a spear, and two more damsels with a "toblier" (? tailleor, plate) of gold and jewels. After them comes the fairest woman ever God created, and with her a maiden weeping. The spear is laid on the table, by it the "toblier" wherein are three drops of blood. In the box borne by the fair lady is a piece of bread, one third part of which she breaks off and gives to the old man. Gawain recognising in her Gansguoter's sister, stays no longer, but asks what these wonders mean. Straightway knights and dames all with mighty shout leap from table, and great joy arises. The old man says what he has seen is the Grail ; none saw it before save Parzival, and he asked not. By his question Gawain has delivered from long waiting and suffering both those which are dead and those which live. The old man himself and his companions are really dead, though they seem it not, but the lady and her damsels are living ; for their unstained womanhood God has granted them to have the Grail, and therewith yearly to feed the old man. All Gawain's adventures latterly have come from the Grail. Now he has ended all, he is to take as prize of his knighthood the sword which will help him in every danger. After him no man shall see the Grail ; further concerning it he must not ask, nor may know more. At daybreak the old man's tale ends, and he with his whole court vanish, leaving only the lady with her five damsels. [After releasing Kay, and undergoing other adventures, Gawain returns to Arthur's court.]

The Petit Saint Graal or Didot-Perceval.*—*Prologue.*—After
the choosing of Arthur to be King, Merlin comes to the court, and tells
how Arthur is Uther-Pendragon's son, brought up by Antor as his
son. All rejoice at this, especially Gauvain, son of Lot. After dinner
the barons bring Merlin to Arthur, and tell him how he was the prophet
of Uther-Pendragon, and had made the Round Table. Arthur promises
to honour Merlin. The latter calls him apart with Gauvain and Key, and
tells him how, in the time of Uther-Pendragon, the Round Table was
made after the pattern of one Joseph constructed when he separated the
good from the evil. Two Kings of Britain before had been Kings of
France, and conquered Rome ; Queen Sibyl and Solomon had prophesied
Arthur should be third, and he, Merlin, was the third to assure him of it.
But this could only be if Arthur established the Round Table as Merlin
directed. Now the Grail had been given Joseph by our Lord himself, and
at His command Joseph led a great folk into the desert. And when evil
befell them Joseph, at our Lord's command, made a table ; whereat one
place was left empty in remembrance of Judas. But Moyses, a false
disciple, sat therein, but sank into the abyss, whereout he shall not come
until the time of Antichrist. Our Lord made the first table ; Joseph, the
second ; he, Merlin, the third. The Grail was given into the keeping of
the rich Fisher King ; but he was old, full of sickness, and should not win
health till a knight came, having sat at the Round Table, true man of God
and of Holy Church, and the best knight in the world for feats of arms.
He must ask the rich fisher of what use is the Grail ; then the King would
be cured of his infirmity, the enchantments of Britain would cease, and the
prophecy be fulfilled. Should Arthur do this, great good would come of it ;
he, Merlin, must go, as he could not often show himself to the people.
Whereupon he departs to Ortoberland, to Blaise, his master, who writes
down these things, and by his writings we know them. The son of Alein
le Gros is a child named Percevaux, and as Alein is dying he hears the
voice of the Holy Ghost saying, Know thou art near thy end, and wilt soon
come into the fellowship of Jesus Christ. Brons, thy father, dwells in
these isles of Ireland, and with him is the Grail. And he may not die
until thy son finds him, to whom he shall commend the grace of the vessel,
and teach the secret words Joseph taught him, then shall he be cured of
his infirmities. And I command thy son that he go to the court of Arthur,
where he shall be taught how he may find the house of his grandfather.
Alein dies, and Percevaux mounts his horse and comes to Arthur's court,
and asks arms from him, and stays there and is much loved.

(1) Arthur proposes holding a tournament at Easter, the greatest the
world had seen, to honour the Round Table. Perceval at first takes no part

---

* In the solitary MS. which gives this version, it follows, as has already
been stated, prose versions of Robert de Borron's undoubted poems, " Joseph of
Arimathea " and " Merlin."

in the tournament ; but afterwards, for love of Aleine, niece of Gauvain, who incites him thereto, and sends him a suit of red armour, he enters the lists unknown, and overbears all opponents, so that all say he should fill the empty place at the Round Table.   Perceval claims the empty place from the King, and when refused threatens to return to his land and never visit the court again.   Arthur yields, and Perceval seats himself.   Then the rocks and the earth groan dolorously, and a voice reproaches Arthur with having disobeyed Merlin's command.   Were it not the goodness of Alein le Gros Perceval had died the death of Moys.   Now should Arthur know the vessel our Lord gave Joseph was in the keeping of the rich fisher, and he was ill and infirm, and until the best knight in the world should come might not die.   And when that knight should come to the rich fisher and ask concerning the vessel, then should he be cured, but die within three days after giving the vessel to that knight, and teaching him the secret words handed down by Joseph.   Thus the enchantments of Britain should cease. (2) Perceval swears not to lie one night where he had lain the night before till he find the rich fisher.   Gauvain, Sagremors, Beduers, Hurgains, and Erec swear the same.   The knights set forth amid general lamentation.   They part at a chapel, and the story follows Perceval.   (3) He comes, after two days, upon a damsel weeping over a knight, Hurganet, one of the Round Table, who had gone forth on the Grail Quest.   He had delivered her from a giant, and ridden with her into a tent where they found knights and ladies, who warned them not to await the owner, the "Orgoillos Delandes," who would kill him.   And whilst speaking a dwarf entered, scourge in hand, who threw down the tent.   The Lord of the Tent then appeared, clad in red armour, and slew Hurganet.   Perceval determines to avenge his death ; rides to the tent with the damsel ; is warned of its inmates ; is surprised by the dwarf, who smites the damsel with his scourge, where-upon Perceval fells him to the ground.   The Knight of the Tent appears ; after a desperate struggle Perceval overcomes him and sends him with the damsel to Arthur's court.   She had fain stayed with him, but he thought of other things.   (4) Perceval comes to the finest castle in the world, enters, and finds no inhabitant.   Only a chessboard he finds.   He begins to move the pieces, and they play against him, and he is checkmated three times running.   Full of anger he prepares to throw the chessmen into the castle moat—suddenly a damsel shows herself and reproaches him.   He will abstain if she comes to him.   She consents, and after her squires and maidens have disarmed Perceval he joins her.   Overcome by her beauty he requests her love.   She will grant it him if he capture the white stag of the wood.   She lends him her hound, and recommends him to take the utmost care of it.   Perceval chases the stag, captures it, and, having cut off its head, starts back.   But meanwhile an old woman has carried off the hound.   She will only give it up if Perceval will go to a grave whereunder is a knight painted, and say : "Felon, he that put you there."   Perceval complies ; whereupon appears a knight on a black horse armed in black. They strive, and Perceval overcomes him.   But meantime a second knight

has carried off both the stag's head and the hound from the old woman.
Perceval's adversary flees to the tomb, which closes upon him, and Perceval
follows the second knight after a vain attempt to get help from the old
woman.   (5) Him he found not ; but after feats longer than I can tell,
comes to his father's house, where he was born.   He only finds his sister
and a niece.   The former tells him concerning her brother, who went to
Arthur's court ; whereupon their mother died of grief.   Perceval reveals
himself, and is amazed at what she relates concerning the Grail and its
guardian, and asks if he may come to behold it.   She answers, Yes ; whereupon he vows not to rest till he have found it.   She attempts to dissuade
him, but he remains firm.   She then urges him to go to their uncle, who is
a hermit, to whom he may confess the sin of his mother's death, and who
will advise him concerning the Quest.   (6) Both proceed thither.   He
rejoices to see them, and asks if Perceval has been to the house of his
father, guardian of the vessel named Grail, and, on hearing that he has not,
tells him how at the table which Joseph and himself had made, the voice
of the Holy Ghost had come to them, telling them to go westward, and
ordering the rich fisher, his father, to come to that land where the sun goes
down (avaloit), telling him he should not die till the son of Alein had
become the best knight in the world.   Perceval had been chosen to do his
Lord's service ; he is to slay no knight nor to lie with any woman, that
being luxurious sin.   His sins have prevented his reaching Brons.   He is
to be careful to keep himself from sin and felony, being of a race our Lord
so loved that He committed His blood to their keeping.   Much else he says,
and on the morrow Perceval and his sister ride forth.   (7) They meet a
knight who challenges them.   Perceval, thinking of the damsel who had
given him the hound, at first pays no attention, but then overcomes and
slays him.   Perceval is much grieved at having so soon broken his uncle's
injunction. On the morrow he leaves his sister, promising to return so soon
as he may.   (8) He meets a knight, accompanied by a damsel the most
wonderfully ugly nature ever made, whereat he signs himself and laughs.
The knight, indignant, challenges him, but is overcome and sent with the
damsel to Arthur's court.   Kay makes mock of them ; but Arthur reproves
him and receives them courteously.   They remain at the court, and know
that she was the most beautiful woman in the world !   (9) Perceval comes
to a ford and is challenged by its guardian, whom he overcomes.   His name
is Urban of the Black Thorn ; his lady had set him to guard the ford.   Her
castle vanishes with a great noise, and she comes to her lover's aid with
her maidens in shape of birds.   Perceval slays one who becomes a woman,
and is carried off by the others to Avallon.   (10) Perceval comes to a tree
at the crossing of four roads, among its branches he sees two naked children of seven years old.   They speak to him concerning the Grail, and
direct him to take the road to the right.   They vanish, and a voice tells
him to heed their counsel.   (11) Perceval comes to a river whereon are
three men in a boat, and the master of the boat bids him go down the
stream till he should come to his house.   Perceval rides a whole day with-

out finding it, and curses the fisher. At last he comes to a castle with lowered drawbridge, enters, and is robed in scarlet by two squires. Meanwhile four attendants have carried the Fisher King, father of Alein, and grandfather of Perceval, into the hall. The King wished to do Perceval what honour he might. They eat, and whilst at table a squire comes out of a chamber, and brings in both hands a lance, whence flows a drop of blood. Him follows a damsel bearing two silver plates and clothes ; then a squire with a vessel in which was our Lord's blood. All bow as he passes, and Perceval had fain asked, but he fears to displease the King, minding him of the worthy man to whom he had confessed, and who forbade his speaking too much and enquiring overmuch—for a man of idle words is displeasing to our Lord. All night Perceval thinks of the lance and of the Grail, and in the morning, on waking, finds neither man nor woman. He sets forth to seek some one, but in vain, and is greatly distressed. (12) He finds a damsel weeping bitterly, who, seeing him, cries out : " Percevaux le Gallois, be accursed, unhappier art thou than ever, having been in the house of the rich Fisher King, and not having asked concerning the Grail. Thy Lord hates thee ; and 'tis wonder the earth do not open beneath thee." Had he not seen Grail and lance pass ? Had he asked what one did with them, the King, cured of his infirmity, would have returned to his youth ; our Lord's prophecy to Joseph been fulfilled, and the enchantments of Britain undone. But Perceval is neither wise, valiant, nor true man enough to have charge of the blood. But he shall come again and ask concerning the Grail, and his grandfather shall be cured. (13) The damsel departs, and Perceval, unable to find his grandfather's house, rides on and comes to a tree under which a damsel is sitting, and in whose branches the stag's head, which had been carried off from him, is hanging. Perceval takes it, and when his hound following a stag comes up, takes possession of it likewise. But the knight who had taken them appears. Perceval fights with and overcomes him ; learns that he is the brother of the Knight of the Tomb, who lives therein with his love, sister of the damsel for whose sake Perceval had hunted the stag. To her Perceval now returns, gives her hound and stag's head, and then departs refusing the offer of her love, even to stop one night with her. (14) Perceval wanders for seven years achieving many feats, and sending more than one hundred knights prisoners to Arthur ; but, not being able to find his grandfather's house, he falls into such melancholy as to lose his memory, so that he minds him no more of God, and never enters Church. One Good Friday, fully armed, he meets a knight and ladies in penitents' dress, who reproach him for going armed on a day that our Lord was crucified. Perceval repents ; returns to his uncle, the hermit ; learns that his sister is dead, and does penitence. The songmen, in their pleasing rhymes, say nothing of this ; but we tell you of it as we find it in the tale Merlin made Blaise write down. (15) Perceval rides forth and meets seven squires of Melianz de Liz, who is going to a tournament at the White Castle, the damsel of which is to be the victor's prize. All the knights of the Round Table will be there, having returned that Whitsuntide from the Quest of the Grail without achieving aught. Perceval leaves the squires and come to a castle where he puts up. His host urges him to take part in the tournament. The morrow they ride forth and look on ; Melianz wears the scarf of the lady of the castle ; he and Gauvain prove themselves the best knights, the onlooking ladies know not to whom to award the prize. The next day, Perceval, having resolved upon taking part, accepts the scarf of his host's daughter, overcomes all adversaries, and sends steeds to the lady in return for her scarf. Being asked by his host if he will not woo the damsel of the White Castle, Perceval answers he may not take wife. Then appears an old man who reproaches Perceval for going to a tournament, and with forgetting his vow to sleep no two nights in the same house till the Quest be accomplished. He is Merlin, come from Hortoblande, to say that owing to the prayers of Perceval's uncle, our Lord wills that the latter may have his blood to keep. He is to go to his grandfather. Perceval asks when he shall get there. " Before a year," is the answer. " 'Tis a long time." " Not so," says Merlin, who leaves him, and tells all to Blaise, from whose writing we know of it. (16) That same night Perceval comes to his grandfather's house, is received by the Fisher King, and as they sit at table the Grail appears, and the relics with it, and when Perceval sees it he asks to what use is the vessel put ? Forthwith the King is cured, and his being changed. Perceval must say first who he is before learning such holy things. Upon learning it is his grandson before him, the King leads him to the Grail, and tells him with this lance Longis pierced the side of Jesus Christ, whom he knew in the flesh. In this vessel is the blood, Joseph caught as it ran to the ground. It is called Grail because it is agreeable to worthy men ; none may sin in its presence. Then Brons, kneeling, prays, and the voice of the Holy Ghost tells him the prophecy will be fulfilled ; and he is to teach Perceval the secret words our Lord on the cross told Joseph, and Joseph told him. He does, but I cannot and may not say what these words were. Then angels carry him off ; and Perceval remains, and the enchantments of Britain and of the whole world cease. And that same day Arthur and his knights sitting at the Round Table are aware of a great noise, and the seat is made whole again which had broken under Perceval. Merlin appears to Blaise, tells him his work is ended, and takes him to Perceval, who was right glad of his company.

Epilogue.—Merlin comes to Arthur's court and relates all that had taken place. The knights, finding the Quest of the Grail is over, and mindful of Merlin's former words, urge Arthur to invade the continent. He does so, overcomes Frollo, King of France ; refuses tribute to the Emperor of Rome, overcomes him, but is recalled to England on learning Mordret's treachery. The latter is slain ; but Arthur, wounded mortally, is carried to Avallon to be healed of Morguen, his sister. Lastly, Merlin tells Perceval how he will withdraw from the world, and be no more seen of men. And the tale says no more of Merlin and the Grail.

The Mabinogi of Peredur ab Evrawc.—Evrawc, Earl of the North, has seven sons, six of whom, like himself, fall in tournaments and combats. His wife carries off her youngest son, Peredur, to the desert, and forbids horses or arms being shown to him. He grows up strong and active, and can outrun his mother's goats and hinds. (1) One day he sees three knights passing—Gwalchmai, the son of Gwyar, and Geneir Gwystyl, and Owain, the son of Urien. His mother declares them to be angels; whereupon he determines to join them. He questions Owain concerning his accoutrements and the use of his weapons. His mother swoons away at the thought of his leaving her; but he picks out a horse and saddles it. Before leaving, his mother counsels him to repeat his paternoster wherever he sees a church; to take food and drink if none offer them; to aid when any outcry is, especially a woman's; if he sees a fair jewel to take it and give it to another; to pay his court to fair women whether they will or no. (2) After two days and nights Peredur comes to a tent, where he finds a damsel. Half of the food and drink she has he takes, half leaves to her; asks her for her ring at leaving, which she gives him. Her lord returning, is jealous, and sets forth to avenge his supposed wrong. (3) Peredur journeys on to Arthur's court. A knight has been there before him, and grievously insulted Gwenhwyvar by dashing a goblet of wine in her face, and carrying the goblet out, and has dared any to avenge the insult; but all hang their heads. Peredur enters the hall and demands knighthood. On Kai's protesting he is too meanly equipped, a dwarf, who, with his female companion has been a year at Arthur's court without speaking, salutes him as the flower of knighthood. Kai strikes him for this, and kicks the female dwarf, who repeats the salutation. Kai bids Peredur seek the knight and win back the goblet, then shall he have knighthood. Peredur does so, and slays the knight. Owain, who has followed, shows him how to undo the armour and to clad himself in it, and bids him back to Arthur. But Peredur refuses, he will not come back to the court till he have avenged the injury done by Kai to the dwarf and dwarfess. (4) Peredur overcomes sixteen knights and sends them to Arthur with the same message. (5) Peredur comes to a castle by a lake, and sees a venerable man sitting by the lake and his attendant fishing, and the old man is lame. And Peredur enters the castle, and is practised in the use of weapons, and learns courtesy and noble bearing; and the old man is his uncle—his mother's brother. He is to leave his mother's habits and discourse, and if he sees aught to wonder at, not to ask the meaning of it. (6) Peredur leaves his uncle and comes to a castle where dwells a second uncle of his—brother likewise of his mother. His strength is tested by his having to cut through an iron staple with a sword. Twice he does it and the broken pieces re-unite, but the third time neither would unite as before. He has arrived at two-thirds of his strength, and when he attains his full power none will be able to contend with him. Whilst talking, two youths enter the hall bearing a mighty spear with three streams of blood flowing from the point to the ground. All wail and lament; but as Peredur is not vouchsafed the meaning of what he sees he forbears to ask concerning it. Then enter two maidens with a salver in which a man's head swims in blood. The outcry redoubles. Peredur retires to sleep. (7) On the morrow, with his uncle's permission, he rides forth, finds a beautiful woman lamenting over the corpse of a knight. She reveals herself as his foster-sister ; calls him accursed for causing his mother's death by leaving her ; and tells him it is her husband she mourns for, slain by the Knight of the Glade. Peredur meets the latter, overcomes him, and makes him take his foster-sister in marriage. (8) Peredur comes to a castle where are eighteen youths and five maidens, and he had never seen one of so fair an aspect as the chief of the maidens. A flask of wine and six loaves are brought by two nuns, and that must suffice for all. The youths press the maiden to offer herself to Peredur as his wife or lady love. She refuses ; but consents when they threaten leaving her to her enemies. She comes weeping to Peredur and relates how she is besieged by an earl who seeks her hand. She implores his aid, and offers to place herself in his hands. Peredur bids her go sleep, he will assist her, The next day he overthrows the master of the household of the earl. To save his life the latter must deliver up one-third of the besieged maiden's lands. The second day it fares the same with the earl's steward ; the third with the earl himself. Peredur thus wins back all his hostess' lands, and tarries with her three weeks ; but for her love he would not have stayed so long. (9) Peredur next meets the Lady of the Tent, ill-entreated of her husband concerning him. Him he overcomes, compels to acknowledge her innocence, and sends both to Arthur. (10) Peredur comes to the castle of a tall and stately lady, who bids him escape from the sorceresses of Glouces-ter, who will attack the castle that night ; but he resolves to remain, and defends one of the watch when overtaken by a sorceress. The latter hails him by his name. She foreknows she is to suffer harm from him. If he will go with her he shall learn chivalry and the use of arms. Peredur consents on her promising to refrain from injuring the countess, and stays with her three weeks. (11) Peredur comes to a hermit's cell. In the morning it has snowed. A hawk has killed a fowl in front of the cell, but is scared away by Peredur's horse ; a raven has alighted on the bird. Peredur likens the blackness of the raven and the whiteness of the snow and the redness of the blood to the hair and the skin and the two red spots on the cheeks of the lady he loves best. Whilst thus lost in thought, Arthur and his household come up with him, but fail to recognise him. A youth accosts him, but receives no answer ; whereupon he thrusts at Peredur but is struck to the ground. Twenty-four youths essay the same, and are repulsed in like manner. Kai then comes and speaks angrily, but Peredur breaks his arms for him. Gwalchmai then approaches him courteously, learns his name, and brings him to Arthur, who does him honour. Thus all return to Caerlleon. (12) Peredur solicits the love of Angharad Law Eurawc, and when she denies him, vows to speak to no Christian till she loves him. (13) Peredur comes to the castle of a huge grey man, a heathen, after slaying a lion, his porter. The grey man's daughter warns him of her father, and at his request brings his horse and arms to his lodging. Peredur overcomes the vassals, and slays the sons of the grey man, and sends the whole household to Arthur to be baptized. (14) Peredur slays a serpent lying upon a gold ring, and wins the ring. For a long time he speaks to no Christian, and loses colour and aspect through longing for Arthur and his lady love. He returns to Arthur's court, but none know him, and he suffers Kai to thrust him through the thigh without his saying a word. He overcomes many knights, and at length Angharad Law Eurawc confesses her love for him. He remains at Arthur's court. (15) Peredur comes to the castle of a huge, black, one-eyed man. The latter's daughter warns him against her father. But Peredur stays, overcomes the latter, and learns how he lost his eye. On the Mound of Mourning is a cairn, in the cairn a serpent with a stone in its tail, the virtue whereof is to give as much gold to the possessor as he may desire. In fighting the serpent he had lost his eye. He directs Peredur to the serpent, and is slain by him. Peredur refuses the love of the maidens of the castle, and rides forth. (16) He comes to the palace of the son of the King of the Tortures. Every day the Addanc of the Lake slays them. Whilst at discourse a charger enters the hall with a corpse in the saddle. They anoint the corpse with warm water and balsam, and it comes to life. The same happens with two other youths. The morrow they ride forth anew against the Addanc, refusing Peredur, who would go with them ; but he follows and finds seated on a mound the fairest lady, who, if he will pledge her his love, will give him a stone by which he may see the Addanc and be unseen of it. He promises, and she gives him the stone, telling him to seek her in India. Peredur passes through a valley wherein is a flock of white sheep, and one of black, and when they cross the river flowing through the valley they change colour. He learns of their shepherd the way to the Addanc's cave, slays it, meets his three companions of the night before, who tell him it was predicted that he should slay the monster, offers them its head, refuses their sister whom they proffer him in marriage ; accepts the services of a youth, Etlym Gleddyv Coch, who wishes to become his attendant, and rides forth. (17) He comes to the court of the Countess of Achievements, over-throws her three hundred knights ; but learning she loves Etlym resigns her to him. (18) Peredur, accompanied by Etlym, comes to the Mound of Mourning, slays two out of the three hundred knights he finds guarding the serpent, slays the latter, repays the remaining hundred knights all they have spent, gives Etlym the stone and sends him back to his love. (19) Peredur comes to a valley wherein are many coloured tents, lodges with a miller, from whom he borrows food and lodging, and learns that a tournament is forward. He overcomes all the knights present, and sends their horses and arms to the miller as repayment. The Empress of the Tournament sends for him, he repels her messengers thrice, the fourth time he yields. She reveals herself as the lady who had helped him against the Addanc, and she entertains him for fourteen years. (20) Arthur

is at Caerlleon-upon-Usk, with him his knights, and among them
Peredur. There enters, riding upon a yellow mule, a maiden of hideous
aspect. She greets all save Peredur, to whom she reproaches his silence
at the court of the Lame King ; had he asked the meaning of the streaming
spear and of the other wonders the King would have regained health and
the dominions peace—all his misfortunes are due to Peredur. She then
tells of a castle where are five hundred and seventy knights, each with the
lady he loves best—there may fame be acquired; and of a castle on a lofty
mountain where a maiden is detained prisoner, whoso should deliver her
should attain the summit of the fame of the world. Gwalchmai sets forth
to release the imprisoned maiden, Peredur to enquire the meaning of the
bleeding lance. Before they leave a knight enters and defies Gwalchmai to
single combat, for that he had slain his lord by treachery. (21) Gwalchmai
meets a knight who directs him to his own castle, where he is welcomed by
his sister. The steward of the castle accuses him to the knight of being the
slayer of his, the knight's, father. Gwalchmai demands a year to acknowledge or deny the accusation. (22) Peredur, who, seeking tidings of the
black maiden, but finding none, has wandered over the whole island, meets
a priest who chides him for being in armour on Good Friday. Peredur
dismounts, asks the priest's blessing, and learns of a castle where he may
gain tidings of the Castle of Wonders. (23) Peredur proceeds thither, and
meets the King of the castle, who commends him to his daughter, by whom
he is well received. A little yellow page accuses him to the King of winning his daughter's love, and advises that he should be thrown into prison.
But the damsel befriends him, and assists him to take part in a tournament,
where, for three days, he overthrows all opponents. The King at last
recognises him, and offers him his daughter ; but he refuses and sets forth
for the Castle of Wonders. (24) On arriving there he finds the door open,
and in the hall a chessboard and chessmen playing by themselves. He
favours one side which loses, whereupon he casts the chessboard in the
lake. The black maiden comes in and reproaches him—he may find the
chessboard again at the Castle of Ysbidinongyl, where a black man lays
waste the dominions of the Empress. Him Peredur overcomes, but spares
his life ; this the black maiden chides him for, and he slays him ; but the
black maiden still refuses him access to the Empress unless he can slay a
stag, swift as the swiftest bird, with one sharp horn in his forehead. She
gives him a little dog belonging to the Empress which will rouse the stag.
With its aid he slays the latter, but a lady, riding by, carries off the dog,
and chides him for slaying the stag. He can only win her friendship by
going to a cromlech which is in a grove, and challenging to fight three
times a man who dwells there. Peredur complies, and fights with a black
man clad in rusty armour ; but when he dismounts his adversary disappears. (25) Peredur, riding on, comes to a castle where sits a lame
grey-headed man, and Gwalchmai by him. A youth enters the hall and
beseeches Peredur's friendship—he had been the black maiden who came
to Arthur's court, and who had chid Peredur concerning the chessboard ;

he was the youth who came with the bloody head in the salver, and the head was that of Peredur's cousin slain by the sorceresses of Gloucester, who also lamed Peredur's uncle, and he, the speaker, was Peredur's cousin. Peredur seeks aid of Arthur, and they start against the sorceresses. One of the latter slays three of Arthur's men ; whereupon Peredur smites her, and she flees, exclaiming this was Peredur, who had learnt chivalry of them, their destined slayer. She and all her companions are slain. Thus is it related concerning the Castle of Wonders.

The Thornton MS. Sir Perceval.—(1) Percyvelle is son of Percyvelle and Acheflour, Arthur's sister. His father is slain in a tournament by the Red Knight whom he had previously overcome in a former tournament. His mother takes to the woods, brings up her son without instruction till he is fifteen years, when she teaches him to pray to God. (2) He then meets with three knights of Arthur's court —Ewayne, Gawayne, and Kay. He takes them for gods. Learning that they are knights, he determines to go to Arthur's court and become a knight himself, catches a wild horse, and, returning to his mother, announces his attention. She counsels him to be always of measure, to salute knights when he meets them, and at his departure gives him a ring for token. (3) He sets forth, and finding on his way a house makes him-self free of it, eats, drinks, and finding a lady sleeping on a bed takes from her her ring, leaving his mother's in its place. (4) Coming to Arthur's hall he rides into it and up to the King so that his mare kisses Arthur's forehead. He demands knighthood at Arthur's hands, threatening to slay him if refused. Arthur sees the likeness to his father, laments over the latter's untimely fate, and recalls that books say the son should avenge the father's bane. Percyvelle bids him let be his jangling and dub him knight. Whilst sitting down to table the Red Knight comes in, carries off Arthur's cup (five years long had he done so) none daring to hinder him. At the King's lament Percyvelle engages to slay the Red Knight, and bring the cup back if knighthood be granted him. The King promises, Percyvelle follows the ravisher, who scorns him, but is slain by a dart flung at him. He captures the knight's steed, and not being able otherwise to remove his armour, and recalling his mother's injunction " out of the iron burn the tree " kindles a fire to burn the body. Gawayne, who has followed him, shows him how to unlace the armour ; when that is removed Percyvelle casts the body into the fire to roast. He refuses to return to Arthur, looking upon himself as great a lord as the King, but sends the cup back through Gawayne and rides on. (5) He meets an old witch, mother to the Red Knight, who addresses him as her son ; her he spears and casts into the fire. (6) He meets ten knights, who flee, taking him for the Red Knight, but on his raising his vizor the oldest knight, reassured, relates how the Red Knight bore him and his sons enmity, and how, fifteen years before, he had slain his brother. Learning that Percyvelle had burnt his enemy, he invites him to his castle. (7) Whilst at meat a

messenger comes in from the Maiden-land begging help from the Lady
Lufamour against a " Sowdane," who would have her to wife. Percyvelle
starts forth with three of the old knight's sons, whom, however, he sends
back each after a mile. Meanwhile, the King at Carebedd, mourning for
Percyvelle, receives Lufamour's messages, gains from him tidings of Percyvelle, and sets forth with his court to follow him. Percyvelle, coming to
the Sowdane's camp, is set upon by the guard, but slays them all, and then
lays him down to rest under the castle wall. In the morning Lufamour's
men make her aware of the slaughter wrought upon her enemies. She
perceives Percyvelle and sends her chamberlain, Hatlayne, to bid him to
her chamber. Whilst at table together tidings are brought that the enemy
have nearly taken the town. Percyvelle sallies forth alone and soon leaves
not one alive. He is then ware of four knights—Arthur, Ewayne, Gawayne,
Kay. He pricks against them and Gawayne receives his onslaught. They
recognise each other, and all proceed to Lufamour's castle. The next day
the Sowdane challenges all comers ; Percyvelle, dubbed knight by Arthur,
slays him, and thereafter weds Lufamour. (8) After a year he thinks on
his mother's loneliness, and sets forth to seek her. Hearing a damsel
lamenting in the wood, he finds her bound to a tree, for that a year before,
while sleeping, a stranger had robbed her of a ring leaving his own in its
stead. Now her ring was of a stone of such virtue that neither death nor
hurt could come to the wearer. He releases her, overcomes the Black
Knight who had bound her, reconciles them and claims his own ring for
the ring he had taken. But the Black Knight has given it to the lord of
the land—a giant. (9) Percyvelle slays the giant, and claims the ring of
the porter. The latter tells him how his master, loving a fair lady, had
offered her that same ring, but she, exclaiming that he had killed her son,
rushed into the forest and was since then bereft of her senses. Percyvelle
puts on a goat's skin, and after nine days search finds her. A magic
drink of the giant's throws her into a three days' sleep, after which, restored
to her right mind, she goes home with her son. He afterwards goes to
the Holy Land, and is there slain.

The Queste del Saint Graal.—[*Furnivall's text (F.) has been
taken as the basis of the present summary. Words and passages not found
in the Welsh translation (W) are italicised ; words or passages found in the
Welsh translation instead of those in Furnivall are in parentheses. The
variants from Birch-Hirschfeld's Summary (B.H.) are given in the notes.*]

(1) On Whitsun Eve the companions of the Round Table being assembled at Camelot, a *damsel* (youth) comes in great haste, asks for Lancelot
and bids him *from King Pelles* (for the sake of whatever he loved most)
accompany her to the forest. Notwithstanding Guinevere's opposition
he does so, and comes to a nunnery where he finds his two cousins,
Boort and Lionel. Three nuns then bring Galahad, a child the like of
whom might scarce be found in the world ; one asks Lancelot to knight
him, he consents, and on the morrow Lancelot and his companions return to

Camelot ; his cousins think the child must be Lancelot's son, but Lancelot answers no word. (2) At the Round Table the seat of each knight is marked, but on the Seat Perillous it is written that *four hundred and fifty-four* (four hundred and fifty) years have passed since the Lord's Passion, and that on this Whitsun Day the seat shall find its master. Lancelot covers these words, and, whilst at Kay's reminding, the court awaits an adventure before sitting down to meat, a youth tells them of a stone floating on the water. It is a block of red marble, in which sticks a sword, and upon it written that none may draw the sword save the best knight in the world. Lancelot declares that the wonders of the Holy Grail are about to begin, and refuses to essay the adventure; Gawain, Perceval, and others try, but fail ; they then sit down to table served by twelve kings ; an old man enters, leading a knight in vermeil armour, whom he proclaims the desired knight, of the seed of David and kin of Joseph of Arimathea, who shall achieve the adventures of the Holy Grail. He draws near the Seat Perillous, on which is now written, " This is Galahad's seat," sits himself therein, dismisses the old man, *and bids him greet, " My uncle, King Pelles, and my grandfather, the rich fisher."** (3) Great honour is done to the new knight, whom Lancelot recognises as his son, and Bors and Lionel as the youth begot by Lancelot upon the daughter *of the Fisher King* (King Pelles). The Queen is told that the knight is come, and her ladies say he *shall end the wonders of Great Britain, and through him the Maimed King shall be healed.* Galahad is then urged by Arthur to essay the adventure of the sword, consents, easily draws out the sword, and asks for a shield. (4) A damsel appears, weeps for Lancelot as having lost his place as the best knight in the world, and tells the King from Nasciens, the hermit, that on that day he would send the Holy Grail to feed the companions of the Round Table. A tournament is ordered, in which Galahad is held the best, as he over-throws all save Lancelot and Perceval. After vespers the court sits down to table, a clap of thunder is heard, followed by the brightest of sunbeams, so that all are as if lighted by the Holy Ghost. None know whence the light comes, and none has power to say a word. The Holy Grail enters, covered with white samite, but none may see who carries it ; the hall is filled with sweet odours, and as the Grail passes along the tables each seat is filled with such meat as each one longs for. Then it departs, none may say how, and those can now speak who before could say no word. (5) All return thanks to God for the grace vouchsafed them, and Gawain tells them that heretofore no man had been served with whatever he might desire save *at the Maimed King's* (at the court of King Peleur). But they could not behold the Grail openly, and Gawain declares he will go on quest of it for a year and a day. The knights of the Round Table make a like vow. Arthur is much distressed, as he knows many will die on the quest. The Queen and her ladies weep likewise, and propose to join their

---

* Birch-Hirschfeld, in his Summary (p. 37, l. 22) or his MS. authority, B.M., xix, E. iii., has transposed the relationships.

knights, but an old priest tells them from Nasciens, the hermit, that no knight entering on the quest of the Holy Grail is to have with him his lady or damsel—the quest is no earthly one. On the morrow, at King Bandamagus' suggestion, all the questers, Galahad first, swear to maintain the quest for a year and a day and longer if need be. After the Queen has taken leave of Lancelot, and Arthur has vainly tried to force a shield on Galahad, the questers set off together and pass the first night at Vagan's Castle. On the morrow they ride forth and separate. (6) After five days Galahad comes to an abbey where he find King Bandamagus and Ywain "li aoutres." The abbey contains a shield which no knight save the destined one may take and go unslain or unhurt. King Bandamagus would take it, but is overthrown by a White Knight ; Galahad then takes it, and his right to do so is admitted by the White Knight, who tells him as follows concerning it :—Forty-three years after our Lord's Passion, Joseph of Arimathea, who took our Lord's body down from the Cross,* came to the city Sarras, where dwelt King Evelac, then a Saracen, who was at war with his neighbour, Tholomes. Josephes, Joseph's son, warned Evelac against going forth to battle unprepared, and, in answer to the King's questions what he should do, told him of the new law and Gospel truth and the Saviour's death, and fixed on his shield a cross of sandal. He was to uncover this on the fourth day's fighting, and to call on the Lord. When he did so he beheld a bleeding, crucified figure. He won the battle, and on his telling the story his brother-in-law, Nasciens, received baptism. The shield then restored to a man his lost hand. Evelac was baptized, and guarded the shield in lordly fashion. Josephes came with his father to Great Britain, where King Crudel threw them with many other Christians into prison. Mordrains† and Nasciens than invaded Great Britain, released Josephes and remained with him in the land. When Josephes was on his deathbed, and Evelac asked him for a remembrance, then he bade King Mordrains bring his shield, and with the blood streaming from his nose marked on it a cross ; this would always remain red, and no knight should with impunity unhang the shield till Galahad should come, last of Nasciens' line. Where Nasciens lay buried, there the shield was to be kept. (7) Galahad draws near a tomb in the abbey graveyard, whence issues a voice telling him not to approach and drive it out. But he does so, and a smoke in man's form comes out ; on opening the tomb a dead knight's body is found lying therein, this is cast out. These things are a symbol: the hard tombstone signifies the *hard-heartedness of the world* (the hardship which

---

* And buried it, adds B. H. in his Summary, whether on MS. authority or not I cannot say, but the Welsh translation has—"there was a period of 240 years" (an obvious mistake on the part of the translator) "after the passion of J. C. when Jos. of A. came ; he who buried J. C. and drew him down from the cross."

† Thus was Evelach called as a Christian, adds B. H. Here W. agrees with Furnivall.

Jesus Christ had in this world) ;* the dead body those dead in sin, and as in Christ's time when they slew Him and were harried out of their land by Vespasian as a punishment; the smoke was a devil who fled from Galahad because he was a virgin.   (8) On the morrow Galahad rides forth accompanied by Melians, a youth who had begged to be allowed to serve him, and whom he had knighted.   They separate at a cross road, Melians takes the left hand road in spite of warning, comes to a tent where hangs a golden crown, seizes it, meets a strange knight who overthrows and had slain him but for Galahad coming to the rescue and overcoming first one, then a second assailant.   Melians is taken to an abbey to be tended, and learns that the two knights who almost overpowered him were his pride in taking the left hand path, his covetousness in carrying off the crown of gold.   (9) Galahad enters a hermitage to pray there, and hears a voice bidding him proceed to the Castle of Maidens and rid it of its bad customs.   He encounters on the way seven knights whom he must overcome, such was the custom of the castle.   He forces them to flight, and an old priest brings him the keys of the castle.   He finds therein numberless maidens, and learns that the former lord of the castle had been, with his son, slain by the seven knights, who had striven before-hand to carry off his daughter.   She foretold that as they had gained the castle for a maiden's sake, they would lose it through a maiden, and be over-come by a single knight, whereupon they determined to make prisoner every maiden passing that way.   Galahad delivers the captives, and puts a daughter of the former duke in possession of the castle.   He learns then that the seven brothers have been slain by Gawain, Gheriot, and Ywain. (10) The story now returns to Gawain.   He passes by the abbey where Galahad found the shield, then that where Melians lay ill, is reproached by a friar with being too sinful to be with Galahad, meets Gheheries, his brother, meets Ywain on the morrow, meets the seven brothers who attack them and are slain ; then Gawain comes alone to a hermitage, confesses for the first time since fourteen years, is admonished by the hermit, learns that the Castle of Maidens signifies hell, the captives the good souls wrongfully therein confined before Christ's coming, the seven knights the seven sins.   Gawain is pressed, but vainly, to make penitence.   (11) The story returns to Galahad.   After wandering for awhile without adventures he meets Lancelot and Perceval.   They do not recognise him, not knowing his *arms* (shield),† and attack him.   He overcomes them, but learning from the words of a recluse, who sees the combat, that she really knows him, and, fearing recognition, he hurries off.‡   (12) Perceval stays with the recluse, and Lancelot starts in pursuit of the Unknown Knight.

---

* Here Birch-Hirschfeld's Summary agrees with W.

† B. H. agrees with W.

‡ According to B. H., the recluse tells him he has fought with his friends, whereupon, ashamed, he hurries off.

He comes in the night to a stone cross near which stands (an old)*
chapel. He dismounts and enters, but an iron rail hinders his progress ; through it he sees an altar whereon *burn seven candles* (a silver
candlestick, a wax taper).† He leaves the chapel, unsaddles his horse,
and lies down to sleep by the cross. Then comes a sick knight on a
bier drawn by two horses, dolourously lamenting. He looks at Lancelot,
but says no word, thinking him asleep, nor does Lancelot say aught, but
remains half asleep. And the sick knight laments, " *When may I have
solace from the holy vessel for the pain I suffer for such a small fault* (was
ever so much pain as is upon me who have done no evil at all)?‡ But
Lancelot says no word, nor when the candlestick comes towards the
cross and the Holy Grail approaches the sick knight, who prays he may
be made whole to join likewise the quest. Then crawling to the table
whereon the vessel stands, and *touching his eyes with* (kissing) it, feels
relief and slumbers. The Grail disappears and Lancelot still says never a
word, for which aftertimes much mischance was his. The sick knight arises
well, a squire appears and *arms* him (with Lancelot's sword and helm),§
and brings him Lancelot's steed, and the knight swears never to rest till
he knows why the Holy Grail appears in so many places of the Kingdom
of Logres, and by whom it was brought to England. So he departs, and
his squire carries off Lancelot's armour. Lancelot awakes wondering
whether what he has seen be dream or truth. And he hears a voice
saying—harder than stone, bitterer than wood, more despised than the
fig tree—he must away, not pollute the spot where is the Holy Grail. He
wanders forth weeping, comes to a hermit, confesses his great sin, his love
for Guinevere, is admonished to tear it from his heart, when there may
still be hope for him. Lancelot promises, and has the adventure at the
chapel explained to him, and stays with the hermit for penance and instruction. (13) The story now returns to Perceval. The recluse orders he be
well taken care of, she loves him well, he is her nephew. She dissuades
him from fighting Galahad as he wishes, does he wish to die and be killed
as his brothers *for their outrages* (in their combats and tournaments) ? He
and Galahad and Bors will achieve the Quest. She is his aunt, formerly
Queen of the Waste Land. *He asks about his mother whom he fears he has
badly treated, and learns she died when he went to Arthur's court.*‖ He asks
further concerning the knight with the red arms, and is told as follows :—
Since Christ's coming were three chief tables ; first, the table at which
Christ often ate with his Apostles ; second, the table of the Holy Grail,
established in semblance and remembrance of the first, by which so many

---

* B. H. here agrees with W.
† B. H. has *five* candles.
‡ B. H. : " When will the Holy Vessel come to still the pain I feel ? Never
suffered man as I."
§ B. H. agrees with W.
‖ B. H. agrees with Furnivall.

miracles were wrought in this land in the time of Joseph of Arimathea, in the beginning when Christianity was brought to this country. He came with four thousand poor companions. One day, wandering in a forest, they had nothing to eat, but an old woman brought *twelve* (ten) loaves, these they bought and they were wroth with one another when they came to divide them. Joseph angry, took the twelve loaves, made the people sit, and by virtue of the Holy Grail multiplied the loaves to their need. At that table was a seat where Josephes, son of Joseph, might sit, but none other, for, as the history tells, the place was blessed by our Lord himself. Now two brothers, relatives of Josephes, envied him his leadership, saying they were of as good seed as he, and one sat in Josephes' seat, and was straightway swallowed up by the earth, whence the seat was called the Dreaded Seat. Last came the Round Table, made by Merlin's counsel, to show the roundness of the world and of the firmament. And Merlin foretold that by companions of this table should the truth of the Grail be known, and that three should achieve it, two virgins and one chaste, and the one should surpass his father as man surpasses wolf, and he should be master, and for him Merlin made a great and wonderful seat, wherein none might sit unharmed save he, and it was known as the Seat Perillous. And as at Whitsuntide the Holy Spirit came to the Apostles in guise of fire, so at Whitsuntide Galahad came clad in red armour. And on the day he came the questing for the Grail began, which might not cease till the truth concerning it *and the lance* was known. To find Galahad, Perceval must first try Castle *Gher* (Goth) where dwells a cousin of Galahad, *and then Castle Corbenic where dwells the Maimed King.* (14) His aunt then tells how after that her husband fell in war against King Laban she withdrew into that wild place. And her son went to serve King Pelles, their relative, and since two years she only knows of him that he is following tournaments throughout Great Britain. (15) On the morrow Perceval comes to a monastery, and seeing mass being performed would enter but cannot, and sees a sick bed with a man or woman lying on it, whom, as he rises when the body of our Lord is raised, he sees to be an old man crowned, with his body full of wounds and crying out, "Father, forget me not." He seems as if he were over *four hundred* (one hundred and four) years old. Perceval asks concerning these wonders, and is told as follows :—When Joseph of Arimathea came to this land, the Saracen, King Crudel, hearing of the Grail by which he lived, threw him and his son Josephes and some hundred others into prison for forty days, and forbade food to be given them. But they had the holy vessel with them. When Mordrains and his brother-in-law, Seraphe, heard these things, they assembled their host, landed in Britain, overcame Crudel, and freed Joseph. On the morrow Evelac, as he was called before he became Christian, desired to see the Holy Grail plainly, and though warned to desist pressed forward to do so, and was struck blind and helpless. He accepted his punishment submissively, but only prayed to Christ that he might survive till *the good knight should come, the* *best* of his seed* (the knight who is to achieve the adventures of the Holy Grail). A voice answered his prayer should be granted, and then he should receive the light of his eyes and his wounds should be made whole. This happened *four hundred* (one hundred and four) years before, and it was that King Evelac whom Perceval had seen, and during that while he had fed on nought else save the Lord's body. (16) Perceval riding forth on the morrow is attacked by twenty knights, sore pressed, and only rescued by the Red Knight's help, who then disappears. (17) Perceval, having lost his horse, asks one vainly from a passing squire, from whom it is shortly afterwards carried off by another knight, whom Perceval, mounted on the squire's cob, attacks but is overthrown. (18) At night a woman appears and offers him a horse if he will do her will— she is, in truth, the enemy. He agrees, she mounts him, he comes to a river, and, before essaying to ford it, makes the sign of the cross, whereupon the horse rushes howling into the water. (19) Perceval, rescued from this peril, finds himself on a wild island mountain, full of savage beasts ; he helps a lion against a snake and wins its service. He is ill at ease on his island, but he trusts God, and is not like those men of Wales where sons pull their fathers out of bed and kill them to save the disgrace of their dying in bed. (20) That night, sleeping by the lion's side, Perceval dreams of two women visiting him, one mounted on a lion, the second on a serpent ; this one reproaches him for killing the serpent. On the morrow an old man comes ship-borne, comforts Perceval with good counsel, and interprets his dream : the dame on the lion was Christ's new law, she on the serpent the old law. (21) A damsel then appears, warns Perceval against the old man, prepares for him a rich banquet with good wine, not British, as in Great Britain they only drink cervoise and other home-made drinks, and excites his passion. He is on the point of yielding, but seeing the cross-handled pommel of his sword crosses himself, and the damsel disappears in flames. Perceval pierces his thigh with his sword in his contrition. The old man reappears, exhorts, explains the various features of his temptation, and finally takes him away with him in his ship. (22) The story now returns to Lancelot. After three exhortations from the hermit he sets forth, and first meets a servant, who assails him bitterly as an unfaithful traitorous knight, in that having openly seen the Holy Grail doing its wonders before him, he yet moved not from his seat. (23) He comes to a hermit's hut and finds the hermit lamenting over the dead body of his companion, who, at his nephew, Agaran's, request, had left the hermitage to aid him against his enemies, and had been treacherously slain by the latter. These things are told by a devil, which had entered into the dead hermit's body. Lancelot is admonished at great length, receives stripes, puts on the dead hermit's hair shirt, and finally leaves with the advice that he should confess every week. (24) He meets a damsel who encourages him, but tells him he will find no lodging for the night.

---

* B. H., the *ninth*.

He dismounts at the foot of a cross at the cross-ways, and has a vision of a man surrounded with stars, crowned and accompanied by seven Kings and two knights, who pray to be taken to heaven ; a man descending from heaven orders one of the knights away, whilst to the other he gives the shape of a winged lion, so that he flies up to heaven and is admitted. * (25) Lancelot meets the knight who had carried off his arms, and who attacks, but is overthrown by him. (26) *He comes to a hermitage, confesses, tells his vision, and learns that it has a great meaning in respect of his lineage, which must be expounded at much length : forty-two years after the Passion of Christ, Joseph of Arimathea left Jerusalem, came to Sarras, helped Evelac, who received baptism at the hands of Josephes, together with his brother-in-law, Seraphe (who took the name Nasciens), and who became a pillar of the holy faith, so that the great secrets of the Holy Grail were opened to him, which none but Joseph had beheld before, and no knight after save in dream. Now Evelac dreamed that out of his nephew, son of Nasciens, came forth a great lake, whence issued nine streams, eight of the same size, and the last greater than all the rest put together ; our Lord came and washed in the lake which King Mordrains thus saw flowing from Celidoine's belly. This Celidoine was the man surrounded by stars in Lancelot's vision, and this because he knew the course of the stars and the manner of the planets, and he was first King of Scotland, and the nine streams were his nine descendants, of whom seven Kings and two knights :—first, Warpus ; second, Chrestiens ;† third, Alain li Gros ; fourth, Helyas ; fifth, Jonaans, who went to Wales and there took to wife King Moroneus' daughter ; sixth, Lancelot, who had the King of Ireland's daughter to wife ; seventh, Bans. These were the seven Kings who appeared to Lancelot. The eighth stream was Lancelot himself, the elder of the knights of the vision. The ninth stream was Galahad, begot by Lancelot upon the Fisher King's daughter, lion-like in power, deepest of all the streams.‡* (27) Lancelot comes to a castle with a meadow before it, whereon a throng of black armoured knights is tourneying against knights in white armour. Lancelot goes to the help of the former,§ but is captured, and on being released rides off lamenting. At night, as he sleeps, a man comes from heaven and reproaches him with his ill faith. A hermitess expounds the allegorical meaning of the adventure. The white knights are those of Eliezer, son of King Pelles, the black those of Argastes, son of King Helain ; this symbolised the Quest, which was a tournament between the heavenly knights and the earthly ones, and in that Quest none might enter who was black with sin ; and Lancelot though sinful, having entered thereon had joined the black knights, and his capture by the others was

---

* B. H., the vision is that of a crowned old man, who with two knights worships the cross.

† B. H., Nasciens.

‡ B. H. has all this passage, save that the references to the vision at the cross-ways seem omitted.

§ B. H., the latter.

his overthrow by Galahad, and his lamentation his return to sin, and it was our Lord who reproached him in his vision ; let him not depart from truth. (28) Lancelot comes to Lake Marchoise, is attacked by a knight in black armour, who kills his horse and rides off; he lays down on the shore and awaits trustfully God's help. (29) The story returns to Gawain. After journeying many days adventureless, he meets Hector de Mares. Neither has heard aught of Lancelot, Galahad, or Bohors. Travelling together they come to a deserted chapel, where, passing the night, Gawain dreams he sees in a meadow one hundred and fifty bulls all spotted, save three, one being dingy, the two others being pure white. Of the one hundred and forty-seven who set off to find better pasture many die and some return, of the three one returns, but two remain between whom strife arises and they separate. Hector dreams that he and Lancelot, being companions, are attacked by a man who knocks Lancelot off his horse and sits him on an ass, after which Lancelot, coming to a fair fountain, would drink of it, but it vanishes ; he, Hector, keeping his horse comes to a castle, the lord of which refuses him admission for that he is too high mounted. Whilst telling one another their dreams, a hand with a taper appears and vanishes, and a voice tells them that, poor of belief as they are, they cannot attain the Holy Grail. On their way to find a hermit who may explain these wonders, Gawain is attacked by and kills a knight, Ywains the Adulterer, son of King Urien. They then come to the hermit, Nasciens, who explains the bulls as the companions of the Round Table, the spotted ones those stained by sin, the three unspotted ones are the achievers, two white, virgins—Galahad and Perceval—one dingy, having once sinned carnally, Bors. The last part of the dream may not be explained, as evil might come of it. In Hector's dream the two horses are Pride and Ostentation. Lancelot's being seated on an ass signifies the putting off of pride, the fountain is the Holy Grail. Both knights are too full of sin to continue in the quest of the Grail. They ride forth and meet with no adventure worth notice. (30) The story returns to Bors. After first coming to a hermit, who exhorts him to abandon the Quest if he do not feel himself free from sin, to whom he confesses, from whom he receives absolution, and to whom he vows to eat nought save bread and water till the Quest be achieved, he comes to a castle whose mistress is sore oppressed by her sister, against whose champion, Priadam the Black, she has vainly sought a defender. Bors promises to come to help. He passes the night at the castle and will not sleep in the rich bed she offers him, though in the morning he tumbles it as if he had lain in it. He overcomes Priadam, and reinstates the lady in her lordship. (31) On the morrow he meets his brother, naked, bound on a hack, being beaten with thorns by two knights. At the same moment passes a very fair maiden being carried off by a knight, and she cries to him for help. He is in anguish, but goes to the maiden's help, wounds her would-be ravisher, and restores her to her friends. (32) He then hurries after his brother, but meets a seeming monk who makes him believe his brother is dead, and gives him an explanation of dreams he has had. He then comes to a tower and is welcomed by its inmates. A damsel offers him her love, and when he refuses threatens with twelve other damsels to throw herself from the tower. Bors is full of pity, but thinks they had better lose their souls than he his. They fall from the tower, Bors crosses himself, and the whole vanishes, being a deceit of 'the devil. His brother's corpse that had been shown him is also gone. (33) On the morrow he comes to an abbey, where he learns that his brother lives, and where all his dreams and adventures are allegorically explained. He then meets Lionel, his brother, who reproaches him bitterly for his conduct, and falls upon him with intent to kill. First a hermit, then a passing knight, Calogrenant, would stop him, but he slays both. Bors is at length, in spite of prayers and entreaties, compelled to draw in self defence, but a voice tells him to flee, and a fiery brand comes from heaven between them. Bors follows the command of the voice directing him towards the sea, where Perceval awaits him. He comes to a ship covered with white samite, and finds therein Perceval, who at first does not know him again, and who tells him all that he has passed through. (34) The story returns to Galahad. After count-less adventures he finds himself one day opposed to Gawain and Hector de Mares in a tournament ; he deals the former such a blow as knocks him out of his saddle. (35) He is brought to the ship wherein are Perceval and Bors by a damsel, who accompanies them until, fourteen days' sail from Logres, they come to a desert isle off which is another ship, on which is written* that those who would enter should see they were full of faith. The damsel then tells Perceval she is his sister, *daughter of King Pellehem.* They enter the ship and find a rich bed with a crown at its head; and at its foot a sword six inches out of the scabbard, its tip a stone of all the colours in the world, its handle of the bones of two beasts, the serpent Papagast, the fish Orteniaus ; it is covered with a cloth whereon is written that only the first of his line would grasp the sword. Perceval and Bors both essay vainly. Galahad, on being asked, sees written on the blade that he only should draw who could strike better than others. The damsel tells the story of the sword as follows :—When the ship came to the Kingdom of Logres there was war between King Lambar, father to the Maimed King, and King Urlain, heretofore Saracen, but newly baptised. Once Urlain, discomfited, fled to the ship, and, finding therein the sword, drew it and slew King Laban† with it, and that was the first blow struck with the sword in the Kingdom of Logres, and there came from it such pestilence and destruction in the land of the two kingdoms that it was afterwards called the Waste Land. When Urlain re-entered the ship he fell down dead. (36) Galahad, further examining the sword, finds the scabbard of serpent's skin, but the hangings of poor stuff. On the scabbard is written that the wearer must surpass his fellows, and the hangings be changed only by a King's daughter and she a maid ; on turning the sword

* B. H., in Chaldee.
† B. H., Labran slays Urban.

over, the other side is found black as pitch, and bearing words that he who should praise it most should blame it most in his greatest need. Perceval's sister explains this as follows : Forty years after our Lord's Passion, Nasciens, Mordrains' brother-in-law, came to the Turning Isle, and found this ship, and therein bed and sword, this last he coveted, but had not the hardihood to draw it, though he stayed eight days food and drinkless longing for it ; on the ninth day a tempest drove him to another island, where, assailed by a giant, he drew the sword, and though it snapped in two and thus fulfilled the inscription, yet he overcame the giant. He afterwards met Mordrains and told him of these wonders ; Mordrains reunited the fragments, then, in obedience to a voice, they left the ship, but in going Nasciens was wounded for having dared to draw a sword of which he was not worthy, thus he who praised it most had most reason to blame it. As for the other words, *King Pelles,** *called the Maimed King* (a lame King who was my, *i.e.*, the damsel's, uncle) once came to this ship on the shore of the sea over against Ireland, and entering it found the sword, drew but was wounded through the thighs by a lance, *and might not be healed till Galahad come.*† (37) They then examine the bed and find it has three spindles ; that in front, snow white ; that behind, blood red ; that above, emerald green, and lest this be thought a lie the story turns from its straight path to explain about these spindles. After Eve, yielding to the devil's advice, had caused Adam to sin, and both knew themselves carnal and were ashamed, and were driven forth from Paradise, Eve kept the branch of the Tree of Life which she had plucked, and planted it and it grew to a tree with branches and leaves white in token that Eve was a virgin when she planted it. Sitting one day beneath the tree, God commanded them to know one another carnally, and when they were ashamed to set about such foul work sent darkness over them. Abel was thus begotten, and the Tree of Life turned green. Afterwards Cain slew Abel underneath that same tree and it turned red. At the Deluge it remained unharmed and lasted till Solomon's time. Whilst the wise King was pondering over the malice of his wife and of all women, a voice told him a woman of his line should bring men more joy than her sex had caused sorrow, and that a virgin knight should be the last of his lineage. His wife, whom he consults as to how he shall let this knight know he had foreknowledge of his coming, advised the building of the ship, and the taking of David's sword to be fitted with a new hilt of precious stones, and a new pommel and scabbard, and placed in the ship together with Solomon's crown on a rich bed ; she furthermore had three spindles made from the Tree of Life and from trees grown from it. And when all was ready Solomon saw in dreams angels coming from heaven and putting the different inscriptions on the sword and ship. (38) The story speaks now of other things. New hangings had not been put on the sword, this

---

* The 1488 text has Urban.
† B. H., Thus was the King wounded, and he was Galahad's grandfather.

was to be done by a damsel.   Perceval's sister supplies hangings made of
her own hair, and names the sword "The Sword of Strange Hangings,"
and the scabbard " Memory of Blood," and Galahad girds on the sword.
(39) On the morrow they set sail and come to Castle Carchelois, in the
March of Scotland, the inmates whereof attack them but are all slain.
Galahad is sorry for those he has killed, but a priest tells him they are
heathens, and he has done the best work in the world, as the three knights
who held the castle had ravished their own sister and wounded their father,
Count Ernous, to death.   Before the latter dies he urges Galahad *to go to
the assistance of the Maimed King* (to undertake other adventures).*   (40) On
the morrow they meet a white stag led by four lions ; these come to a
hermitage, hear mass, the stag becomes a man and sits on the altar, the
lions a man, an eagle, a lion, and an ox, all winged.   (41) On the morrow
Perceval takes Galahad's sword, which he will wear from henceforth.
They come to a castle, the inmates of which demand that Perceval's sister
should pay the custom of the castle, which is to give a dishful of blood
from her right arm.   The three companions protect Perceval's sister
against overwhelming odds till nightfall, when, learning that the blood is
asked to heal the Lady of the Castle suffering from leprosy, Perceval's
sister sacrifices herself.   Before dying she gives directions that her body
is to be put in a ship and buried in the Palace Spiritual in Sarras.   Bors
then leaves his two companions to succour a wounded knight pursued by
a knight and a dwarf ;† and Perceval and Galahad, after seeing the castle
they had thus left destroyed by fire from heaven in vengeance of the
blood of the good maidens which had there been shed, likewise separate.
(42) The story returns to Lancelot.   He is at the Water of Marcoise,
surrounded by the forest and high rocks, but he does not lose faith in
God ; in obedience to a voice he goes on board a passing ship and finds
therein Perceval's sister, whose story he learns from the letter at her head.
After a month's journeying a knight joins them who proves to be Galahad,
and they pass together half a year achieving marvellous adventures.   After
Easter, at the new time when the birds sing their sweet and varied songs,
they come to land, and a knight in white arms bids Galahad leave his
father, which he does.   (43) After a month's further wandering on the
sea, Lancelot comes to a castle guarded by two lions,‡ against whom he
would at first defend himself, but is reproved for trusting his strength
rather than his Creator.   Entering, he comes to a room wherein are the
Holy Vessel, and a priest celebrating mass ; Lancelot is warned not to
enter, but when he sees that the priest about to raise the body of God has
a man put into his hands, he cannot refrain from pressing forward to his
aid, but is struck down by a fiery wind and remains fourteen days dumb,

---

* It does not appear from B. H.'s Summary whether his text agrees with
F. or W.

† B. H., seven knights.

‡ B. H., that was the Castle of Corbenic where the Holy Grail was kept.

food- and drinkless. He finds he is in Castle Corbenic, and a damsel tells him his quest is ended. King Pelles rejoices to see him, at dinner the Holy Grail fills the tables so that living man could not think of greater plenty ; whilst at dinner Hector de Mares comes to the castle door, but is ashamed to enter, hearing that Lancelot is within, and rides off pursued by the reproaches and taunts of those of the castle. Lancelot returns to Arthur's court, passing on the way the tomb of Bandamagus, whom Gawain had slain. (44) The story returns to Galahad. He comes to an abbey wherein is King Mordrains, who knows his approach, and asks that he may die in his arms ; Galahad takes him on his breast, Mordrains dies and all his wounds are found healed. (45) Galahad cools the boiling fountain by putting his hand in it. (46) Galahad delivers from the tomb where he had been burning three hundred and fifty-four years his relative, Symeu, who thus expiated his sin against Joseph of Arimathea. (47) Galahad rides five years before he comes to the *house of the Maimed King* (the court of King Peleur), and during all the five years Perceval bears him company, and within that time they *achieve the great adventures of the Kingdom of Logres* (cast out the evil adventures of the Island of Britain). (48) One day they met Bors, who in the five years had not been in bed four times. The three come to *Castle Corbenic** (the court of King Peleur) *where they are greeted by King Pelles, and where Eliezer, King Pelles' son, brings the broken sword with which Joseph had been pierced through the thighs ; Bors cannot rejoin the pieces, Perceval can only adjust them together, Galahad alone can make the sword whole, and it is then given to Bors.* (50) At vesper-time a hot wind strikes the palace, and a voice orders all unfit to sit at Christ's table to depart, as the true knights were to be fed with Heaven's food. All leave save *King Pelles, Eliezer, his son, and his niece, the most religious maid on the earth* (a young maiden) ; to them enter nine knights† and salute Galahad : three are from *Gaul* (Wales), three from Ireland, three from Denmark. *Then four damsels bring in on a wooden bed a man, crowned, in evil plight, who greets Galahad as his long-expected deliverer.* A voice orders out of the room him who has not been a companion of the Quest, and straightway *King Pelles and Eliezer and* the damsel depart. From heaven comes a man clad like a Bishop and borne in a chair by four‡ angels, who place him before the table upon which stands the Holy Grail. Upon his forehead is written that he was *Joseph* (son of Joseph of Arimathea) first Bishop of of Christendom, whereat they wonder, as they know that man lived three hundred years before. He kneels before the altar and opens the door of the *ark* (chamber), and four angels‡ issue, *two bearing burning lights, the third a cloth of red samite, the fourth a lance bleeding so hard that the drops*

---

* B. H., the Castle of the Maimed King.

† B.H., ten. Obviously a mistake on the part of his text, as the nine with the three Grail questers make up twelve, the number of Christ's disciples.

‡ B. H., three.

run into a box he holds in his other hand (two with torches, the third with the lance, the fourth holding the box into which the blood drops); the candles are placed on the table, the cloth is placed on the holy vessel so that the blood fell into it. Joseph then celebrates the Sacrament, and on his raising the wafer, as it were a child descends from heaven and strikes itself into the wafer, so that it takes man's form. Joseph then kisses Galahad and bids him be fed by the Saviour's own hand, and vanishes. But there comes out of the holy vessel, a man with hands bleeding and feet and body, and says He will reveal His secrets, and give the high food so long desired and toiled for. He gives the Sacrament to Galahad and his companions, and explains that the Grail is the dish of the Last Supper, and Galahad shall see it more fully in the City of Sarras, whither it is going, Britain being unworthy of it, and whither he is to follow it with Perceval and Bors ; *but as he must not leave the land without healing the Maimed King he is to take some of the blood of the lance and therewith anoint his legs.* Galahad asks why all may not come with him ; but Christ says they are twelve who have eaten as the Apostles were twelve, and they must separate as the Apostles separated. *Galahad then heals the Maimed King, who goes into an abbey of white monks.* (51) The three companions, after sending messages to Arthur's court *through Estrois de Gariles and Claudius, son of King Claudas,*† coming to Solomon's ship, herein they find the Holy Grail, set sail ; on landing bury Perceval's sister, heal a cripple to help them carry the Grail-table, are cast in prison by King *Escorant* for a year, are fed by the Holy Grail ; at *Escorant's* death Galahad is made King, fashions a tree of gold and precious stones over the Grail and prays before it every morning as do his companions. (52) On the anniversary of Galahad's crowning the three see before the holy vessel a man clad like a Bishop, who begins mass and calls Galahad to see what he has so longed to see, and at the sight Galahad trembles very greatly, and he thanks God for letting him see that which tongue may not describe nor heart think, and he begs that he may pass away from this earthly life to the heavenly one. The Bishop then gives him the body of God, and reveals himself as Josephus, son of Joseph of Arimathea. Galahad kisses Perceval and Bors, and sends greetings to Lancelot through Bors, his soul then leaves his body and angels take it away. A hand from heaven then comes to the vessel and takes it and the lance, and bears it heavenwards, so that since there was no man bold enough to say he has seen the Holy Grail (except Gwalchmai once). (52) *Galahad's body is buried. Perceval goes into a hermitage, where Bors stays with him for a year and two months ; Perceval dies, and is buried by Bors in Galahad's tomb ; Bors left alone in a place as strange as Babylon, sets sail for Britain, and comes to Camelot, when all are greatly joyed to see him ; he tells the adventures of the Holy Grail ; they are written down and kept in the Abbey of Salisbury, and*

---

* B. H. agrees with F.

† One cannot see from B. H. whether his text agrees with F. or W.

from these Master Walter Map drew to make his book of the Holy Grail for the love of King Henry his lord, who had the story translated from Latin into French. The story now is silent and tells no more concerning the adventures of the Holy Grail. *

Grand St. Graal.—(1) The writer salutes all who have faith in the Holy Trinity. He does not name himself for three reasons : lest his declaration that he received the story from God Himself be a stumbling block ; lest his friends pay less honour to the book if they know the author ; lest if he have made any blunder all the blame fall upon him.

(2) In the year 717 after the Passion of Christ, as the writer lies in his hut in one of the wildest parts of White Britain, on Good Friday Eve and doubts of the Trinity, Christ appears to him and gives him a little book not larger than a man's palm, and this book will resolve all his doubts ; He Himself has written it, and only he who is purified by confession and fasting may read it. On the morrow the writer opens it and finds therein four sections, headed each as follows : This is the book of thy lineage ; here begins the book of the Holy Grail ; here is the beginning of the terrors ; here begin the marvels. As he reads lightning and thunder come and other wonders. On Good Friday, as he is celebrating the service, an angel raises him in spirit to the third heaven, and his doubts concerning the Trinity are set at rest. When his spirit returns to his body he locks up the book ; but on Easter Sunday, when he would read further, finds it gone ; a voice says he must suffer to have the book back again, must go to the plains of Walescog, follow a wonderful beast to Norway, and there find what he seeks. He obeys, the beast leads him first to a hermit's, then past the pine of adventures to a knight's castle, on the third day to the queen's lake and a nunnery. After exorcising a hermit possessed of the devil. he finds the book, and on his return Christ commands him to make a fair copy before Ascension Day. He sets to work at once, on the fifteenth day after Easter.† The book begins as follows : Few believe on Christ at

---

* B. H. agrees with F.

† It will be advisable to give here the well-known passage from the chronicle of Helinandus, which has been held by most investigators to be of first-rate importance in determining the date of the Grand St. Graal. The chronicle ends in the year 1204, and must therefore have been finished in that or the following year, and as the passage in question occurs in the earlier portion of the work it may be dated about two years earlier (Birch-Hirschfeld, p. 33). " Hoc tempore (717–719) in Britannia cuidam heremitae demonstrata fuit mirabilis quaedam visio per angelum de Joseph decurione nobili, qui corpus domini deposuit de cruce et de catino illo vel paropside, in quo dominus caenavit cum discipulis suis, de quo ab eodem heremita descripta est historia quae dicitur gradale. Gradalis autem vel gradale gallice dicitur scutella lata et aliquantulum profunda, in qua preciosae dapes divitibus solent apponi gradatim, unus morsellus post alium in diversis ordinibus. Dicitur et vulgari nomine greal, quia grata et acceptabilis

His crucifixion, among whom is Joseph of Arimathea, as the Holy Scripture of the Grail testifies. He is in all things a good man. He lives in Jerusalem with his wife and a son, Josephes (not the same Josephes who so often quotes the Scripture, but not less learned than he), he it was who passed his father's kin across sea to White Britain, since called England, without rudder or sail, but in the fold of this shirt. Joseph, having much loved the Lord, longs after His death to possess somewhat having belonged to Him ; goes to the house of the Last Supper, and carries off the dish wherein He had eaten. Having been a knight of Pilate's for seven years, he craves a boon of him, which is Christ's body. Pilate grants it ; Joseph descends the body from the Cross, places it in a sepulchre, and, fetching the dish from his house, collects in it the blood flowing from the body,* and finishes laying the body in the tomb. The Jews hear of this, are angered, seize Joseph, throw him into prison in the most hideous and dirtiest dungeon ever seen, feed him at first on bread and water, but when Christ is found to have arisen, Caiaphas, Joseph's jailor, lets him starve. But Christ brings the holy dish that Joseph had sent back to his house with all the blood in it. Joseph is overjoyed. Christ comforts him, and assures him he shall live and carry His name to foreign parts. Joseph thus remains in prison. Meanwhile his wife, though often pressed to marry, refuses until she shall have had sure tidings of her husband ; as for his son he will only marry Holy Church. (3) Forty years go by ; after Christ's death Tiberius Cæsar reigned ten years, then Caius, one year ; then Claudius, fourteen years ; then Noirons, in whose reign S.S. Peter and Paul were crucified, fourteen years ; then Titus, and Vespasian, his son, a leper. The freeing of Joseph befalls in the third year of Titus' reign and in this wise : Titus has vainly sought a leech to heal Vespasian. At last a strange knight from Capernaum promises his help and tells how he in his youth had been healed of the leprosy by a prophet. The Emperor on hearing this sent to Judea to seek out that prophet ; his messenger comes to Felix, and orders him to

---

est in ea comedenti, tum propter continens, quia forte argentea est vel de alia preciosa materia, tum propter contentum .i. ordinem multiplicem dapium preciosarum. Hanc historiam latine scriptam invenire non potui sed tantum gallice scripta habetur a quibusdem proceribus, nec facile, ut aiunt, tota inveniri potest."

The Grand St. Graal is the only work of the cycle now existing to which Helinandus' words could refer ; but it is a question whether he may not have had in view a work from which the Grand St. Graal took over its introduction. Helinandus mentions the punning origin of the word " greal " (infra, p. 76), which is only hinted at in the Grand St. Graal, but fully developed elsewhere, e.g., in the Didot-Perceval and in Borron's poem.

Another point of great interest raised by this introduction will be found dealt with in Appendix B.

* The MS. followed by Furnivall has an illustration, in which Joseph is represented as sitting under the Cross and collecting the blood from the sides and feet in the basin.

have proclamation made for aught Christ has touched ; hereupon an old woman, Marie la Venissienne, brings the cloth upon which the Saviour's likeness had painted itself when she wiped His face. The messenger returns to Rome with this cloth and the mere sight of it heals Vespasian, who straightway resolves to avenge Christ's death. He goes to Jerusalem, Joseph's wife appears before him, accuses the Jews of having made away with her husband ; none of the Jews know where he is save Caiaphas, who reveals the secret on condition that he is to be neither burnt or slain. Vespasian himself goes down into the prison and finds it as light as though one hundred candles had burnt in it. He tells Joseph who he is, whereat the latter wondered, not thinking he had been longer than from Friday to Sunday, not once had it been dark. A voice tells Joseph not to fear, and that he will find the Holy Vessel at his home. Joseph returns to Jerusalem with Vespasian, and points out to him the abettors of Christ's death, whom Vespasian has burnt. Caiaphas is set adrift in a boat. (4) The night before Vespasian returns to Rome, Christ appears to Joseph and commands him to go forth and fill foreign lands with his seed ; he must be baptised, and must go forth without money or aught but the dish ; all heart can want or wish he shall have, all who accompany him must be baptised likewise. Joseph is baptised by St. Philip, then Bishop of Jerusalem, as is also Vespasian, concerning whom the story is now silent. (5) Joseph preaches to his friends and relatives and converts seventy-five of them. They leave Jerusalem and come to Bethany, where the Lord appears to Joseph, promises him aid as once to the Jews in the wilderness, commands him to make a wooden ark for the dish, which he is to open when he wants to speak to Him, but no one is to touch it save Joseph and his son Josephes ; Joseph does as commanded, his troop is miraculously fed, and on the eleventh day they come to the town of Sarras, between Babilone and Salavandre, whence the Saracens have their name, and not from Sara. (6) Joseph and his seventy-five companions enter the city and go to the Temple of the Sun, to the seat of judgment, where the Saracens are assembled with their lord, Evalach the Unknown ; he had been a man of prowess in his youth, but was now old ; seven days before, the Egyptians had beaten his army, and the council is now devising how vengeance may be taken therefor. Joseph is greatly joyed at these events, and when the council advises peace assures the King of victory, but he must destroy his images and believe on Him who died on the Cross. Evalach asks how one who could not save himself could save another. Joseph, in answer, tells of Christ's birth, life, death, descent into hell, resurrection, ascension, and of the sending of the Holy Ghost. Evalach cannot understand either the Incarnation or the Trinity, and although Joseph explains that the Virgin conceived by the overshadowing of the Holy Ghost through her ear, and that her virginity was no more hurt than is water when a sunbeam enters it, remains stubborn and calls his learned men to his aid, but Joseph confounds these, and Evalach lodges the Christians for the night and gives them good beds. (7) Evalach dreams of a tree-stock whence spring three

equal trunks and though three yet are truly one, also of a room with a
secret door of marble, through which a child passes without opening it ; a
voice tells him this is a type of the miraculous conception of Christ.   (8)
Meanwhile, Joseph, unable to sleep, prays for comfort and adjures the Lord
by all His mercies to help Evalach ; he is told by a voice he shall be sent
for to explain the King's dream.   Joseph then goes to sleep with his wife,
Helyab, but not as lustful folk do, for there was nothing between them
till the Lord commanded the begetting of Galahad, and then, so full of love
to the Saviour were they that they had no desire.   From Galahad came
the high race which honoured the land of White Britain, now called England.   (9) The morrow morning Joseph and his company worship before
the ark (now the place wherein they were had been called the Spiritual
Palace by Daniel) when a soft sweet wind comes and the Holy Ghost
descends and Christ speaks and urges all to love Him ; He tells Josephes to
draw near and take charge of His flesh and blood; Josephes opens the door
of the ark and sees a man all in red, and with him five angels, each six
winged, all in red, each with a bloody sword in his left, and in their rights
severally, a cross, nails, lance, sponge, and scourge ; Josephes sees Christ
nailed to the Cross, and the blood running down from His side and feet
into the dish ; he would enter the ark but angels restrain him.   Joseph,
wondering at his son's state, kneels before the ark and sees therein an altar
covered with white cloths, under which is a red samite one, covering three
nails, a lance head all bloody, and the dish he had brought, and in the
middle of the altar an exceeding rich vessel of gold and precious stones ;
seven angels issue from the ark with water and watering pot (2), gold
basins and towels (2), and gold censers (3), an eighth carrying the holy
dish, a ninth a head so rich and beautiful as never mortal eye saw, a tenth
a sword, three more with tapers, lastly Jesus.   The company of angels go
over the house sprinkling it with holy water, because it had heretofore
been dwelt in by devils.   Christ tells Josephes he is to receive the sacrament of His flesh and blood, and be made sovran shepherd over His new
sheep ; bishop's vestments are brought out of the ark.   Josephes is seated
in a chair, which afterwards made a Saracen King's eyes fly out of his head,
is consecrated, an angel keeps the holy oil wherewith all Kings of Britain
were anointed till the time of Uther Pendragon, of whom none of the
many that have told his history have rightly known why he was so called ;
the meaning of the episcopal vestments is explained to Josephes, and his
duties set forth.   (10) Josephes then goes into the ark and celebrates the
sacrament using Christ's words only, whereat bread and wine become flesh
and blood, and in place of the bread a child, which, though as bidden, he
divides into three parts yet is eaten as one whole ; an angel puts patina
and chalice into the dish ; Joseph and his company receive the sacrament
in the form of a child ; Christ bids Josephes celebrate the sacrament daily ;
tells him that he and Joseph are to go with Evalach's messengers now nigh
at hand.   Leucans, Josephes' cousin, is appointed guardian of the ark.
(11) Joseph and his son go before the King and overcome all the heathen

clerk's objections ; Josephes tells Evalach he will be given over to his
enemies for three days, and shall only escape by believing on Christ ; the
heathen idols are smashed by a devil at the compelling of Josephes' two
angels. A messenger brings the news that King Tholomes has entered
and is capturing the land, and he will not rest till he be crowned at Sarras.
Josephes tells the King this ill-hap is to mind him of his lowly origin, he
is son of a shoemaker in an old city of France, Meaux, and was one of a
tribute of one hundred youths and one hundred maidens claimed by
Augustus Cæsar from France, as here dwelt a prouder folk than elsewhere,
and the two daughters of the Count of the Town, Sevain, were among the
tribute, and Evalach was among their servants. When Felix was named
Governor of Syria by Tiberius he had taken Evalach with him, and held
him in high honour until one day, angry with Felix's son, Evalach slew him
and had to fly, after which he entered the service of Tholome Cerastre,
King of Babylon, who had given him the land he now ruled. Josephes
further explains the King's dreams, and when the latter declares himself
willing to believe, asks for his shield, upon which he fixes a red cross and
tells him to look on it in his need and pray to God and he shall be saved.
(12) Evalach marches with his army against Tholomes, is joined by his
brother-in-law, Seraphe (whom he thought hated him most of any man
in the world) at the Queen's entreaty ; numerous combats ensue between
the two armies ; Seraphe performs prodigies of valour ; Evalach is taken
prisoner, and in his need looks on the shield, sees thereon Christ crucified,
prays to God for help, a White Knight appears, overcomes Tholomes, who
is taken prisoner, and Evalach's army is victorious. (13) Meanwhile
Josephes, remaining in Sarras, has been counselling Queen Sarraquite,
secretly a Christian, since her mother was cured of a bloody flux, and since
Christ appeared to her when she was afraid of the hermit her mother had
led her to for baptism because he had such a long beard ; she dares not
avow her faith for fear of her husband. Josephes tells her of the battle
which has taken place and of the White Knight. (14) Evalach and Seraphe
return ; the King asks at once after the Christians, and learns that he
owes his victory to the Lord to whom also Seraphe owed his strength in
battle ; the shield is uncovered, a man with a wounded arm is healed by
it, and then the cross vanishes ; Seraphe turns Christian, is baptised and
receives the name Nasciens, he is straightway healed of his wounds,
exhorts Evalach to believe, and tells of Tholomes' death. Evalach is
baptised, and re-christened Mordrains, or Slow-of-Belief. After baptising
the town and destroying all images, Josephes leaves three of his companions in charge of the Grail Ark, and goes with the rest to Orcanz, turns
out of an image a devil who had slain Tholomes, and converts more of
the heathen folk. (15) Meanwhile Mordrains has ordered his people to be
baptised or to leave his land ; many take the latter course and are met outside the town by a devil who wounds them grievously, whereupon Josephes
hurries to their aid, but is met by an angel with a lance and smitten
through the thigh for having left his baptising work to trouble himself

about contemners of God's law, and the mark of the wound should stay with him all his life, and the iron spear head remain in the wound so that ever after he limped, and he had later to smart for it, as the tale will show in due season. Many more people are converted, Bishops are left in the land and holy relics at Sarras. (16) Josephes brings Mordrains, Sarraquite, and Nasciens to the holy shrine, and shows them the vessel wherein is Christ's blood. Nasciens thinks he has never seen aught to match it, and he gives it a name that since it has never lost. For, says he, nothing he had seen before but somewhat displeased him (li degraast), but this pleases him (li grée) entirely; he further tells how once when a young man, hunting, as he stood deep in thought a voice made itself heard, saying "Thou shall't never accomplish what thou thinkest on until the wonders of the Grail are disclosed," and he knows now this must be the Grail as every wish of his heart is accomplished. And he draws nearer and lifts the vessel's lid and looks therein, but straightway falls to trembling, feeling he can no longer see. And he knew that the blindness was to punish his curiosity, and turning to Josephes tells him that the iron shall not be drawn out of that wound inflicted by the angel at Orcanz, nor he himself recover his sight until Josephes, wounded, himself comes to draw out the iron.

So they stand lost in thought, till a voice is heard, "After my vengeance my healing" and an angel appears, touches Josephes' thigh with the lance shaft, whereupon the head comes out, and from it drop great drops of blood which the angel collects in a vessel, and wherewith he anoints Josephes' wound, making it whole, and Nasciens' eyes, restoring to him his sight. And the angel tells them that the meaning of the lance is that of the beginning of the wonderful adventures which shall befall in lands whither God purposes leading them ; when the true knights should be separated from the false ones, and the earthly knighthood become a heavenly one. And at the beginning of those adventures the lance would drop blood as then, but beforehand none ; and then wonders would happen all over the world where the lance was, great and terrible wonders, in recognition of the Holy Grail and of the lance ; and the marvels of the Grail should never be seen save by one man alone ; and by the lance wherewith Josephes was struck should but one other man be struck, and he a King of Josephes' kin, and the last of the good men ; he should be struck through the two thighs, and only healed when the Grail wonders were disclosed to the Good Knight, and that one should be last of Nasciens' kin. Thus, as Nasciens was the first to behold the wonders of the Grail, that one should be the last ; so saith the true crucified one, adding, " Upon the first and last of My new ministers will I spend the vengeance of the adventurous lance in token of Myself having received the lance stroke whilst on the Cross." And so many days as Josephes had born the lance head in his wound so many days should the marvellous adventures last. Now these days (*years*)* were twenty-two. (17) Josephes explains

---

* MS. reading.

Mordrains' vision, and makes him destroy the image of a woman he had kept in a secret chamber, known, so he thought, only to himself. (18) Josephes and his company go forth from Sarras, but the tale tells nothing of them in this place, but keeps straight on. On the following night Mordrains dreams that, sitting in Sarras at table, of a sudden a thunderbolt strikes crown from his head and the first mouthful from his lips ; a great wind carries him up into a far land where he is fed by a lion and lioness, and after a while an eagle carries off Nasciens' son to a land whereof the inhabitants bow down before him, and out of this nephew's belly comes a great lake giving rise to nine streams, eight of equal breadth and depth, the ninth as wide and deep as the remainder put together, and rushing and turbulent, and at first foul and muddy, but afterwards clear and pure as a precious stone ; then comes down from heaven a man in likeness of one crucified, who bathes hands and feet in the lake and eight streams, but in the ninth his whole body. (19) Mordrains tells his vision to Nasciens and confesses to former treacherous and jealous feelings he had against him ; they seek counsel of the priests, but none can expound the vision, and as they sit together a great tumult is heard and the sound of a horn announcing " the beginning of dread," and they fall senseless to the ground ; but Mordrains is caught up by the Holy Ghost and borne off. (20) Meanwhile Nasciens is accused by Kalafier, a Christian-hater, of having made away with Mordrains, and is cast into prison with Kalafier for gaoler. (21) Meanwhile Mordrains has been carried off by the Holy Ghost to an island lying between Babylon, Scotland, and Ireland, a high land from which the western sea can be looked over as far as Spain ; it was once a pirates' lair, but Pompey drove them thence. To Mordrains comes a noble man who gives his name as Tout-entour, comforts him, and exhorts him to steadfastness in the faith ; when he leaves a fair woman appears and tempts the King, who luckily does not pay heed to her, and well for him, as he learns from the noble man that she is Lucifer in disguise. He is assailed by many temptations ; storm, thunder, and lightning affright him ; the wonderful bird Phœnix attacks him and snatches the bread from his lips ; Lucifer again visits him and shows him Nasciens' dead body, but it is only an invention ; finally, all these trials withstood, the noble man comes again and expounds the dream of the nine streams : the lake is a son of Nasciens, from whom descend nine Kings, all good men and true, but the ninth surpassing all in every virtue ; he is the knight to whom the wonders of the Grail shall be shown, and Christ shall bathe Himself wholly in him. (22) Meanwhile Nasciens has been kept in prison together with his son, Celidoine (Heaven-given) by Kalafier. But a miraculous hand appearing from out a cloud strikes off Nasciens' fetters, and carries him out of the dungeon ; Kalafier pursues but is struck down by the hand ; on his death bed he orders that Celidoine be cast from the battlements, but nine hands bear him up in mid air, whilst Kalafier, slain by fire from heaven, goes to eternal death. Sarraquite, overjoyed to hear of her brother's escape, sends out messengers to meet them. Meanwhile Nasciens' wife, Flegentyne, has set out in search of her husband accompanied by the old knight, Corsapias, and his son, Helicoras. (23) Now Nasciens has been carried fourteen days journey off to the Turning Isle (concerning which many wonders are told) ; all of these things are true, as Christ Himself has written the book of the Holy Grail, and He never wrote aught else save the Lord's Prayer for the disciples and the judgment upon the woman taken in adultery. And no man is bold enough to say that since the Resurrection Christ wrote aught else save this " haute escripture del S. Graal." (24) A ship comes to Nasciens' isle which he would enter but for words warning him against it unless he be full of faith. However, crossing himself he enters [and finds therein the same wonders as those described in Queste, Inc. 35, 36, 37, viz. :— the sword and the three spindles, precisely the same story about which is told as in the Queste]. (25) Nasciens deeming there must be magic in this, the ship splits in twain, and had well nigh drowned him, but he regains the isle swimming, and on the morrow an old man comes in a ship and gives him an allegorical explanation of what has befallen him. (26) Meanwhile Celidoine, carried off by the hands to the land of the heathen King Label, wins his favour by expounding a dream, converts him, but at his death is cast adrift by the heathen barons in a boat with a lion, and after three days comes to Nasciens' island. (27) The two rejoice on their meeting, and leave the island together in Solomon's ship, come after four days to another island, where Nasciens, attacked by a giant, seizes Solomon's sword but it breaks in his hand, nevertheless, with another sword he overcomes the giant. He chides Solomon's sword, but Celidoine says it is some sin of his made it break. Thereafter they see a ship approaching wherein is Mordrains. There is rejoicing between the three, and much telling of past adventures. Nasciens shows the broken sword to Mordrains, who, taking it in his hands, joins it together, whereupon a voice bids them leave the ship ; Nasciens, not obeying fast enough, is wounded in the shoulder by a fiery sword in punishment of his having drawn Solomon's sword. (28) The messengers sent out by Sarraquite in search of Nasciens have, meantime, had many adventures, have come across the daughter of King Label, suffered shipwreck, and been thrown upon a desert isle formerly the home of the great physician, Ypocras (of whom a long story is told how he was tricked by a Roman lady), been tempted in divers fashions, but at last they are led to Mordrains, Nasciens, and Celidoine. (29) On the third night a priest clad in white comes walking on the sea, heals Nasciens' wound, and sends off Celidoine in another ship. The remainder come to land, Mordrains and Sarraquite are reunited ; Nasciens' wife, Flegentyne, is sent for ; and Label's daughter is christened by Petrone, a holy man and kinsman of Joseph. She was after Celidoine's wife, as my lord Robert of Borron testifies, who translated this history from Latin into French after the holy hermit to whom our Lord first gave it. (30) Nasciens sets forth in search of his son, his knights follow on his track, and two are struck dead for their sins. Nasciens comes again to Solomon's ship, is tempted by the devil in the shape of a fair damsel, goes on board the ship and dreams as

follows :—Celidoine is in the promised land with all those who had left
Sarras ; he, Nasciens, shall go thence likewise and never depart thence, nor
shall the ship until it take back the last of his line to Sarras, together with
the Holy Grail, and that shall be after three hundred years ; and thereafter Celidoine leads before him nine persons, all in guise of Kings, save the
eighth who was like a dog, and the ninth turns into a lion, and at his death
the whole world mourns over him.   And the names of these, Nasciens'
descendants, are : Celidoine, Marpus, Nasciens, Alains li Gros, Ysaies,
Jonans, Lancelot, Bans, Lancelot, like unto a dog until his end, Galahad,
foul at the source, but afterwards clear, in whom Christ shall bathe Himself
wholly, and who shall end all the adventures.   On the morrow it is
explained to Nasciens that the eighth of his descendants likens a dog on
account of his sins, and the ninth is foul at the beginning as engendered in
fornication and not as Holy Church wills.   (31) The story, after touching
on Flegentyne, who retires to her own land, returns to Joseph, who, with
his son, Josephes, and his companions, has been wandering about.   Joseph is
ordered by a voice from heaven to beget a son, whose name shall be Galaad.
At length the company comes to the sea shore and laments that it has no
ships ; Joseph rebukes them, and says those may pass who have kept chaste,
whereupon four hundred and sixty come forward to confess their lechery.
Josephes is told to put forward the Grail-bearers, to take the shirt off his
back, and having spread it on the water, all the pure companions shall
find place on it.   This happens, and all find place save Symeu and his son,
who are not as they should be, and who sink and are well nigh drowned.
The chosen company arrive on the morrow in Great Britain, then full of
Saracens and infidels.   Josephes then prays for the remainder of the
company ; a heavenly voice says they shall come in good time, and that
this is the promised land in which they shall multiply and become the
worthiest race anywhere.   (32) Meantime Nasciens has been led in
Solomon's ship to those of Joseph's followers who had been left behind,
as the history of the Holy Grail testifies.   After being warned against
fresh falling into sin they are brought over to Joseph, and are fed with as
much meat as they could want.   But the fifth day the company, not having
eaten for a day, come to the tent of a poor woman, wherein are twelve loaves
about which they dispute.   Josephes, referred to, breaks each loaf in three,
and having placed the Holy Grail at the head of the table by its power the
bread suffices for more than five hundred people.   (33) Hereafter the
company comes to Castle Galafort, where Celidoine is found disputing
with the Saracen wise men.   The Christians are well received by Ganort,
and shortly afterwards he and his people are baptised, one hundred and
fifty who refuse being drowned.   Over their bodies a tower is built, the
Tower of Marvels, and thereafter, it is prophesied, a King named Arthur
should reign, and from one blow of a sword adventures should arise,
lasting twelve years, until the last descendant of Nasciens should end
them, and till that time no knight of Arthur's house should enter the tower
without having to fight as good a man as himself ; thus should it be till

he who was to end the adventures appeared. So they build the tower, and it lasts until Lancelot destroys it, as the "Tale of Arthur's Death" relates. (34) Joseph's wife bears a son, who receives the name of Galahad, of the Castle of Galafort. (35) The King of Northumberland, hearing of Ganort's conversion, summons him to the court, and on his refusal attacks him, but is defeated and slain by the Christians. (36) Josephes, his father, and one hundred and fifty of the Christians, leaving Galafort, come to Norgales, and are thrown into prison by King Crudel, who says, "Let them be for forty days, and see if their vessel will feed them." Our Lord comes to comfort them, and bids them be of good cheer, He will send an avenger to slay these dogs. (37) Our Lord, in the likeness of one crucified, then appears to Mordrains, bids him set forth with wife and children and King Label's daughter and Nasciens' wife and go to Great Britain, there to avenge him on King Crudel. Mordrains hearkens, and shortly after sets forth with all his household, leaving his land in charge of Duke Ganor. On the way a devil carries off the captain of the ship, who had lusted after Queen Flegentyne. They arrive in Britain and rejoin their friends ; great is the joy ; Nasciens' queen is like to have died of joy, and swoons twelve times. (38) Mordrains sends word to Crudel to set the Christians free, and on his refusal marches against, overthrows, and slays him, but is grievously wounded, though he suffers no pain. Josephes and his companions are freed, and thanksgivings are made before the Grail. On the morrow, as Josephes is officiating before the holy vessel, Mordains presses near to see it, in spite of a warning voice ; he loses his sight and the power of his body ; he confesses his folly, but prays he may not die till the Good Knight's coming, the ninth of Nasciens' descendants. A voice promises him this, and that when the Good Knight comes he shall recover his sight and his wounds be healed ; but three hear this promise beside Mordrains himself, Joseph, Josephes, and Nasciens. (39) Mordrains is brought to Galafort, where Celidoine marries King Label's daughter and begets a son, Nasciens. Mordrains then, after giving his wife and shield into Nasciens' keeping, retires to a hermitage, and builds a monastery of the White Monks, and stays there till Perceval sees him and Galahad, too, as the "Tale of the Holy Grail" tells. (40) Josephes leaves Galafort, and, coming to Camelot, converts many of the people, whereat King Agrestes, being grieved, is baptised with false intent, and after Josephes' departure persecutes the Christians, and is punished by madness and death. Josephes returning, buries the martyrs, whose blood had blackened a cross, which keeps the name of the "Black Cross," till the Good Knight, Lancelot of the Lake's son comes. (41) Josephes comes to a hill called Hill of the Giant ; 'tis a Friday, and Brons is sitting next him at the Grail-table, but between the two is space for a man to sit, and Brons, Josephes' kinsman, asks him why he does not invite some one to fill it. Josephes answers, only he who is a holier man than any present can fill that place, as it typifies Christ's seat at the Last Supper, and is empty waiting His coming, or whom He shall send. Such of the company as are in mortal sin take this saying as presumption and fable, and Moys declares his willingness to sit in it if his companions will ask Josephes' leave. They do so, and though Josephes minds them how Moys might hardly come to Britain, and though he solemnly warns Moys himself, he gives his leave. Moys takes the seat, and at once seven flaming hands from heaven seize upon him and carry him off to a far place burning like a dry bush. The people repent, and, in answer to their enquiries, Josephes tells them the day shall come when they shall know where Moys is. (42) After the meal Josephes, at Brons' request, has the latter's twelve sons up before him, and asks them whether they will be wedded or not. Eleven choose wedding, but the twelfth virginity and the service of the Holy Grail. Josephes, overjoyed, having married the other eleven, appoints him guardian of the Grail at his death, and he might leave the guardianship afterwards to whom he would. (43) Josephes and his companions pass through Britain converting the heathen. Now the Grail only gives food to such as are not in sin, and once as the troop is encamped by a lake, Peter, a kinsman of Josephes', bears it through the ranks, and all are fed with the best food, save the sinners ; these complain, and beg Josephes to pray for them, whereupon he bids Brons' youngest son, the same he had chosen as Grail-keeper, Alains le Gros (not that Alains, Celidoine's son, *he* was king and wore a crown, but this one never) take the net from the Grail-table and fish with it in the pond. Alains does so and catches one fish, a big one, but say they, 'Twill not be enough ; however, Alains, having shared it in three, and having prayed it might suffice, all are fed. Alains is called in consequence the Rich Fisher, and all the Grail-keepers after him bear this name, but they were more blessed than he, being crowned Kings whereas he never wore crown. (44) Joseph, leaving his companions, comes into the Forest of Broceliande, meets a Saracen who would lead him to his sick brother, but is himself slain by a lion. Joseph is thrown in prison and wounded in the thigh by the men of the sick knight's castle, but, obtaining leave to visit the sick knight, heals him, and brings back to life the Saracen slain by the lion ; both brothers are baptised ; a fragment of the sword remaining in the wound, Joseph draws it out, and laying it with the remainder of the sword prophecies it shall not be made whole till he come who shall achieve the adventures of the Holy Grail. (45) Joseph, returning to his companions, finds them in doubt as to how they shall cross a great water, they pray for guidance, and a white hart appears, followed by four stags, and leads them across, all save Chanaan, who crosses later in a fisherman's boat. Josephes, in answer to Alain and Pierron, explains the hart and lions as Christ and the Evangelists, and Christ would appear in that wise afterwards to Arthur, Mordred, and Lancelot. (46) The Christians come to a house where burns a great fire, out of which is heard a lamentable voice ; it is that of Moys ; at Josephes' prayer rain falls from heaven and quenches half the flames, but he may not be wholly delivered until the Good Knight, Galahad, come. (47) The Christians come into the land of King Escos, whence Scotland has its name. The Holy Grail refuses meat to Chanaan and to Symeu, Moys' father, whereat enraged,

Symeu attacks Pierre and wounds him, and Chanaan slays his twelve brethren. Symeu is carried off by devils, whilst Chanaan's grave bursts out in flames, which may not quench till Lancelot come. (48) Meanwhile Pierre's wound having become worse, he is left behind with a priest, who leads him to the sea shore, and, at his request, places him in a boat ; this carries him to the isle of the heathen king, Orcanz, whose daughter finding him on the sea shore dying, has pity on him and tends him secretly till he is healed. Her father requires a champion, Pierre offers himself, conquers, converts, and baptises Orcanz, who takes the name Lamer, and marries his daughter, and King Luces comes to the wedding and is overjoyed. From him came Gauvain, son of King Lot of Orcanie. Mordred was no true son of Lot's, but of Arthur's. Gauvain is thus of the seed of Joseph of Arimathea. (49) Josephes after fifteen years' wanderings comes back to Galafort, and finds his brother Galahad grown up ; by Josephes' advice the men of Hocelice take Galahad for their king, and he became the ancestor of Ywain, son of Urien. Once whilst riding he comes to Symeu's fiery grave, which may not be quenched till Galahad, the Good Knight, comes. At Galahad's death he is buried in an abbey he founds to allay Symeu's pains, and the tombstone of his grave may not be lifted until by Lancelot. (50) Joseph dies shortly after Galahad's crowning, and Josephes, feeling death near, pays a last visit to Mordrains, who begs for a token from him. Josephes asks for the king's shield, and with blood gushing from his nose marks on it a red cross, gives it to Mordrains, and says no one shall hang it on his neck without rue till Galahad do so ; the shield is placed on Nasciens' tomb. On the morrow Josephes dies ; his body is carried afterwards into Scotland to still a famine, and is buried in the Abbey of Glays. (51) Before his death he has confided the Grail to Alain. The latter comes with his brethren, one of whom, Josue, is unmarried, to the Terre Foraine, converts the King and people, and marries Josue to his daughter. Here is the resting-place of the Holy Grail ; a lordly castle is built for it, hight Corbenic, which is Chaldee, and signifies "holy vessel." At Josue's wedding, such is the power of the Holy Grail, that all present are as filled as if they had eaten the finest meats they could think of. And that night the King, baptized Alfasem, sleeping in the castle, beholds the holy vessel covered with crimson samite, and a man all flaming tells him no mortal may sleep where the Holy Grail rests, and wounds him through both thighs, and bids others beware of sleeping in the Palace Adventurous. And afterwards many a knight essayed the adventure, but lost his life, till Gauvain came, and he, though he kept his life, had such shame and mischance as he had not had for the Kingdom of Logres' sake. (58) Alain and Alfasem die ; Josue becomes King and Grail-keeper, and after him Aminadap, Catheloys, Manaal, Lambor, all Kings and known as the Fisher, and Lambor fighting with his enemy, Bruillant, pursues him to the sea shore, and Bruillant finds there Solomon's ship and enters it, and finds the sword with which he slays Lambor, and this was the first blow struck with that sword in Great Britain, and such great woes sprang therefrom that no labourers worked, nor wheat grew, nor fruit trees bore, nor fish was found in the waters, so that the land was known as the Waste Land. But Bruillant falls dead for drawing the sword. After Lambor, Pelleans, wounded in the two thighs in a battle of Rome, whence he was always called the Maimed King, and he might not heal till Galahad the Good Knight come ; and from him descends Pelles, and on his daughter does Lancelot of the Lake beget Galahad. (59) Nasciens, Flegentyne, and Sarraquite die on the self-same day. Celidoine reigns, and is followed by Marpus, he by Nasciens, Alain li Gros, Ysaies, Jonas, Lancelot, Bans, Lancelot of the Lake. Here the story ends of all the seed of Celidoine, and returns to speak of Merlin, which my lord Robert of Borron thus begins.*

---

* I have not thought it necessary to give a summary of the prose romance Perceval le Gallois. One will be found in Birch-Hirschfeld, pp. 123–134. The version, though offering many interesting features, is too late and unoriginal to be of use in the present investigation.

In making up the slips, the summary of Borron's poem dropped out. In order not to disturb the page form, which was fixed before the omission was noticed, it has been inserted after the Grand St. Graal with a subpagination.

Robert de Borron's Poem: Joseph of Arimathea.—

(1) Before Christ's coming all folk went to Hell, but He came born of a Virgin that He might bring them out of Hell. He took flesh what time Judæa was under Rome and Pilate governed it. Now a soldier of Pilate's loved Christ but dared not show it. Of Christ's few disciples one was bad, his chamberlain, and he betrayed Him to the Jews. (2) On Thursday Jesus gathers His disciples; Judas' question, the washing of the feet, the kiss of betrayal follow. When the Jews carry off Jesus, one of them takes the very fair vessel wherein He made His sacrament, and gave it to Pilate, who keeps it till he learns Jesus' death. (3) Joseph is angry hereat, and claims pay for his and his five knights five years' free service, and his pay is Christ's body. Pilate grants it him, and Joseph hastens to the Cross, but the guards deny him, whereon he complains to Pilate, who sends Nicodemus to see he obtain it, and also gives Joseph the vessel. (4) Joseph and Nicodemus descend the body, and wash it, which makes the blood flow afresh. Joseph puts the blood in the vessel, wraps the body in a fine cloth and entombs it. The descent into Hell and the Resurrection follow. (5) The Jews are incensed against Joseph and Nicodemus; the latter escapes, but Joseph is thrust into a horrible and dark prison. To him Christ appears with His vessel, in a great light, and instructs Joseph, telling him for his love to Him he shall have the symbol of His death and give it to keep to whom he would; He then gives Joseph the great, precious vessel wherein is His holiest blood. Joseph wonders, having hidden it in his house. Joseph is to yield the vessel to three persons only, who are to take it in the name of the Trinity. No Sacrament shall ever be celebrated but Joseph shall be remembered. But Joseph must be taught concerning the Sacrament; the bread and wine are Christ's flesh and blood, the tomb is the Altar; the grave-cloth the Corporal, the vessel wherein the blood was put shall be called Chalice, the cup-platten signifies the tombstone. All who see Joseph's vessel shall be of Christ's company, have fulfilment of their heart's wish and joy eternal. (*The author adds:* I dare not, nor could not, tell this but that I had the great book wherein the histories are written by the great clerks, therein are the great secrets written which are called the Graal.) Christ leaves Joseph, who remains in prison, no man heeding him (6) until, when Vespasian, the Emperor's son, was a leper, a pilgrim comes to Rome and tells of Christ's cures, and lays his head Vespasian could be cured could anything of Christ's be brought to Rome. The Emperor sends messengers, who hear Pilate's story of the Crucifixion and about Joseph. The Jews are called together, and one tells of Verrine, who is brought before the messengers, and she relates how she wiped Christ's face and thus got the likeness of Him. They take her to Rome, Vespasian is healed, and sets forth to revenge Christ's death. He kills many Jews, burning some. One Jew offers to find Joseph, and tells the story of his imprisonment. Vespasian is let down into the prison and finds Joseph alive, who, to his amazement, welcomes him by name, and

reads him a lecture on Biblical history and Christian Faith. Vespasian is converted, and sells the Jews at the rate of thirty for a penny. (7) Joseph exhorts his kin, among them his sister, Enygeus, and brother-in-law, Hebron. They agree to believe, and to follow him. He sets off with them and they dwell for long in far-off lands. For awhile things go well, but then all the host does turns to naught; 'tis on account of carnal sin. The host complains to Hebron that they and their children die of hunger. (8) Hebron reports this to Joseph, who goes weeping and kneels before the vessel and asks why his followers suffer? A voice from the Holy Ghost answers he is not in fault, but he is to set the vessel before the people, and to mind him how He, Christ, had eaten with His disciples, and how the false disciple was detected. In the name of that table whereat Christ last ate, Joseph is to prepare another, and then to call his brother-in-law, Brons, and make him go into the water to catch a fish, and the first he catches Joseph is to put it on the table, and then to take the vessel, put it on the table, cover it with a towel, and then place Hebron's fish opposite it. The people are then to be called, who will soon see wherein they have sinned. And Joseph is to sit where Christ sat at the Last Sacrament, with Brons at his right. And Brons is to draw back one seat, to signify the seat of Judas, and the seat thus left empty is not to be filled until Enygeus have a child by Brons, her husband, and when that child is born there shall be his seat. The people is then to be bidden sit down to the grace of our Lord. Joseph does all this; part of the people sit, part do not, the sitters are filled with sweetness and the desire of their heart, the others feel nought. One of the sitters, named Petrus, asks if they feel nothing, and tells them it is because they are defiled with sin. The sinners then depart, but Joseph bids them come back day by day. Thus Joseph detects the sinners, and thus is the vessel first proved. (9) Joseph tells the sinners it severs them from the others, as it holds no company with nor has love towards any sinner. The sinners ask the name of the vessel: it is called *Graal*, as it agreeable to all who see it. Now all this is verity, hence we call this the Story of the Grail, and it shall be henceforth known as the Grail. (10) One sinner remains, Moyses, a hypocrite (here a gap which can be filled up from the prose versions: Moyses seats himself in the empty seat, whereupon the earth opens and swallows him). (11) Joseph prays to Christ that as He came to him in prison, and promised He would come to his aid when in trouble, so now He would show him what has become of Moyses. The voice tells Joseph again about the empty seat, and how that the one at Joseph's table was not to be filled until the third man come, whom Hebron should beget and Enygeus bear, and *his* son should fill the seat. Moyses had stayed behind only to deceive, he had his deserts, no more should be heard of him in fable or song until *he* come who should fill the empty seat. (12) In course of time Brons and Enygeus have twelve sons and are greatly bothered with them, and ask Joseph what is to be done with them. Joseph prays before the vessel;

eleven will marry, one remain single ; this one is Alain. Joseph is told by the voice when he consults the vessel about this nephew, to relate all about Christ's death and about the vessel, to tell Alain that from him shall issue an heir who is to keep the vessel ; Alain is to take charge of his brethren and sisters and go westwards. An angel will bring a letter for Petrus to read, telling him to go whither he lists; he will say : the vale of Avaron ; thither shall he go and wait for the son of Alain, and shall not pass away until that one come, and to him shall Petrus teach the power of the vessel, and say what has become of Moyses, and then may he die. (13) All happens as foretold by the voice ; the letter comes for Petrus, who declares his intention of departing for the vale of Avaron, bidding the host pray God he may never go against His will. Alain leaves with his brethren, and, as Joseph taught him, preaches the name of Jesus Christ. (14) Petrus stays one day more ; it is, says an angel, the Lord sends to Joseph, that he may see and hear the things of the vessel. The angel continues : The Lord knows Brons for a worthy man, and 'twas, therefore His will he should go fishing ; he is to keep the vessel after Joseph, who must instruct him properly especially concerning the holy words which God spake to Joseph in the prison, which are properly called the Secrets of the Grail ; Brons is to be called the Rich Fisher from the fish he caught ; all the people are to go westwards ; Brons is to wait for the son of his son, and to give him the vessel, then shall the meaning of the blessed Trinity be made known ; after the vessel has been given to Brons, Petrus is to go, as he may then truly say he has seen Hebron, the Rich Fisher, put in possession of the vessel ; when all this is done, Joseph is to go to perfect joy and life pardurable. (15) On the morrow Joseph tells them the angel's message, save the words of Christ in the prison, which he tells to the Rich Fisher alone. The latter is then put in possession of Grail and headship ; Joseph stays three days with him, then the Good Fisher goes away—in the land where he was born—and Joseph remains.*

Master Robert de Borron should doubtless tell where Alain went, Hebron's son, and what became of him ; what life Petrus led, and what became of him ; what became of the long-lost Moyses ; where the Rich Fisher went, and where he stayed. It were well to assemble these four things, but this no man could do save he had first heard tell the greatest history of the Grail, which is all true ; and in this time I tell it to my Lord Walter, never had the great history of the Grail been told by mortal man. If God gives me strength I will assemble these four parts if I can find them in a book, meanwhile I must go on to the fifth and forget the four. (Then follows the Merlin).

---

* *Cf.* p. 78 as to this passage.

Robert de Borron's Poem: Merlin.—(In order to give all the materials for the discussion of Birch-Hirschfeld's theory of the Grail legend in the next chapter, a brief summary of the Merlin is added. A full one may be found in Birch-Hirschfeld, pp. 166, *et seq.*)

The devil, incensed at Christ's victory over him, in revenge begets by fraudful malice upon a virgin, a son, who is to be the wisest of mankind, and to oppose Christ's teaching. This is Merlin, who at eighteen months is able to save his mother, threatened with the doom of unchastity. Afterwards he is brought to King Vortigern, to whom he expounds the mystery of the unfinished tower. Vortigern is driven from his throne by Pendragon, with whom Merlin stands in high honour ; equally so with his successor, Uter Pendragon, for whom he builds the Round Table, leaving one place empty to be filled in the time of Uter's successor. He then helps the King to satisfy his passion for Yguerne, and takes charge of Arthur, their son. When the latter grows up to be a youth he fulfils the adventure of the sword in the anvil, and is proclaimed King. " And I, Robert of Borron, writer of this book, may not speak longer of Arthur till I have told of Alain, son of Brons, and how the woes of Britain were caused ; and as the book tells so must I what man Alain was, and what life he led, and of his seed and their life. And when I have spoken of these things I will tell again of Arthur."

(Then follows in one solitary MS., the Didot-Perceval summarised above, p. 28. As will be seen, it does not tell what man Alain was, nor does it refer to him at all save in the most passing way).

CHAPTER III.

The legend formed of two portions : Early History of Grail, Quest—**Two forms** of each portion distinguished—Grouping of the various versions —Alternative hypotheses of development—Their bearing upon the alleged Celtic origin of the Grail—Closer examination of the various accounts of the Grail : The first use made of it and its first possessor ; its solace of Joseph ; its properties and the effect produced by it ; its name ; its arrival in England ; the Grail-keeper and his relationship to the Promised Knight—Three different stages in the development of the Queste—The work and the qualification of the Promised Knight —Conclusions : Priority over Early History of Quest—Chronological arrangement of the versions.

THE information afforded by the summaries enables us to take a general view of the legend as a whole, and to attempt a more accurate chronological classification of its varying forms. It will have been seen that the legend is formed of two distinct portions : the one dealing with the origin and wanderings (Early History) of the Grail, the other with its Quest. The two portions are found combined in the Joseph and Didot-Perceval and in the Grand St. Graal and Queste considered each as one organic whole. Versions A, Chrestien and his continuators; C, Didot-Perceval taken by itself; D, Queste; F, Wolfram, and G, Perceval le Gallois, treat only of the Quest. Versions B, Metrical Joseph, and E, Grand St. Graal, only of the Early History. But in nearly all the the versions, no matter of which portion, references are to be found to the other, and when the versions are carefully examined, it is found that of each portion there exist two entirely different forms. Taking the Early History first, versions A, B, C, D, E, and G, in so far as they deal with it at all, relate much as follows: the Grail is the vessel which our Lord used at the Last Supper, which, given by Pilate to Joseph, served the latter to receive the blood flowing from the body of the dead Christ, sustained him miraculously during his captivity, was, after his release, used by him to test the faith of his followers, and was brought to England by Joseph (A, D, E), by Brons (B, C), and was finally confided by Joseph to his brother-in-law, Brons, to be kept until the coming of the latter's grandson (versions B and C), or was left in charge of Alain, son of Brons, from whom it passed to his brother Josue, in whose line it remained until the Good Knight should come (version E). But F, Wolfram makes the Grail a vessel of " lapsit exillit " (*i.e.*, lapis herilis, or lapsus ex coelis, or lapis electrix), which, after the fall of the rebel angels, was given in charge to Titurel and his dynasty, and by them preserved in the Grail Castle, Montsalvatch, guarded by a sacred order of Knighthood whom it chooses itself. So far, therefore, as the Early History is concerned all the versions, save one, are in the main of the same class, the differences between them being, apparently, ones of development and not of origin.

Turning now to the Quest, two classes are likewise to be distinguished : in the first the hero is Perceval, in the second there are three heroes, Galahad, Perceval, and Bors, chief of whom is Galahad. To the first class belong versions A, Chrestien, etc., C, Didot-Perceval ; F, Wolfram ; and G, Perceval le Gallois ; whilst D, Queste, alone of the versions which recount the Quest only, belongs to the other class. It is followed, however, by E, Grand St. Graal, in so far as the latter has any reference to the Quest. In the other Early History version, namely B, Metrical Joseph, the name of the hero who is to achieve the Quest is not mentioned, but the indications concerning him agree more closely with the march of the story in C, Didot-Perceval, than with those of D, Queste; it must therefore be ranged in the first class. The main incident in the versions of this class is the hero's visit to the castle of a sick king, his beholding there the Grail in company with other relics, his neglect on the first visit to ask the meaning of what he sees, his punishment, second visit to the Grail Castle, and attainment of his end, whether healing of the Sick King or winning of the Grail kingship. The two versions, H, Peredur, and I, Sir Perceval, which belong to the Grail cycle, though they do not mention the Grail, and although I, Sir Perceval, does not contain the above-mentioned incident, must likewise be placed in this class, as must also the

Gawain episodes of Diu Crone. In the second class this main incident is missing, though several of its less important features are present in altogether different connection. The story in D, Queste, is largely made up of adventures tallying often detail for detail with those in the Early History version, E, Grand St. Graal, with which it shares similarity in the Quest form.

Whilst each portion of the legend exists in two forms, the great majority of versions in both cases belong to one form. Looking for the moment upon D and E as one whole, there is in both cases only one minority-version, viz., for the Early History, F, Wolfram, for the Quest D-E, Queste, Grand St. Graal. And each of these is only in a minority as far as one portion of the legend is concerned, D-E, agreeing with the majority in the Early History, and F in the Quest. Taking the average of all the versions there results what may be called the *Joseph of Arimathea form* as the type of the Early History; the *Perceval form* as the type of the Quest. As a rule, it may be confidently assumed that the larger number of versions represent an older form, an assumption strengthened so far as the Early History is concerned by the fact that the minority version, F, Wolfram, can historically be proved to be one of the latest in date of all the versions, and, so far as the Quest is concerned, by the following considerations:—The minority version, D-E, has three heroes, of whom Perceval is second in importance only to the chief hero, Galahad, indeed he occupies as large a space in the narrative. This position can be due only to his being the original achiever of the Quest. It is obviously inadmissible that seven or eight versions should have conspired to pick out one only, and that one the second, of the three heroes of the Queste, and should have made him the sole hero, whilst it is easy to understand that the author of D, Queste, dissatisfied for certain reasons with the older forms of the story, yet not daring to alter it so far as to entirely burke the original hero, should have taken the course he did.

Two alternative hypotheses now naturally suggest themselves. The two parts of the legend may really form one organic whole, although more frequently found asunder than combined, or the one part may be an explanatory and supplementary after-thought.

If the first hypothesis be accepted, it is natural to look upon the Metrical Joseph and the Didot-Perceval as the first and last parts of a trilogy, which, as presenting the legend in its fullest and most orderly shape, has a claim to being the oldest form of the story, and the main, if not the only, source of all other versions. If, on the other hand, the second hypothesis be exact, if one part of the legend be later than the other, and has been artificially welded into one with it, that version in which this fusion is most perfect, instead of being the earliest is, with greater likelihood, one of the latest forms. How do these alternative hypotheses affect the special object of these studies—the investigation of the alleged Celtic element in the Grail romances? In this way. If the Early History be an integral part of the romance, the probabilities in favour of a purely Christian legendary origin for the Grail itself are immensely increased, and the utmost the Celtic partisan could hope to show was that a Christian legend had somehow or other been strongly influenced by Celtic popular traditions. But if the reverse be true the probabilities are at once in favour of the Christian legendary element being the intruding one, and the chief aim of the Celtic partisan will be to disengage the present versions of the Quest from the traces left upon them by the Early History, and to accumulate as many parallels as possible between the residuum and admittedly genuine Celtic tradition. It by no means follows, however, that the acceptance of the second hypothesis involves the acceptance of the Celtic origin of the Grail. The romance as we have it—Quest, Early History—may be the fusion of two elements, one of which, the Christian legendary, may claim *all* that is connected with the mystic vessel. Were it otherwise our task would be greatly simplified. For the mere fact that what may be called the non-Grail members of the cycle, *i.e.*, H, Peredur, and I, Sir Perceval, know nothing of the Early History, gives no uncertain hint as to which portion of the romance is the original, and which the accretion. Two points have then to be investigated —the relationship one to the other of Early History and Quest; and, if the Quest is found to be the older portion, whether the Grail really belongs to it, or whether its presence in the various forms of the story as we now have them may not be due to the

Early History.   An examination of the various passages in which the Grail is mentioned will furnish material towards settling the first point.   Such an examination may profitably omit all reference to Wolfram, to the prose Perceval le Gallois, from which little is apparently to be gained respecting the oldest forms of the legend, and to Heinrich von dem Türlin's version of the Gawain episodes. It must also neglect for the nonce the two non-Grail members of the cycle (the Mabinogi and Sir Perceval) as their testimony is either of little or of the highest value according as the Quest is or is not found to be the oldest portion of the romance.   With these exceptions all the versions furnish elements of comparison, though little is to be got, as far as the point under discussion is concerned, from what is apparently the latest section of the Conte du Graal, Gerbert's poem.

The consideration of the second point will necessitate comparison of the various Quest forms among themselves, and the examination of numerous Celtic stories which present analogies with them.

The Grail : the first use made of it and its first Possessor.

We learn nothing from Chrestien respecting the early history of the Grail, nor is Gautier more communicative if the Mons MS. version be followed.   The intercalation, A IIᴀ, however, and Manessier give full details.   According to the former :

. . .   c'est icel Graal por voir
Que nostre Sires tant ama
Que de son saint sanc l'anora
Au jor que il fu en croix mis. (16–19)

According to the latter :

C'est li vassiaus, ce saciés-vous,
Ù ens li sains sans présious
Nostre Segnor fu recéus
Quant de la lance fu férus. (35,017–20)

We learn from the former that " Josep le fist fère " (v. 22), and that he used it to collect the blood that flowed from each foot of our Lord as He hung on the Cross (verses 30–39), whilst the latter leaves it uncertain who the first possessor was, and who held the

Grail to receive our Lord's blood. The information given in versions B, is as might be expected, much fuller. B I, Metr. Jos., which calls it "un veissel mout gent," tells how Christ used it, He "feisoit son sacrement" in it; how it was found by a Jew, who delivered it up to Pilate, by whom it was given to Joseph, and by him used to receive the blood which bursts forth again from Christ's wounds when the body has been taken down from the Cross.—C, Didot-Perceval: Brons, after relating how Longis pierced the Lord's body as it hung on the Cross, says of the Grail, "en cest vessel gist le sanc que Joseph recueilli qui decoroit par terre" (p. 483).—E, Grand St. Graal: Joseph himself finds the vessel out of which Christ had eaten, takes it home, and when he has received the body from Pilate, fetches the vessel and collects in it all the blood flowing from the wound he can (I, pp. 23, 24). Curiously enough, the very MS. which gives this version has an illustration of Joseph sitting under the Cross and collecting the blood as it drops from the wounds in side and feet. Three different accounts of how the Grail came into Joseph's possession and to what use he put it thus exist:—

(1) The Grail is the vessel in which Christ's blood was received as He hung upon the Cross (Pseudo-Gautier, Manessier, Didot-Perceval, and an illustration in a MS. of the Grand St. Graal); Joseph had had it made (Pseudo-Gautier).

(2) The Grail is the vessel which had been used by Christ at the Last Supper. It is used as a receptacle for the blood of Christ after His body has been taken down from the Cross (Metr. Jos.).

(3) Same as No. 2, with minor alterations, such as that it was Joseph who found the holy vessel himself (Grand St. Graal),

The Grail: its Solace of Joseph.

Chrestien and Gautier are again silent, but from A IIA, Pseudo-Gautier, we learn that Joseph was wont to pray before the Grail, that he was, in consequence, imprisoned in a high tower by the Jews, delivered thence by the Lord, whereupon the Jews resolve

to exile him with Nicodemus, and that sister of his who had a
likeness of Christ (verses 60–110). Manessier, in the Mons MS.
version, passes this over, but A IIIA, has the following important
passage :—

> En une charte orrible et lède
> Fu mis Joseph sanz nul arreste ;
> . . . .
> XL ans ilecques estut
> C'onques ne menja ne ne but ;
> Mais Damediex li envoioit
> Le Saint Graal que il véoit
> II foiées ou III le jor ; (V. pp. 153–4.)

In the B versions this episode is one of capital importance.   B I.,
Joseph is put into prison, because the Jews suspect him of having
stolen away Christ's body.   To him in the dungeon, "qui estoit
horrible et obscure " (v. 703), appears Christ, who hands him
the Grail, whereat he is surprised, as he had hidden it in a house
where none knew of it (v. 860), and addresses him as follows :—

> En ten povoir l'enseigne aras
> De ma mort et la garderas
> Et cil l'averunt à garder
> A cui tu la voudras donner. (847–50)

These will be three—

> Joseph, bien ce saras garder,
> Que tu ne le doiz commander
> Qu'a trois persones qui l'arunt.
> Ou non dou Père le penrunt
> Et dou Fil et dou Saint-Esprit (871–75)

The offices Joseph rendered to Christ's body were symbolical of
the Sacrament : the sepulchre is the altar ; the sheet in which the
body was wrapped the corporal ; the vessel in which the blood was
received shall be called chalice ; and by the patina upon which if
rests is signified the tombstone (v. 901–912).   Finally Christ
promises Joseph that :—

> Tout cil qui ten veissel verrunt,
> En ma compeignie serunt ;
> De cuer arunt emplissement
> Et joie pardurablement. (917–20)

The prose versions repeat this account in the main, but with
some important additions, thus : B II, Cangé MS., adds after
Christ's last words, " Lors li aprant Jhésu Christ tex paroles que
jà nus conter ne retraire ne porroit, etc. (I, 227) ; when Christ
hands the vessel to Joseph, " Tu tiens lou sanc as trois personnes
en une déité, qui degota des plaies de la char au fil, etc. (I, 225–26);
after the description of the Grail, " lou Graal c'est à dire sor lou
caalice." . . In C, Didot-Perceval, the Holy Ghost, speaking
to Brons, commands him to reveal to Perceval, " icelles paroles
segroies qu'il (*i.e.*, Christ) aprist à Joseph en la prison," which,
adds the narrator, "je ne vous puis dire ne ne doi" (I, 483).
E, Grand St. Graal: The Jews, angry at Joseph's having taken
Christ's body down from the Cross, throw him into "la plu
hideuse chartre qui onques fust veue" and when they hear of the
Lord's resurrection propose to starve him ; but Christ comes to him,
brings him for comfort " la sainte esceuele que ostoie en sa maison
a tot le sanc qu'il Auoit requelli," and comforted him much, and
assured him that he should not die in prison but come out safe and
sound, and his name be glorified.   And Joseph "fu en la prison
. . . . tant qu'il demoura xlii ans (pp. 25–26).*   Here again
are three distinct accounts :—

(1) That of Pseudo-Gautier, which merely mentions Joseph's
devotions to the Grail, and does not connect that devotion
with any solace during his captivity.

(2) That of the B versions, in which Christ Himself brings the
holy vessel to the captive, and connects it with certain
promises and recommendations which He makes to him ;
the vessel shall remain with his seed, but it is to be in
charge of three persons, a symbol of the Trinity. The
services rendered by Joseph to Christ's body are connected with the Mass. The late (prose) drafts of this
version insist still more upon the sacramental nature of the
Grail.

(3) The Grand St. Graal and Pseudo-Manessier introduce a

---

* It is forty-two years, according to D. Queste (p. 119), after the Passion
that Joseph comes to Sarras.

fresh element—the Grail is the material means by which Joseph is sustained (forty years according to the one, forty-two years according to the other version) without food or drink.

The great importance of the incident in the B versions is most remarkable when contrasted with the comparative indifference displayed by the other versions, and notably by the Grand St. Graal, which, at the first blush, looks so like a mere amplification of B, still more remarkable the agreement between the prose versions of B, with C, Didot-Perceval, respecting Christ's words to Joseph against B I, Metr. Jos. It is difficult to decide which of the two versions is the older; B I, after Christ's words, has the following important passage :—

> Ge n'ose conter ne retreire,
> Ne je ne le pourroie feire,
> Neis, se je feire le voloie,
> Se je le grant livre n'avoie
> Où les estoires sunt escrites,
> Par les granz clers feites et dites :
> Lá sunt li grant secré escrit
> Qu'en numme le Graal et dit.

which may either have been the reason why the prose versions, followed by the Didot-Perceval, speak as they do about the secret words, or may be the versifier's excuse for giving those secret words themselves, *i.e.*, the explanation of the mysteries of the Grail in its relation to the Sacrament, in which case the verse would be later than the prose forms.* Finally, it would seem that Pseudo-Manessier, A IIIₐ, and the Grand St. Graal drew their information one from the other or from a common source.

---

* It is plain that B I is abridged in the passage dealt with, from the following fact : Joseph (v. 2,448, etc.) praying to Christ for help, reminds Him of His command, that when he (Joseph) wanted help he should come "devant ce veissel precieus Où est votre sans glorieus." Now Christ's words to Joseph in the prison say nothing whatever about any such recommendation; but E, Grand St. Graal, does contain a scene between our Lord and Joseph, in which the latter is bidden, "Et quant tu vauras à moi parler si ouuerras l'arche en quel lieu que tu soies" (I, 38–39) from which the conclusion may be drawn that B I represents an abridged and garbled form of the prototype of E.

Properties and Effect of the Grail.

In Chrestien these seem to be of a purely physical nature ; the Grail is borne uncovered through the hall at every meal (4,470–79), it feeds the Fisher King's father—

> D'une seule oiste li sains hom
> Quant en ce Greal li aporte
> Sa vie sostient et conforte
> Tant sainte cose est li Graaus.   (7,796–99)

the most direct testimony in Chrestien to its sacred nature. In Gautier, likewise, the physical properties are insisted upon in the following passages :—

> Lors vit parmi la sale aler
> La rice Gréail ki servoit
> Et mist le pain a grant esploit.   (20,114–16)

> Moult mangièrent à grant loisir ;
> Adonques véissiés servir
> Le Gréail moult honestement.   (20,142–43)

but in verses 28,078–81 a remarkable spiritual effect is attributed to it—

> Car li diables ne deçoit
> Nul homme ki le jor le voie,
> Ne ne le met en male voie
> Por faire pécié creminal.

In A IIA, Pseudo-Gautier, the physical side alone is insisted upon—

> Et de quanqu'il lor ert mestiers
> Les fornissoit à tel plenté
> Com s'il n'eust néant cousté ;   (12–14)

> Et li Graaux par tot aloit
> Et pain et vin par tot portoit
> Et autres mès a grant planté.   (171–74)

Manessier makes no special reference to the properties of the Grail. In the B versions it is the spiritual power of the Grail which is dwelt upon.   Christ's words to Joseph have already been quoted (*supra*, p. 71), and the use which the latter puts the Grail to, and which is specially indicated to Joseph by the Holy Ghost, is in accordance with them.   The Grail is to serve him as a touchstone to distinguish the sinners of his company—

> Car il n'a à nul pecheour
> Ne compaignie ne amour ;   (2,629-30)

whereas to those who have not defiled themselves with sin it brings

> La douceur, l'accomplissement
> De leur cueurs tout entièrement ;   (2,565-67)

so that according to them—

> . . . . . Cuers ne pourroit,
> A pourpenser ne soufiroit
> Le grant delit que nous avuns
> Ne la grant joie en quoi nous suns.   (2,609-12)

This testing power of the Grail is especially brought into play when the vessel is placed on the table in connection with the fish which Brons caught, and which won him the name of the Rich Fisher.

C, Didot-Perceval, has only one reference, "ne il ne covient mie en sa compagnie pechier" (I, 483), agreeing with B and with Gautier's lines 28,079-80.

In D, Queste, we revert to the physical gifts of the Grail. "And as soon as it entered the door of the hall the whole court was filled with perfumes . . . . and it proceeded to every place in the hall.   And as it came before the tables it filled them with every kind of meat that a man would wish to have."   When it comes in, " Every one looked at each other, and there was not one that could say a single word;" when it goes out, "Every one recovered his speech " (D II, pp. 442–43).   There is no allusion to a gathering at which the Grail is used to test the state of grace of its devotees. E, Grand St. Graal, shows a curious mixture of the two ideas; the Grail feeds its worshippers, but only those who are "de sainte vie," to them it bring "toutes le boines viandes ke cuers d'omme pourroit penser," but "li pecheour n'auoient ke mangier."   This version shows itself here, as in so many other passages, one of the latest in date, embodying and reconciling as it does the conceptions of the older versions—conceptions which it is difficult to derive, either from a common source or from one another.   If it were not for the solitary phrase of Gautier's, lines 28,079, etc. (a passage which

affords the strongest proof against the homogeneity of that part of
the Conte du Graal which goes under Gautier's name), there would
be an unbroken chain of testimony as to the food-giving power of
the Grail on the part of the earlier A versions, supported by the
Queste in opposition to the spiritual gifts insisted on by the B and
E, Grand St. Graal, forms. It is in any case difficult to believe that
if the writer of the Queste, with his strong tendency to mystic
allegory, had had before him the highly spiritual presentment of
the Grail-power found in B, he would have neglected it in favour
of the materialistic description he uses. In one point this version
differs from all others, the dumbness with which the Grail strikes
those to whom it appears.*

Name of Grail.

Whilst the majority of versions afford no explanation of the
name of the Grail, B and C attach a curious punning meaning to
it, thus B I, Metr. Jos. :

> Par droit Graal l'apelera ;
> Car nus le Graal ne verra,
> Ce croi-je, qu'il ne li agrée ;   (2,659–61)

and C, Didot-Perceval, " Et por ce l'anpelon-nos Graal, qu'il agrée
as prodes homes " (p. 483).   E, Grand St. Graal, seems to follow
these versions in Nasciens' words, " Car tout mi pense sont
accompli, puis ke ie voi chou qui en toutes choses me plaist et
m'agrée " (I, 212).   Is such a punning explanation more con-
sonant with the earliness or the lateness of the versions in which it
is found ?   If the meaning of " Gréal " as cup or vessel was a
perfectly well-established one, it is difficult to see why in the first
treatment of the subject it should have been necessary to explain
the word at all.

Arrival of the Grail in England.

Neither A I, Chrestien, nor A II, Gautier, give any indication
how the Grail came to England ; not until we come to A II A,

---

* In the Mabinogi of Branwen, the daughter of Llyr, the warriors cast into
the cauldron of renovation come forth on the morrow fighting men as good as
they were before, except that they are not able to speak (Mab., p. 381).

Pseudo-Gautier, do we learn anything on the subject. It is there related (v. 139–48) how Joseph and his companions take ship and sail till they come to the land promised Joseph by God—the White Isle, namely, a part of England; and how (v. 161–66) Joseph, finding that "sa vitaille li falloit," prays God to lend him that Grail in which he had collected the holy blood. The prayer is granted and the Grail appears and feeds the company. A III, Manessier, simply says that Joseph, after leaving Sarras, carried the Grail about with him, then in a singularly enigmatic passage (the Fisher King is speaking) :—

> Et, quant il furent départis,
> Il s'en ala en son païs,
> Et tout partout ù il aloit
> La loi Jhésucrist essauçoit.
> Puis vint en cest païs manoir,
> Od lui le saint Gréal, por voir.
> Josep qui en Dieu se fia
> Icest païs édéfia. (35,123–30)

The B versions account is much more elaborate, and demands the most careful analysis. In B I, Metr. Jos., the first mention of the West is found in Christ's words to Joseph concerning his nephew, Alain, who is to keep the Grail, to take charge of his brothers and sisters, and

> Puis s'en ira vers occident
> Es plus loiteins lius que pourra ; (3,100–01)

further that Petrus is likewise to go " ès vaus d'Avaron (3,123), it being added that—

> Ces terres trestout vraiement
> Se treient devers occident. (3,125–26)

Effectively we learn (v. 3,262, etc.) that Alain leads his brothers into strange lands. But the Grail remains behind, and in v. 3,353, etc., an angel declares it necessary that all the people should go to the West, that Brons should have the vessel, that he should go straight to the West, and that Petrus, after seeing the Grail safe in Brons' keeping, is to go likewise. Joseph follows the angel's command, and three days after he has committed the Grail to Brons' hands

> Ainsi Joseph se demoura.
> Li boens Pescherres s'en ala
> (Dont furent puis meintes paroles
> Contées, ki ne sunt pas foles)
> En la terre lau il fu nez,
> Et Joseph si est demourez.   (3,455–60)

A puzzling passage, as it is difficult to be sure whether line 3,459 refers to the Fisher or to Joseph, a point of obvious importance, as in the latter case it would indicate that Joseph in this version does not go West. On turning to the prose versions, some remarkable variations are found in the corresponding passages; thus B II, Cangé MS. (I, 265) after relating how Brons finds wives for his children, adds, "Mais ancor estoit la crestientez moult tenue et moult novele en ce païs que l'an apeloit la bloe Bretaigne que Joseph avoit novellement convertie à la créance de Jhésu-Christ," words which would seem to indicate that the writer imagined Joseph and his company *already* in England. The corresponding passage to v. 3,445–60 runs thus : Ensinc se departirent, si s'en ala li riches peschierres dont maintes paroles furent puis, en la grant Bretaigne et ensinc remest Joseph et fina en la terre et ou païs où il fu envoiez de par Jhésu-Crist (275). B III, Didot MS, accentuates the punning reference to Avalon in the angel's message to Joseph, "Come li monde . . . . . va en avalant covient-il que toute ceste gent se retraie en occident" (p. 330). The final passage runs thus : "Eynsi se despartirent Joseph et Bron : et Joseph s'en ala en la terre et el pais où il fust nez et ampris la terre" (p. 332). Thus the testimony of these versions favours the application of v, 2,459 in Metr. Jos. to Joseph. From C, Didot-Perceval, we obtain an account similar in parts to that of the B versions, the most direct reference being in the speech of the hermit, Perceval's uncle, " Biaus niès, sachès que à la table là où Joseph fist et je meismes oïmes la voiz de saint esperit qui nos comenda venir en loingteines terres en occident, et comenda le riche péchéor mon père que il venist en cestes parties, là ou li soleil avaloit" (449–50), where the punning reference to Avalon is again prominent, and where, apparently, the passage of Joseph himself to England is not indicated. An entirely different form of the legend is found in D and E. In the former (D II, 450)

it is briefly stated, " And afterwards it happened to Joseph, and
Joseph his father, and a number of his family with them, to set
out from the city of Sarras, and they came as far as Great
Britain "; again, p. 467, Perceval's aunt relates how when Joseph
of Arimathea came, and his son Joseph with him, to Great Britain,
there came with them about 4,000 people, all of whom are fed by
ten loaves, placed on the table, on the head of which is the Grail.
E, Grand St. Graal, dwells specially upon Josephe ; he is referred
to in I, p. 22, as having passed "le lignage ioseph son père outre mer
iusqu'en la bloie bertaigne qui ore a nom engleterre," and II, 123,
etc., gives a full account of how the passage is effected ; how the
Grail-bearers are sent first, and supported through the water by
its power ; how, when Josephe takes off his shirt, and his father
Joseph puts his foot upon it, it swells until it holds 250 persons:
These two accounts agree better with that of A IIA, Pseudo-
Gautier, than with any of the others ; indeed, a passage in the latter
(v. 125–29), which tells how Joseph committed the portrait of our
Lord, made by Verrine, to the mercy of the sea, may have given
the hint for the miraculous shirt story of the Grand St. Graal.
In this version, too, as in D, Queste, we first hear of the passage to
England, and then the Grail appears at the miraculous feeding of
the travellers. The versions thus fall into two clearly-defined
groups, Joseph being the Grail-bearer in the one, Brons in the
latter. The latter class is represented by the Metrical Joseph and
the Didot-Perceval alone, if we except the Berne MS. form of a
portion of the Conte du Graal, which, in its finish, has obviously
copied the Metrical Joseph. To the former class belong all the
other versions. Nay, more, one of the prose forms of Borron's
poems is interpolated, so as to countenance the Joseph-account of
the bringing of the Grail to England. Moreover, Borron's account
of the whole transaction is ambiguous and obscure; at first Alain
is the destined hero, long passages being devoted to him, and the
keeping of the mystic vessel being expressly reserved to him.
Yet he leaves, quite quietly, nothing more being heard of him,
and the same machinery of angelic messages is set in motion for
Brons, to whom, henceforth, the chief *rôle* is assigned. Does not
this show that there were from the outset two accounts of the

evangelisation of Britain, one, attributing it to Joseph, of wider popularity, and followed solely by the majority of the romances, whilst Borron, who gave greater prominence to the other account, has maladroitly tried to fuse the two into one? In any case it would be remarkable were the legend of purely Christian origin, and were the Metrical Joseph its earliest form, and source of the other forms, that its testimony on such an important point should be contradicted by nearly every other version.

Do the foregoing facts throw any light upon the question whether the two sections of the romance are originally independent, and which is the earlier? It is the later forms of the Quest alone which mention Joseph. But if he be really the older of the two personages to whom, in the Early History, the evangelisation of Britain is attributed, this would of itself go a long way to proving that the two portions of the romance only came into contact at a late stage of their development, and that the Quest is the older. It is otherwise if Brons be looked upon as the original Grail-bringer; the same causes which led to his exclusion from the other versions of the Early History might have kept him out of most versions of the Quest, and his presence in one Quest version could be claimed as a proof of the homogeneity of the romance. For the present, it is sufficient to mark the fact that what may be called the Brons form of the Early History is in a minority.

The Grail-Keeper and his relationship to the Promised Knight.

In the A versions the Grail-keeper is the Fisher King, uncle to the hero of the Quest, Perceval. The relationship is first plainly put in Chrestien, where the hermit, speaking to Perceval of the Grail, says—

> Cil qui l'en sert, il est mes frere
> Ma sœur et soie fu ta mère,
> Et del rice Pescéour croi
> Que il est fius à celui roi
> Qui del Graal servir se fait. (7,789–94)

The origin of his name is fully explained in the passage (v. 4,685–98), which tells of his being wounded in battle by a lance-thrust through his two thighs, of his sufferings, and of his only solace being fishing from a boat. How the Grail came into his possession C does not say. Gautier has no occasion to mention these facts, but from Manessier we learn that Joseph, having converted the land, died therein; that the Fisher King is of his seed, and that if God wills the Grail will never have its dwelling elsewhere than with him (35,130–36); that he, the Fisher King, had a brother, Goon Desert, treacherously slain by Partinal, who broke his sword in the murderous act. Goon's body and the fragments of the sword being brought by his niece to the Fisher King, he wounds himself with them, "parmi les gambes en traviers," and may not be healed until a knight should come to weld the fragments together and avenge his brother's death.

Pseudo-Gautier tells how Joseph, dying, prays that the Grail may remain with his descendants—

> Si fist il, c'est verité fine,
> Qu' après sa mort n'en ot sésine
> Nus hom, tant fust de son lignage
> Se il ne fu del haut parage.
> Li riches Peschéor, por voir,
> En fu estret et tuit si oir
> Et des suens fu Greloguevaus
> Ausi en réfu Percevaus.   (183–90)

Manessier disagrees, it will have been noticed, with Chrestien respecting the cause of the Fisher King's wound, and neither he nor the other continuators of Chrestien make any mention of that enigmatic personage the Fisher King's father, so casually alluded to by Chrestien (v. 7,791-99). Perceval according to them is a direct descendant of Joseph, Brons being as entirely ignored here as in the transport of the Grail to England.

In the B versions the Grail-keeper is Brons, and the Promised Knight is his son or grandson, for a close examination again shows that two varying accounts have been embodied in one narrative. In the passage where the Holy Ghost, speaking to Joseph, tells him of the empty place to be left at the table he is to make, the following lines occur :—

> Cil lius estre empliz ne pourra
> Devant qu' Enygeus avera

Un enfant de Bron seu mari,
Que tu et ta suer amez si ;
Et quant li enfès sera nez,
La sera ses lius assenez ;   (2,531–37)

followed closely by the prose versions : B II, Cangé MSS., "ne icil leux ne pourra estre ampliz tant que le filz Bron et Anysgeus ne l'accomplisse" (I, 254) ; B III, Didot MS., "Cist leus ne porra mie estre ampliz devant ce que li fist Bron l'ampleisse (I, 316). But afterwards a fresh account appears ; in the second message of the Holy Ghost, Joseph is told :

Que cist luis empliz ne sera
Devant que li tierz hons venra
Qui descendra de ten lignage
Et istera de ten parage,
Et Hebruns le doit engenrer
Et Enygeus ta sueur porter ;
Et cil qui de sen fil istra,
Cest liu méismes emplira.   (2,789–96)

In the corresponding passages both B II and III have the following significant addition, " et I. autre (*i.e.*, place) avoc cestui qui el nom de cestui sera fondé " (I, 261), " raemplira ce leu et I. autre qui en leu decestu isera fondez " (I, 322), which effectually disposes of M. Hucher's attempt (I, 254, note) to harmonise the two accounts by the remark that in the first one " il ne s'agit pas de la Table ronde où c'est Perceval qui remplit le lieu vide." Henceforth the legend follows the second account. To Alain, son of Brons, is revealed that

. . . de lui doit oissir
Un oir malle, qui doit venir. (3,091–92)

Petrus is to wait for " le fil Alein," Brons is to wait for " le fil sen fil," and when he is come to give him the vessel and Grail (3,363–67). B II, Cangé MS., again makes a characteristic addition to the promise to Alain " et si li di que de lui doit issir un oirs masles, à cui la grace de mon veissel doit repairier " (I, 267).

C, Didot-Perceval, follows the second account of B. Perceval is son to Alain li Gros, grandson to Brons, the rich Fisher King, " et cil rois péchéors est en grant enfermetez, quar il est vieil home et plains de maladies" (I, 418), and nephew to the hermit, "un des fiz Bron et frère Alein" (I, 448), though curiously enough when he tells Brons that he knows him to be father of his father, the latter addresses him as "bieaux niès" (I, 483). In any case whether B and C do or do not afford proof of a nearer relationship than that of grandson and grandfather between the Grail-keeper and the achiever of the Quest, the chronology which bridges over 400 years in two generations is equally fantastic.

In D, Queste, no less than three different accounts are to be distinguished, corresponding certainly to three stages in the development of this version due to the influence of other versions of the legend. The earliest is that preserved in D II, the Welsh translation of a now lost French original. The Promised Knight is Galahad, son of Lancelot, grandson, on the mother's side, of King Pelles (ch. iv). The Grail is kept at the court of King Peleur (ch. lxvii), the name of which is apparently Corbenic (ch. lxiv). The Lame King is mentioned by Perceval's sister (ch. xlix), as a son of King Lambar, who fought with King Urlain and slew him, and in consequence of that blow the country was wasted; afterwards (ch. l.) his lameness is set down to his folly in attempting to draw the magic sword, for which, though there was not in Christendom a better man than he, he was wounded with a spear through the thigh. She also speaks of him here as her uncle. The Grail quest is not connected in any way with the healing of this Lame King. In the text printed by Furnivall, Galahad is first introduced as Lancelot's son and Pelles' grandson, but when he comes to Arthur's court he bids his returning companion, "salues moi tous chiaus del saint hostel et mon *oncle le roi pelles* et mon *aioul le riche peschéour*." Guinevere's ladies, according to this version, prophesy that Galahad will heal the Lame King. A long account, missing in D I, is given by the hermit to Lancelot of his ancestry as follows (p. 120) :—Celidoine, son of Nasciens, had nine descendants, Warpus, Crestiens, Alain li Gros, Helyas, Jonaans, Lancelot, Ban, Lancelot himself, Galahad, in whom Christ will bathe himself entirely. Perceval is son of a King Pellehem (p. 182). The Lame King is Pelles, "que l'on apièle lo roi mehaignié" (p. 188) ; he is at Corbenic when Lancelot comes there. When Galahad and his companions arrive at his court a sick man wearing a crown is brought in, who blesses Galahad as his deliverer. After the appearance of the Grail, Galahad heals him by touching his wound with the spear. The third account, from the version of the Queste printed with the Lancelot and the Mort Artur in 1488, at Rouen, by Gaillard le Bourgeois,* makes Galahad send greetings to the Fisher King and to his *grandfather, King Pelles;* it adds to Perceval's sister's account of how Pelles was wounded, the words, "he was Galahad's grandfather;"† it adds to the account of Lancelot's visit to the Grail Castle, the words, "this was Castle Corbenic, where the Holy Grail was kept." Before discussing these differences it is advisable to see what the Grand St. Graal says on these points. Here Alain, the Fisher King, son of Brons, is a virgin, and when Josephe commits the Grail to his care he empowers him to leave it to whom he likes (II, 360–39.) In accordance with this Alain leaves the Grail to his brother Josue, with the title of Fisher King. Josue's descendants are Aminadap, Catheloys, Manaal, Lambor (who was wounded by Bruillans with Solomon's sword, whence arose such a fierce war that the whole land was laid desert).‡ Pelleans, wounded in battle in the ankle, whence he had the name Lame King, Pelles, upon whose daughter Lancelot begets Galahad, who is thus, on the mother's side, ninth in descent from Brons, brother to Joseph. Galahad's descent is likewise given from Celidoine, son of Nasciens, as follows : Marpus, Nasciens, Alains li Gros, Ysaies, Jonans, Lancelot, Bans, Lancelot, Galahad, who in thus counting Celidoine is tenth in descent from Nasciens, Joseph's companion, (vol. ii, ch. xxxix.) So far the story is fairly consistent, although there is a difference of one generation between father's and mother's genealogy. But ch. 17, in a very important passage,

---

* The version summarised by Birch-Hirschfeld.

† Curiously enough this very text here prints Urban as the name of the Maimed King ; Urban is the antagonist of Lambar, the father of the Maimed King in the original draft of the Queste, and his mention in this place in the 1488 text seems due to a misprint. In the episode there is a direct conflict of testimony between the first and second drafts, Lambar slaying Urlain in the former, Urlain Lambar in the latter.

‡ This account agrees with that of the second draft of the Queste, in which Urlain slays Lambar.

introduces a different account. The angel is expounding to
Josephe and Nasciens the marvels of the lance; to Josephe he says,
" de cheste lance dont tu as este ferus; ne sera iamis ferus ke vns
seus hom. Et chil sera rois, et descendra de ton lignaige, si serra li
daerrains des boins. Chil en sera ferus parmi les cuisses ambedeus,"
and will not be healed till the Good Knight come, "et chil . .
serra li daerrains hom del lignaige nascien. Et tout ausi com
nasciens a este li premiers hom qui les meruelles du graal a veues;
autresi sera chil li daerrains qui les verra.* Car che dist li urais
crucefis. 'Au premier home du precieus lignaige, et au daerrain, ai
iou deuise à demonstrer mes meruelles.' Et si dist enchore après.
' Sour le premier et sour le daerrain de mes menistres nouuiaus qui
sont enoint et sacre a mon plaisir, espanderai iou la venianche de
la lanche auentureuse' (I, 216–17), i.e., the last of Josephe's line
shall be the only man wounded by the lance, the last of Nasciens'
line shall be the deliverer. But according to Galahad's genealogy,
given above, it is not the last of Josephe's line (represented by his
cousin Josue) who is the Wounded King, for Galahad himself is as
much the last in descent from Josephe as from Nasciens, and even
if we take the words to apply only to the direct male descendants
of Josue, there is still a discrepancy, as not Pelles, but Pelleant,
his father, is the " roi mehaigniés." If the Wounded King were
really the last of Josephe's line, i.e., Pelles, Galahad would be
his grandson, as Percival is to Brons. Taking the two versions
D. and E. together, some idea may be gathered from them
of the way in which the legend has grown, and of the shifts to
which the later harmonisers were put in their attempts to reconcile
divergent accounts. In the first draft of the Queste, Galahad has
nothing to do with the Lame King, the latter remains Perceval's
uncle, the very relationship obtaining in Chrestien. Galahad has
supplanted Perceval, but has not stepped into the place entirely.
The second draft of the Queste endeavours to remedy this by
clumsily introducing the Lame King and his healing, missing in the
first draft, into the great Grail scene at the end, an idea foreign

---

* Only one beholder of the Quest is alluded to, although in the Queste,
from which the Grand St. Graal drew its account, three behold the wonders of
the Grail.

to the original author of the Queste, who, having broken with
Perceval as chief hero, also broke with the distinctive Quest
incident as far as the chief hero is concerned. But a strange
blunder is committed; the second draft, anxious to make Galahad's
grandfather both Fisher and Lame King, actually speaks of Pelles
as Galahad's uncle, in direct contradiction to its own indication.
The third draft corrects this mistake, and tries by different
explanatory interpolations to confirm the relationship of Galahad to
the Lame King, and the identity of his castle with the Grail
Castle. The author of the Grand St. Graal now appears on the
scene, appropriates the story about King Lambar, father to the
Lame King, Percival's uncle, makes him an ancestor of Galahad,
and gives a name to his son, Pelleant (which name creeps back
into the second draft of the Queste as that of Perceval's father), and
thus derives Galahad on the mother's side from Brons, although it
escapes him that he thus gives the lie to the prophecy which he
puts in the angel's mouth, that it is the last of Josephe's seed who
is to be lamed by the lance, and that he has not given his Lambor
fictitious ancestors enough to equalize the genealogies.

We are thus led back to the relationship of uncle and nephew
as the earliest subsisting between the Grail King and the achiever
of the Quest, and we find in those versions which supplant
Perceval by Galahad a story told of the former's great uncle, King
Lambar, by no means unlike that told of his uncle in the A versions,
and that there, as here, the cause of the woe brought upon the
hero's family is one of the magic talismans which the hero is in
quest of and by means of which he is to achieve his quest. We
further notice that in so far as the Early History influences the
Quest forms, it is the later versions in which its influence is apparent, and it is the Joseph, not the Brons form, which exercises this
influence. Not until we come to the Grand St. Graal, an obvious
and bold attempt to embody previous versions in one harmonious
whole, does the Brons form make itself felt.

Work of the Promised Knight.

In Chrestien we can only guess at what the results of the
successful achievement of the Quest would have been by the

reproaches addressed to the hero upon the failure of his first visits to the Grail Castle ; he would have mended all things, and—

> Le bon roi ki est mehaigniés ;
> Que tous eust regaengniés
> Ses membres, et tière tenist,
> Et si grans bien en avenist ; (4,763–67)

many evils will flow from his failure, and the cause of it is the sin he has committed in leaving his mother, who thereupon died of grief (4,768–71); again the Loathly Damsel reproaches him that the Rich King would have been healed of his wound, he would have kept in peace his land, which he never may again, for now

> Dames en perdront lor maris
> Tières en seront essilies,
> Et pucièles deconsellies ;
> Orfenes, veves en remanront
> Et maint Chevalier en morront. (6,056–60)

Gautier de Doulens gives a vivid description of the effect of Gawain's partially successful visit to the Grail King; the character of the landscape changes at once—

> N'estoit pas plus que mienuis,
> Le soir devant, que Dex avoit
> Rendu issi com il devoit
> As aiges lor cors el païs ;
> Et tout li bos, ce m'est avis,
> Refurent en verdor trové,
> Si tos com il ot demandé
> Por coi si sainnoit en l'anstier
> La lance ; si devoit puplier
> Li règnes ; mais plus ne pupla
> Por tant que plus ne demanda. (20,344–55)

All the country folk both bless and curse Gawain.

> Sire, mors nous as et garis,
> Tu dois estre liés et maris ;
> Car grant aise nos as doné,
> S'en devons tout mercier Dé ;
> Et si te devons moult hair
> Pour con que nel vosis öir
> Le Greail, por coi il servoit,
> Ne de la joie ki devoit
> Là venir ne poroit nus dire,
> Si en doit avoir duel et ire. (20,357–66)

In Manessier, when Perceval has finally accomplished the
Quest by the slaying of Partinal, and has come for the third time
to the Grail Castle (though even then he only reaches it after
long wanderings and lights upon it by chance), news whereof is
brought to the King;—

> Li rois, à grant joie et grant feste
> Est maintenant salis en piés
> Et se senti sain et haitiés.   (44,622-24)

Perceval is crowned King after his uncle's death, and reigns
for seven years.

Thus, in the A versions, the healing of the Maimed King, and
the consequent restoration to fertility and prosperity of his land,
such are the tasks to be achieved by the hero of the Quest.   In
the B versions an entirely different series of conceptions is met
with.   Brons, the Fisher King, is to wait for his grandson, and to
hand him the vessel which he received from Joseph.   When this
is done the meaning of the Trinity is to be known—*

> Lors sera la senefiance
> Accomplie et la demonstrance
> De la benoite Trinité,
> Qu'avons en trois parz devisée.   (3,371-74)

Besides this, the Promised Knight is to visit Petrus, who may
not pass away till he comes, and from whom he is to learn the
power of the vessel, and the fate of Moys (v. 3,127-36).   Finally,
when he comes he is to fill the empty seat, and to find Moys, of
whom it is said—

> De lui plus ne pallera-on
> Ne en fable ne en chançon,
> Devant que cil revenra
> Qui li liu vuit raemplira :
> Cil-méismes le doit trouver.   (2,815-19)

Here the only indication which can possibly be tortured into a
hint of the waiting of a sick king for his deliverer is the reference
to Petrus.   It is not a little remarkable that when the latter is

---

* This, of course, belongs to the second of the two accounts we have found
in the poem respecting the Promised Knight, the one which makes him the
grandson and not the son merely of Brons.

leaving for England, he asks for the prayers of the company that he may not fall into sin, and lose the love of God (v. 3320–35) Does this presuppose a version in which he *does* sin, and is consequently punished by disease, from which only the Promised Knight may heal him?

On turning to C, a totally distinct account of what the Quest achiever is to do presents itself. He seats himself, it is true, in the empty seat, but it goes nigh with him that he suffers the fate of Moys, from which he is only preserved by the great goodness of his father, Alain (p. 427). He does not find Moys; Petrus is not once mentioned by name, nor does Perceval visit anyone who may not die till he come, and from whom he learns the power of the vessel, saving always the Fisher King, for the references to whom see *supra*, p. 83. This Fisher King is "veil home et plains de maladies, ne il n'aura james santé devant un chevalier que yà à la Table ronde aserra, sera prodons vers Deu et vers sainte eglise et ait fait tant d'armes que il soit le plus alosez del monde. Et lors vendra à la maison au riche roi péchéor et quant il aura demandé de quoi li Graus sert, tantost sera li roi gariz de de sa'nfermeté et cherront li enchentement de Bretaigne et sera la prophétic accomplie" (p. 419). Again, p. 427 "li riches rois péchéors est chéuz en grant maladie et en grant enfermeté, ne il peust morir devant que uns de XXX chevalier, qui ci sunt asis, ait tant fait d'armes et de chevalerie qu'il soit li mieudres chevalier del monde." Again, p. 427, "Et quant il (*i.e.*, the Fisher King) sera gariz, si ira, dedanz li III jorz, de vie à mort, et baillera à celui chevalier, le vesseau et li aprendra le segroites paroles qui li aprist Joseph ; et lors ampliz de la grace du Sainct Esprit et cherront li enchentement de la Bretaigne et les afaires." Again, when Perceval has come for the second time to the Fisher King's, and has asked the question and learnt the secret words, he remained there " et moult fust prodons et chéirent les enchentement de la terre de Bretaigne et par tout le monde." Here, then, are the Sick King, the mysterious question, the healing, and the effect upon the land (note how the enchantments of Britain are insisted upon), as in the A versions. The only points of contact with B are that Brons is like Petrus in not being able to die till Perceval come, and that his infirmity seems to be ascribed mainly to his age, and not to a wound, which at first sight seems to agree better with the vague indications of B than with the positive statement of A.

Two accounts, each fairly definite and consistent, are thus forthcoming respecting the object of the Quest, the one represented by A and C, the other by B. What light is thrown upon the matter by the remaining versions, and which of these two accounts do they support?   Neither from the Queste, D, nor from the Grand St. Graal, E, can any clear conception of the Quest be gathered.   Both have a great deal to say about the adventures and the wonders of the Grail, but absolutely nothing comes of the achievement so far as the Grail itself, or as Galahad and his two companions are concerned.   It goes to the East, they with it, they become hermits and die.   But in proportion as the main object of the Quest becomes less definite, the number of secondary objects increases.   In D, Queste, Galahad is to achieve the adventure of the Seat Perillous (ch. iii, iv) ; he is to wear the shield left by Joseph to Mordrains (ch. x) ; he is to release from life Mordrains himself, struck with blindness for approaching too near the Grail (ch. xxiii) ; he (according to the second draft of the Queste), is to release King Pelles (his grandfather, according to draft 3), wounded through both ankles for trying to draw the sword ; he is to release Simei, burning in a fiery grave for that he once sinned against Joseph of Arimathea (ch. lxvi).   To this sufficiently long list the Grand St. Graal adds the resoldering of the sword broken by Joseph—" Ha espée, iamais ne sera resaudée deuant ke chil te tenra qui les hautes auentures del Saint Graal devra asoumir" (II, 264) ; the delivery of Moys from out the furnace where he burns, not for always "ains trouuera enchore merchi et pardon.   Mais che qu'il a mesfait, espanira il en tel manière qu'il en sera en fu iusc' a tant ke li boines chiualiers uenra (II, 277).   Moys likewise speaks of Galahad as one who "achieura les auentures de la grant bertaigne" (II, 279–80).   Finally, Pelleur wounded (mehaigniés de ii cuisses) "en vne bataille de rome" is to be released, "il ne peut garir de la plaie deuant ke galaad, li tres boins chiualers, le vint visiter.   Mais lors sans faille gari il" (II, p. 373).

The Queste knows nothing of Petrus, but in the Grand St. Graal he turns up at the end in the same casual way as Brons, and converts King Luces (II, 3356-3), *i.e.* is thus brought into connection with Geoffrey of Monmouth's form of the conversion of Britain legend.

The foregoing statement confirms all that has previously been urged as to the lateness of both Queste and Grand St. Graal. The author of the former again shows himself a daring, but not over skilful, adapter of older legends, the author of the latter an unintelligent compiler, whose sole aim it is to lengthen out his story by the introduction of every incident he can lay his hands upon. But although late, they may nevertheless throw light upon the question which, of the two strongly differentiated accounts of the object of the Grail quest which have been noted, has the better claim to be looked upon as the older one. The Conte du Graal and the Didot-Perceval agree, as has been seen, against the Metrical Joseph, in making the main object of the Grail-seeker the healing of a maimed or the release from life of a supernaturally old King. This *motif*, it is not too much to say, is the pivot upon which in the Conte du Graal all turns; in the Metrical Joseph it is barely hinted at.

The Queste, if looked at closely, is found to bear witness to the Conte du Graal form. As is seen from the summary (*supra*, p. 41, Inc. 12) it has the very incident upon which so much stress is laid in Chrestien's poem, the visit to the Sick King, the omitted question, the consequent misfortune. True, all this has been transferred from the original hero, Perceval, to the father of the new hero Galahad, and, true, the final object which the Queste proposes, in so far as it proposes any definite object, to its Grail-seeker is of a different character. But the fact that this object is not stated in the same way as in the Metrical Joseph, whilst that found in the Conte du Graal *is* embodied though in a different connexion, points unmistakably to what may be called the healing *motif* as the older one. Here, again, the Metrical Joseph is in a minority, and it is not even followed by that very version, the Didot-Perceval, which has been ascribed to the same author, and claimed as an integral portion of the same trilogy.*

---

* The object of the Quest according to Heinrich von dem Türlin will be found dealt with in Chapter VII.

Qualifications of the Promised Knight.

Neither Chrestien, Gautier, nor Manessier lay any stress upon special qualifications in the quest-hero for the achievement of his task. In Chrestien, as already stated, (*supra*, p. 87), it is exclusively the sin of which Perceval has been guilty in leaving his mother which prevents his achieving the Quest at his first visit to the Grail Castle (v. 4,768–71 and 7,766–74), whilst the continuator make no attempt at any explanation of the hero's repeated failures. Not until Gerbert does a fresh *motif* show itself in the poem, but then it is a remarkable one; if Perceval has been hitherto unable to attain the goal he has so long striven for, it is because he has been unfaithful to his first love, Blanchefleur (VI, p. 182); he must return and wed her before he is fit to learn the full secret of the Grail.*

The other Quest versions are on this point in striking contrast to Chrestien. The words of C, Didot-Perceval, have already been noted, (*supra*, p. 89). Again the damsel, reproaching the hero after his first failure, addresses him thus :—"Mès je sai bien por quoi tu l' ás perdu, por ceque tu ni es pas si sage ne si vaillant, ne n'as pas fet tant d'armes ; ne n'ies si prodons que tu doies avoir le sanc nostre (sire) en guarde" (p. 467).

It is significant to note in this connection that it is only after Perceval has overcome all the best knights of the Round Table, including Gawain (the companion hero, as will be shown later, of the oldest form of the story), and thereby approved himself the best knight of the world, that Merlin appears and directs him to the Grail Castle.† The talk about Holy Church would seem to be an addition, and the original ideal a purely physical one.

In the Queste the qualification of the hero has become the

---

* This is one of a remarkable series of points of contact between Gerbert and Wolfram von Eschenbach.

† It almost looks as if the author of C were following here a version in which the hero only has to go once to the Grail Castle ; nothing is said about Perceval's first unsuccessful visit, and Merlin addresses Perceval as if he were telling him for the first time about matters concerning which he must be already fully instructed.

main feature of the legend, the pivot upon which everything turns. The one thing necessary is that the hero should be a virgin, and the story is one long glorification of the supreme virtue of chastity. Yet even here the warlike deeds of Galahad are dwelt upon in a way that points to a different ideal. Traces, though slight ones, may be found in C, Didot-Perceval, of the importance attached to the chastity of the hero; thus his hermit uncle admonishes him, " ne vous chaille de gésir aveuc fame, quar cest un peché luxurious et bien sachiez, que la pichié que vous avez fait, vous ont neu à trover la maison Bron," and in the adventure with the damsel of the hound, although he had (p. 440) solicited her favours, and she had promised them if he brought her the head of the white stag, yet (p. 470) when he returns to her and she offers herself to him, he pleads his quest as a reason for not even passing one night with her. In Gautier de Doulens, on the contrary, everything passes in accordance with the orthodox custom of the day—when knights were as punctual in demanding as ladies scrupulous in granting the fulfilment of such bargains. But here, again, references to chastity seem to be additions, and rather unskilful ones, whilst in the Queste they are the vital spirit of the story.

What results from the foregoing is much as follows :-—

The Perceval form of the Quest is certainly the older of the two, and underlies in reality the Galahad form. When cleared from the admixture of Christian mystic elements it appears as a coherent and straightforward story, in which nothing necessarily presupposes the Early History. The influence of the latter is, however, distinctly traceable. As far as Chrestien himself is concerned, nothing can be asserted with certainty as to the origin, extent, and nature of that influence; in the case of his continuators it can be definitely referred to that form of the Early History which is represented by the Queste and the Grand St. Graal (save in the solitary instance of the Berne fragment of Gautier de Doulens). The later in date the sections of the Conte du Graal, the more strongly marked is the influence of the Early History, and *pari passu* the increasing prominence given to the Christian mystic side of the Grail.

Of the Early History two forms can be distinguished. In the one, Joseph and the group of persons whom he converts in the East are made the means of bringing Christianity to Britain. The Grail is dwelt upon almost solely in its most material aspect. This form is closely connected with the Galahad Quest, and its chronology has been elaborately framed to correctly bridge over the difference in time between the Apostolic and Arthurian ages. It has also affected, as remarked above, the later versions of the Perceval Quest. The second or Brons form knows nothing of the companions of Joseph, who is only indirectly the means of the conversion of Britain, the real evangelists being kinsmen of his who bear decided Celtic names. These kinsmen are related as grandfather and father (or simply father or uncle), to a hero whose exploits are to be dealt with in a sequel. There is strong insistence upon the spiritual character of the Grail, which is obviously intended to play an important part in the promised sequel. No traces of this form are to be found in any version (saving always the above-mentioned fragment of Gautier), until we come to the Grand St. Graal, with which such portions as do not conflict with the Joseph form are embodied.

The Didot-Perceval, although formally in contact with the Brons Early History, is not really the sequel announced in that work. It differs profoundly from it in the most essential feature of the story, the nature of the task laid upon the hero. Upon examination this appears to be of the same nature as that of the Conte du Graal, with a seasoning of the Christian mystic element. It was, however, *intended* for a sequel to the Metrical Joseph, a fact which may be taken as a proof that Borron never completed his plan of a Joseph-Merlin-Grail trilogy of which we possess the first two parts.

The first of the two points marked for investigation at the outset of this chapter may thus be considered settled. The Quest is originally independent of and older than the Early History. And although in no instance can the versions of the former be said to be entirely free from the influence of the latter, yet in the older forms the traces are such as to be easily separated from the prin i-tive elements of the story.

The versions which have been examined may now be arranged in the following order :—

(1) Chrestien's portion of the Conte du Graal. The oldest form of the Perceval Quest, but presupposing an Early History.

(2) Gautier de Doulens followed Chrestien, in all probability, almost immediately. Even less can be gathered from him than from Chrestien respecting the earliest form of the Early History, but this is probably represented by

(3) Pseudo-Gautier, which in all likelihood gives the outline of the work made use of by Queste and Grand St. Graal. Pseudo-Gautier is almost certainly some years later than Gautier, as the Berne MS. scribe found it necessary to seek for information in

(4) Borron's poem, probably written towards the end of the twelfth century, but which for some reason remained unknown for a time, although it afterwards, as evidenced by the number of MSS., became popular. There is every reason to believe that Borron knew nothing of any other Early History. His work, as we have it, is abridged and arranged. Meanwhile

(5) Queste had appeared. The author probably used the same Early History as Pseudo-Gautier. He knew the Conte du Graal, and wrote in opposition to it with a view to edification. He certainly knew nothing of Borron's poem, or he could not have failed, with his strong mystical tendencies, to dwell upon the spiritual and symbolic character of the Grail.

(6) The Grand St. Graal, an earlier draft of the work, now known under that title. Probably an enlarged version of the hypothetical original Early History ; wanting all the latter portions relating to Brons and his group, which were added to it when Borron's poem became known. This work must have appeared before 1204 (in which year it is referred to by Helinandus), and, as Chrestien wrote his poem about 1189-90, it follows that at least half-a-dozen works belonging to the Grail cycle came out in the last twelve years of the twelfth century.

(7) Manessier and

(8) Gerbert brought out independent endings to the Conte du Graal from 1216 to 1225. It was probably shortly after this time that Borron's poem became known, and that it was incorporated with the Grand St. Graal, which assumed the shape under which it has come down to us.

(9) The Didot-Perceval is probably the latest in date of all the members of the cycle.

Before proceeding to examine our second point, which is whether the Grail itself really belongs to the original form of the Quest, or has been introduced into the Quest versions from the Early History, it will be advisable to summarise the opinions and researches of previous investigators. Light will thus be thrown upon many points of interest which have not received special examination in these pages. A theory of the origin and development of the cycle, which is in many respects directly opposed to the conclusions we have reached, will also be fully set forth, and an opportunity will thus be given for testing by adverse criticism the soundness of our method of investigation, and of the results to which it has led us.

CHAPTER IV.

SKETCH OF THE LITERATURE CONNECTED WITH THE GRAIL CYCLE.

Villemarqué—Halliwell—San Marte (A. Schulz)—Simrock—Rochat—
Furnivall's reprint of the Grand St. Graal and of Borron—J. F. Camp-
bell—Furnivall's Queste—Paulin Paris—Potvin's Conte du Graal—
Bergmann—Skeat's Joseph of Arimathea—Hucher : Grail Celtic, date
of Borron—Zarncke, Zur Geschichte der Gralsage ; Grail belongs to
Christian legend—Birch-Hirschfeld develops Zarncke's views : Grand
St. Graal younger than Queste, both presuppose Chrestien and an
earlier Queste, the Didot-Perceval, which forms integral part of
Borron's trilogy ; Mabinogi later than Chrestien; various members of
the cycle dated—Martin combats Birch-Hirschfeld : Borron later than
Chrestien, whose poem represents oldest stage of the romance, which
has its roots in Celtic tradition—Hertz—Criticism of Birch-Hirschfeld.

MONSIEUR TH. DE LA VILLEMARQUÉ'S researches form a convenient
starting point, both on account of the influence they exercised
upon later investigation, and because he was the first to state with
fulness and method the arguments for the Celtic origin of the
legend. They appeared originally in the volume entitled " Contes
populaires des anciens Bretons précédés d'un essai sur l'origine des
épopées chevaleresques de la Table Ronde " (Paris, 1842), and com-
prising a French translation of the Mabinogion of Geraint and
Peredur, with introductory essays and detailed explanatory notes.
The translation of Peredur is preceded by a study of Chrestien's
poem, in which the following conclusions are stated : The Grail is
Celtic in origin, the French term being equivalent to the Welsh
per, and having a like meaning, basin. It is the Druidic basin
alluded to by Taliessin, the same which figures in the Mabinogi
of Branwen, which appears in the oldest folk-tales of Brittany, and
which is sought for in the twelfth century Mabinogi by Peredur,
i.e., the Basin-Seeker. The original occult character of the Druidic
basin, and of the lance, the bardic symbol of undying hatred to

the Saxon, disappears in the Mabinogi, the tone and character of which are purely romantic. Composed among a people comparatively unused to the chivalrous ideal, it breathes, however, a rude and harsh spirit. But such as it is, it forms the groundwork of Chrestien's poem. Comparison between the two demonstrates the simple character of the Welsh romance, and shows how the French poet sought to transform it by an infusion of feudal courtliness and religious mysticism. In its last stage of development the story reverts to its pristine, occult, and mystic character.

Much of what M. de la Villemarqué says is sound and telling; but, unfortunately, although well aware that the French poem is the work of three men and not of one, he yet treats it as an organic whole, and thus deprives the larger part of his comparison of all value. Moreover, he supports his thesis by arguments based upon a Breton poem (the story of which is similar to that of Perceval's youth), ascribed without the shadow of evidence to the end of the tenth century.

In 1861 M. de la Villemarqué reprinted his work with extensive additions, under the title of " Les Romans de la Table Ronde et les Contes des Anciens Bretons." The section summarised above remained substantially unaltered, but considerable extension was given to the author's views concerning the mode of development of the romances. The points chiefly insisted upon are: the similarity of metre between the Welsh poem and the French metrical romances; the delight of the Plantagenet kings in the Welsh traditions and the favour showed them; and the early popularity of the Welsh and Breton singers. Villemarqué's last word upon the subject is that the Welsh storytellers received from the ancient bards a pagan tradition, which, changed in character and confounded with the Mystery of the Sacrament, they handed on to the romance writers of Northern France and Germany, who gave it a fresh and undying life.

Villemarqué's views were worked up by Mr. Baring Gould in his essay on the Sangreal ("Curious Myths of the Middle Ages," 1867) and in this form or in their original presentment won wide acceptance as the authoritative exposition of the Celtic origin of the cycle.

In England, Mr. Halliwell, when editing, in 1844, the Thornton Sir Perceval, derived it from Chrestien and his continuators, in spite of the omission of Lance and Grail, on account of the sequence of incidents being the same. The Mabinogi is alluded to as an adaptation of Chrestien. The supposition that Perceval's nick-name, "le Gallois," implies the Welsh origin of the story is rejected as absurd.

In Germany the Grail-cycle formed the subject of careful investigation on the part of San Marte (A. Schulz) for some years prior to 1840. From 1836 to 1842 he brought out a modern German translation of Wolfram von Eschenbach's Parzival, accompanied by an elaborate essay on the genesis of the legend, and in 1841, "Die Arthur-Sage und die Mährchen des rothen Buchs von Hergest." In the latter work a careful analysis of the Mabinogi leads to the following conclusions :—Locale and persons are purely Welsh ; tone and character are older than the age of the Crusades and Knighthood ; it may be looked upon with confidence as the oldest known source of the Perceval *sage*. In comparing the Mabinogi with Kiot's (*i.e.*, Wolfram's) version, stress is laid upon the task imposed upon Peredur, which is held to be different in character and independent in origin from the Grail Quest in Kiot. The Thornton Sir Perceval is claimed as the representative of an early Breton *jongleur* poem which knew nothing of the Grail story. In the former work Wolfram von Eschenbach's poem is accepted, so far as its framework is concerned, as a faithful echo of Kiot's, the Provencal origin of which is proved by its Oriental and Southern allusions. The Provencals may have obtained the Peredur *sage* direct from Brittany, they at any rate fused it with the Grail legend. Their version is an artistic whole, whereas the North French one is a confused string of adventures. Chrestien's share in the latter is rightly distinguished from that of his continuators, and these are dated with fair accuracy. Robert de Borron is mentioned, but as a thirteenth century adapter of earlier prose versions; the Grand St. Graal is placed towards the middle of the thirteenth century. In analysing the Joseph of Arimathea form of the legend, the silence of the earlier British historians concerning Joseph's evangelisation of Britain is noted, and 1140 is given as the earliest date of this part of the legend. The captivity of Joseph arises probably from a confusion between him and Josephus. There is no real connection between the Joseph legend and that of the Grail. Wolfram's Templeisen agree closely with the Templars, one of the main charges against whom was their alleged worship of a head from which they expected riches and victuals, and to which they ascribed the power of making trees and flowers to bloom.*

San Marte's translation of Wolfram was immediately (1842) followed by Simrock's, whose notes are mainly directed against his predecessor's views on the origin and development of the Grail legend. The existence of Kiot is contested ; the *differentia* between Wolfram and Chrestien are unknown to Provencal, but familiar to German, poetry. The Grail myth in its oldest form is connected with John the Baptist. Thus in the Mabinogi the Grail is represented by a head in a platter ; the head the Templars were accused of worshipping has probably the same origin ; the Genoese preserved the Sacro Catino, identified by them with the Grail, in the chapel of St. John the Baptist; Chrestien mentions with especial significance, St. John's Eve (Midsummer Eve). The head of St. John the Baptist, found, according to the legend, in the fourth century, was carried later to Constantinople, where in the eleventh century it is apparently used to keep an emperor from dying (even as of the Grail, it is told, no one could die the day he saw it). If Wolfram cuts out the references to the Baptist, *en revanche* he brings Prester John into the story. The essential element in the Grail is the blood in the bowl, symbol of creative power as is the Baptist's head, both being referable to the summer equinox. Associated with John the Baptist is Herodias, who takes the place of an old Germanic goddess, Abundia, as John does of Odin or Baldur.† The essence of the myth is the reproductive power of the blood of the slain god (Odin-Hackelberend, Baldur,

---

* It is remarkable, considering the scanty material at his disposal, how accurate Schulz' analysis is, and how correct much of his argumentation.

† Wagner has admirably utilised this hint of Simrock's in his Parsifal, when his Kundry (the loathly damsel of Chrestien and the Mabinogi) is Herodias. *Cf. infra*, Ch. X.

Adonis, Osiris). As the Grail may only be seen by those to whom God's grace is granted, so in the German folk-tale the entrance to the hollow mounds wherein lies treasure or live elves is only visible to Sunday children or pure youths. Thus, too, no man may find the grave of Hackelberg (Odin). Such caves, when entered, close upon the outgoing mortal as the Grail Castle portcullis closes upon Parzival. Many of Gauvain's adventures appear in German folk-tradition. As to Parzival's youth "it cannot be doubted that we have here a variation of the Great Fool folk-tale (Dummling's Märchen) found among all people. It is hard to say what people possessing this tale brought it into contact, either by tradition or in writing, with the Grail story, but that people would have the first claim among whom it is found in an independent form." The Mabinogi explanation of the Grail incident is unacceptable, and the Mabinogi itself is later than Chrestien, as is shown by its foolish invention of the witches of Gloucester, and by its misrendering the incident of the dwarves greeting Peredur. In the original folk-tale the ungainly hero wàs *laughed at*, not greeted. The Thornton Sir Perceval may possibly contain an older version of Perceval's youth than any found elsewhere. Wolfram's poem represents, however, the oldest and purest form of the Grail myth, which, originally pagan, only became fully Christianised in the hands of the later North French poets.

Simrock's speculations, though marred by his standing tendency to claim over much for German tradition, are full of his usual acute and ingenious, if somewhat fanciful, learning. His ignorance of Celtic tradition unfortunately prevented his following up the hint given in the passage quoted above which I have adopted as one of the mottoes of the present work.

In 1855 Rochat published (" Ueber einen bisher unbekannten Percheval li Gallois," Zurich) selections from a Berne MS. containing part of Gautier de Doulens' continuation of Chrestien (v. 21,930 to end, with thirteen introductory and fifty-six concluding original lines, *cf*. p. 19), and entered at some length into the question of the origin and development of the Grail legend. The Mabinogi, contrary to San Marte's opinion, is placed after Chrestien. Villemarqué's ballad of Morvan le Breiz is the oldest form of the

Perceval *sage*, then comes the Thornton Sir Perceval, a genuine popular production derived probably from a Welsh original. In spite of what San Marte says, the Grail incident is found in the Mabinogi, and it might seem as if Chrestien had simply amplified the latter. On San Marte's theory of the (Southern) origin of the Grail myth, this, however, is impossible, and the fact that the Mabinogi contains this incident is a proof of its lateness.

Up to 1861 all writers upon the Grail legend were under this disadvantage, that they had no complete text of any part of the cycle before them,* and were obliged to trust largely to extracts and to more or less carefully compiled summaries. In that year Mr. Furnivall, by the issue for the Roxburghe Club of the Grand St. Graal, together with a reprint of Robert de Borron's poem (first edited in 1841 by M. Franc. Michel), provided students with materials of first-rate importance. His introductory words are strongly against the Celtic origin of the story, and are backed up by a quotation from Mr. D. W. Nash, in which that "authority who really knows his subject" gives the measure of his critical acumen by the statement that the Mabinogi of Peredur can have nothing to do with the earliest form of the legend, because "in Sir T. Malory, Perceval occupies the second place to Galahad." In fact, neither the editor nor Mr. Nash seems to have tried to place the different versions, and their assertions are thus of little value, though they contributed, nevertheless, to discredit the Celtic hypothesis. San Marte, in an essay prefixed to the first volume, repeated his well-known views respecting the source of Wolfram's poems, and, incidentally, protested against the idea that the Mabinogi is but a Welshified French romance.

In 1862 the accomplished editor of the " Popular Tales of the West Highlands," Mr. J. F. Campbell, published in his second volume (p. 152) some remarks on the Story of the Lay of the Great Fool, which ended thus, " I am inclined . . . . to consider this ' Lay ' as one episode in the adventures of a Celtic hero, who, in

---

* Excepting, of course, the late fifteenth and early sixteeth century Paris imprints, which represented as a rule, however, the latest and most interpolated forms, and Mons. Fr. Michel's edition of Borron's poem.

the twelfth century became Perceval le chercheur du basin. He too, was poor, and the son of a widow, and half starved, and kept in ignorance by his mother, but, nevertheless . . . in the end he became possessed of that sacred basin, le Saint Graal, and the holy lance, which, though Christian in the story, are manifestly the same as the Gaelic talismans which appear so often in Gaelic tales, and which have relations in all popular lore—the glittering weapon which destroys, and the sacred medicinal cup which cures." I have taken these words as a motto for my studies, which are, indeed, but an amplification of Mr. Campbell's statement. Had the latter received the attention it deserved, had it, for instance, fallen into the hands of a scholar to whom Simrock's words quoted on p. 101 were familiar, there would, in all probability, have been no occasion for the present work.

The publication of texts was continued by Mr. Furnivall's issue, in 1864, for the Roxburghe Club, of the Quête del Saint Graal from a British Museum MS. The opening of twelve MSS. from the Bibliothèque Nationale is likewise given, and shows substantial unity between them and Mr. Furnivall's text. In 1868 Mons. Paulin Paris published, in the first volume of his " Romans de la Table Ronde," a general introduction to the Round Table cycle, and a special study upon the Metrical Joseph and the Grand St. Graal. A large share of influence is assigned to Celtic traditions through the medium of Breton *lais*. The Early History of the Grail is a British legend, and embodies the national and schismatic aspirations of the British Church. The date given in the prologue to the Grand St. Graal, and repeated by Helinandus, is accepted as the genuine date of a redaction of the legend substantially the same as that found later in the Grand St. Graal. The word " Grail " is connected with the Latin *gradale*, modern gradual, and designated the book in which the tradition was first written down. The Grand St. Graal is anterior to Chrestien's poem, and Robert de Borron's poem in the first draft preceded the Grand St. Graal, and was written between 1160 and 1170, but he subsequently revised it towards 1214, as is shown by his alluding, l. 3,490, " O mon seigneur, Gauter *en peis* " (where the underlined words are equivalent to the Latin *in pace*) to Gautier of Montbeliard in the past tense. From

1868 to 1870 M. Potvin brought out his edition of the Conte du Graal, and of the prose Perceval le Gallois from Mons MSS. In the after-words priority is claimed for the latter romance over all other members of the cycle, and three stages are distinguished in the development of the legend—Welsh national—militant Christian—knightly—the prose romance belonging to the second stage, and dating substantially from the eleventh century. The lance and basin are originally pagan British symbols, and between the lines of the Grail legend may be read a long struggle between heretic Britain and orthodox Rome. The Perceval form of the Quest is older than the Galahad one. The Joseph of Arimathea forms are the latest, and among these the Grand St. Graal the earliest.

Conclusions as paradoxical as some of these appear in Dr. Bergmann's " The San Grëal, an Enquiry into the Origin and Signification of the Romance of the S. G.," Edinburgh, 1870. The idea of the Grail is due entirely to Guyot, as also its connection with the Arthurian cycle. Chrestien followed Guyot, but alters the character of the work, for which he is reproved by Wolfram, who may be looked upon as a faithful representative of the earlier poet. Chrestien's alterations are intended to render the poem more acceptable in knightly circles. On the other hand Walter Map found Guyot too secular and heretical, and wrote from a purely eccle-siastical standpoint the Latin version of the legend in which the Grail is associated with Joseph of Arimathea. This version forms the basis of Robert de Borron, author of the Grand St. Graal and of the continuators of Chrestien. Although Bergmann denies the Celtic origin of the Grail itself, he incidentally accepts the authen-ticity of the Mabinogi of Peredur, and admits that the whole framework of the story is Celtic.

In the endeavour to prove the paradox that one of the latest, most highly developed, and most mystic of all the versions of the legend (viz., Wolfram's) really represents the common source of them all, Bergmann is compelled to make the most gratuitous assumptions, as a specimen of which may be quoted the statement that the *roi-pecheur* is originally the *sinner* king, and that it is by mistake that the North French *trouvères* represent him as a *fisher*.

Bergmann's views passed comparatively unnoticed. They are,

indeed, alluded to with approval in Professor Skeat's edition of Joseph of Arimathea, a fourteenth century alliterative abridgement of the Grand St. Graal (E. E. Text Soc., 1871). In the editor's preface the Glastonbury traditions concerning the evangelisation of Britain by Joseph are taken as a starting point, two parts being distinguished in them, the one *legendary*, tallying with William of Malmesbury's account, and, perhaps, of considerable antiquity, the other *fabulous*, introducing the personages and incidents of the romances and undoubtedly derived from them. Some twenty years after the publication of the " Historia Britonum " Walter Map probably wrote a Latin poem, from which Robert de Borron, the Grand St. Graal, and, perhaps, the other works of the cycle were derived. " Grail " is a bowl or dish. Chrestien may have borrowed his Conte du Graal from Map ; the " Quest " is probably an after-thought of the romance writers.

Speculations such as these were little calculated to further the true criticism of the Grail cycle. Some few years later, in 1875, the then existing texts were supplemented by M. Hucher's work, so often quoted in these pages. In an introduction and notes displaying great research and ingenuity, the following propositions are laid down :—The Grail is Celtic in origin, and may be seen figured upon pre-Christian Gaulish coins. Robert de Borron's poem may be called the Petit St. Graal, and its author was a lord of like-named territory near Fontainebleau, who between 1147 and 1164 made large gifts to the Abbey of Barbeaux, which gifts are confirmed in 1169 by Simon, son of said Robert. About 1169 Robert came to England, met Walter Map, and was initiated by him into the knowledge of the Arthurian romance, and of the legend of the Holy Grail. Between 1170 and 1199 he entered the service of Walter of Montbeliard and wrote (in prose) the Joseph of Arimathea and the Merlin. At a later period he returned to England, and wrote, in conjunction with Map, the Grand St. Graal. This is shown by MS. 2,455 Bibl. Nat. (of the Grand St. Graal) : " Or dist li contes qui est estrais de toutes les ystoires, sî come Robers de Borons le translatait de latin en romans, à l'ayde de maistre Gautier Map." But Hélie de Borron, author of the Tristan and of Guiron le Courtois, calls Robert his friend and

kinsman. Hélie has been placed under Henry III, who has been
assumed to be the Henry to whom he dedicates his work; if so
can he be the friend of Robert, who wrote some fifty years earlier?
Hélie should, however, be placed really under Henry II. Robert
wrote originally in prose; the poem contains later etymological
and grammatical forms, though it has occasionally preserved older
ones; besides in v. 2,817 etc. (*supra*, p. 83) it refers to the deliverance of Moys by the Promised Knight, and thus implies
knowledge of the Grand St. Graal; this passage is omitted by
most of the prose versions, thus obviously older. Then the poem
is silent as to the Christianising of Britain mentioned by one prose
version (C.). We may accept Borron's statement as to his having
dealt later with the histories of Moys and Petrus, and as to his
drawing his information from a Latin original. Merlin is the
pivot of Borron's conception. In comparing the third part of his
trilogy (Joseph of Arimathea, Merlin, Perceval) with Chrestien
it must be born in mind that Chrestien reproduces rather the
English (Joseph—Galahad), than the French (Brons—Perceval)
form of the Quest, and this, although the framework of Chrestien
and Robert's Perceval is substantially the same. Chrestien's work
was probably preceded by one in which the Peredur story as found
in the Mabinogi was already adapted to the Christianised Grail
legend. There are frequent verbal resemblances between Robert
and Chrestien (*i.e.*, Gautier, Hucher never distinguishing between
Chrestien and his continuators) which show a common original
for both. It is remarkable that Chrestien should never mention
Brons, and that there should be such a difference in the stories of
the Ford Perillous and the Ford Amorous. It is also remarkable
that Robert, in his Perceval, should complain that the *trouvères*
had not spoken of the Good Friday incident which is to be found
in Chrestien.

M. Hucher failed in many cases to see the full significance of
the facts he brought to light, owing to his incorrect conception of the
development of the cycle as a whole, and of the relation of its com-
ponent parts one to the other. He made, however, an accurate survey of the cycle possible. The merit of first essaying such a survey
belongs to Zarncke in his admittedly rough sketch, "Zur Geschichte

der Gralsage," published in the third volume (1876) of Paul and
Braune's Beitraege.—The various forms may be grouped as follows :
(1) Borron's poem, (2) Grand St. Graal, (3) Quête, (4) Chrestien,
(5 and 6) Chrestien's continuators, (7) Didot MS. Perceval, (8)
Prose Perceval li Gallois. Neither the Spanish-Provencal nor the
Celtic origin of the legend is admissible; it has its source wholly
in the apocryphal legends of Joseph of Arimathea, in which two
stages may be distinguished; the first represented by the Gesta
Pilati and the Narratio Josephi, which tell how Christ appeared to
Joseph in prison and released him therefrom ; the second by the
Vindicta Salvatoris, which combines the legends of the healing
of Tiberius with that of Titus or Vespasian. Joseph being thus
brought into contact with Titus, the space of time between the
two is accounted for by the forty years captivity, and the first hint
was given of a miraculous sustaining power of the Grail. Borron's
poem is still purely legendary in character; the fish caught by the
rich fisher is the symbol of Christ; the incident of the waiting for
the Promised Knight belongs, however, not to the original tradition but to a later style of Christian mysticism. The Grand St.
Graal and the Quête extend and develop the *donnée* of the poem,
whilst in Chrestien tone, atmosphere, and framework are profoundly modified, yet there is no reason to postulate for Chrestien
any other sources than Nos. 1–3, the differences being such as he
was quite capable of deliberately introducing. As for No. 7 (the
Didot-Perceval) it is later than Chrestien and his continuators, and
has used both. Wolfram von Eschenbach had only Chrestien for
his model, Kiot's poem being a feigned source. The legend of
the conversion of Britain by Joseph is no genuine British tradition;
William of Malmesbury's account of Glastonbury is a pamphlet
written to order of the Norman Kings, and incapable of serving
as a representative of Celtic tradition. The passages therein
relating to Joseph are late interpolations, disagreeing with the
remainder of his work and disproved by the silence of all contemporary writers.

Zarncke's acute article was a praiseworthy attempt to construct
a working hypothesis of the growth of the cycle. But it is full of
grave misconceptions, as was, perhaps, inevitable in a hasty survey

of such an immense body of literature. The versions are "placed" most incorrectly. The argumentation is frequently marred by *a priori* reasoning, such as that Chrestien, the acknowledged leading poet of the day, could not have copied Kiot, and by untenable assertions, such as that Bran, in the Mabinogi of Branwen, the daughter of Llyr, is perhaps a distant echo of Hebron in Robert de Borron's poem. He had, however, the great merit of clearing the ground for his pupil, A. Birch-Hirschfeld, and urging him to undertake what still remains the most searching and exhaustive survey of the whole cycle : "Die Sage vom Gral," etc. As Birch-Hirschfeld's analysis is at present the only basis for sound criticism, I shall give his views fully :—The Grand St. Graal, as the fullest of the versions dealing with the Early History of the Grail, is the best starting-point for investigation. From its pronounced religious tone monkish authorship may be inferred. Its treatment of the subject is not original as is shown by (1) the repetition *ad nauseam* of the same motive (*e.g.*, that of the lance wound four times), (2) the pedigrees, (3) the allusions to adventures not dealt with in the book, and in especial to the Promised Knight. The testimony of Helinand (see *supra*, p. 52), which is of first-rate importance, does not allow of a later date for the Grand St. Graal than 1204. On turning to the Queste it is remarkable that though sometimes found in the MSS. in conjunction with the Grand St. Graal it is also found with the Lancelot, and, when the hero's parentage is considered, it seems more likely that it was written to supplement the latter than the former work. This supposition is adverse to any claim it may lay to being held the earliest treatment of the subject, as it is highly improbable that the Grail legend occupied at the outset such an important place in the Arthurian romance as is thus accorded to it. Such a claim is further negatived by the fact that the Queste has three heroes, the second of whom is obviously the original one of an older version. In estimating the relationship between the Grand St. Graal and the Queste it should be borne in mind that the latter, in so far as it deals with the Early History, mentions only Joseph, Josephe, Evelach (Mordrain) and Seraphe (Nascien), from whom descends Galahad ; that it brings Joseph to England, and that it does not

give any explanation of the nature of the Grail itself. It omits
Brons, Alain, the explanation of the name " rich fisherman," the
name of Moys, although his story is found in substantially the same
shape as in the Grand St. Graal, and is silent as to the origin of the
bleeding lance. If it were younger than and derived from the Grand
St. Graal alone, these points, all more important for the Early
History than the Mordrain episodes would surely have been dwelt
upon. But then if the Grand St. Graal is the younger work, whence
does it derive Brons, Alain, and Petrus, all of whom are introduced
in such a casual way ? There was obviously a previous Early History
which knew nothing of Josephe or of Mordrain and his group,
the invention of the author of the Queste, whence they passed
into the Grand St. Graal, and were fused in with the older form of
the legend. There is, moreover, a positive reference on the part of
the Grand St. Graal to the Queste (vol. ii., p. 225). The author
of the Queste introduced his new personages for the following
reasons : He had already substituted Galahad for the original hero,
and to enhance his importance gives him a fictitious descent from
a companion of Joseph. From his model he learnt of Joseph's
wanderings in the East, hence the Eastern origin of the Mordrain
group. In the older form the Grail had passed into the keeping
of Joseph's nephew, in the Queste the Promised Knight descends
from the nephew of Mordrain ; Brons, as the ancestor of the original
Quest hero necessarily disappears in the Queste, and his place is in
large measure taken by Josephe. The priority of the Queste over
the Grand St. Graal, and the use of the former by the latter may
thus be looked upon as certain. But if Mordrain is the invention
of the Queste, what is the meaning of his illness, of his waiting for
the Promised Knight, of the bleeding lance, and of the lame king
whom it heals ? These seem to have no real connection with the
Grail, and are apparently derived from an older work, namely,
Chrestien's Conte du Graal.

Chrestien's work, which ended at v. 10,601, may be dated as
having been begun not later than 1189 (*vide supra*, p. 4). Its
unfinished state accounts for its having so little positive information
about the Grail, as Chrestien evidently meant to reserve this information for the end of the story. But this very freedom with which

the subject is handled is a proof that he had before him a work whence he could extract and adapt as he saw fit; moreover we have (Prologue, v. 475, etc.) his own words to that effect. With Chrestien's account of the Grail—a bowl bejewelled, of wondrous properties, borne by a maiden, preceded by a bleeding lance, accompanied by a silver plate, guarded by a king wounded through both ankles (whose only solace is fishing, whence his surname), ministering to the king's father, sought for by Perceval, nephew to the fisher king, its fate bound up with a question which the seeker must put concerning it—may be compared that of the Queste, in which nothing is known of a question by which the Grail kingship may be obtained (although it relates the same incident of Lancelot), which knows not of one wounded king, centre of the action, but of two, both of secondary importance (though possibly Chrestien's Fisher King's father may have given the hint for Mordrain), in which the lance is of minor importance instead of being on the same level as the Grail. Is it not evident that the Queste took over these features from Chrestien, compelled thereto by the celebrity of the latter's presentment ? The Queste thus presupposes the following works : a Lancelot, an Early History, a Quest other than that of Chrestien's, and finally Chrestien as the lame king and lance features show. It thus falls between 1189 (Chrestien begun) and 1204 (Grand St. Graal ended).

With respect to the three continuators of Chrestien it would seem that Gautier de Doulens' account of the Grail, as found in the Montpellier MS., knowing as it does only of Joseph, and making the Fisher King and Perceval descendants of his, belongs to an older stage of development than that of Manessier and Gerbert, both of whom are familiar with the Mordrain group, and follows that of the original version upon which both the Queste and the Grand St. Graal are based. There is nothing to show that Gautier knew of the Queste, whilst from Gautier the Queste may have possibly have taken Perceval's sister and the broken sword. Gautier would thus seem to have written immediately after Chrestien, and before the Queste, i.e., about 1195. As for the date of the other two continuators, the fact of their having used the Queste is only one proof of the lateness of their composition (as to the date of which see *supra*, p. 4). It must be noted that whilst in their account of the Grail Chrestien's continuators are in substantial accord with the Queste versions, and yet do not contradict Chrestien himself, they add considerably to his account of the lance. This is readily explained by the fact that as Chrestien gave no information respecting the origin of either of the relics, they, the continuators, had to seek such information elsewhere; they found all they could wish respecting the Grail, but nothing as to the lance, the latter having been first introduced by Chrestien, and the Queste versions knowing nothing respecting it beyond what he told. Thus, thrown upon their own resources, they hit upon the device of identifying the lance with the spear with which Jesus was pierced as He hung on the Cross. This idea, a most natural one, may possibly have been in Chrestien's intent, and *may* have been suggested to him by the story of the discovery of the Holy Lance in Antioch half a century before. It must, however, be admitted that the connection of the lance with the Grail legend in its earliest form is very doubtful, and that Celtic legends may possibly have furnished it to Chrestien, and indicated the use to which he intended putting it. The analysis, so far, of the romances has resulted in the presupposition of an earlier form; this earlier form, the source or basis of all the later versions of the legend, exists in the so-called Petit St. Graal of Robert de Borron. Of this work, found in two forms, a prose and a poetic one, the poetic form, *pace* Hucher, is obviously the older, Hucher's proofs of lateness going merely to show that the sole existing M.S. is a recent one, and has admitted new speech-forms;* moreover the prose versions derive evidently from one original. The greater simplicity of the poem as compared with the Grand St. Graal proves its anteriority in that case; Paulin Paris' hypothesis that the poem in its present state is a second draft, composed after the author had made acquaintance with the Grand St. Graal, is untenable, the poem's reference (v. 929 etc.) to the " grant livre " and to the " grant estoire dou Graal," written by " nul home qui fust

---

* Hucher's argument from v. 2817 (*supra* p. 106) that the poem knew of the Grand St. Graal is, however, not met.

mortal" (v. 3,495-6) not being to the Grand St. Graal, but having, on the contrary, probably suggested to the writer of the latter his fiction of Christ's being the real author of his work. The Grand St. Graal used the poem conjointly with the Queste, piecing out the one version by help of the other, and thereby entirely missing the sequence of ideas in the poem, which is as follows : Sin, the cause of want among the people; the separation of the pure from the impure by means of the fish (symbol of Christ) caught by Brons, which fish does not feed the people, but, in conjunction with the Grail, severs the true from the false disciples ; punishment of the self-willed false disciple; reward of Brons by charge of the Grail. In the Grand St. Graal, on the contrary, the fish is no symbol, but actual food, a variation which must be laid to the account of the Queste. In a similar way the two Alains in the Grand St. Graal may be accounted for, the one as derived from the poem, the second from the Queste. As far as conception is concerned, the later work is no advance upon the earlier one. To return to Borron's work, which consists of three sections ; there is no reason to doubt his authorship of the second, Merlin, or of the third, Perceval, although one MS. only of the former mentions the fact, and it is, moreover, frequently found in connection with other romances, in especial with the Lancelot ; as for Perceval, the silence of the unique MS. as to Borron is no argument, as it is equally silent in the Joseph of Arimathea section. All outward circumstances go to show that Borron divided his work into three parts, Joseph, Merlin, Perceval. But, if so, the last part must correspond in a fair measure to the first one; recollect, however, that we are dealing with a poet of but little invention or power of giving unity to discordant themes, and must not expect to find a clearly traced plan carried out in every detail. Thus the author's promise in Joseph to speak later of Moses and Petrus seems not to be fulfilled, but this is due to Borron's timidity in the invention of new details. What *is* said of Moses does not disagree with the Joseph, whereas a later writer would probably follow the Grand St. Graal account ; as for Petrus he is to be recognised in the hermit Perceval's uncle. There may be some inconsistency here, but Borron *can* be inconsistent, as is shown by his treatment of Alain,

who at first vows to remain virgin, and afterwards marries.
But a graver argument remains to be met; the lance occurs in
Perceval—now *ex hypothesi* the first introduction of the lance is
due to Chrestien. The lance, however, only occurs in two passages, both obviously interpolated. The identity of authorship is
evident when the style and phraseology of the two works are
compared; in both the Grail is always *li graaux* or else *li veissel*,
not as with the later versions, *li saint graaux;* both speak of *la
grace dou graal;* in both the Grail is *bailli* to its keeper, who has
it *en guarde;* the empty seat is *li liu vit*, not the *siège perilleux*.
The central conception, too, is the same—the Trinity of Grail-
keepers symbolising the Divine Trinity. The secret words given
by Christ with the Grail to Joseph in prison, by him handed on to
Brons, are confided at the end of the Perceval by Brons to the hero
—and there is no trace of the Galahad form of the Quest, as
would inevitably have been the case had the Perceval been posterior
in date to the Queste. As the Perceval is connected with the
Joseph, so it is equally with the Merlin; it is remarkable that
neither Merlin nor Blaise play a prominent part in the Queste
versions, but in Borron's poem Merlin is the necessary binding
link between the Apostolic and Arthurian ages. Again the whole
character of the Perceval speaks for its being one of the earliest
works of the cycle; either it must have used Chrestien and
Gautier or they it; if the former, is it credible that just those adventures which were necessary to supply the ending to the Joseph
could have been picked out? But it is easy to follow the way in
which Chrestien used the Perceval; having the three-part poem
before him he took the third only for his canvas, left out all that
in it related to the first two parts, all, moreover, that related to
the origin and early history of the Grail; the story of the childhood
is half indicated in the Perceval, and Chrestien may have had
Breton lays with which to help himself out; all relating to the
empty seat is left out as reaching back into the Early History; the
visit to Gurnemanz is introduced to supply a motive for the hero's
conduct at the Grail Castle; the wound of the Fisher King is
again only an attempt of Chrestien's to supply a more telling
motive; as for the sword Chrestien invented it; as he also did the

Grail-messenger, whose portrait he copied from that of Rosette la Blonde. The order of the last episodes is altered by Chrestien sensibly for the better, as, with him, Perceval's doubt comes first, then the Good Friday reproof, then the confession to and absolution by the hermit; whereas in the Perceval the hero after doubt, reproof, and absolution rides off again a-tourneying, and requires a second reproof at Merlin's hands. It is easy to see here which is the original, which the copy   Chrestien thus took with clear insight just what he wanted in the Perceval to fit out his two heroes with adventures.* As for Borron's guiding conception, his resolve to have nothing to do with the Early History made him neglect it entirely; he only cared to produce a knightly poem, and we find, in consequence, that he has materialised all the spiritual elements of his model. Gautier de Doulens' method of proceeding was much simpler : he took over all those adventures that Chrestien purposely left out, and they may be found brought together (verses 22,390–27,390) with but few episodes (Perceval's visit to Blanche-fleur, etc.) entirely foreign to the model amongst them.† The Perceval cannot be later than Gautier, as otherwise it could not stand in such close relationship to the Joseph and Merlin; it must, therefore, be the source of the Conte du Graal, and a necessary part of Borron's poem, which in its entirety is the first attempt to bring the Joseph of Arimathea legend into connection with the Arthur *sage*. The question as to the origin of the Grail would thus seem answered, the Christian legendary character of Borron's conception being evident ; but there still remains the possibility that that conception is but the Christianised form of an older folk-myth. Such a one has been sought for in Celtic tradition. The part played by Merlin in the trilogy might seem to lend colour to such an hypothesis, but his connection with the legend is a purely artificial one. Nor is the theory of a Celtic origin strengthened by reference to the Mabinogi of Peredur. This knows nought of Merlin, and is nearer to Chrestien than to the Didot-Perceval, and may, indeed, be looked upon as simply a clumsy retelling of the

---

* *Vide* p. 200, for Birch-Hirschfeld's summary comparison of the two works, and *cf. infra* p. 127.

† *Cf. infra* p. 128, for a criticism of this statement.

Conte du Graal with numerous additions. A knowledge of the
Didot-Perceval on Chrestien's part must be presupposed, as where
could he have got the Fisher King and Grail Castle save from a
poem which dealt with the Early History of the Grail, a thing
the Mabinogi does not do. But, it may be said, Chrestien used
the Mabinogi conjointly with Borron's poem. That the Welsh tale
is, on the contrary, only a copy is apparent from the following
considerations :—It mixes up Gurnemanz and the Fisher King; it
puts in the mouth of Peredur's *mother* an exclamation about the
knights, "Angels they are my son," obviously misread from *Perceval's* exclamation to the same effect in Chrestien's poem ; Perceval's
love-trance over the three blood drops in the snow is explained in
Chrestien by the hero's passion for Blanchefleur, but is quite
inexplicable in the Mabinogi ; again, in the Welsh tale, the lance
and basin episode is quite a secondary one, a fact easily explained if
it is looked upon as a vague reminiscence of Chrestien's unfinished
work ; moreover the Mabinogi lays great stress upon the lance,
which has already been shown to belong to a secondary stage in
the development of the legend. Again the word Graal occurs
frequently in old Welsh literature, and invariably in its French
form, never translated by any equivalent Welsh term. As for the
name Peredur, it is understandable that the Welsh storyteller
should choose the name of a national hero, instead of the foreign
name Perceval ; the etymology Basin-Seeker is untenable. There
is no real analogy between the Grail and the magic cauldron of
Celtic fable, which is essentially one of renovation, whereas the
Grail in the second stage only acquires miraculous feeding, and in
the third stage healing powers. It is of course not impossible
that such adventures in the Mabinogi, as cannot be referred
directly to Chrestien, may belong to a genuine Peredur *sage.*

The question then arises—was Robert de Borron a simple
copyist, or is the legend in its present form due to him, *i.e.*, did *he*
first join the Joseph of Arimathea and Grail legends, or had he a
predecessor ? Now the older Joseph legends know nothing of his
wandering in company of a miraculous vessel, Zarncke having
shown the lateness of the one commonly ascribed to William of
Malmesbury. Nor is it likely Borron had before him a local French

legend as Paulin Paris (Romania, vol. i.) had supposed ; would he
in that case have brought the Grail to England, and left Joseph's
fate in uncertainty ?   The bringing the Grail to England is simply
the logical consequence of his conception of the three Grail-keepers
(the third of British blood), symbolising the Trinity, and of the
relation of the Arthurian group to this central conception ; where
the third Grail-keeper and the third of the three wondrous tables
were, there the Grail must also be.   What then led Borron
to connect the sacramental vessel with the Joseph legend ?   In
answering this question the later miraculous properties of the
Grail must be forgotten, and it must remembered that with Borron
it is only a vessel of " grace ;" this is shown in the history of
(Moys) the false disciple, which obviously follows in its details the
account of the Last Supper, and of the detection of Judas by means
of the dish into which Jesus dips a sop, bidding the betrayer take
and eat.   Borron's first table being an exact copy of the Last Supper
one, *his* holy vessel has the property of that used by Christ.   In
so far Borron was led to his conception by the story as told in the
canonical books ; what help did he get from the Apocrypha ?
His mention of the Veronica legend and certain details in his presentment of Vespasian's vengeance on the Jews (*e.g.*, his selling
thirty for a penny) show him to have known the Vindicta Salvatoris, in which Joseph of Arimathea appears telling of his former
captivity from which Christ Himself had delivered him.   Thus
Borron knew of Joseph's living when Vespasian came to Jerusalem.
From the Gesta Pilati he had full information respecting the imprisonment of Joseph ; he combined the accounts of these two
apocryphal works, substituting a simple visit of Christ to Joseph
for the deliverance as told in the Gesta Pilati, and making Vespasian the deliverer, whereto he may have been urged by Suetonius'
account of the freeing of *Josephus* by Vespasian (Vesp. ch. v.).
But why should Joseph become the Grail-keeper ?   Because the
fortunes of the vessel used by the Saviour symbolise those of the
Saviour's body ; as *that* was present at the Last Supper, was
brought to Pilate, handed over to Joseph, was buried, and after
three days arose, so with the Grail.   Compare, too, Christ's words
to Joseph (892, etc.) in which the symbolical connection of the laying

in the grave and the mass is fully worked out. Thus Joseph who laid Christ's body in the grave is the natural guardian of the symbol which commemorates that event, thus, too, the Grail is the natural centre point of all the symbolism of mass and sacrament, and thus the Grail found its place in the Joseph legend, ultimately becoming its most important feature. Need Perceval's question detain us ? May it not be explained by the fact that as Joseph had to apply twice for Christ's body, so his representative, the Grail-seeker, had to apply twice for the symbol of Christ's body, the Grail ? But it is, perhaps, best to consider the question and the Fisher King's weakness as inventions of Borron's, possibly derived from Breton sources, the ease with which the hero fulfils a task explained to him beforehand favouring such a view. Borron, it must be noticed, had no great inventive power ; in the Joseph he is all right so long as he has the legend to follow ; in the Merlin and the Perceval he clings with equal helplessness to the Breton sagas, confining himself to weaving clumsily the adventures of the Grail into the regular Arthur legend.

The question as to the authorship of the Grand St. Graal and the Queste, the latter so confidently attributed to W. Map, may now profitably be investigated. Map, who we know flourished 1143–1210 (see *supra*, p. 5), took part in all the political and social movements of his time. If we believe the testimony of the MSS. which ascribe to him the authorship of the following romances : (1) the Lancelot, in three parts ; (2) the Queste ; (3) the Mort Artur ; (4) the Grand St. Graal, he would seem to have shown a literary activity quite incompatible with his busy life, when it is remembered how slow literary composition was in those days. Nor can it be reconciled with the words of Giraldus Cambrensis,* although Paulin Paris (Rom. i. 472) has attempted such a reconciliation by the theory that the words *dicere* and *verba dare* referred to composition in the vernacular, and that Map was

---

* Opera V. 410: Unde et vir ille eloquio clarus W. Mapus, Oxoniensis archidiaconus (cujus animae propitietur Deus) solita verborum facetia et urbanitate praecipua dicere pluris et nos in hunc modum convenire solebat : "Multa, Magister Geraldc, scripsistis et multum adhuc scribitis, et nos multa diximus. Vos scripta dedistis et nos verba."

opposing not his *oratorical* to Gerald's *literary* activity, but his
French to Gerald's *Latin* works. Against this initial improbability
and Gerald's positive testimony must be set, it is true, the witness
of writers of the time and of the MSS. The most important
is that of Hélie de Borron in his prologue to Guiron le Courtois.*
After telling how Luces de Gast was the first to translate from the
Latin book into French, and he did part of the story of Tristan, he
goes on : "Apriés s'en entremist maistre Gautiers Map qui fu
clers au roi Henry et devisa cil l'estoire de monseigneur Lancelot
du Lac, que d'autre chose ne parla il mie gramment en son livre.
Messiers Robers de Borron s'en entremist après. Je Helis de
Borron, par la prière monseigneur de Borron, et pour ce que com-
paignon d'armes fusmes longemeut, en commençai mon livre du
Bret." Again in the epilogue to the Bret,† "Je croi bien touchier sor
les livres que maistres Gautiers Maup fist, qui fit lou propre livre
de monsoingnour Lancelot dou Lac ; et des autres granz livres que
messires Robert de Berron fit, voudrai-je prendre aucune flor de la
matière . . . en tel meniere que li livres de monsoingnour Luces
de Gant et de maistre Gautier Maapp et ciz de monsoingnour Robert
de Berron qui est mes amis et mes paranz charnex s'acourderont
au miens livres—et je qui sui appelex Helyes de Berron qui fui
engendrez dou sanc des gentix paladins des Barres qui de tous tens
ont été commendeour et soingnor d'Outres en Roménie qui ores
est appelée France." Now Hélie cannot possibly belong to the
reign of Henry II (+ 1189) as asserted by Hucher (p. 59), as he
speaks of Map in the past tense (*fu* clers), and Map outlived
Henry, moreover the mention of Romenie proves the passage to
have been written after the foundation of the Latin Empire in
1304. Hélie's testimony is thus not that of an immediate contemporary, and it only shows that shortly after Map's death the
Lancelot was ascribed to him. It is, moreover, in so far tainted,
that he speaks with equal assurance respecting the great Latin
book which of course never existed ; nor can we believe him when
he says that he was the comrade of Robert de Borron, as this latter

---

* Printed in full, Hucher, I. 156, etc.
† Printed by Hucher, I. p. 35, etc.

wrote before Chrestien, and must have been at least thirty years
older than Hélie, who in the Guiron (written about 1220) calls
himself a young man. How is it with the testimony of the MSS. ?
Those of the Lancelot have unfortunately lost their colophon,
owing to the Queste being almost invariably added; those of the
Queste show as a rule a colophon such as the one quoted by Paulin
Paris from the Bibl. Nat., MS. 6,963 (MSS. Franç. II., p. 361) :
" Maistre Gautiers Map les estrait pour son livre faire dou Saint-
Graal, pour l'amor del roy Henri son seignor, qui fist l'estore
translater dou latin en françois." A similar statement occurs in
a MS. of the Mort Artur (Bib. Nat. 6,782.). Both are equally
credible. Now as the King can only be Henry II (+1189) and as
the Queste preceded the Mort Artur it must be put about 1185,
and Chrestien's Conte du Graal about 1180, an improbably early
date when it is recollected that the Conte du Graal is Chrestien's
last work. The form, too, of these colophons, expressed as they are
in the third person, so different from the garrulous first person
complacency with which Luces de Gast and Hélie de Borron
announce their authorship, excites the suspicion that we have here
not the author's own statement, but that of a copyist following a
traditional ascription. Whether or no Map wrote the Lancelot,
it may safely be assumed that he did not write the Queste, or *a
fortiori* the Grand St. Graal. The tradition as to his authorship
of these romances may have originated in Geoffrey's mention of
the Gualterus archidiaconus Oxenfordensis, to whom he owed his
MS. of the Historia Regum Britanniae. A similar instance of
traditional ascription on the part of the copyist may be noted in
the MSS. of the Grand St. Graal, the author of which is declared
to be Robert de Borron. The ordinary formulæ (quoted *supra*,
p. 5) should be compared with Borron's own words in the
Joseph (*supra*, p. 5) and the difference in form noted. What
proves these passages to be interpolations is that the author of the
Grand St. Graal especially declares in his prologue that his name
must remain a secret. The colophons in question are simply to be
looked upon as taken over from the genuine ascription of Borron's
poem, and there is no positive evidence as to the authorship of
either the Queste or the Grand St. Graal; both works are pro-

bably French in origin, as is shown by the mention of Meaux in the Grand St. Graal. As for the date of Borron's poem, a *terminus ad quem* is fixed by that of the Conte du Graal (1180); and as the poem is dedicated to Gautier of Montbeliard, who can hardly have been born before 1150, and who must have attained a certain age before he could become Robert's patron, it must fall between the years 1170 and 1190.

The results of the investigation may be summed up as follows : the origin of the Grail romances must be sought for in a Christian legend based partly upon the canonical, partly upon the uncanonical, writings. This Christian legend was woven into the Breton sagas by the author of the oldest Grail romance ; the theories of Provençal Spanish, or Celtic origin are equally untenable, nor is there any need to countenance the fable of a Latin original. Chronologically, the versions arrange themselves thus :—

(1) Between 1170 and 1190 (probably about 1183) Robert de Borron wrote his trilogy : Joseph of Arimathea— Merlin—Perceval. Sources : Christian legend (Acta, Pilati, Descensus Christi, Vindicta Salvatoris) and Breton sagas (Brut ?). Here the Grail is simply a vessel of grace.

(2) About 1189 Chrestien began his Conte du Graal, the main source of which was the third part of Borron's poem. Marvellous food properties attributed to the Grail ; introduction of the bleeding lance, silver dish, and magic sword.

(3) Between 1190 and 1200 Gautier de Doulens continued Chrestien's poem. Main sources, third part of (1) and first part of same for Early History—introduction of broken sword.

(4) Between 1190 and 1200 (but after Gautier?) the Queste du St. Graal written as continuation to the Lancelot. Sources (1) and (2) (for lance) and perhaps (3). New personages, Mordrain, Nascien, etc., introduced into Early History.

(5) Before 1204 Grand St. Graal written, mainly resting upon (4) but with use also of first part of (1).

(6) Between 1214 and 1220. Manessier's continuation of the Conte du Graal. For the Early History (5) made use of.

(7) Before 1225 Gerbert of Montreuil's additions to Manessier. Both (4) and (5) used.

(8) About 1225 Perceval li Gallois ; compiled from all the previous versions.*

That part of Birch-Hirschfeld's theory which excited the most attention in Germany bore upon the relationship of Wolfram to Chrestien (see *infra*, Appendix A). In other respects his theory won very general acceptance. The commendatory notices were, however, of a slight character, and no new facts were adduced in support of his thesis. One opponent, however, he found who did more than rest his opposition upon the view of Wolfram's relationship to Chrestien. This was E. Martin, who ("Zeitschrift für d. Alterthums-kunde," 1878, pp. 84 etc.) traversed most of Birch-Hirschfeld's conclusions. Whilst accepting the priority of Queste over Grand St. Graal he did not see the necessity of fixing 1204 as a *terminus ad quem* for the latter work as we now have it, as Helinandus' statement might have referred to an older version ; if the Grand St. Graal could not be dated neither could the Queste. As for the Didot-Perceval there was nothing to prove that it was either Borron's work or the source of Chrestien and Gautier. Birch-Hirschfeld's arguments to show the interpolation of the lance passages were unsound ; it was highly improbable either that Chrestien should have used the Perceval as alleged, or that Borron, the purely religious writer of the Joseph, should have changed his style so entirely in the Perceval. Moreover, Birch-Hirschfeld made Borron dedicate a work to Gautier of Montbeliard before 1183 when the latter must have been quite a young man, nor was there any reason to discredit Hélie de Borron's testimony that he and Robert had been companions in arms, a fact incredible had

---

* The remainder of Birch-Hirschfeld's work is devoted to proving that Chrestien was the only source of Wolfram von Eschenbach, the latter's Kiot being imagined by him to justify his departure from Chrestien's version ; departures occasioned by his dissatisfaction with the French poet's treatment of the subject on its moral and spiritual side. This element in the Grail problem will be found briefly dealt with, Appendix A.

the one written forty years before the other. The work of Chrestien and his continuators must be looked upon as the oldest we
had of the Grail cycle. It was likely that older versions had been
lost. A Latin version might well have existed, forms such as
Joseph de Barimaschie (*i.e.*, ab Arimathea) pointed to it. Martin
followed up this attack in his " Zur Gralsage, Untersuchungen,"
Strasburg, 1880. A first section is devoted to showing that Wolfram must have had other sources than Chrestien, and that in
consequence such portions of his presentment as differ from Chrestien's must be taken into account in reconstructing the original
form of the romance. The second and third sections deal with
Heinrich von dem Türlin's " Die Crone," and with the earliest form
of the tradition. Gawain's second visit to the Grail Castle, as told
of by Heinrich (*supra*, p. 26) has features in common with the
widely-spread traditions of aged men slumbering in caves or
ruined castles, unable to die until the right word is uttered which
breaks their spell. This conception differs from the one found in
all the other versions inasmuch as in them the wonder-working
question releases, not from unnaturally prolonged life, but from
sore disease. Can a parallel be found in Celtic tradition to this
sufferer awaiting deliverance ? Does not Arthur, wounded well
nigh to death by his nephew Modred, pass a charmed life in Avalon,
whither Morgan la Fay carried him for his healing, and shall he
not return thence to free his folk ? The original conception is
mythic—the summer god banished by the winter powers, but destined to come back again. The *sage* of Arthur's waiting, often in
some subterranean castle, is widely spread, two of the earliest
notices (those of Gervasius of Tilbury, in the " Otia Imperialia," p.
12 of Liebrecht's edition, and of Caesarius of Heisterbach) connect
it with Etna—the tradition had followed the Norman Conquerors
of Sicily thither—and from Sicily it would seem to have penetrated
to Germany, being first found in German tradition as told of
Frederick II. Again Gerald (A.D. 1188) in the "Itinerarium Cam-
briae " (Frankfort, 1603, p. 827, L. 48) tells of a mountain chain
in the South-East of Wales : "quorum principalis Cadair Arthur
dicitur i. Cathedra Arthuri, propter gemina promontorii cacumina
in cathedrae modum se praeferentia. Et quoniam in alto cathedra

et in ardua sita est, summo et maximo Britonum Regi Arthuro
vulgari nuncupatione est assignata." The Eildon Hills may be
noted in the same connection, "in which all the Arthurian chivalry
await, in an enchanted sleep, the bugle blast of the adventurer
who will call them at length to a new life" (Stuart Glennie,
"Arthurian Localities," p. 60). If the Grail King is Arthur, the
bleeding lance is evidently the weapon wherewith he was so sorely
wounded. And the Grail? this is originally a symbol of plenty,
of a joyous and bountiful life, hence of Avalon, that land of ever-
lasting summer beyond the waves, wherein, as the Vita Merlini
has it, they that visit Arthur find "planitiem omnibus deliciis
plenam." Of those versions of the romance in which the Christian
conception of the Grail is predominant, Robert de Borron's poem
(composed about 1200) is the earliest, and in it, *maugre* the
Christianising of the story, the Celtic basis is apparent: the Grail
host go a questing Avalonwards ; the first keepers are Brons and
Alain, purely Celtic names, the former of which may be compared with Bran ; the empty seat calls to mind the *Eren stein* in
Ulrich von Zatzikhoven's Lanzelot, whereof (verse 5, 178) *ist gesaget
daz er den man niht vertruoc an dem was valsch oder haz.* Admitting the purely Christian origin of the Grail leads to this difficulty :
the vessel in which Christ's blood was received was a bowl, not
an open or flat dish like that used in commemoration of the Last
Supper. Evidently the identification of the Grail with the Last
Supper cup is the latest of a series of transformations. Nor can
the Christian origin of the legend be held proved by the surname
of Fisher given to the Grail-keeper. True, neither Chrestien nor
Wolfram explains this surname, whilst in Borron's poem there is at
least a fish caught. But if the fish had really the symbolic meaning ascribed to it would not a far greater stress be laid upon it ?
In any case this one point is insufficient to prove the priority of
Borron, and it is simpler to believe that the surname of Fisher had
in the original Celtic tradition a significance now lost. Birch-
Hirschfeld's theory supposes, too, a development contrary to that
observed elsewhere in mediæval tradition. The invariable course
is from the racial-heathen to the Christian legendary stage. Is
it likely that in the twelfth century, a period of such highly

developed mystic fancy, an originally Christian legend should lose
its mystic character and become a subject for minstrels to exercise
their fancy upon ?   In the earlier form of the romance there is an
obvious contrast between the task laid upon the Grail quester and
that laid upon Gawain at Castle Marvellous.   The first has suffered
change by its association with Christian legend ; but the second,
even in those versions influenced by the legend, has retained its
primitive Celtic character.   The trials which Gawain has to undergo
may be compared with those imposed on him who seeks to penetrate
into the underworld, as pictured in the Purgatorium S. Patricii, in
the Visio Tnugdali, etc.   This agrees well with the presentment
of Castle Marvellous, an underworld realm where dwell four
queens long since vanished from Arthur's court, and which, according to Chrestien (verse 9,388), Gawain, having once found, may no
longer leave.   One of these queens is Arthur's mother, whom a
magician had carried off, a variant it would seem of the tradition
which makes Arthur's father, Uther, win Igerne from her husband
by Merlin's magic aid.   Many other reminiscences of Celtic tradition may be found in the romances—Orgeleuse, whom Gawain
finds sitting under a tree by a spring, is just such a water fairy
as may be met with throughout the whole range of Celtic folk-lcre,
and differs profoundly from the Germanic conception of such
beings.

W. Hertz, in his " Sage vom Parzival und dem Gral " (Breslau,
1882) following, in the main, Birch-Hirschfeld, lays stress upon
the two elements, "legend" and "sage" out of which the romance
cycle has sprung.   He does not overlook many of the weak points
in Birch-Hirschfeld's theory, e.g., whilst fully accepting the fish
caught by Bron as the symbol of Christ, he notices that the incident as found in Robert de Borron, whom he accepts as the first
in date of the cycle writers, is not of such importance as to justify
the stress laid upon the nickname "rich fisher," by all the ex
hypothesi later writers.   The word "rich" must, he thinks, have
originally referred to the abundant power of conversion of heathen
vouchsafed to the Grail-keeper, but even Robert failed to grasp
the full force of the allusion.   Against Birch-Hirschfeld he maintains that the connection of Joseph with the conversion of Britain

in all the versions shows that the legend must have assumed definite shape first on British soil, and he looks upon the separatist and anti-papal tendencies of the British Church as supplying the original impulse to such a legend. The Grail belongs originally wholly to the "Legend;" only in the later versions and in Wolfram, owing to the latter's ignorance of its real nature, does it assume a magic and popular character. The lance, on the other hand, is partly derived from the Celtic *sage*. The boyhood of Perceval is a genuine folk-story, a great-fool tale, and had originally nothing to do with the Grail, as may plainly be seen by reference to the Thornton Sir Perceval, the most primitive form of the story remaining, the Mabinogi, and the modern Breton tale of Peronnik, deriving directly or indirectly from Chrestien. As for the question, although it presented much that seemed to refer it to folk-tradition, as for instance in Heinrich von dem Türlin's version, where Gawain's putting the question releases the lord of the castle and his retainers from the enchantment of life-in-death, yet the form of the question, "Je vos prie que vous me diez que l'en sert de cest vessel," shows its original connection with the Grail cultus, and necessitates its reference to the "Legend." Existing versions fail, however, to give any satisfactory account of the question. It is a matter of conjecture whether in the earliest form of the legend (which Hertz assumes to have been lost) it was found in the same shape as in the Didot-Perceval.

Birch-Hirschfeld's theory has already been implicitly criticised in Chapter III. The considerations adduced therein, as well as Martin's criticisms and Hertz's admissions, preclude the necessity of examining it in further detail. Formally speaking, the theory rests upon the assumption that we have Borron's work substantially as he wrote it, an assumption which, as shown by the difference in *motif* between the Metrical Joseph and the Didot-Perceval, is inaccurate. Again, the theory does not account for the silence of all the other versions respecting Brons and that special conception of the Grail found in Borron's poem. Nor does it offer any satisfactory explanation of the mysterious question which Birch-Hirschfeld can only conjecture to have been a meaningless invention, *eine harmlose Erfindung*, of Borron's. In fact, only such portions of the cycle are exhaustively examined as admit of reference to the alleged originating idea, and a show of rigorous deduction is thus made, the emptiness of which becomes apparent when the entire legend, and not one portion only, is taken into account. Despite the learning and acuteness with which it is urged, Birch-Hirschfeld's theory must be rejected, if it were only because, as Martin points out, it postulates a development of the legend which is the very opposite of the normal one. We cannot admit that this vast body of romance sprang from a simple but lofty spiritual conception, the full significance of which, unperceived even by its author, was totally ignored, not only, were that possible, by Chrestien and his continuators, but by the theologising mystics who wrote the Grand St. Graal and the Queste—aye, and even by the latest and in some respects the most theologically minded of all the writers of the cycle, the author of the Prose Perceval le Gallois and Gerbert. We must say, with Otto Küpp (Zacher's Zeitschrift, XVII, 1, p. 68), "die jetzt versuchte christliche Motivierung ist ganz unglücklich geraten und kann in keiner Weise befriedigen."

The field is thus clear for an examination of the Quest with a view to determining whether the Grail really belongs to it or not. The first step is to see what relationship exists between the oldest form of the Quest and what have been called the non-Grail members of the cycle—i.e., the Mabinogi of Peredur ab Evrawc and the Thornton MS. Sir Perceval. As preliminary to this inquiry, an attempt must be made to determine more closely the relationship of the Didot-Perceval to the Conte du Graal—whether it be wholly derived from the latter, or whether it may have preserved through other sources traces of a different form of the story than that found in Chrestien.*

---

* I have not thought it necessary, or even advisable, to notice what the "Encyclopædia Britannica" (Part XLI, pp. 34, 35) and some other English "authorities" say about the Grail legends.

CHAPTER V.

Relationship of the Didot-Perceval to the Conte du Graal—The former not the source of the latter—Relationship of the Conte du Graal and the Mabinogi—Instances in which the Mabinogi has copied Chrestien—Examples of its independence—The incident of the blood drops in the snow—Differences between the two works—The machinery of the Mabinogi and the traces of it in the Conte du Graal—The stag-hunt —The Mabinogi and Manessier—The sources of the Conte du Graal and the relation of the various parts to a common original—Sir Perceval —Steinbach's theory—Objections to it—The counsels in the Conte du Graal—Wolfram and the Mabinogi—Absence of the Grail from the apparently oldest Celtic form.

In examining the relationship of the Didot-Perceval to the Conte du Graal, the sequence of the incidents is of importance. This is shown in the subjoined table (where the numbers given are those of the incidents as summarized, chapter II), in which the Didot-Perceval sequence is taken as the standard.

DIDOT-PERCEVAL.	CHRESTIEN.	GAUTIER DE DOULENS.
Inc.	Inc.	Inc.
2. Perceval sets forth in quest of the rich fisher.	11. Only after the reproaches of the loathly damsel does Perceval first set forth in quest of the Grail.	... ...
3. Finds a damsel weeping over a knight. Adventure with dwarf and the Orgellos Delande.	8. In so far as finding a damsel weeping over a dead knight, and (9) for overcoming the Orgellous de la Lande.	9. In so far as a damsel is found lamenting over a knight.
4. Arrival at the Chessboard Castle. Adventure of the stag hunt and loss of the hound.	... ...	7 and 8.
5. Meeting with sister; instruction concerning the Grail; vow to seek it.	... ...	12.
6. Meeting with, confession to, and exhortation from her-mit uncle.	15. *After* the Good Friday in-cident.	12.

DIDOT-PERCEVAL.	CHRESTIEN.	GAUTIER DE DOULENS.
Inc.	Inc.	Inc.
7. Disregard of uncle's exhortations (slaying a knignt), through thinking of damsel of the Chessboard.	... ...	12. In so far as a knight is slain, but *before* the meeting with the hermit.
8. Meeting with Rosette and Le Beau Mauvais (the loathly damsel).	... ...	11.
9. Adventure at the Ford with Urbains.	... ...	9. Ford Amorous; *entirely different adventure.*
10. The two children in the tree.	... ...	20. *One* child.
11. First arrival at Grail Castle.	7	... ...
12. Reproaches of the wayside damsel.	8. In so far as in both the hero is reproached by a wayside damsel.	... ...
13. Meeting with the damsel who had carried off the stag's head and hound, and second visit to Castle of the Chessboard.	... ...	13 and 18. Many adventures being intercalated.
14. Period (7 years) of despair ended by the Good Friday incident.	15	... ...
15. Tournament at Melianz de Lis. Merlin's reproaches.	13. But told of Gawain not of Perceval.	... ...
16. Second arrival at Grail Castle. Achievement of Quest.	... ...	22.

The different sequence in the Didot-Perceval and Chrestien may be explained, as Birch-Hirschfeld explains it, by the freedom which Chrestien allowed himself in re-casting the work; but why should Gautier, who, *ex hypothesi*, simply took up from Chrestien's model such adventures as his predecessor had omitted, have acted in precisely the same way? If the theory were correct we should expect to find the non-Chrestien incidents of the Didot-Perceval brought together in at least fairly the same order in Gautier. A glance at the table shows that this is not the case. In one incident, moreover, the Didot-Perceval is obviously right and Gautier obviously wrong, namely, in his incident 12, where the slaying of the knight before the hero's meeting the hermit takes away all point from the incident. An absolutely decisive proof that that portion of the Conte du Graal which goes under Gautier's name (though it is by no means clear that all of it is of the same age or due to one man), cannot be based upon the Didot-Perceval as we now possess it, is afforded by the adventure of the Ford

Amorous or Perillous, which in the two versions is quite dissimilar. This incident stands out pre-eminent in the Didot-Perceval for its wild and fantastic character. It is a genuine Celtic *märchen*, with much of the weird charm still clinging to it that is the birthright of the Celtic folk-tale. It is inadmissible that Gautier could have substituted for this fine incident the commonplace one which he gives.

If, then, it is out of the question that Gautier borrowed directly from the Didot-Perceval, how are the strong resemblances which exist in part between the two versions to be accounted for ? Some of these resemblances have already been quoted (*supra*, p. 75), the remainder may be usefully brought together here.*

First arrival at the Castle of the Chessboard—

DIDOT-PERCEVAL.	GAUTIER.
Li plus biaux chasteaux del monde et vit le pont abeissié et la porte defermé (p. 439).	Le bel castiel que je vos dis . . . . Et vit si bièles les entrées Et les grans portes desfremées (22,395, etc.) ;

The damsel exhorts him not to throw the chessman into the water—

Votre cors est esmeuz à grant vilainie faire (p. 440).	Car çou serait grans vilonie (22,503).

Perceval having slain the stag, sees its head carried off—

Si vint une veille sor un palestoi grant aléure et prist le brachet et s'en ala or tot (p. 442).	Une pucièle de malaire Vint cevauçant parmi la lande Voit le braket, plus ne demande Par le coler d'orfrois le prist . . . . Si s'en aloit grant aléure (22,604, etc.).

On Perceval threatening to take it away from her by force she answers—

Sire Chevalier, force n'est mie droit et force me poez bien faire (p. 443).	Force à faire n'est mie drois Et force me poés vos faire (22,640).

In the subsequent fight with the Knight of the Tomb, he, overcome—

Se torna vers le tonbel grant aléure et li tombeaux s'enleva contre moult et chevalier s'en feri enz (p. 444).	Que fuiant vait grant aléure Vers l'arket et la sepouture Si est entrés plus tost qu'il pot (22,723, etc.).

* They are brought together by Hucher, vol. i, p. 383, etc.

In the description of Rosette (the loathly damsel)—

DIDOT-PERCEVAL.	GAUTIER.
Ele avoit le col et les mains plus noires et le vier, que fer. . . (p. 453).	Le col avoit plus noir que fer (25,409).

When the loathly damsel and her knight come to Arthur's court, Kay jests as follows :—

| Lors pria (*i.e.*, Kay) le chevalier par la foi que il devoit, le roi, qui li déist où il l'avoit prise et si en porroit une autre tele avoir, si il l'aloit querre (p. 457). | Biaus sire, Dites moi, si Dex le vos mire, Si plus en a en vostre terre, Une autèle en iroie querre Si jou le quidoie trover (25,691 etc.). |

These similarities are too great to be accidental. It will be noticed, however, that they bear chiefly upon two adventures : that of the chessboard and stag hunt, and that of the loathly maiden. As to the latter, it is only necessary to allude to Birch-Hirschfeld's idea that Rosette is the original of the damsel who reproaches Perceval before the court with his conduct at the Grail Castle, a theory to state which is to refute it. The former adventure will be closely examined in the following section. There is no need to suppose direct borrowing on the part of one or the other versions to account for the parallel in these two incidents; a common original closely followed at times by both would meet the requirements of the case. It is difficult to admit that the author of the Didot-Perceval used Gautier's continuation and not Chrestien's original, especially when the following fact, strangely overlooked by both Birch-Hirschfeld and Hucher, is taken into account: Perceval on his first arrival at the Grail Castle keeps silence (as will be seen by a reference to the summary, *supra*, p. 31), because, "li souvenoit du prodome qui li avoit deffandu que ne fust trop pallier," etc. As a matter of fact, the "prodome" had forbidden nothing of the sort, and this casual sentence is the first allusion to the motive upon which Chrestien lays so much stress as explaining his hero's mysterious conduct at the Grail Castle. Evidently the Didot-Perceval, which, to whoever considers it impartially, is an obvious abridgment and piecing together of material from different sources, found in one of its sources an episode corresponding to that of Gonemans in Chrestien. But its author, influenced probably by the

Galahad version of the Quest, substituted for the "childhood" opening of this hypothetical source the one now found in his version, and the Gonemans episode went with the remainder of that part of the story. When the hero comes to the Grail Castle, the author is puzzled; his hero knows beforehand what he has to do, sets out with the distinct purpose of doing it, and yet remains silent. To account for this silence the author uses the motive belonging to a discarded episode, but applies the words to his hermit, forgetting that he had put no such words into his mouth, and that, attributed to him, the injunction to keep silence became simply meaningless. Is the model treated in this way by the Didot-Perceval Chrestien's poem? Hardly, for this reason. After the Good Friday incident occurs the remarkable passage, quoted (*supra*, p. 31), as to the silence of the *trouvères* respecting it. Chrestien gives the incident in full, and the author of the Perceval could have had no reason for his stricture, or could not have ventured it had he been using Chrestien's work. Two hypotheses then remain; the unknown source may have been a version akin to that used by Chrestien and Gautier, or it may have been a summary abridgment of the Conte du Graal, in which, *inter alia*, the Good Friday incident was left out. In either case the presence of the passage in the Perceval is equally hard of explanation; but the first hypothesis is favoured by the primitive character of the incident of the Ford Perillous, and several other features which will be touched upon in their place. The Didot-Perceval would thus be an attempt to provide an ending for Borron's poem by adapting to its central *donnée* a version of the Perceval *sage* akin to that which forms the groundwork of the Conte du Graal, its author being largely influenced by the Galahad form of the Quest as found in the *Queste*. If this view be correct, the testimony of Perceval (wherever not influenced by Borron's poem or the *Queste*) is of value in determining the original form of the story, the more so from the author's evident want of skill in piecing together his materials. It will, therefore, be used in the following section, which deals with the relationship of the Conte du Graal and the Mabinogi of Peredur ab Evrawc.

Relationship of the Conte du Graal and the Mabinogi.—As was seen in Chapter IV, opinion began with Monsieur de Villemarqué by accepting the Mabinogi as the direct source of the Conte du Graal, and has ended with Zarncke and Birch-Hirschfeld in looking upon it as a more or less direct copy. The most competent of living scholars in this matter, M. Gaston Paris, has expressed himself in favour of this opinion in his recent article on the Lancelot story (Romania, 1886).* Before dealing with the question as presented in this form, Simrock's view, differing as it does from that of all other investigators, deserves notice. He, too, looks upon the Mabinogi as derived from Chrestien, and yet bases his interpretation of the myth underlying the romance upon a feature, the bleeding head in the dish, found only in it. But if the Mabinogi have really preserved here the genuine form of the myth, it must represent an older version than Chrestien's, and if, on the other hand, Chrestien be its only source, the feature in question cannot belong to the earliest form of the story. Simrock's theory stands then or falls in this respect by the view taken of the relationship between the two versions, and need not be discussed until that view has been stated.

To facilitate comparison, the incidents common to the two stories are tabulated as under, those of the Mabinogi being taken as the standard :—

MABINOGI.		CONTE DU GRAAL.
Inc.	Inc.	*Chrestien.*
1. Encounter with the knights.	1.	
2. Adventure with the damsel of the tent.	2.	
3. Avenging of the insult to Guinevere; incident of the dwarves; departure from Court.	3 and 4.	
5. Arrival at house of first uncle (found fishing); instruction in arms.	5.	Gonemans.
6. Arrival at house of second uncle (Grail Castle). First sight of the talismans (head in basin and lance).	7.	Uncle found fishing; talismans, Grail and lance.

---

* In the preface to the second volume of his edition of Chrestien's works (Halle, 1887), W. Förster distinguishes Peredur from the Lady of the Fountain and from Geraint, which he looks upon as simple copies of Chrestien's poems dealing with the same subjects. Peredur has, he thinks, some Welsh features.

MABINOGI.	CONTE DU GRAAL
Inc.	Inc.
7. Reproaches of foster-sister whom he finds lamenting over a dead knight.	8. Reproached by his cousin; also instructed by her about the magic sword.
8. Adventure with the damsel of the besieged castle who offers herself to hero.	6. Blanchefleur, Gonemant's niece.
9. Second meeting with the lady of the tent.	9.
10. First encounter with the sorceresses of Gloucester, who are forced to desist from assailing hero's hostess.	
11. Adventure of the drops of blood in the snow.	10.
20. Reproaching of Peredur before the Court by the loathly damsel.	11.
21. Gwalchmai's adventure with the lady whose father he had slain.	14.
22. Peredur's meeting the knight on Good Friday, and confession to priest.	15. Hermit, hero's uncle.
	Gautier.
24. Arrival at the Castle of Wonders (Chessboard Castle); stag hunt; loss of dog; fight with the black man of the cromlech.	Inc. 7, 8, and partly 13 and 18.
25. Second arrival at the (Grail) castle; achievement of the Quest by destruction of sorcesses of Gloucester. "Thus it is related concerning the Castle of Wonders."	22. In so far as Gautier ends his part of the story here with the hero's second arrival at the Grail Castle, but no similarity in the incidents.

The sequence is thus exactly the same in the Mabinogi and in Chrestien, with the single exception of the Blanchefleur incident, which, in the French poem precedes, in the Welsh tale follows, the first visit to the Grail Castle. The similarity of order is sufficient of itself to warrant the surmise of a relation such as that of copy to original. If the Mabinogi be examined closely, much will be found to strengthen this surmise. Thus, Birch-Hirschfeld has pointed out that when Peredur first sees the knights, and on asking his mother what they may be, receives the answer, "Angels, my son "; this can only be a distorted reminiscence of Perceval's own exclamation,

> . . . Ha! sire Dex, Merchi!
> Ce sont angle que je voi ci! (1,349-50).

as the hero's mother would be the last person to describe thus the knights whom she has done her best to guard her son from knowledge of. Again, Simrock has criticised, and with reason, the incident of Peredur's being acclaimed by the dwarf on his arrival at Arthur's court as the chief of warriors and flower of knighthood. In the corresponding incident in Chrestien, the hero is told laughingly by a damsel that he should become the best knight in the world, and she had not laughed for ten years, as a fool had been wont to declare. This is an earlier form than that of the Mabinogi, and closer to the folk-tale account. Thus, to take one instance only, in Mr. Kennedy's Giolla na Chroicean Gobhar (Fellow with the Goat-skin) [Fictions of the Irish Celts, p. 23], the hero comes to the King of Dublin, as Peredur to Arthur, clad in skins and armed with a club. " Now, the King's daughter was so melancholy that she didn't laugh for seven years, but when she saw Tom of the Goat-skin knock over all her father's best champions, then she let a great sweet laugh out of her," and of course Tom marries her, but not until he has been through all sorts of trials, aye, even to Hell itself and back. In Chrestien, the primitive form is already overlaid; we hear nothing further of the damsel moved to laughter nor of the prophetic fool; and in the Mabinogi it seems obvious that the hailing of the hero, added in Chrestien to the older laughter, has alone subsisted. Birch-Hirschfeld takes exception likewise to the way in which Peredur's two uncles are brought upon the scene, the first one, corresponding to Gonemans in Chrestien, being found fishing instead of the real Fisher King, the lord of the Castle of the Magic Talismans, whilst at the latter's, Peredur has to undérgo trials of his strength belonging properly to his stay at the first uncle's. Evidently, says Birch-Hirschfeld, there has been a confusion of the two personages. Again, when Peredur leaves his second uncle on the morrow of seeing the bleeding head and spear, it is said, " he rode forth with his uncle's permission." Can these words be a reminiscence of Chrestien's ?

> Et trueve le pont abaiscié,
> C'on li avoit ensi laissié
> Por ce que rien nel detenist,
> De quele eure qu'il venist
> Que il ne passat sans arriest (4,565–69).

We shall see later on that in the most primitive form of the unsuccessful visit to the Castle of the Talismans the hero finds himself on the morrow on the bare earth, the castle itself having vanished utterly. The idea of permission being given to leave is diametrically opposed to this earliest conception, and its presence in the Mabinogi seems only capable of explanation by some misunderstanding of the story-teller's model.

The Blanchefleur incident shows some verbal parallels, "The maiden welcomed Peredur and put her arms around his neck."

> Et la damosele le prent
> Par le main débonnairement (3,025–26)
> Et voit celi ajenouillie
> Devant son lit qui le tenoit
> Par le col embraciet estroit (3,166–68).

Can, too, the "two nuns," who bring in bread and wine, be due to the "II Abéies," which Perceval sees on entering Blanchefleur's town ? It may be noticed that in this scene the Welsh story-teller is not only more chaste, but shows much greater delicacy of feeling than the French poet. Peredur's conduct is that of a gentleman according to nineteenth century standards. Chrestien, however, is probably nearer the historical reality, and the conduct of his pair—

> S'il l'a sor le covertoir mise
> *   *   *   *
> Ensi giurent tote la nuit.

is so singularly like that of a Welsh *bundling* couple, that it seems admissible to refer the colouring given to this incident to Welsh sources. Another scene presenting marked similarities in the two works is that in which the hero is upbraided before the court by the loathly damsel. In the Mabinogi she enters riding upon a *yellow* mule with *jagged thongs*: in Chrestien—

> Sor une *fauve mule* et tint
> En sa main destre une escorgie (5,991–2).

" Blacker were her face and her two hands than the blackest iron covered with pitch."

> Ains ne véistes si noir fer
> Come ele ot les mains et le cor (5,998–99).

" And she greeted Arthur and all his household except Peredur."

> Le roi et ses barons salue
> Tout ensamble comunalment
> Fors ke Perceval seulement (6,020–3).

In the Mabinogi, Peredur is reproached for not having asked about the streaming spear; in Chrestien " la lance qui saine " is mentioned first although the Grail is added. Had Peredur asked the meaning and cause of the wonders, the " King would have been restored to health, and his dominions to peace."

> Li rices rois qui moult s'esmaie
> Fust or tos garis de sa plaie
> Et si tenist sa tière en pais (6,049–51).

Whereas now " his knights will perish, and wives will be widowed, and maidens will be left portionless "—

> Dames en perdront lor maris,
> Tières en seront essilies,
> Et pucièles desconsellies ;
> Orfenes, veves en remauront
> Et maint chevalier en morront (6,056, etc.).

In the " Stately Castle " where dwells the loathly damsel, are five hundred and sixty-six knights, and " the lady whom he loves best with each," in " Castle Orguellos " five hundred and seventy, and not one " qui n'ait s'amie avoeques lui." " And whoever would acquire fame in arms and encounters and conflicts, he will gain it there if he desire it."

> Que la ne faut nus ki i alle,
> Qui la ne truist joste u batalle ;
> Qui viout faire chevalerie,
> Si là le quiert, n'i faura mie (6,075, etc.).

" And whoso would reach the summit of fame and honour, I know where he may find it. There is a castle on a lofty mountain, and there is a maiden therein, and she is detained a prisoner there, and whoever shall set her free will attain the summit of the fame of the world."

> Mais ki vorroit le pris avoir
> De tout le mont, je quic savoir
> Le liu et la pièce de terre
> U on le porroit mius conquerre ;
> *   *   *   *   *
> A une damoisièle assise ;
> Moult grant honor aroit conquise,
> Qui le siège en poroit oster
> Et la pucièle délivrer (6,080, etc.).

In this last case certainly, in the other cases probably, a direct influence, to the extent at least of the passages quoted, must be admitted. But before concluding hastily that the Welsh story-teller is the copyist, some facts must be mentioned on the other side. Thus the incident of the blood drops in the snow, which Birch-Hirschfeld sets down as one of those taken over by the Mabinogi, with the remark that the Welsh story contains no trace of a passion as strong as Perceval's for Blanchefleur, has been dealt with by Professor H. Zimmer in his " Keltische Studien," vol. ii, pp. 200. He refers to the awakening of Deirdre's love to Noisi by similar means, as found in the Irish saga of the Sons of Usnech (oldest MS. authority, Book of Leinster, copied before 1164 from older MSS.) as evidence of the early importance of this *motif* in Celtic tradition. The passage runs thus in English : " As her foster-father was busy in winter time skinning a calf out in the snow, she beheld a raven which drank up the blood in the snow ; and she exclaimed, ' Such a man could I love, and him only, having the three colours, his hair like the raven, his cheeks like the blood, his body like the snow.' "

Now the Mabinogi says, almost in the same words—the black-ness of the raven and the whiteness of the snow, and the redness of the blood he compared to the hair and the skin and the two red spots upon the cheek of the lady that best he loved. In Chrestien there is no raven, and the whole stress is laid upon the *three* drops of blood on the snow, which put the hero in mind of the red and white of his lady's face. As Zimmer justly points out, the version of the Mabinogi is decidedly the more primitive of the two; and that, moreover, as the incident does not figure at all in what Birch-Hirschfeld presumes to be Chrestien's source, the Didot-Perceval, the following development of this incident must, *ex hypothesi*, have taken place. In the Didot-Perceval the hero is once upon a time lost in thought. To explain this, Chrestien invents the incident of the three drops of blood in the snow; the Mabinogi, copying Chrestien, presents the incident in almost as primitive a form as the oldest known one! Here, then, the Mabinogi has preserved an older form than Chrestien, alleged to have been its source in all those parts common to both. Nor is it certain that the fact of Peredur's undergoing the sword-test in the Talisman Castle *does* show, as Birch-Hirschfeld maintains, that the Welsh story-teller confused the two personages whom he took over from Chrestien, Gonemans and the Fisher King. The sword incident will be examined later on; suffice here to say that no explanation is given in the Conte du Graal of the broken weapon; whereas the Mabinogi does give a simple and natural one. But these two instances cannot weaken the force of the parallels adduced above. In determining, however, whether these may not be due to Chrestien's being the borrower, the differences between the two versions are of even more importance than the similarities.

What are these? The French romances belonging to the Perceval type of the Grail quest give two versions of the search for the magic talismans, that of the Conte du Graal and that of the Didot-Perceval. The latter pre-supposes an early history which, as already shown, cannot be looked upon as the starting point of the legend without postulating such a development of the latter as is inadmissible on *a priori* grounds, and as runs counter to many well-ascertained facts. The former is not consistent with itself, Manessier's finish contradicting Chrestien's opening on such an essential point as the cause of the maimed king's suffering. Still the following outline of a story, much overlaid by apparently disconnected adventures, may be gathered from it. A hero has to seek for magic talismans wherewith to heal an uncle wounded by his brother, and at the same time to avenge him on that brother. What, on the other hand, is the story as told in the Mabinogi?

A hero is minded by talismans to avenge the death of a cousin (and the harming of an uncle); it is not stated that the talismans pass into his possession. It is difficult to admit that either of these forms can have served as direct model to the other. If the Mabinogi be a simple copy of the Conte du Graal, whence the altered significance of the talismans? whence also the machinery by means of which the hero is at last brought to his goal, and which is, briefly, as follows? The woe which has befallen Peredur's kindred is caused by supernatural beings, the sorceresses of Gloucester; his ultimate achievement of the task is brought about by his cousin, who, to urge him on, assumes the form (1) of the black and loathly damsel; (2) of the damsel of the chessboard, who incites him to the Ysbydinongyl adventure, reproves him for not slaying the black man at once, and then urges him into the stag hunt; (3) of the lady who carries off the hound and sends him to fight against the black man of the cromlech; " and the cousin it was who came in the hall with the bloody head in the salver and the lance dripping blood." The whole of the incidents connected with the Castle of the Chessboard, which appear at such length in both the Conte du Graal and the Didot-Perceval, but without being in any way connected with the main thread of the story, thus form in the Mabinogi an integral portion of that main thread. Would the authors of the Conte du Graal have neglected the straight-forward version of the Welsh tale had they known it, or could, on the other hand, the author of the Mabinogi have worked up the disconnected incidents of his alleged model into an organic whole? Neither hypothesis is likely. Moreover the Conte du Graal and the Didot-Perceval, if examined with care, show distinct traces of a machinery similar to that of the Welsh story. Thus in Chrestien, Perceval, on arriving at the Fisher King's, sees a squire bringing into the room a sword of such good steel that it might break in but one peril, and this the King's niece (*i.e.*, Perceval's cousin) had sent her uncle to bestow it as he pleased; and the King gives it to the hero for—

. . . biaus frère ceste espée
Vous fu jugie et destineé (4,345-6).

After Perceval's first adventure at the Grail Castle it is his

" germaine cousine " (4,776) who assails him with her reproaches; she knows all about the sword (4,835–38) and tells him, how, if it be broken he may have it mended (4,847–59). So far Chrestien, who furthermore, be it noted, makes Blanchefleur Perceval's lady-love, likewise his cousin, she being niece to Gonemans (3,805–95). A cousin is thus beloved of him, a cousin procures for him the magic sword, a cousin, as in the Mabinogi, incites him to the fulfilment of the quest, and gives him advice which we cannot doubt would have been turned to account by Chrestien had he finished his poem. Turning now to Gautier, in whose section of the poem are to be found the various adventures growing out of the chessboard incident, this difference between the Mabinogi and himself may be noted. In the former, these adventures caused by Peredur's cousin serve apparently as tests of the hero's strength and courage. The loss of the chessboard is the starting-point of the task, and the cousin reappears as the black maiden. Nothing of the sort is found in Gautier. True, the damsel who reproaches Perceval is in so far supernatural, as she is a kind of water-nix, but it is love for her which induces the hero to perform the task; she it is, too, who lends him the dog, and she is not identified with the " pucelle de malaire" who carries it off (22,604, etc.). But later on Perceval meets a knight who tells him that a daughter of the Fisher King's (thus also a cousin of Perceval) had related to him how a knight had carried off a stag's head and hound to anger another good knight who had been at her father's court, and had not asked as he should concerning the Grail, for which reason she had taken his hound and had refused him help to follow the robber knight (23,163, etc.). This makes the " pucelle de malaire " to be Perceval's cousin, and she plays the same *rôle* as in the Mabinogi. True, when later on (Incident 13) Perceval finds the damsel, nothing is said as to her being the Fisher King's daughter; on the contrary, as will be seen by the summary, a long story is told about the Knight of the Tomb, brother to her knight, Garalas, and how he lived ten years with a fay. She is here quite distinct from the lady of the chessboard to whom Perceval returns later. The version found in the Didot-Perceval agrees with the Mabinogi as against Gautier in so far that the hero is in love with the mistress of the castle, and not with the damsel who reproaches him for throwing away the chessmen. This reproaching damsel is not in any way identified with the lady who carries off the hound, who is described as " une vieille," and of whom it is afterwards told " elle estoit quand elle voloit une des plus belles damoiselles du monde. Et est cele meismes que mon frère (the brother of the Knight of the Tomb, who here, as in Gautier, is the lover of a fay) amena à la forest," *i.e.*, she is the fay herself, sister to the lady of the Chessboard Castle, who hated her and wished to diminish her and her knight's pride (p. 469). Here, again, a connection can be pieced out between the various personages of the adventure; and it appears that the hero is driven to his fight against the Knight of the Tomb by a fair damsel transformed into a mysterious hag.* The Mabinogi thus gives one consistently worked-out conception— transformed hag=Peredur's cousin—which may be recovered partly from that one of the two discordant versions found in Gautier which makes the pucelle de malaire to be the Fisher King's daughter, hence Perceval's cousin, and connects the stag hunt with the Grail incident, partly from the Didot-Perceval, which tells how the same pucelle de malaire is but playing a part, being when she wills one of the fairest maids of the world. Now we have seen that the stag hunt is just one of those portions of the story in which are found the closest verbal similarities between Gautier de Doulens and the Didot-Perceval. It is, therefore, perplexing to find that there is not more likeness in the details of the incident. But the similarities pointed out concern chiefly the first part of the incident, and are less prominent in the latter part (the hero's encounter with the Knight of the Tomb). This, taken together with the difference in the details of the incident just pointed out, strengthens the opinion expressed above, that the Didot-Perceval and Gautier

---

* It is perhaps only a coincidence that in Gautier the " pucelle de malaire " is named Riseut la Bloie, and that Rosette la Blonde is the name of the loathly damsel whom Perceval meets in company of the Beau Mauvais, and whom Birch-Hirschfeld supposes to have suggested to Chrestien *his* loathly damsel, the Grail messenger. But from the three versions one gets the following :—Riseut (Gautier), loathly damsel (Didot-Perceval), Grail messenger (Chrestien),= Peredur's cousin, who in the Mabinogi is the loathly Grail messenger, and the protagonist in the stag-hunt.

are not connected directly but through the medium of a common source, the influence of which can be seen distinctly in certain portions of either story, and that when this source fails they go widely asunder in their accounts. That such an hypothesis is not unreasonable is shown by the fact that Gautier has two contradictory forms of this very story, one of which, that which makes the hound-stealing damsel a daughter of the Fisher King, is on all fours with the Mabinogi, whilst the other is more akin to, though differing in important respects from, that of the Didot-Perceval. In this case, at least, Gautier must have had two sources, and if two why not more?

It may be urged in explanation of the similarities between Gautier and the Mabinogi, that the author of the latter used Gautier in the same free way that he did Chrestien, but that getting tired towards the close of his work he abridged in a much more summary fashion than at first. If the comparison of the versions of the stag hunt found in either work be not sufficient to refute this theory, the following consideration may be advanced against it: if the Mabinogi derives entirely from the Conte du Graal, how can the different form given to the Grail episode be accounted for?—if it only knew Chrestien, where did it get the chessboard adventure from, and if it knew Gautier as well as Chrestien why did it not finish the Grail adventure upon the same lines as it began, *i.e.*, partly in conformity with its alleged model?

Is Manessier any nearer than Gautier to the Mabinogi in the later portion of the tale? The chief points of the story told by him may be recapitulated thus :—The Grail damsel is daughter of the Fisher King, the damsel of the salver, daughter of King Goon Desert, his brother (*i.e.*, both are cousins to Perceval); Goon Desert, besieged by Espinogre, defeats him, but is treacherously slain by his nephew Partinal, the latter's sword breaking in the blow. Goon's body is brought to the Fisher King's castle, whither the broken sword is likewise brought by Goon's daughter to be kept until a knight should come, join together the pieces, and avenge Goon's death. In receiving the sword the Fisher King wounds himself through the thighs, and may not be healed until he be avenged on Partinal. Perceval asks how he may find the murderer, the blood vengeance (faide = O.H.G. Fehde) being on him. Perceval fights with Partinal, slays him, cuts off his head as token of his victory, returns to the Fisher King's castle, lighting upon it by chance, heals the Fisher King by the mere sight of the head, which is fixed on a pike on the highest battlements. At the death of his uncle Perceval succeeds him as King of the Grail Castle. Here, then, as in the Mabinogi, the story turns definitely upon a blood feud; the same act which brings about the death of one relative of the hero, also causes, indirectly, it is true, the laming of another, even as in the Mabinogi the same supernatural beings kill Peredur's cousin and lame his uncle; the cousin reappears again, bringing the magic sword by whose aid alone the hero can accomplish the vengeance, and uttering the prediction the fulfilment of which will point out the destined avenger. Finally, if the Mabinogi seems to lay special stress upon the head of the murdered man, Manessier lays special stress upon the head of the murderer. Now it is quite evident that the Mabinogi cannot have copied Manessier. It has been alleged that the Welsh story-teller, adapting Chrestien to the taste of his fellow countrymen, substituted a blood feud for the Grail Quest, but what reason would he have had for thus dealing with Manessier? He had simply to leave out the Christian legendary details, which in Manessier are, one can hardly say, adapted to the older form of the story, to find in that older form a clear and straightforward account with no admixture of mystical elements. It is impossible to explain the strong general similarity of outline with the equally marked divergences of detail (Sorceresses of Gloucester instead of Partinal, etc.,) except by saying that both, though going back to a common legendary source, are unconnected one with another.

The facts thus dealt with may be recapitulated as follows:— There is marked similarity in general outline between the Mabinogi and the Conte du Graal in the adventures common to both; in that portion of the Conte du Graal due to Chrestien there occur, moreover, many and close verbal parallels, and the corresponding part of the Mabinogi is told at greater length than the remainder of the incidents common to both works. That which answers in the Mabinogi to the Grail Quest forms a clear and straightforward whole, the main features of which may be recovered from the Conte du Graal, but in varying proportions from the various sections of that work. Thus the indications of this Mabinogi talisman quest, the central intrigue, as it may be called, of the tale, are in Chrestien of the slightest nature, being confined to passing hints; in Gautier they are fuller and more precise, though pointing to a version of the central intrigue different, not only in details but in conception, from that of the Mabinogi; in Manessier alone is there agreement of conception, although the details still vary. Finally, those portions of the Mabinogi which are in closest verbal agreement with Chrestien contain statements which cannot easily be reconciled with this central intrigue.

These facts seem to warrant some such deductions as these. Bearing in mind that the Mabinogi is an obvious piecing together of all sorts of incidents relating to its hero, the only connecting link being that of his personality, its author may be supposed, when compiling his work, to have stretched out his hand in all directions for material. Now a portion of the Peredur *sage* consisted of adventures often found elsewhere in the folk-tale cycles of the Great Fool and the Avenging Kinsman—cycles which, in Celtic tradition, at least, cover almost the same ground as the one described by J. G. von Hahn under the title, "Die Arische Aussetzung und Rückkehr-Formel." In the original of the Mabinogi this portion probably comprised the childhood and forest up-bringing, the visit to Arthur with the accompanying incidents, the training by the uncle (who *may* have been the Fisher King), the arrival at the (bespelled) castle, where the hero is to be minded of his task by the sight of certain talismans and of his cousin's head, the reproaches of the loathly damsel, her subsequent testing of the hero by the adventures of the chessboard, stag hunt, etc., the hero's final accomplishment of the task, vengeance on his kindred's enemies, and removal of the spells. There would seem to have been no such love story as that frequently found in stories of the Great Fool class, *e.g.*, in the Irish one (*supra*, p. 134). This original was probably some steps removed from being a genuine popular version; the incidents were presented in a way at once over-concise and confused, and some which, as will be seen in the

next chapter, the living folk-tale has preserved were left out or
their significance was not recognized. What more natural than
that the author of the Mabinogi in its present form, knowing
Chrestien, should piece out his bare, bald narrative with shreds and
patches from the Frenchman's poem ? The moment Chrestien fails
him, he falls back into the hurried concision of his original. His
adaptation of Chrestien is done with singularly little skill, and at
times he seems to have misunderstood his model. He confines his
borrowing to matters of detail, not allowing, for instance, Chrestien's
presentment of the Grail incident to supersede that of his Welsh
original. In one point he may, following Chrestien, have made
a vital change. It seems doubtful whether the Welsh source of
the Mabinogi knew of a maimed king, an uncle to be healed
through the hero's agency ; the sole task may have been the
avenging the cousin's death. True the " lame uncle " appears at
the end, but this may be due to some sudden desire for consistency
on the arranger's part. But whether or no he was found in the
Welsh story preserved in the Mabinogi, he certainly played no such
leading part as in the Conte du Graal. The two stories deal with
the same cycle of adventures, but the object of the hero is not the
same in both, and, consequently, the machinery employed is not
quite the same. The present Mabinogi is an unskilful fusion of
these two variations upon the one theme.*

Light is also thrown by this investigation upon the question of
Chrestien's relationship to his continuators. Birch-Hirschfeld's
theory that the Didot-Perceval was the source of Chrestien
and Gautier has already been set aside. Apart from the reasons
already adduced, the fact that it does not explain from whence
Manessier got his ending of the story would alone condemn it. It
must now be evident that Chrestien and two of his continuators drew
from one source, and this a poem of no great length probably, the
main outlines of which were nearly the same as those of the Welsh
proto-Mabinogi given above, with this difference, that the story
turned upon the healing of the uncle and not the avenging the

---

* I have not thought it necessary to discuss seriously the hypothesis that
Chrestien may have used the Mabinogi as we now have it. The foregoing statement of the facts is sufficient to negative it.

cousin's death. This poem, which seems also to have served, directly or indirectly, as one of the sources of the Didot-Perceval, had probably departed from popular lines in many respects, and *may*, though this would be an exceedingly difficult question to determine, have begun the incorporation of the Joseph of Arimathea legend with its consequent wresting to purposes of Christian symbolisms of the objects and incidents of the old folk-tale.

Such an incorporation had almost certainly begun before Chrestien's time, and was continued by him. There can be little doubt that he dealt with his model in a free and daring spirit, altering and adding as seemed best to him. This alone explains how Manessier, slavishly following the common original, tells differently the cause of the lame king's wound. Gautier, who lacked Chrestien's creative power, though he often equals him in the grace and vivacity of his narrative, seems to have had no conception of a plan ; the section of Conte du Graal which goes under his name is a mere disorderly heap of disconnected adventures brought together without care for consistency. But for this very reason he is of more value in restoring the original form of the story than Chrestien, who, striving after consistency, harmony, and artistic development of his tale, alters, adds to, or retrenches from the older version. Gautier had doubtless other sources besides the one made use of by Chrestien. This does not seem to be the case with Manessier, who, for this portion of the story, confined himself to Chrestien's original, without taking note of the differences in *motif* introduced by his predecessor. What is foreign to it he drew from sources familiar to us, the Queste and Grand S. Graal, from which more than two-thirds of his section are derived.

In working back to the earliest form of the Perceval-*sage*, Mabinogi and Conte du Graal are thus of equal value and mutually complementary. Both are second-hand sources, and their testimony is at times sadly corrupt, but it is from them chiefly that information must be sought as to the earlier stages of development of this legendary cycle. They do not by themselves give any satisfactory explanation of the more mysterious features of the full-blown legend, but they do present the facts in such a way as to put out of court the hypothesis of a solely Christian legendary origin.

Before proceeding further it will be well to see if the English Sir Perceval has likewise claims to be considered one of the versions which yield trustworthy indications as to the older form of the story. This poem, described by Halliwell as simply an abridged English version of the Conte du Graal, has, as may be seen by reference to Ch. IV, been treated with more respect by other investigators, several of whom, struck by its archaic look, have pronounced it one of the earliest versions of the Perceval *sage*. It has quite lately been the object of elaborate study by Paul Steinbach in his dissertation: "Uber dem Einfluss des Crestien de Troies auf die altenglische literatur," Leipzig, 1885. The results of his researches may be stated somewhat as follows: the two works correspond incident for incident down to the death of the Red Knight, the chief differences being that Perceval is made a nephew of King Arthur, that the death of his father at the hands of the Red Knight is explained as an act of revenge on the part of the latter, that Arthur recognizes his nephew at once, and tells him concerning the Red Knight, and that the burning of the Red Knight, only hinted at in Chrestien's lines—

> Ains auroie par carbonees.
> Trestout escarbellié le mort, etc. (2,328–9).

is fully told in the English poem. After the Red Knight incident the parallelism is much less close. The English poem has incidents to itself: the slaying of the witch, the meeting with the uncle and nine cousins, the fight with the giant for the ring, the meeting with and restoring to health the mother. Of the remaining incidents, those connected with Lufamour are more or less parallel to what Chrestien relates of his hero's adventure with Blanchefleur, and that of the Black Knight, with that of the Orgellous de la Lande in Chrestien. Of the 2,288 verses of the English poem the greater part may be paralleled from Chrestien, thus:—

P. of G.			Cr.	P. of G.			Cr.
1–160..	..	..	485–940	433–80 ..	..	..	1,829–1,970
161–188..	..	..	941–1,206	481–600..	..	..	2,091–2,170
169–256..	..	..	1,207–82				⌈ 2,055–90
257–320..	..	..	1,283–1,554	601–56 ..	..		⟨ 2,135–59
321–432..	..	..	1,555–1,828				⌊ 2,171–2,225

P. of G.	Cr.	P. of G.	Cr.
657-740..	.. 2,268-2,312	953-1,012 ⎱	⎰ 2,900-3,960
741-820.	.. 2,313-2,398	1,125-1,380 ⎬ ..	⎨ 4,088-94
1,061-1,108	.. 4,000-4,060	1,541-1,760 ⎰	⎱
1,109-1,124	.. 5,511-553	1,761-1,808	4,095-4,150
1,381-1,540	.. 5,600-5,891	1,809-1,951	4,865-5,375

the incidents comprised v. 821–952 and 1,953–2,288, being the only one entirely unconnected with Chrestien. This general agreement between the two works shows the dependence of the one on the other. But while evidently dependent, the English poem, as is shown by the differences between it and its French original, belongs at once to a less and to a more highly developed stage of the Perceval *sage*. The differences are thus of two kinds, those testifying to the writer's adherence to older, probably Breton, popular traditions and those due to himself, and testifying to the skill with which he has worked up his materials and fitted portions of Chrestien's poem into an older framework. Of the first kind are : the statement that Perceval meets with three knights instead of five as in Chrestien, the English poem agreeing here with the Mabinogi ; the mention of his riding on a *mare* and of his being clad in goat-skins, the English poem again agreeing rather with the Mabinogi than with Chrestien, and showing likewise points of contact with the Breton ballads about Morvan lez Breiz, printed by Villemarqué in the Barzaz Breiz. The combat with the giant may likewise be paralleled from the Lez Breiz cycle in that hero's fight with the Moorish giant. These points would seem to indicate knowledge on the author's part of popular traditions concerning Perceval forming a small cycle, of which the departure from, and return to the mother were the opening and closing incidents respectively. This form of the story must have been widely spread and popular to induce the author to leave out as much as he has done of Chrestien's poem in order to bring it within the traditional framework. He accomplished his task with much skill, removing every trace of whatever did not bear directly upon the march of the story as he told it. In view of this skill differences which tend to make the story more consequent and logical may fairly be ascribed to him. Such are : the making Perceval a nephew of Arthur, the mention of a feud between the Red Knight and

Perceval's father, the combat with the witch arising out of Perceval's wearing the Red Knight's armour, and the other adventures which follow eventually from the same cause, the feature that the ring taken by Perceval from the lady in the tent is a magic one, endowing its wearer with supernatural strength, the change made between this ring and his mother's which prepares the final recognition, etc. The original poem probably ended with the reunion of mother and son, the last verse, briefly mentioning the hero's death, being a later addition. To sum up, Sir Perceval may be looked upon as the work of a folk-singer who fitted into the old Breton framework a series of adventures taken partly from Chrestien, partly from the same Breton traditions which were Chrestien's main source, and with remarkable skill avoided all such incidents as would not have accorded with the limits he had imposed upon himself.

Against this view of Steinbach's it might be urged that a writer as skilful as the author of Sir Perceval is assumed to be could easily have worked Chrestien's Grail episode into his traditional framework. A more plausible explanation, assuming the theory to be in the main correct, might be found in the great popularity in this country of the Galahad form of the Quest, and the consequent unwillingness on the author's part to bring in what may have seemed to him like a rival version. Steinbach has not noticed one curious bit of testimony to the poem's being an abridgment of an older work, more archaic in some respects than Chrestien. When the hero has slain the Red Knight he knows not how to rid him of his armour, but he bethinks him—

> . . . "My moder bad me
> Whenne my dart solde brokene be,
> Owte of the irene brenne the tree,
> Now es me fyre gnede" (749-52).

Now the mother's counsel, given in verses xxv-vi are solely that he should be "of mesure," and be courteous to knights; nothing is said about burning the tree out of the iron, nor does any such counsel figure either in Chrestien or in the Mabinogi, which in this passage has copied, with misunderstandings, the French poet.* The use of Chrestien by the author of Sir Perceval seems, however, uncontestable; and, such being the case, Steinbach's views meet the difficulties of the case fairly well. It will be shown farther on, however, that several of the points in which the German critic detects a post-Chrestien development, are, on the contrary, remains of as

---

* THE COUNSELS. *Chrestien* (v. 1,725, etc.): aid dames and damsels, for he who honoureth them not, his honour is dead; serve them likewise; displease them not in aught; one has much from kissing a maid if she will to lie with you, but if she forbid, leave it alone; if she have ring, or wristband, and for love or at your prayer give it, 'tis well you take it. Never have comradeship with one for long without seeking his name; speak ever to worthy men and go with them; ever pray in churches and monasteries (then follows a dissertation on churches and places of worship generally). *Mabinogi* (p. 83): wherever a church, repeat there thy Paternoster; if thou see meat and drink, and none offer, take; if thou hear an outcry, especially of a woman, go towards it; if thou see a jewel, take and give to another to obtain praise thereby; pay thy court to a fair woman, *whether she will or no*, thus shalt thou render thyself a better man than before. (In the italicised passage the Mabinogi gives the direct opposite of Chrestien, whom he has evidently misunderstood.) *Sir Perceval* (p. 16): "Luke thou be of mesure Bothe in haulle and boure, And fonde to be fre." "There thou meteste with a knyghte, Do thi hode off, I highte, and haylse hym in hy" (He interprets the counsel to be of mesure by only taking half the food and drink he finds at the board of the lady of the tent. The kissing of the lady of the tent which follows is in no way connected with his mother's counsel.) *Wolfram:* "Follow not untrodden paths; bear thyself ever becomingly; deny no man thy greeting; accept the teaching of a greybeard; if ring and greeting of a fair woman are to be won strive thereafter, kiss her and embrace her dear body, for that gives luck and courage, if so she be chaste and worthy." Beside the mother's counsels Perceval is admonished by Gonemans or the personage corresponding to him. In *Chrestien* (2,838, *et seq.*) he is to deny mercy to no knight pleading for it; to take heed he be not over-talkful; to aid and counsel dames and damsels and all others needing his counsel; to go often to church; not to quote his mother's advice, rather to refer to him (Gonemans). In the *Mabinogi* he is to leave the habits and discourse of his mother; if he see aught to cause him wonder not to ask its meaning. In *Wolfram* he is not to have his mother always on his lips; to keep a modest bearing; to help all in need, but to give wisely, not heedlessly; and in especial not to ask too much; to deny no man asking mercy; when he has laid by his arms to let no traces thereof be seen, but to wash hands and face from stain of rust, thereby shall ladies be pleased; to hold women in love and honour; never to seek to deceive them (as he might do many), for false love is fleeting and men and women are one as are sun and daylight.—There seems to me an evident progression in the ethical character of these counsels. Originally they were doubtless purely practical and somewhat primitive of their nature. As it is, Chrestien's words sound very strange to modern ears.

old and popular a form of the story as we can work back to. Accepting, then, the hypothesis that Sir Perceval, like the Mabinogi, has been influenced by Chrestien, what is the apparent conclusion to be drawn from the fact that the former omits the Grail episode altogether, whilst the latter joins Chrestien's version to its own, presumably older one, so clumsily as to betray the join at once? May it not be urged that Chrestien's account is obviously at variance with the older story as he found it? may not the fact be accounted for by the introduction of a strange element into the thread of the romance? This element would, according to Birch-Hirschfeld, be the Christian holy-vessel legend, and it would thus appear that the Grail is really foreign to the Celtic tradition. Let me recapitulate briefly the reasons already urged against such a view. The early history of the Grail, that part in which the Christian element prevails, must certainly be regarded as later than the Quest, to which it could not have given rise without assuming such a development of the romance as is well nigh incredible—the Quest versions, moreover, all hang together in certain respects, and point unmistakably to Celtic traditions as their source. These traditions must then be examined further to see if they contain such traces of the mystic vessel as are wanting in the Mabinogi and the English poem, and as may have given rise to the episode as found in the French romances. As Perceval is the oldest hero of the Quest, and as the boyhood of Perceval, forming an integral part of all the oldest Quest versions presents the strongest analogies with the folk-tale of the Great Fool, it is this tale which must now be examined.

CHAPTER VI.

The Lay of the Great Fool—Summary of the Prose Opening—The Aryan
Expulsion and Return Formula—Comparison with the Mabinogi,
Sir Perceval, and the Conte du Graal —Originality of the Highland,
tale—Comparison with the Fionn legend—Summary of the Lay of the
Great Fool—Comparison with the stag hunt incident in the Conte
du Graal and the Mabinogi—The folk-tale of the twin brethren—
The fight against the witch who brings the dead to life in Gerbert
and the similar incident in the folk-tale of the Knight of the Red
Shield—Comparison with the original form of the Mabinogi—
Orginality of Gerbert.

ONE of the most popular of the poetic narratives in the old heroic
quatrain measure still surviving in the Highlands is the " Lay of
the Great Fool" (Laoidh an Amadain Mhoir), concerning which,
according to Campbell, vol. iii., p. 150, the following saying is
current:—" Each poem to the poem of the Red; each lay to the
Lay of the Great Fool; each history to the history of Connal" (is
to be referred as a standard). This Lay, as will be shown presently, offers some remarkable similarities with the central Grail
episode of the quest romances, but before it is investigated a prose
opening often found with it must be noticed. This prose opening
may be summarised thus from Campbell, vol. iii., pp. 146, *et seq.*

There were once two brothers, the one King over Erin, the
other a mere knight. The latter had sons, the former none.
Strife broke out between the two brothers, and the knight and his
sons were slain. Word was sent to the wife, then pregnant, that
if she bore a son it must be put to death. It was a lad she had,
and she sent him into the wilderness in charge of a kitchen wench
who had a love son. The two boys grew up together, the knight's
son strong and wilful. One day they saw three deer coming towards them; the knight's son asked what creatures were these—
creatures on which were meat and clothing 'twas answered—it
were the better he would catch them, and he did so, and his foster-

mother made him a dress of the deer's hide. Afterwards he slew his foster-brother for laughing at him, caught a wild horse, and came to his father's brother's palace. He had never been called other than " Great fool," and when asked his name by his cousin, playing shinty, answered, " Great Fool." His cousin mocked at him, and was forthwith slain. On going into the King's (his uncle's) presence, he answered in the same way. His uncle recognised him, and reproaching himself for his folly in not having slain the mother with the father, went with him, as did all the people.

In my article on the Aryan Expulsion and Return Formula among the Celts ("Folk-Lore Record," vol. iv.), I have shown that this tale is widely distributed in the Celtic Heldensage as well as in the Celtic folk-tale. Before noticing the variants, a word of explanation may be necessary. The term, Arische Aussetzungs-und Rückkehr-Formel, was first employed by J. G. v. Hahn in his Sagwissenschaftliche Studien (Jena, 1876), to describe a tale which figured in the heroic literature of every Aryan race known to him. He examined fourteen stories, seven belonging to the Hellenic mythology, Perseus, Herakles, Oedipus, Amphion and Zethos, Pelias and Neleus, Leukastos and Parrhasius, Theseus ; one to Roman mythic history, Romulus and Remus ; two to the Teutonic Heldensage, Wittich-Siegfried, Wolfdietrich ; two to Iranian mythic history, Cyrus, Key Chosrew ; two to the Hindu mythology, Karna, Krishna. I was able to recover from Celtic literature eight well-defined variants, belonging to the Fenian and Ultonian cycles of Irish Heldensage (heroes, Fionn and Cu-Chulaind); to Irish mythic history, Labraidh Maen ; to the folk-tale still living in the Highlands, Conall and the Great Fool; to the Kymric Heldensage, Peredur-Perceval, Arthur, and Taliesin An examination of all these tales resulted in the establishing of the following standard formula, to the entirety of which it will of course be understood none of the tales answer :—

    I. Hero born—

        (a) Out of wedlock.

        (b) Posthumously.

        (c) Supernaturally.

        (d) One of twins,

II. Mother, princess residing in her own country.

III. Father—

(a) God ⎫
          ⎬ from afar.
(b) Hero ⎭

IV. Tokens and warning of hero's future greatness.

V. He is in consequence driven forth from home.

VI. Is suckled by wild beasts.

VII. Is brought up by a (childless couple), or shepherd, or widow.

VIII. Is of passionate and violent disposition.

IX. Seeks service in foreign lands.

IXA. Attacks and slays monsters.

IXB. Acquires supernatural knowledge through eating a fish, or other magic animal.

X. Returns to his own country, retreats, and again returns.

XI. Overcomes his enemies, frees his mother, seats himself on the throne.

I must refer to my article for a full discussion of the various Celtic forms of this widely-spread tale, and for a tabular comparison with the remaining Indo-European forms analysed by J. G. von Hahn. Suffice to say here that the fullest Celtic presentment of the *motif* is to be found in the Ossianic Heldensage, the expelled prince being no other than Fionn himself. The Celtic form most closely related to it is that of the Great Fool summarised above, the relationship of Peredur-Perceval with which is evident. In both, the father being slain, the mother withdraws or sends her son into the wilderness; in both he grows up strong, hardy, ignorant of the world. Almost the same instances of his surpassing strength and swiftness are given; in the Mabinogi by celerity and swiftness of foot he drives the goats and hinds into the goat-house; in the Highland folk-tale he catches the wild deer, and seeing a horse, and learning it is a beast upon which sport is done, stretches out after it, catches and mounts it; in Sir Perceval he sees—

. . . A fulle faire stode
Offe coltes and meres gude,
Bot never one was tame (v. xxi.).

and "smertly overrynnes" one.—The Great Fool then comes to his uncle, in whom he finds the man who has killed his father. Sir Perceval likewise comes to his uncle, and gets knowledge from him of his father's slayer; in Chrestien and the Mabinogi no relationship is stated to exist between Arthur and the hero. The manner of the coming deserves notice. In the Conte du Graal, entering the hall the hero salutes the King twice, receives no answer, and, turning round his horse in dudgeon, knocks off the King's cap.

In the English poem—

> At his first in comynge,
> His mere withowtenne faylynge,
> Kiste the forehevede of the Kynge,
> So nerehande he rade (v. xxxi.).

He then demands knighthood or—

> Bot (unless) the Kyng make me knyghte,
> I shall him here slaa (v. xxxiii.).

In the Great Fool the horse incident is wanting, but the hero's address to his uncle is equally curt: "I am the great fool . . . and if need were it is that I could make a fool of thee also." The incident then follows of the insult offered to Arthur by the Red Knight. Here, be it noted, the Mabinogi version is much the ruder of the three, "the knight dashed the liquor that was in the goblet upon her (Gwenhwyvar's) face, and upon her stomacher, and gave her a violent blow in the face, and said," &c.; in Chrestien the incident is not directly presented, but related at second-hand, and merely that the discourteous knight took away the goblet so suddenly that he spilt somewhat of its contents upon the queen, and that she was so filled with grief and anger that well nigh she had not escaped alive; in Sir Perceval the knight takes up the cup and carries it off. Now it is a *lieu commun* of Celtic folk-tales that as a King is sitting at meat, an enemy comes in mounted, and offers him an insult, the avenging of which forms the staple of the tale. A good instance may be found in Campbell's lii., " The

Knight of the Red Shield." As the King is with his people and his warriors and his nobles and his great gentles, one of them says, "who now in the four brown quarters of the Universe would have the heart to put an affront on the King?"—then comes the rider on a black filly, and, "before there was any more talk between them, he put over the fist and he struck the King between the mouth and the nose." It is noteworthy that this tale shows further likeness to the Mabinogi-Great Fool series, generally, in so far as it is the despised youngest who out of the three warriors that set off to avenge the insult succeeds, even as it is the despised Peredur who slays the Red Knight, and specially in what may be called the prophecy incident. With the exception of the opening incidents, this is the one by which the "formula" nature of the Perceval *sage* is most clearly shown. In the Mabinogi it is placed immediately after the hero's first encounter with the sorceresses of Gloucester: "by destiny and foreknowledge knew I that I should suffer harm of thee," says the worsted witch. The Conte du Graal has only a trace of it in the Fisher King's words as he hands the magic sword to Perceval—

> . . . Biaus frère, ceste espée
> Vous fu jugie et destinée (4345-6),

whilst in Sir Perceval a very archaic turn is given to the incident by Arthur's words concerning his unknown nephew—

> The bokes say that he mone
> Venge his fader bane (v. xxxvi.).

This comparison is instructive as showing how impossible it is that Chrestien's poem can be the only source of the Mabinogi and Sir Perceval. It cannot be maintained that the meagre hint of the French poet is the sole origin of the incident as found in the Welsh and English versions, whilst a glance at my tabulation of the various forms of the Aryan Expulsion and Return formula ("Folk-Lore Record," vol. iv.) shows that the foretelling of the hero's greatness is an important feature in eight of the Celtic and five of the non-Celtic versions, i.e., in more than one-third of all the stories built up on the lines of the formula. It is evident that here at least Mabinogi and Sir Perceval have preserved a trait almost effaced in the romance.   In the above-mentioned Highland tale the incident is as follows: the hero finds "a treasure of a woman sitting on a hill, and a great youth with his head on her knee asleep"; he tries to wake the sleeper, even cuts off his finger, but in vain, until he learns how it was in the prophecies that none should rouse the sleeping youth save the Knight of the Red Shield, and he, coming to the island, should do it by striking a crag of stone upon his breast.   This tale, as already remarked, shows affinity to the Perceval saga in two incidents, and is also, as I have pointed out ("Folk-Lore Record," vol. v., Mabinogion Studies), closely allied to a cycle of German hero and folk-tales, of which Siegfried is the hero.   Now Siegfried is in German that which Fionn is in Celtic folk-lore, the hero whose story is modelled most closely upon the lines of the Expulsion and Return formula.   We thus find not only, as might be expected, affinity between the German and Celtic hero-tales which embody the formula, but the derived or allied groups of folk-tales present likewise frequent and striking similarities.*

Another Highland tale (Campbell, lviii., The Rider of Grianaig) furnishes a fresh example of this fact.   Here, also, the deeds to be done of the hero were prophesied of him.   But these deeds he would never accomplish, save he were incited thereto and aided therein by a raven, who in the end comes out as a be-spelled youth, and a steed, a maiden under spells, and the spells will not go off till her head be off.   Even so Peredur is urged on and helped by the bewitched youth. In other respects, there is no likeness of plan and little of detail†

---

* In the notes to my two articles in the "Folk-Lore Record" will be found a number of references establishing this fact.

† The hero renews his strength after his various combats by rubbing himself with the contents of a vessel of balsam.   He has moreover to enter a house the door of which closes to of itself (like the Grail Castle Portcullis in Wolfram), and which kills him.   He is brought to life by the friendly raven.   The mysterious carlin also appears, "there was a turn of her nails about her elbows, and a twist of her hoary hair about her toes, and she was not joyous to look upon."   She turns the hero's companions into stone, and to unspell them he must seek a bottle of living water and rub it upon them, when they will come out alive.   This is like the final incident in many stories of the Two Brothers class.   Cf. note, p. 162.

to the Mabinogi, certainly no trace of direct influence of the Welsh story upon the Highland one.

It may, however, be asserted that all of these tales are derived more or less directly from the French romance. This has been confidently stated of the Breton ballad cycle of Morvan le Breiz (Barzaz Breiz) and of the Breton Märchen, Peronik l'idiot (Souvestre, Foyer Breton), and I have preferred making no use of either. In the matter of the Scotch and Irish tales a stand must be made. The romance, it is said, may have filtered down into the Celtic population, through the medium of adaptations such as the Mabinogi or Sir Perceval. Granted, for argument sake, that these two works are mere adaptations, it must yet follow that the stories derived from them will be more or less on the same lines as themselves. Is this so? Can it be reasonably argued that the folk-tale of the Great Fool is a weakened copy of certain features of the Mabinogi, which itself is a weakened copy of certain features of the French poem? Is it not the fact that the folk-tale omits much that is in the Mabinogi, and on the other hand preserves details which are wanting not alone in the Welsh tale but in Chrestien. If other proof of the independent nature of these tales were needed it would be supplied by the close similarity existing between the Great Fool opening and the Fionn legend. This is extant in several forms, one of which, still told in the Highlands (Campbell's lxxxii.), tells how Cumhall's son is reared in the wilderness, how he drowns the youth of a neighbouring hamlet, how he slays his father's slayer, and wins the magic trout the taste of which gives knowledge of past and to come, how he gets back his father's sword and regains his father's lands, all as had been prophesied of him. Another descendant of the French romance it will be said. But a very similar tale is found in a fifteenth century Irish MS. (The Boyish Exploits of Finn Mac Cumhall, translated by Dr. J. O'Donovan in the Transactions of the Ossianic Society, vol. iv.); Cumhall, slain by Goll, leaves his wife big with a son, who when born is reared by two druidesses. He grows up fierce and stalwart, overcomes all his age-mates, overtakes wild deer he running, slays a boar, and catches the magic salmon of knowledge. An eighteenth century version given by Kennedy ("Legendary Fictions," p. 216) makes Cumhall offer violence to Muirrean, daughter of the druid Tadg, and his death to be chiefly due to the magic arts of the incensed father. It will hardly be contended that these stories owe their origin to adaptations of Chrestien's poem. But in any case no such contention could apply to the oldest presentment of Fionn as a formula hero, that found in the great Irish vellum, the Leabhar na h'Uidhre, written down from older materials at the beginning of the twelfth century. The tract entitled "The cause of the battle of Cnucha" has been translated by Mr. Henessey ("Revue Celtique," vol. ii., pp. 86, *et seq.*). In it we find Cumhall and Tadhg, the violence done to the latter's daughter, the consequent defeat and death of Cumhall, the lonely rearing of Fionn by his mother, and the youth's avenging of his father. I must refer to my paper in the "Folk-Lore Record" for a detailed argument in favour of the L.n.H. account being an euhemerised version of the popular tradition, represented by the Boyish Exploits, and for a comparison of the Fionn *sage* as a whole with the Greek, Iranian, Latin, and Germanic hero tales, which like it are modelled upon the lines of the Expulsion and Return formula. I have said enough, I trust, to show that the Fionn *sage* is a variant (a far richer one) of the theme treated in the boyhood of Perceval, but that it, and *a fortiori* the allied folk-tales are quite independent of the French poem. It then follows that this portion of Chrestien's poem must itself be looked upon as one of many treatments of a theme even more popular among the Celts than among any other Aryan race, and that its ultimate source is a Breton or Welsh folk-tale.

The genuine and independent nature of the Great Fool prose opening being thus established, it is in the highest degree suggestive to find in the accompanying Lay points of contact with the Grail Legend as given in Chrestien. Three versions of this Lay have been printed in English, that edited by Mr. John O'Daly (Transactions of the Ossianic Society, vol. vi., pp. 161, *et seq.*); Mr. Campbell's (West Highland Tales, vol. iii. pp. 154, *et seq.*) and Mr. Kennedy's prose version (Bardic Stories of Ireland, pp. 151, *et seq.*). O'Daly's, as the most complete and coherent, forms the staple of the following summary, passages found in it alone being italicised.*

Summary of the Lay of the Great Fool.—(1) There was a great fool who subdued the world by strength of body; (2) *He comes to the King of Lochlin to win a fair woman, learns she is guarded by seven score heroes, overthrows them, and carries her off;* (C. and K. plunging at once *in medias res,* introduce the Great Fool and his lady love out walking) (3) The two enter a valley, are meet by a " Gruagach " (champion, sorcerer), in his hand a goblet with drink; (4) The Great Fool thirsts, and though warned by his lady love drinks deep of the proffered cup; the " Gruagach " departs and the Great Fool finds himself minus his two legs; (5) The two go onward, and ("swifter was he at his two knees than six at their swiftness of foot;" C.) A deer nears them followed by a white hound, the Great Fool slays the deer and seizes the hound; (6) whose owner coming up claims but finally yields it, and offers the Great Fool food and drink during life; (7) The three fare together (the glen they had passed through had ever been full of glamour) till they come to a fair city filled with the glitter of gold, dwelt in solely by the owner of the white hound and his wife, " whiter than very snow her form, gentle her eye, and her teeth like a flower"; (8) She asks concerning her husband's guests, and, learning the Great Fool's prowess, marvels he should have let himself be deprived of his legs;

---

* O'Daly's version consists of 158 quatrains; Campbell's of 63. The correspondence between them, generally very close (frequently verbal), is shown by the following table :—

O'D., 1, 2.	C., 1, 2.	O'D., 68, 69.	C., 46, 47.
—	C., 3.	O'D., 70.	C., 49.
O'D., 3.	C., 4.	O'D., 71.	C., 48.
O.D., 4–15.	—	—	C., 50.
O'D., 16.	C., 4.	O'D., 72.	C., 52.
O'D., 17–24.	C., 5–12.	O'D., 73.	—
O'D., 25.	—	O'D., 74.	C., 53.
—	C., 13–15.	O'D., 75.	C., 54.
O'D., 26–47.	C., 16–36.	O'D., 76–80.	C., 55–59.
O'D., 48–56.	—	O'D., 81–134.	—
O'D., 57–61.	C., 37–40.	O'D., 135, 136.	C., 60, 61.
O'D., 62.	—	—	C., 62.
O'D., 63–65.	C., 41–43.	O'D., 137.	—
O'D., 66.	C., 45.	O'D., 138.	C.. 63.
O'D., 67.	C., 44.	O'D. 139–158.	—

(9) The host departs, leaving his house, wife, and store of gold in the Great Fool's keeping, he is to let no man in, no one out should any come in, nor is he to sleep; (10) Spite his lady love's urgings the Great Fool yields to slumber, when in comes a young champion and snatches a kiss from the host's wife, ("She was not ill pleased that he came," C.); (11) The Great Fool's love awakening him reproaches him for having slept—he arises to guard the door, in vain does the intruder offer gold, three cauldrons full and seven hundred townlands, he shall not get out; (12) *At the instigation of the host's wife* the intruder restores the Great Fool's legs, but not then even will the hero let him go—pay for the kiss he must when the host returns; threats to deprive him of his legs are in vain, as are likewise the entreaties of the host's wife (All this is developed with great prolixity in O'Daly, but there is nothing substantial added to the account in C.); (13) Finally the intruder discloses that he himself is the host, and he was the Gruagach, whose magic cup deprived the Great Fool of his legs, and he is, "*his own gentle brother long in search of him, now that he has found him he is released from sorcery.*" The two kiss (C. and K. end here). (14) The two brothers fare forth, encounter a giant with an eye larger than a moon and an iron club, wherewith he hits the Great Fool a crack that brings him to his knees, but the latter arising closes with the giant, kills him and takes his club, the two then attack four other giants, three of whom the Great Fool slays with his club, and the fourth yields to him. The brothers take possession of the giant's castle and all its wealth.

There are obvious similarities between the Lay and the story found in the Mabinogi and the Conte du Graal. A stag hunt is prominent in both, and whilst engaged in it the hero falls under "illusion," in both too the incident of the seizure of the hound appears, though in a different connection. Finally in the Lay, as in the Mabinogi, the mover in the enchantment is a kinsman whose own release from spells depends upon the hero's coming success-fully out of the trials to which he exposes him. But while the general idea is the same, the way in which it is worked out is so different that it is impossible to conceive of the one story having been borrowed from the other. What can safely be claimed is that the Great Fool, counterpart of Peredur-Perceval in the adventures of his youth and up-bringing, is also, to a certain extent, his counterpart in the most prominent of his later adventures, that of the stag hunt. It is thus fairly certain that all this part of the Conte du Graal is, like the *Enfances*, a working up of Celtic folk-tales. The giant fight which concludes the Lay may be compared with that in Sir Perceval and in Morvan le Breiz, and such a comparison makes it extremely likely that the incident thus preserved by independent and widely differing offshoots from the same folk-tale stem, belongs to the oldest form of the story.

The analogies of the Lay with the Perceval *sage* are not yet exhausted. In virtue of the relationship between the two chief characters, the Lay belongs to the "twin-brother cycle." This group of folk-tales, some account of which is given below,* is closely

---

* Of this widely spread group, Grimm's No. 60, Die zwei Brüder, may be taken as a type. The brethren eat heart and liver of the gold bird and thereby get infinite riches, are schemed against by a goldsmith, who would have kept the gold bird for himself, seek their fortunes throughout the world accompanied by helping beasts, part at crossways, leaving a life token to tell each one how the other fares ; the one delivers a princess from a dragon, is cheated of the fruit of the exploit by the Red Knight, whom after a year he confounds, wins the princess, and, after a while, hunting a magic hind, falls victim to a witch. His brother, learning his fate through the life token, comes to the same town, is taken for the young king even by the princess, but keeps faith to his brother by laying a bare sword twixt them twain at night. He then delivers from the witch's spells his brother, who, learning the error caused by the likeness, and thinking advantage had been taken of it, in a fit of passion slays him, but afterwards, hearing the truth, brings him back to life again. Grimm has pointed out in his notes the likeness between this story and that of Siegfried (adventures with Mimir, Fafnir, Brunhilde, and Gunnar). In India the tale figures in Somadeva's Katha Sarit Sagara (Brockhaus' translation, ii., 142, *et seq.*). The one brother is transformed into a demon through accidental sprinkling from a body burning on a bier. He is in the end released from this condition by his brother's performing certain exploits, but there is no similarity of detail. Other variants are *Zingerle* (p. 131) where the incident occurs of the hero's winning the king's favour by making his bear dance before him ; this I am inclined to look upon as a weakened recollection of the incident of a hero's making a princess *laugh*, either by playing antics himself or making an animal of his play them (*see supra*, p. 134, Kennedy's Irish Tale). Grimm also quotes *Meier* 29 and 58, but these are only variants of the dragon-killing incident. In the variant of 29, given p. 306, the hero makes the king laugh, and in both stories occurs the familiar incident of the hero coming unknown into a tournament and overcoming all enemies, as in Peredur (Inc. 9). *Wolf.*, p. 269, is closer, and here the hero is counselled by a grey mannikin whom

related on the one hand to the " dragon slayer " group of *märchen*, on the other hand to the Expulsion and Return formula tales. In many versions of the latter (the most famous being that of Romulus and Remus) the hero is one of twins, and, after sharing for a while with his brother, strife breaks out between them. In the folk-tale this strife leads to final reconciliation, or is indeed a means of unravelling the plot. In the hero-tale on the other hand the strife mostly ends with the death or defeat of the one brother. It would seem that when the folk-tale got associated with a definite hero (generally the founder and patron of a race) and became in brief a hero-tale, the necessity of exalting the race hero brought about a modification of the plot. If this is so the folk-tale group of the " two brothers " must be looked upon as older than the corresponding portion of the Expulsion and Return hero-tales, and not as a mere weakened echo of the latter. To return to the twin-brother features. The Peredur-Perceval *sage* has a twin-sister, and is parallel herein to the Fionn *sage* in one of its forms

---

he will unspell if he succeeds. *Stier*, No. I. (not p. 67, as Grimm erroneously indicates) follows almost precisely the same course as Grimm's 60, save that there are three brothers. *Graal*, p. 195, has the magic gold bird opening, but none of the subsequent adventures tally. *Schott*, No. 11, is also cited by Grimm, but mistakenly ; it belongs to the faithful-servant group. Very close variants come from Sweden (Cavallius-Oberleitner, V*a*, V*b*) and Italy (Pentamerone, I. 7 and I. 9). The Swedish tales have the miraculous conception opening, which is a prominent feature in tales belonging to the Expulsion and Return group (*e.g.*, Perseus, Cu-Chulaind, and Taliesin), but present otherwise very nearly the same incidents as Grimm. The second of the Italian versions has the miraculous conception opening so characteristic of this group of folk-tales, and of the allied formula group, the attainment of riches consequent upon eating the heart of a sea dragon, the tournament incident (though without the disguise of the hero), the stag hunt, wherein the stag, an inimical wizard haunting the wood, is a cannibal and keeps the captured hero for eating. In the story of the delivery by the second brother, the separating sword incident occurs. The first version opens with what is apparently a distorted and weakened form of the hero's clearing a haunted house of its diabolical inmates (*see infra* Ch. VII., Gawain) and then follows very closely Grimm's Two Brothers, save that the alluring witch is young and fair, the whole tale being made to point the moral, "more luck than wit." Straparola, *a* 3, is a variant of the dragon fight incident alone. It is impossible not to be struck by the fact that in this widely spread group of tales are to be found some of the most characteristic incidents of the Perceval and allied Great Fool group. The only version, however, which brings the two groups into formal contact is O'Daly's form of the Great Fool.

("How the Een was set up"), though curiously enough not to the Great Fool folk-tale (otherwise so similar to "How the Een was set up"), which, as in the Lay, has a brother. But beyond this formal recognition of the incident in the Perceval *sage*, I am inclined to look upon the Perceval-Gawain dualism as another form of it. This dualism has been somewhat obscured by the literary form in which the *sage* has been preserved and the tendency to exalt and idealise *one* hero. In the present case this tendency has not developed so far as to seriously diminish the importance of Gawain; *his* adventures are, however, left in a much more primitive and *märchenhaft* shape, and hence, as will be shown later on, are extremely valuable in any attempt to reach the early form of the story.*

If Simrock's words quoted on the title page were indeed conclusive—"If that race among whom the 'Great Fool' folk-tale was found independent of the Grail story had the best claim to be regarded as having wrought into one these two elements"— then my task might be considered at an end. I have shown that this race was that of the Celtic dwellers in these islands, among whom this tale is found not only in a fuller and more significant form than elsewhere, but in a form that connects it with the French Grail romance. But the conclusion that the Conte du Graal is in the main a working up of Celtic popular traditions, which had clustered round a hero, whose fortunes bore, in part, a striking resemblance to those of Fionn, the typical representative of the Expulsion and Return formula cycle among the Celts, though hardly to be gainsaid, does not seem to help much towards settling the question of the origin of the Grail itself. The story would appear to be Celtic except just the central incident upon which the whole turns. For the English Sir Perceval, which undoubtedly follows older models, breathes no word of search for any magic talisman, let alone the Grail, whilst the Mabinogi, which is also older in parts than the Conte du Graal, gives a different turn

---

* The brother feature appears likewise in Wolfram von Eschenbach, where Parzival's final and hardest struggle is against the unknown brother, as the Great Fool's is against the Gruagach. This may be added to other indications that Wolfram *did* have some other version before him besides Chrestien's.

to and assigns a different *motif* for the hero's conduct.   The avenging of a kinsman's harm upon certain supernatural beings, and the consequent release from enchantment of another kinsman, supply the elements of a clear and consistent action to which parallels may easily be adduced from folk-tales, but one quite distinct from the release of a kinsman through the medium of certain talismans and certain magic formulæ.   Numerous as have been the points of contact hitherto established between Celtic folk belief and the French romance, the parallel would seem to break down at its most essential point, and the contention that the Grail is a foreign element in the Celtic legend would still seem to be justified.   Before, however, this can be asserted, what I have called the central episode of the romance requires more searching and detailed examination than it has had, and some accessory features, which, on the hypothesis of the Christian legendary origin of the Grail, remain impenetrable puzzles must be commented upon. And another instructive point of contact between romance and folk-tale must be previously noticed, connected as it is with stories already dealt with in this chapter.

In the latest portion of the Conte du Graal, the interpolation of Gerbert, the following incident occurs :—The hero meets four knights carrying their wounded father, who turns out to be Gonemans, the same who armed him knight.   He vows vengeance upon Gonemans' enemies, but his efforts are at first of no avail. As fast as in the daytime he slays them, at night they are brought back to life by " Une vieille " who is thus described :—

> La poitrine ot agüe et sèche ;
> Ele arsist ausi come une esche
> Si on boutast en li le fu.*
>
> *   *   *   *
>
> La bouche avoit grant à merveilles
> Et fendue dusqu'as oreilles,
> Qu'ele avoit longues et tendans ;
> Lons et lez et gausnes les dans
> Avoit.   (Potvin vi., 183, 184.)

---

* I cannot but think that these words have connection with the incident in the English Sir Perceval of the hero's throwing into the flames and thus destroying his witch enemy.

She carries with her

II. barisiax d'ivoire gent ;

containing a "poison," the same whereof Christ made use in the
Sepulchre, and which serves here to bring the dead back to life
and to rejoin heads cut off from bodies.   She goes to work thus :—

> A la teste maintenant prise,
> Si l'a desor le bu assise ;

then taking the balm

> Puis en froie celui la bouche
> À cui la teste avoit rajointe ;
> Sor celui n'ot vaine ne jointe
> Qui lues ne fust de vie plaine.

Perceval stops her when she has brought back three of her men
to life ; she recognises in him her conqueror :

> Bien vous connois et bien savoie
> Que de nului garde n'avoie
> Fors que de vous ; car, par mon chief
> Nus n'en péust venir à chief
> Se vous non.   .   .   .

So long as she lives, Perceval shall be powerless to achieve his
Quest.   She wars against Gonemant by order of the King of the
Waste City, who ever strives against all who uphold the Christian
faith, and whose chief aim it is to hinder Perceval from attaining
knowledge of the Grail.   Perceval gets possession of somewhat of
the wonder-working balm, brings to life the most valiant of his
adversaries, slays him afresh after a hard struggle, in which he
himself is wounded, heals his own hurt, and likewise Gonemant's,
with the balsam.   Compare now Campbell's above-cited tale, the
Knight of the Red Shield.   The hero, left alone upon the island by
his two treacherous companions, sees coming towards him " three
youths, heavily, wearily, tired."   They are his foster-brothers, and
from the end of a day and a year they hold battle against the Son
of Darkness, Son of Dimness, and a hundred of his people, and
every one they kill to-day will be alive to-morrow, and spells are
upon them they may not leave this (island) for ever until they kill

them. The hero starts out on the morrow alone against these enemies, and he did not leave a head on a trunk of theirs, and he overcame the Son of Darkness himself. But he is so spoilt and torn he cannot leave the battle-field, and he lays himself down amongst the dead the length of the day. " There was a great strand under him below ; and what should he hear but the sea coming as a blazing brand of fire, as a destroying serpent, as a bellowing bull ; he looked from him, and what saw he coming on the shore of the strand, but a great toothy carlin   .   .   .   there was the tooth that was longer than a staff in her fist, and the one that was shorter than a stocking wire in her lap." She puts her finger in the mouth of the dead, and brings them alive. She does this to the hero, and he bites off the finger at the joint, and then slays her. She is the mother of the Son of Darkness, and she has a vessel of balsam wherewith the hero's foster-brothers anoint and make him whole, and her death frees them from her spells for ever.* This " toothy carlin " is a favourite figure in Celtic tradition. She re-appears in the ballad of the Muilearteach (probably Muir Iarteach, *i.e.*, Western Sea), Campbell, iii., pp. 122, *et seq.*, and is there described as " the bald russet one," " her face blue black, of the lustre of coal, her bone tufted tooth like rusted bone, one deep pool-like eye in her head, gnarled brushwood on her head like the clawed-up wood of the aspen root." In another version of the ballad, printed in the Scottish Celtic Review, No. 2, pp. 115, *et seq.*, the monster is " bald red, white maned, her face dark grey, of the hue of coal, the teeth of her jaw slanting red, one flabby eye in her head, her head bristled dark and grey, like scrubwood before hoar."† The editor of this version, the Rev. J. G. Campbell, interprets the ballad, and correctly, no doubt, " as an inroad of the

---

* I must refer to my Mabinogion Studies, I. Branwen for a discussion of the relation of this tale with Branwen and with the Teutonic Heldensage.

† Another parallel is afforded by the tale of Conall Gulban (Campbell, III., 274). Conall, stretched wounded on the field, sees " when night grew dark a great Turkish carlin, and she had a white glaive of light with which she could see seven miles behind her and seven miles before her ; and she had a flask of balsam carrying it." The dead men are brought to life by having three drops of balsam put into their mouths. The hero wins both flask and glaive.

Personified Sea." There is no connection, save in the personage of the " toothy carlin," between the ballad and the folk-tale.*

It is impossible, I think, to compare Gerbert's description of the witch with that of the Highland " Carlin " without coming to the conclusion that the French poet drew from traditional, popular Celtic sources. The wild fantasy of the whole is foreign in the extreme to the French temperament, and is essentially Celtic in tone. But the incident, as well as one particular feature of it, admits of comparison : the three foster-brothers of the Highland tale correspond to the four sons of Gonemant, who be it recollected, represents in the Conte du Graal, Peredur-Perceval's uncle in the Mabinogi ; in both, the hero goes forth alone to do battle with the mysterious enemy ; the Son of Darkness answers to the King of the Waste City ; the dead men are brought back to life in the same way ; the release of the kinsman, from spells, or from danger of death, follows upon the witch's discomfiture. And yet greater value attaches to the incident as connected with the Mabinogi form of the story ; in Gerbert, as in the Mabinogi, the hero's uncle is sick to death, his chief enemy is a monstrous witch (or witches), who foreknows that she must succumb at the hero's hands.† Something has obviously dropped

---

* *Cf.* my Branwen for remarks on the mythological aspect of the ballad. It should be noted that most of the ballads traditionally current in the Highlands are of semi-literary origin, *i.e.*, would seem to go back to the compositions of mediæval Irish bards, who often sprinkled over the native tradition a profusion of classical and historical names. I do not think the foreign influence went farther than the " names " of some personages, and such as it is is more at work in the ballads than in the tales.

† This may seem to conflict with the statement made above (p. 145), that the Mabinogi probably took over the maimed uncle from Chrestien. But there were in all probability several forms of the story ; that hinted at in Chrestien and found in Manessier had its probable counterpart in Celtic tradition as well as that found in Gerbert. It is hardly possible to determine what was the form found in the proto-Mabinogi, the possibility of its having been exactly the same as that of Gerbert is in no way affected by the fact that the Mabinogi, as we now have it, has in this respect been influenced by Chrestien. Meanwhile Birch-Hirschfeld's hypothesis that Gerbert's section of the Conte du Graal is an interpolation between Gautier and Manessier is laid open to grave doubt. It is far more likely that Gerbert's work was an independent and original attempt to provide an ending for Chrestien's unfinished poem, and that he had before him a different version of the original from that used by Gautier and Manessier.

out from the Mabinogi. May it not be those very magic talismans, the winning of which is the chief element of the French romances, and may not one of the talismans have been the vessel of life-restoring balsam which figures in Gerbert and the Highland tales ?*   The study of subsidiary versions and incidents may thus throw upon the connection of the Grail with the Perceval romance a light which the main Celtic forms of the latter have not hitherto yielded.

The Thornton MS. Sir Perceval differs in this incident from both Manessier and Gerbert.   As in Gerbert and the Highland Tale the hero meets his uncle and cousins ; there is the same fight with the mother of the enemy of his kin, the hideous carlin, but it precedes, as does also the slaying of that enemy, the meeting of uncle and nephews.   There is thus.no room for the healing *motif* for which the unconscious avenging of the father's death is substituted.   These differences bear witness both to the popular and shifting nature of the traditions upon which the romances are based, and to the fact that the avenging of a blood feud was the leading incident of its earliest form.

---

* It occurs also in Peredur (Inc. 16), where the hero comes to the Castle of the Youths, who, fighting every day against the Addanc of the Cave, are each day slain, and each day brought to life by being anointed in a vessel of warm water and with precious balsam.

CHAPTER VII.

The various forms of the visit to the Grail Castle in the romances—Conte
du Graal : Chrestien ; Gautier-Manessier ; Gautier-Gerbert—Didot-
Perceval—Mabinogi—Conte du Graal : Gawain's visit to the Grail
Castle—Heinrich von dem Türlin—Conte du Graal : Perceval's visit
to the Castle of Maidens—Inconsistency of these varying accounts ;
their testimony to stories of different nature and origin being embodied
in the romances—Two main types: feud quest and unspelling quest
—Reasons for the confusion of the two types—Evidence of the confusion in older Celtic literature—The Grail in Celtic literature : the gear
of the Tuatha de Danann ; the cauldron in the Ultonian cycle ; the
Mabinogi of Branwen ; vessel of balsam and glaive of light in the
contemporary folk-tale—The sword in Celtic literature : Tethra ;
Fionn ; Manus—Parallels to the Bespelled Castle ; the Brug of
Oengus, the Brug of Lug, the Brug of Manannan Mac Lir, Bran's
visit to the Island of Women, Cormac Mac Art, and the Fairy Branch ;
Diarmaid and the Daughter of King Under the Waves—Unspelling
stories : The Three Soldiers; the waiting of Arthur; Arthur in Etna ;
the Kyffhäuser Legend, objections to Martin's views concerning it—
Gawain's visit to the Magic Castle and Celtic parallels ; The Son of
Bad Counsel ; Fionn in Giant Land ; Fionn in the House of Cuana ;
Fionn and the Yellow Face—The Vanishing of the Bespelled Castle
—Comparison with the Sleeping Beauty cycle—The "Haunted Castle"
form and its influence on Heinrich's version—The Loathly Grail
Messenger.

THE analysis of the various versions has shown that the Conte du
Graal is the oldest portion of the vast body of French romance
which deals with the Grail, and that it presents the earliest form
of the story. The examination of the theories put forward to
explain the genesis and growth of the legend has shown how
untenable is that hypothesis which makes the Christian legend
the starting point of the cycle. The comparison of the Conte du
Graal with Celtic legends and folk-tales has shown that the former
is in the main a North French retelling of tales current then, as
now, among the Celtic peoples of Britain, and probably of Brittany.

One thing alone remains unexplained, the mysterious Grail itself. Nor has any light been thrown from Celtic sources upon the incident of the hero's visit to the Castle of Talismans, his silence, and the ensuing misfortune which overtakes him. Where this incident does appear in a Celtic version, the Mabinogi, it is not brought in connection with the Grail, and it bears obvious traces of interpolation. The utmost we have been able to do is to reconstruct from scattered indications in different Celtic tales a sequence of incidents similar to that of the French romance. Let us, then, return to what may be called the central incident of the Grail legend in its older and purer form. And let us recall the fact that the hypothesis which finds a Christian origin for the whole legend has no explanation to offer of this incident. Birch-Hirschfeld can merely suggest that Perceval's question upon which all hinges is "eine harmlose Erfindung Borron's," a meaningless invention of Borron's. It is, indeed, his failure to account for such an essential element of the story that forms one of the strongest arguments against his hypothesis.

In the first place it must be noticed that the incident of a hero's visit to a magic castle, of his omission whilst there to do certain things, and of the loss or suffering thereby caused, occurs not once, but many times ; not in one, but in many forms in the vast body of Grail romance, as is seen by the following list, which likewise comprises all the occasions on which one or other of the questers has come near to or succeeded in seeing the Grail :—

(1) CHRESTIEN : (Inc. 7).   Perceval's first visit to the Grail Castle. Question omitted.

(2) GAUTIER : (Inc. 22).   Perceval's second visit to the Grail Castle. Question put—

   Incident breaks off in middle, and is continued in one version by :—

   (2A) MANESSIER, who sends off the hero on a fresh quest, which is finished in

(3) MANESSIER : (Inc. 21). Perceval's third visit to Grail Castle. The question is not mentioned. Hero's final success.

In another version by :—

(4) GERBERT : (Inc. 1-3).   Perceval is sent forth anew upon
  Quest.   He has half put the question and been partially
  successful.

(5) GERBERT : (Inc. 21).   Perceval's third visit to Grail Castle.
  Question not mentioned.   Hero's success.

*Besides these forms of the episode in the Conte du Graal of
which Perceval is the hero, we have—*

(6) GAUTIER : (Inc. 3).   Gauvain's first visit according to one,
  second visit according to another version.   Question half
  put, partial success.

*And finally a somewhat similar incident of which Perceval is
the hero in:*

(7) GAUTIER : (Inc. 12).   Visit to the Castle of Maidens.   Untimely sleep of hero.

So far the Conte du Graal.   Of the versions closely
connected with it we have :

(8 & 9) WOLFRAM VON ESCHENBACH : Two visits of Perceval to
  Grail Castle.   Question omitted at first, put in second, and
  crowned with success.

(10 & 11) MABINOGI OF PEREDUR : (Inc. 6-25).   Two visits of
  hero to Grail Castle.   Question omitted at first.   Second
  visit successful.   No mention of question.

(12 & 13) DIDOT-PERCEVAL : (Inc. 11-16).   Two visits of Perceval
  to Grail Castle.   Question omitted at first, put at second,
  and crowned with success.

In a German romance, which presents many analogies
with that portion of the Conte du Graal which goes
under Gautier's name:

(14) HEINRICH VON DEM TÜRLIN : Gawain's first visit to Grail
  Castle.   Question put.   Success.   Allusion to previous
  unsuccessful visit of Perceval.

Finally in the QUESTE versions we have four variants of
the incident—

(15) QUESTE : (Inc. 12).   Lancelot at the cross-road, omission to
  ask concerning the Grail.

(15) QUESTE : (Inc. 15).   Perceval heals Mordrains.

,,   (Inc. 43).   Lancelot comes to Grail Castle.
Partial fulfilment of his Quest.

,.   (Inc. 48).   The three questers come to the Grail
Castle.

On looking at the list we notice that the Conte du Graal knows
of three visits on the part of the principal hero to the Castle of
Talismans : 1, 2, 3, or 1, 2–4, 5, and of one visit (or two) of the
secondary hero; whilst Wolfram, the Mabinogi, and the Didot-
Perceval know of two only. Heinrich von dem Türlin gives only
one visit to *his* chief hero, though he mentions a former one by the
secondary hero. In Wolfram, and the Didot-Perceval, the incident
may be compared in the Conte du Graal with 1 and 2; in the
Mabinogi with 1 and 5; in Heinrich with 6. The Queste forms of
the incident are obviously dependent upon those of the Conte du
Graal, although they have been strongly modified. As for 7, it
would seem to be a form of the incident which has been entirely
unaffected by the Christian symbolism which has influenced all the
others.

It will be advisable to recapitulate the leading features of the
incident as found in the different versions. Where the summaries
in Chapter II afford detailed information about it, the recapitulation
will be brief, but it will be necessary to give at least one version
at much greater length than heretofore.

In the Conte du Graal (1) the hero finds a King fishing, who
directs him to his castle. Just as he deems the fisher has deceived
him the castle bursts upon his sight. He enters, is led into a
square room wherein is a bed sitting on which is an old man
wrapped in sables; before him is a great fire of dry wood; 400 men
might sit in the hall. The King rises to greet him; as they sit, a
squire enters with a sword which had but two fellows, sent by the
King's niece for the hero to whom it was destined. The hall is
light as it may be. A squire enters holding a lance by the middle;
all can behold the drop of blood which flows from the point upon the
holder's hand. There follow him two squires with candlesticks, each
with ten candles, in either hand; a damsel holding a Grail, which
gives out a light as greater than that of the candles as the sun

outshines the stars; and another damsel with a plate of fine gold. The procession passes from one into the other room. The hero refrains from asking who is served by the Grail. After playing at chess with the King they dine, and again the Grail passes, uncovered, at each dish. The hero would fain ask what was done with it, and is about to do so, but puts off the question. On the morrow he sees no one in the castle, the doors of the rooms he had been in the eve before are shut, no one answers; and, mounting his horse, which he finds ready saddled, he sets forth over the drawbridge, which closes of itself behind him, without learning why lance bleeds or whither the Grail is borne. (2) At the second visit the hero comes into a magnificent room, ornamented with fine gold and stars of silver, wherein on a vermeil couch the rich King is sitting. The hero is fain forthwith to ask about Grail and bleeding lance, but must sit him down by the rich King and tell of his adventures, about the chapel in which lay the dead Knight, and the black hand, the child in the tree and the tree full of candles. The King makes him eat before answering his questions. Whilst at meat a damsel, fairer than flowers in April, enters with the Holy Grail, another with the lance, a squire with the broken sword. The hero asks about these talismans. But first the King answers the questions about the earlier wonders; the talismans he will tell of after meat. The hero insists to know about the sword. The King bids him put it together—can he do so he will learn about the Knight in the Chapel, and after that about the talismans. Save for one flaw the hero succeeds, whereupon the King says he knows no one in the world better than he, embraces him, and yields him up all in his house. The squire who brought the sword returns, wraps it in a cendal, and carries it off.

2A. The King bids the hero eat. Lance and Grail, and a fair silver dish pass before them, the latter held by a damsel. The hero sighs and begs to learn about these three. He is told about lance, Grail, Grail-

4. The hero would hold it sin if he did not ask concerning the Grail. The King first submits him to the sword test.* The existence of the flaw is apparently held to constitute failure, due to the hero's sin

---

* For the second time, if Gerbert's continuation be really intended for our present text of Gautier, and if Potvin's summary of Gerbert is to be relied upon; Birch-Hirschfeld seemingly differs from him here, and makes the King at once mention the flaw.

bearing damsel, dish-bearing damsel, and in answer to further questions, learns the history of the
broken sword, and of the chapel
haunted by the black hand.   After
sleeping in a splendid bed* he sets
forth on the morrow on the sword
quest (the slaying of Partinal).

3. Having accomplished which, and
   lighted chancewise upon the Grail
   Castle, the King, apprised by a
   squire and forthwith healed, meets
   the hero who shows him head and
   shield.   At table lance and Grail
   pass, borne by two maidens; de-
   lectable meats fill the dishes—all
   are filled and satisfied who behold
   the Holy Grail and the lance that
   bleeds.   Thereafter enters a squire
   holding a silver dish covered with
   red samite ; the talismans pass
   thrice; the King thanks the hero
   for having slain his enemy and
   thereby rid him of great torment.
   Asks his name, learns that he is
   his nephew, and offers him his
   kingdom.

in quitting his mother so abruptly.
In the night the hero has a vision,
which warns him to hasten to his
sister's aid.   On the morrow the
Grail Castle has vanished.   Mounting his horse, which stands ready
saddled, he rides forth.   After a
vain essay to gain entrance to a
magnificent castle, in which he
breaks his sword, and thereby
loads upon himself seven further
years of adventure, but learns how
the sword may be made whole
again, he finds the land which the
day before was waste fertile and
peopled.   The peasants hail him:
the townsmen come forth in his
honour—for through him the folk
have won back lands and riches.
A damsel tells him how : at the
Court of the Fisher King he had
asked about the Grail.   At her
castle he has his sword mended.
(Later the hero learns that his
failure to win the Grail comes
from his not having wedded his
lady-love).

5. Hero is directed by a cross to the
   Court of the Fisher King.   The
   latter makes him sit by his side
   and tell his adventures, when he
   would fain learn about the Grail.
   The same procession then passes
   as in (2), save that sword instead
   of being broken is simply described
   as not resoldered.   The hero says
   he has been twice before with the
   King, and reproaches him for not
   having answered his questions,
   although he had resoldered the
   sword to the King's great joy.
   The King then bids him shake the
   sword, which he does, and the flaw
   disappears.   The King is overjoyed, and the hero is now worthy
   of knowing everything.†

In comparing with these versions of the incident that found
in the Didot-Perceval, we find that the hero at his first visit is
welcomed by the squires of the castle, clad in a scarlet cloak,

---

* It may be worth notice that v. 35,473 is the same as Chrestien, v. 4,533.

† It is evident that, although in the MS. in which this version is found it is
followed by Manessier's section, the poem was intended by Gerbert to end here.

and placed upon a rich bed, whilst four sergeants apprise Brons
of his arrival, and the latter is carried into the hall where sits
the hero, who rises to greet him. Brons questions him before
they sit down to meat. The mystic procession is formed by squire
with lance bleeding, damsel with silver dish, squire with the
vessel holding our Lord's blood. On the morrow the hero sees no
one, and finds all the doors open. At his second visit there is no
mention of difficulty in ◦finding the castle. This time the King
rises to greet him; they talk of many things and then sit down
to meat. Grail and worthy relics pass, and the hero asks who
is served by the vessel which the squire holds in his hands.
Straightway the King is healed and changed; overjoyed he first
asks the hero who he is, and, on learning it, tells him concerning
lance and Grail, and afterwards, at the bidding of a heavenly
voice, the secret words which Joseph taught him, Brons.

In the Mabinogi the castle lies on the other side of a meadow.
At his first visit the hero finds the gates open, and in the hall
a hoary-headed man sits, around whom are pages who rise to
receive the hero. Host and guest discourse and eat, seated
beside one another. The sword trial follows, and the hero is
declared to have arrived at two-thirds of his strength. The two
youths with the dripping spear enter, amid the lamentation of the
company, are followed by the two maidens with the salver wherein
is a man's head, and the outcry redoubles. On the morrow the
hero rides forth unmolested.

At the second visit the castle is described as being in a valley
through which runs a river. The grey-headed man found sitting
in the hall with Gwalchmai is described as lame.

So far we have recapitulated the leading features of Perceval's
dealings at the Talismans Castle in the Conte du Graal and in
the most closely allied versions. But Perceval, the chief hero, has,
as we have already seen, an under-study in Gauvain. And the
Gauvain form of the incident deserves as close examination as the
Perceval form.

(6) Gauvain has met a knight, stranger to him, with whom
he travels to Caerleon. Whilst in his company the stranger is slain
by a dart cast by whom no one knows. Before dying he bids

Gauvain take his arms and his horse; he knows not why he has been slain, he never harmed anyone. Gauvain suspects and accuses Kex, upon whom he vows to prove the murder, and sets forth to learn the unknown's name. After affronting the adventure of the black hand* in the chapel and long wanderings, he finds himself one evening at the opening of a dark, tree-covered road at whose further end he spies a light. Tired and fasting he lets his horse go at its will, and is led to a castle where he is received with great honour as though he were expected. But when he has changed his dress the castle folk see it is not he whom they thought. In the hall is a bier whereupon lie cross and sword and a dead knight. Canons and priests raise a great lamentation over the body. A crowned knight enters and bids Gauvain sit by his side. Then the Grail goes through the room, serving out meats in plenty, and acting the part of a steward, whereat Gauvain is astounded. He next sees a lance which drips blood into a silver cup. From out the same room whence come the talismans, the King issues, a sword in his hand, the sword of the dead knight, over whom he laments—on his account the land languishes. He bids Gauvain essay to make the sword whole, but Gauvain cannot, and is told his quest may not be accomplished. After his toils and wanderings Gauvain is sleepy, but he struggles against sleep, and asks about bleeding lance and sword and bier. Whilst the King is answering him he goes to sleep. On awakening he is on the sea shore, arms and steed by his side.† He then meets

---

* Told at other times, and notably by Gautier himself (Inc. 21), of Perceval, where the feature of a dead knight lying on the altar is added.

† According to the Montpellier MS., which here agrees substantially with Potvin's text (the Mons MS.), this is Gauvain's second visit to the Grail Castle. At his first visit he had been subjected to the sword test and had slept. The mystic procession is made up as follows :—Squire with lance ; maidens with plate ; two squires with candlesticks; fair maiden weeping, in her hands a " graal;" four squires with the bier, on which lies the knight and the broken sword. Gauvain would fain learn about these things, but is bidden first to make the sword whole. On his failure he is told

Vous n'avez par encore tant fet
D'armes, que vous doiez savoir, etc.,

and then goes to sleep. His awakening finds him in a marsh.

with the peasantry, and is told of the changed condition of the land in a passage already quoted (p. 87). Had he asked about the Grail " por coi il servoit," the land had been wholly freed.

Heinrich von dem Türlin's account of Gauvain's visit to the Grail Castle differs, as will be seen by the Summary, p. 27, which it is unnecessary to repeat, more from that of Gautier than from the Perceval visit of the Conte de Graal, with which it has the common feature, that the person benefitted by the transaction is the Lord of the Magic Castle. As will already have been noticed it stands alone in the conception that the inmates of the castle are under the enchantment of death-in-life from which the question frees them.

There still remains to be noticed (7) the incident of Perceval's visit to the Castle of Maidens, so closely analogous in certain details to the Grail Castle visit, and yet wholly disassociated from it in the conduct of the story. Perceval, wandering, sees across a river in fair meadow land a rich castle built of marble, yellow and vermeil. Crossing a bridge he enters, and the door at once closes behind him. No one is in the hall, in the centre of which is a table, and hanging to it by a steel chain a hammer. Searching the castle he still finds no one, and no one answers to his call. At length he strikes upon the table three blows with the hammer. A maiden appears, reproaches him, and disappears. Again he waits, and again he strikes three blows. A second damsel appears, and tells him if he strike afresh the tower will fall, and he be slain in its fall. But as he threatens to go on, the damsel offers to open the door and let him forth. He declares he will stay till morning, whereupon the damsel says she will call her mistress. The hero bids her haste as he is not minded to wait long, and warns her that he still holds the hammer. Other damsels then show themselves, disarm and tend the hero, and lead him through a splendid hall into a still more splendid one, wherein a hundred fair and courteous maidens, all of like age and mien, and richly dressed, rise at his approach and hail him as lord. The hero deems himself in paradise, and " sooth 'tis to be in paradise to be with dames and maids; so sweet they are, the devil can make naught of them, and 'tis better to follow them than to hearken to sermons preached in church for money." The dame of the castle bids the hero sit him down by her. "White she is as a lily, rosier than on a May morn a fresh blown rose when the dew has washed it." She asks him his name, and on hearing how he had wandered lonely three days ere meeting with the castle, tells him he might have wandered seven ere finding where to partake of bread and meat. He is well feasted. In reply to his questions about the castle, and how is it no man may be seen in it, he learns he is in the Maidens' Castle, all the inmates of one kin and land, of gentle birth; no mason put his hand to the castle, no serf toiled at it. Four maids built it, and in this wise: Whatever knight passed, and entering, beheld the door closed, and no man meeting him—if craven he struck no blow with the hammer, and on the morrow he went forth unheeded; but if wise and courteous he struck the table, and was richly entertained. As the lady tells this tale the hero, overcome with much journeying, falls asleep and is laid to bed by the maidens. On the morrow he wakes beneath a leafy oak, and never a house in sight.

It is surely superfluous to point out that the foregoing recapitulation of the various forms under which this incident has come down to us gives the last blow to the theory which makes Christian symbolism the starting point, and the Didot-Perceval the purest representative of the legend. We should have to admit not only that the later romance writers entirely misunderstood the sense of their model, but that, whilst anxiously casting about in every direction for details with which to overlay it, they neglected one of its most fertile hints—that of the secret words handed down through Joseph from Christ Himself to the successful Grail quester. What a mine of adventures would not Gautier, Gerbert, and all the other unknown versifiers, who added each his quota to the Conte, have found in those "secret words?" Nay, more, we must admit that so much in love were they with this incident they misunderstood, that they repeated it in half-a-dozen varying forms, and finally eliminated from it every trace of its original element. There are theories which ask too much and which must be set on one side, even if one has nothing equally ingenious and symmetrical to set in their place.

Three things strike one in considering this incident apart from
the other adventures with which it is associated; the want of
consistency in those versions which, formally, are closely related,
an inconsistency which we have already noted in dealing with the
legend as a whole; the repetition of the same incident with almost
similar details, but with a different animating conception; and the
fact that some of the secondary forms testify to that same thread of
story which we have already extracted from the comparison of the
Mabinogi and the Conte du Graal in their entirety. Not only is
the conception of the Quest different in Chrestien and Manessier or
Chrestien-Gerbert, but the details are different, the centre of interest being shifted from the omitted question to the broken sword.
In Manessier the *dénoûment* is brought about without any reference
to the question, in Gerbert the reference is of the most perfunctory
kind.   Again we find the same machinery of Grail, lance, and other
talismans, which in Chrestien-Manessier serves to bring about the
hero's vengeance on his uncle's murderer, in Chrestien-Gerbert
the re-union of the lovers and the winning of the Grail Kingship,
used in the Gawain quest with the evident object of compass-
ing vengeance upon the slayer of the unknown knight.   And,
thirdly, this secondary form is in close agreement with the
Mabinogi—here, as there, the sword test takes place at the Fisher
King's; here, as there, it immediately precedes the passing of
the talismans ; here, as there, it is only partially successful; here,
as there, is a tangible reminder of the object of the quest, in
the dead body of the unknown knight in the one case, in the
head swimming in blood in the other.   And here we may note that
of the two forms in which the *Queste* reproduces this incident,
the one which holds the more prominent position in the narrative,
the one of which Lancelot is the hero, closely resembles that
secondary form in the Conte du Graal which is connected with
Gawain.   The wounded knight whom Lancelot beholds at the
crossways borne into the chapel upon a bier, and clamouring for
the succour of. the Grail, recalls forcibly the dead knight of the
Gawain quest.   It is, perhaps, still more significant that when
the Queste does reproduce the Perceval form, it is only in its
externals, and the mystic vessel, which in the older version is

obviously a means of achieving the quest, has, in the later one, become the end of that quest.

It seems impossible to resist the following conclusions:—The many forms of the incident found in the Grail romances are not variants of one, and that an orderly and logical original; they testify to the fact that in the body of popular tradition which forms the basis of these romances the incident of the visit to a magic castle was a common one, that it entered into the thread of stories, somewhat similar in outline and frequently centered in the same hero, but differing essentially in conception, and that the forms in the romances which are most likely to keep close to the traditional model are those secondary ones with which the innovating spirit, whether due to the genius of the individual artist, or to intruding Christian symbolism, has least concerned itself. There is apparently but one case in the Conte du Graal, that of Perceval's visit to the Castle of Maidens, which has been modified by neither of these influences.

To accept these conclusions is to clear the ground. If we rid our minds of the idea that there is a *Grail legend*, a definite fixed sequence of incidents, we need not be discouraged if we fail to find a prototype for it in Celtic tradition or elsewhere. We shall be prepared to examine every incident of which the Grail is a feature upon its own merits, and satisfied if we can find analogies to this or that one. And by so doing we are more likely to discover the how and why of the development of the legends as we find them in the romances.

Leaving subsidiary details out of account, we may bring all the instances in which the Grail appears under two formulas : that of the kinsman avenging a blood feud by the means of the three magic talismans, sword and lance and vessel ; and that of the visit to the Bespelled Castle, the inmates of which enjoy, thanks to the magic vessel, a supernaturally prolonged life, from which they are released by the hero's question concerning that vessel.   The one we may call the feud quest, the other the unspelling quest. The Proto-Mabinogi belonged, as we have already seen (*supra*, p. 139), to the first class, and accordingly we find that all relating to the question is obviously interpolated from Chrestien. Chrestien's model belonged, in all probability if not wholly, chiefly to the first class, and accordingly we find that Manessier, certainly more faithful than Chrestien to that original, lays no stress upon the question. But in Chrestien himself there is a mixture of the two formulas ; the question and the food-producing qualities of the magic vessel have been incorporated in the feud formula. Once started upon this track the legend continues to mingle the formulas. The mystic procession, which probably owes its form to Chrestien, is repeated with monotonous sameness by his continuators ; the machinery of the feud quest almost invariably doubles that of the visit to the Bespelled Castle, and vice versâ. Thus Heinrich von dem Türlin, along with the most archaic presentment of the unspelling quest, has that procession of the talismans which properly belongs to the feud quest ; and, to complete his conception, we must turn to incidents at present set in the framework of the other formula. For the effect upon the land produced by the hero's action at the Castle of Talismans is obviously analagous to, though of directly contrary nature to, that produced upon the inmates of the Bespelled Castle. They are dead though they seem quick, the land is full of life though it seems waste. The question which frees the one from the spell of life-in-death, frees the other from the spell of death-in-life.* The Didot-Perceval has the complete conception. Perceval's question not only releases Brons, who may not die until then, but it also ends the enchantment of Britain.

The identity of hero in stories originally dissimilar was one reason for the confusion between the two formulas ; the nature of the Grail was another. Its attributes were in all probability not very clearly defined in the immediate models of the French romance writers; these found it enveloped in mysterious haze, which simple story-tellers, such as Gautier, did not try to clear up, and which

---

* It may be conjectured that the magic vessel which preserves to this enchanted folk.the semblance of life passes into the hero's possession when he asks about it, and that deprived of it their existence comes to an end, as would that of the Anses without the Apples of Iduna. I put this into a note, as I have no evidence in support of the theory. But read in the light of this conjecture some hitherto unnoticed legend may supply the necessary link of testimony.

gave free play to the mystic imaginings of those writers who used romance as a vehicle for edification. The one tangible thing about it in stories of the one class, its food producing-power, has left its trace upon every one of the romances. But we shall also find in our survey of Celtic literature that this attribute, as well as that of healing or restoring to life, is found indifferently in stories of both the classes, to the fusion of which we refer the Grail legends in their present form. Another link between the two formulas is formed by the sword. It is almost invariably found associated with the healing vessel of balsam in task stories connected with the feud quest of the Mabinogi and the Conte du Graal; it is also a frequent feature in the legend of the unsuccessful visit to the Bespelled Castle.* Finally, the most important reason for running into one the stories derived from these two formulas, and the one which could hardly fail to lead to the fusion, is to be found in the identity of the myth which underlies both conceptions. The castle to which the avenger must penetrate to win the talismans, and that to which the hero comes with the intent of freeing its lord, are both symbols of the otherworld.

Bearing in mind this double origin of the Grail, and reviewing once more the entire cycle, we note that, whilst it is that presentment of the magic vessel due to the second formula which is most prominent in the romances, the feud quest has furnished more and more varied sequences of incident, and is the staple of the oldest literary Celtic form (the Proto-Mabinogi) and of those North French forms which are most closely akin to it. Here the magic vessel is at best one of three equally potent treasures; as a matter of fact its *rôle* in this section of the romances is, as we have seen,

---

* Nearly all the objections to the view suggested in the text may be put aside as due to insufficient recognition of the extent to which the two formulas have been mingled, but there is one which seems to me of real moment. The wasting of the land which I have looked upon as belonging to the unspelling formula, is traced by the Queste to the blow struck by King Lambar against King Urlain, a story which, as we have seen, is very similar to that which forms the groundwork of one at least of the models followed by the Conte du Graal in its version of the feud quest. It does not seem likely that the Queste story is a mere echo of that found in the Conte du Graal, nor that the fusion existed so far back as in a model common to both. But the second alternative is possible.

inferior to that of the sword. Obviously intended to be the immediate cause of restoration to life or health of the hero's kinsman,
its functions have been minimised until they have been forgotten.
If this is so already in the Proto-Mabinogi and in the model of
the Conte du Graal, we may expect to find that elsewhere in Celtic
tradition the magic vessel is of less account than sword or lance.

We should likewise misconceive the character of popular tradition
if we expected to find certain attributes rigidly ascribed to the
mystic vessel in this or that set of stories. The confusion we have
noted in the romances may be itself derived from older traditions.
Certain it is that in what may be looked upon as the oldest account
of the vessel* in Celtic literature (although the form in which it has
reached us is comparatively modern), there is a vessel of abundance
associated with three other talismans, two of them being sword and
lance. The Tuatha de Danann (the race of fairies and wizards
which plays a part in Irish tradition analogous to that of Gwydion ap
Don, Gwynn ap Nudd, and their kin in Welsh) so runs the tradition preserved by Keating in his History of Ireland (Book I, ed. by
Joyce, Dublin, 1880, p. 117), had four treasures : The Lia Fail,
the stone of Fate or Virtue (" now in the throne upon which is
proclaimed the King of the Saxons," i.e., the stone brought by
Edward I., from Scone) ; the sword that Lug† Lamhfhada (Lug
the Longhanded) was wont to use ; the spear the same Lug used
in battle ; the cauldron of the Dagda, " a company used not ever go
away from it unsatisfied." Keating followed old and good sources,
and although the passage I have underlined is not to be found in
all MSS. of his work (e.g., it is missing in that translated by
Halliday), and although the verse which he quotes, and which probably goes back to the eleventh century, whilst the traditions which

---

* I do not follow M. Hucher upon the (as it seems to me) very insecure
ground of Gaulish numismatic art. The object which he finds figured in pre-
Christian coins may be a cauldron—and it may not—and even if it is a cauldron
it may have no such significance as he ascribes to it.

† Cf. as to Lug D'Arbois de Jubainville, Cycle Mythologique Irlandais;
Paris, 1884, p. 178. He was revered by all Celtic races, and has left his trace in
the name of several towns, chief among them Lug-dunum = Lyons. In so far as
the Celts had departmental gods, he was the god of handicraft and trade ; but
cf. as to this Rhys, Hibb. Lect., p. 427-28.

it embodies may be regarded as a couple of centuries older, does not mention this property of the Dagda's* Cauldron, it may, I think, be assumed that the tradition here noticed is genuine, and that a vessel akin to the Grail, as well as talismans akin to those that accompany the Grail, formed part of the gear of the oldest Celtic divinities.†

This conclusion appears no rash one when we consider the further references to the cauldron in Middle Irish Literature. The Battle of Magh Rath, a semi-historical romance relating to events which took place in the seventh century, is ascribed by its editor, Dr. J. O'Donovan, to the latter half of the twelfth century. It relates (pp. 51, *et seq.*) how the sons of the King of Alba sought to obtain from their father the "Caire Ainsicen" so called, because "it was the caire or cauldron which was used to return his own proper share to each, and no party ever went away from it unsatisfied, for whatever quantity was put into it there was never boiled of it but what was sufficient for the company according to their grade or rank." The mediæval story-teller then goes on to instance similar cauldrons to be met with in the older history of Ireland. These may nearly all be referred to the oldest heroic Irish cycle, the Ultonian, of which Cuchulainn is the most prominent figure. This cycle, in its origin almost if not wholly mythic, was at an early date (probably as early as the eighth century) euhemerised, and its gods and demi-gods made to do duty as historical personages living at the beginning of the Christian era. It is, indeed, not improbable that actual historical events and personages of that period may have coloured and distorted the presentment of the myth ; and it is highly probable that the substance of these stories does go back to that age, as they are almost entirely free from any admixture of

---

* *Cf.* D'Arbois de Jubainville, *op. cit.*, p. 269–290. The Dagda—the good god—seems to have been head of the Irish Olympus. A legend anterior to the eleventh century, and belonging probably to the oldest stratum of Celtic myth, ascribes to him power over the earth : without his aid the sons of Miledh could get neither corn nor milk. It is, therefore, no wonder to find him possessor of the magic cauldron, which may be looked upon as a symbol of fertility, and, as such, akin to similar symbols in the mythology of nearly every people.

† *Cf.* as to the mythic character of the Tuatha de Danann, D'Arbois de Jubainville, *op. cit.*, and my review of his work, Folk-Lore Journal, June, 1884.

Christian elements, and such admixture as there is can be readily detected as the handiwork of the tenth and eleventh century monks by whom these tales were written in MSS. which have for the most part come down to us. The cauldron is found with the same properties as those set forth in the Battle of Magh Rath, in two of the most celebrated tales of this cycle, the Toghail Bruighne da Derga, and the Tale of Mac Datho's pig.

Turning from Irish to Welsh literature we may note that the Grail has frequently been compared with the cauldron of Bran in the Mabinogi of Branwen, the daughter of Llyr. I have dealt with this tale fully (Folk-Lore Record, Vol. V.), and see no reason to depart from the conclusion I then arrived at; namely, that it goes back in the main to the eleventh or tenth century. Here, the revivifying power of the vessel is dwelt upon, " The property of it is that if one of thy men be slain to-day, and be cast therein, the morrow he will be as well as ever he was at his best, except that he will not regain his speech." We cannot fail to recall that in the Queste which, as far as the Grail itself is concerned, must be referred on the whole to the feud quest formula, when the sacred vessel appears the assembled company is struck dumb.*

Later Celtic folk-literature has followed the Mabinogi rather than the older Irish legend in its account of the mystic vessel. Where it appears in the folk-tale its function is to heal or to bring back to life. We may leave out of account for the present the references in the Welsh "bardic" literature to the cauldron of Ceridwen, chief among which is that in the Mabinogi of Taliesin. I am far from thinking that this literature deserves the wholesale condemnation that has been passed upon it, but it has been too little and too uncritically studied to afford, as yet, a firm basis for investigation. We are on surer ground in dealing with the living folk-tale. Thus the tale of Fionn's Enchantment, although belonging more properly

---

* I at one time thought that the prohibition to reveal the "secret words," which is such an important element in Robert de Borron's version, might be referred to the same myth-root as the instances in the text. There is little or no evidence to sustain such a hazardous hypothesis. Nevertheless it is worth while drawing attention in this place to that prohibition, for which I can offer no adequate explanation.

to the other formula, may be noticed here as containing a cup of balsam, the washings of which restore the maimed Fionn to complete health. Mr. Campbell, who has noted the tale, remarks that the cup of healing is common in all the Fenian stories, which is what we should naturally expect, seeing the close connection between Fionn and Peredur (Rev. Celt. I., p. 194). Other instances have already been given in Chapter VI. of the appearance of the vessel of balsam in connection with the glaive of light, and of its use in bringing back to life the hero's enemies. And here it may be noted that almost the very mode in which it is introduced in the folk-tales may be paralleled from the romances. The Grail appears to Perceval and Hector, lying well nigh dead upon the field of battle, and makes them whole, even as the vessel of balsam re-vivifies the dead warriors whom Conall Gulban has just slain, and heals the latter. It is, perhaps, only a coincidence that the angel in the one, the Carlin in the other case, appear in a great flashing of light. But, as a rule, in those task-stories which otherwise present such close similarities to the feud quest of the Proto-Ma-binogi and the Conte du Graal, the mystic vessel has dropped out altogether, and the sword is the chief if not the only talisman. This is the case in Campbell, I., the young King of Easaidh Ruadh, and in XLVI. Mac Iain Direach. In one instance the glaive of light is met with outside the task group, in Campbell XLI., the Widow and her Daughters, variant ii (a Bluebeard story), and here it is found associated with the vessel of balsam. In the folk-tales, then, as in one section of the Conte du Graal, the healing vessel is decidedly of less account than the avenging or destroying weapon. This, as the sword, plays such an important part in the French romances that an examination of its *rôle* in Celtic literature will repay examination.

Besides the already quoted instances in which the sword of light accompanies the vessel of balsam as one of the treasures which reward the hero's quest, but in which it does not otherwise affect the march of the story, we find others in which the sword is either that weapon which causes the woe, the subject of the story, or else is the one means of testing the hero's fitness for his quest. In either case it is parallel to the sword of the Grail romances. Apart from these special instances there are general references in the oldest Irish literature to the quasi-supernatural nature attributed to the sword. Thus the Leabhar Gabhala, or Book of Invasions, the tenth and eleventh century tract in which Irish mythology was euphemerised into an historical relation of the pre-Christian invasion of Ireland, has a passage relating to the sword of Tethra, King of the Fomori,* which spake, and, adds the Christian scribe, the ancient Irish adored swords.† This is borne out by a passage in the Seirglige Conculainn, a story belonging to the Ultonian cycle, which Mr. Whitley Stokes has translated (Rev. Celt. I., 260). The men of Ulster, when showing their trophies, had their swords upon their thighs, "for their swords used to turn against them where they made a false trophy."

The Christian transcriber notes that it was reasonable for the pagan Irish to trust their swords "because demons used to speak from out them." To return to the sword of Tethra. The most famous battle of Irish mystic history is that of Mag-Tured, in which the Tuatha de Danann, the gods of light and life, overcome their enemies the Fomori. Ogma, the champion of the Tuatha de Danann, wins the sword of Tethra, and as he cleans it it tells him the many and great feats it had wrought.

It is, however, in the second of the great heroic cycles of the ancient Irish, the Fenian or Ossianic, that we find the sword put to a use which strongly recalls that of the romances. Not until the hero is able to wield the weapon so that it break not in his hand, or to weld it together so that no flaw appears,‡ is he fit to set

---

* Powers of darkness and death. Tethra their king reigns in an island home. It is from thence that the maiden comes to lure away Connla of the Golden Hair, as is told in the Leabhar na-h-Uidhre, even as the Grail messenger comes to seek Perceval—" 'tis a land in which is neither death nor old age—a plain of never ending pleasure," the counterpart, in fact, of that Avalon to which Arthur is carried off across the lake by the fay maiden, that Avalon which, as we see in Robert de Borron, was the earliest home of the Grail-host

† Cf. D'Arbois de Jubainville, op. cit. p. 188.

‡ When Cuchulainn was opposing the warriors of Ireland in their invasion of Ulster one of his feats is to make smooth chariot-poles out of rough branches of trees by passing them through his clenched hand, so that however bent and knotted they were they came from his hands even, straight, and smooth. Tain bo Cualgne, quoted by Windisch, Rev. Celt., Vol. V.

forth on the quest. In Campbell's LXXVII., " How the Een was
set up," Fionn applies for his sword to Ullamh Lamhfhada*
(Ullamh the Longhanded), who gives him the most likely sword
and the best he found. The hero takes it, shakes it, casts it out
of the wooden handle and discards it. Thrice is this repeated, and
when the right weapon is in Fionn's hand, he quells utterly all he
sees.† Now how had Fionn obtained this sword originally? By
slaying black Arcan, his father's slayer. It may, I think, be looked
upon as certain that in an earlier form of the story, the weapon in
question would turn out to be the one with which the treacherous
deed was done, and Fionn, a counterpart of Peredur in his bringing
up, would also be his counterpart in this incident‡ For the sword
with which Partinal slew Goon Desert is treasured up for the use
of Perceval, but only after a repeated essay is he held worthy of
it.§

The sword incident reappears in a tale of Campbell's, Manus
(Vol. III.), which presents some very remarkable analogies with the
romances. Manus is driven into various adventures by his aunt;

---

* This epithet recalls Lug, of whom it is the stock designation. Now Lug was
par excellence the craftsman's god ; he, too, at the battle of Mag Tured acted
as a sort of armourer-general to the Tuatha de Danann. A dim reminiscence
of this may be traced in the words which the folk-tale applies to Ullamh l.f., " he
was the one special man for taking their arms."

† *Cf.* my Aryan Expulsion and Return formula, pp. 8, 13, for variants of
these incidents in other stories belonging to this cycle and in the allied folk-tales.

‡ This incident is only found in the living Fionn-*sage*, being absent from
all the older versions, and yet, as the comparison with the allied Perceval sage
shows, it is an original and essential feature. How do the advocates of the
theory that the Ossianic cycle is a recent mass of legend, growing out of the lives
and circumstances of historical men, account for this development along the
lines of a formula with which, *ex hypothesi*, the legend has nothing to do?
The Fionn-*sage*, it is said, has been doctored in imitation of the Cuchulainn-*sage*,
but the assertion (which though boldly made has next to no real foundation)
cannot be made in the case of the Conte du Graal. Mediæval Irish bards and
unlettered Highland peasants did not conspire together to make Fionn's
adventures agree with those of Perceval.

§ In the Gawain form of the feud quest found in Gautier, the knight whose
death he sets forth to avenge is slain by the cast of a dart. Can this be brought
into connection with the fact that Perceval slays with a cast of his dart the Red
Knight, who, according to the Thornton romance, is his father's slayer.

an armourer of his grandfather offers to get him a sword ; but all given to him he breaks save the armourer's old sword, and it beat him to break that. The armourer then gives him a cloth, " When thou spreadest it to seek food or drink, thou wilt get as thou usest." Subsequently, helped by a lion, he achieves many feats. He comes to the help of the White Gruagach by fetching the blood of a venemous horned creature belonging to the King over the Great World, by which alone the White Gruagach could be restored to life when the magic trout with which his life was bound up had been slain. Afterwards he accompanies him against his enemy the Red Gruagach, who is slain, and his head stuck on a stake. This Red Gruagach is apparently the father of the aunt who so persecutes Manus.*

This examination of the sword incident shows that the Mabinogi has preserved the original form of the story, and links afresh this portion of the Conte du Graal with the other Celtic stories belonging to the Expulsion and Return formula group, with which it has so much else in common. In all the formula-stories, except those of the Conte du Graal and the Proto-Mabinogi, the hero has to avenge his father, not his uncle; and it is highly suggestive that at least one version of the Perceval cycle (the Thornton romance) follows suit. With this remark we may take leave of the feud quest.

Many and interesting as have been the parallels from the older Celtic literature to the feud quest, they are far outweighed by those which that literature affords to the second formula—the visit to the Bespelled Castle—which we have noted in the romances.

From the recapitulation (*supra*, pp. 173, *et. seq.*) we may learn several things. The castle lies, as a rule, on the other side of a river ; the visitor to it is under a definite obligation ; he must either do a

---

* This prose tale precedes an oral version of one of the commonest Fenian poems, which in its present shape obviously goes back to the days when the Irish were fighting against Norse invaders. The poem, which still lives in Ireland as well as in the Highlands, belongs to that later stage of development of the Fenian cycle, in which Fionn and his men are depicted as warring against the Norsemen. It is totally dissimilar from the prose story summarised above, and I am inclined to look upon the prose as belonging to a far earlier stage in the growth of the cycle, a stage in which the heroes were purely mythical and their exploits those of mythical heroes generally.

certain thing, as, *e.g.*, in Perceval's visit to the Castle of Maidens, strike on the table three blows with the hammer, or he must put a certain question, or again he must abstain from certain acts, as that of falling asleep (Perceval and Gawain) or drinking* (Gawain, in Heinrich von dem Türlin). Disregard of the obligation is punished in various ways. In the case of the Castle of Maidens the craven visitor is allowed to fare forth unheeded without beholding the marvels of the castle; but, as a rule, the hero of the adventure finds himself on the morrow far away from the castle, which has vanished completely. The inmates of this castle fall into two classes—they are supernatural beings like the maidens, who have apparently no object to gain from their mortal visitor, but who love heroism for its own sake, and are as kindly disposed towards the mortal hero in the folk-lore and mythology of the Celts as gods, and especially goddesses, are in the mythic lore of all other races; or they suffer from an over-lengthened life, from which the hero alone can release them. This latter feature, seen to perfection only in Heinrich von dem Türlin, is apparent in the Didot-Perceval, and has, in the Conte du Graal, supplied the figure of the old man, father to the Fisher King, nourished by the Grail.

These features sufficiently indicate that the Magic Castle is the realm of the other world. The dividing water is that across which lies Tír-na n-Og, the Irish Avalon, or that Engelland dwelt in by the shades which the inhabitants of the Belgian coast figured in the west.† In Celtic lore the earliest trace of this realm is found, as is the earliest trace of Grail and sword, in connection with the Tuatha de Danann, that race of dispossessed immortals which lives on in the hollow hill sides, and is ever ready to aid and cherish the Irish mythic heroes. The most famous embodiment of this conception in Irish myth is the Brug na Boine, the dwelling place of Oengus,‡

---

* The prohibition seems to be an echo of the widely-spread one which forbids the visitor to the otherworld tasting the food of the dead, which, if he break, he is forfeit to the shades. The most famous instance of this myth is that of Persephone.

† *Cf.* Procopius quoted by Elton, Origins of English History, p. 84.

‡ Prof. Rhys, Hibbert Lectures for 1886, looks upon him as a Celtic Zeus. He dispossessed his father of the Brug by fraud, as Zeus dispossessed Kronos by force.

son of the Dagda, and the earliest account of it is that contained in the Book of Leinster, the second of the two great Irish vellums written down in the twelfth century. It is a land of Cockayne; in it are fruit trees ever loaded with fruit, on the board a pig ready roasted which may not be eaten up, vessels of beer which may not be emptied, and therein no man dies.* But Oengus is not the only one of the Tuatha de Danann who has such a fairy palace. The dwelling place of Lug is of the same kind, and in the story of the Conception of Cuchulainn,† which tells how the god carried off Dechtire, sister of Conchobor, and re-incarnated himself in her as the great Ulster hero, we learn that when Conchobor and his men go in search of Dechtire and her fifty maidens, they first come to a small house wherein are a man and woman; the house suddenly becomes a splendid mansion,‡ therein are the vanished maidens in the shape of birds (and all sorts of goods, and dishes of divers sorts, known and unknown; never did they have a better night, in the morning they found themselves houseless, birdless in the east of the land, and they went back to Emain Macha).§ Although no prohibition is mentioned the similarity in parts of this story, which, it must be repeated, is older than the introduction of Christianity in Ireland, to the romances is evident. Another famous Brug of the Tuatha de Danann is that of Manannan Mac Lir. Among the visitors was Bran, the son of Febal, whose story may be found in the Leabhar na h' Uidhre, the oldest of the great Irish vellums.‖ One day as he was alone in his palace there came to him soft, sweet music, and he fell asleep. When he awoke a silver branch, covered with flowers, was at his side. A short while after, as he was in the midst of his kinsfolk, his chiefs, and his nobles, an unknown damsel appeared, and bid him to her in the

---

* D'Arbois de Jubainville, *op. cit.*, p. 275. Rhys, *op. cit.*, p. 149.

† M. Duvau, Revue Celtique, Vol. IX., No. 1, has translated the varying versions of the story.

‡ Like many of the older Irish tales the present form is confused and obscure, but it is easy to arrive at the original.

§ The part in brackets is found in one version only of the story. Of the two versions each has retained certain archaic features not to be found in the other.

‖ Summarised by D'Arbois de Jubainville, *op. cit.*, p. 323.

land of *Sidhe*, and then vanished, and with her the branch. Bran set sail, and with him thirty men. After two days' wandering they met Manannan Mac Lir. They continued their journey until they came to an island dwelt in solely by women; their queen it was who had sent for Bran. He stayed with her a while, and then came back to Ireland.

But the most famous of the visits to the Brug of Manannan is that of Cormac Mac Art, whom the Irish legendary annals place in the third century of our era, and bring into connection with Fionn. The story, though only known to us from later MSS., can be traced back to the tenth century at least, as the title of it figures in a list preserved in the Book of Leinster, and as it is apparently alluded to by the eleventh century annalist, Tighernach.* The following summary is from a version, with English translation by Mr. Standish Hayes O'Grady, in the third volume of the Ossianic Society's publications.

Of a time that Cormac was in Liathdruim he saw a youth having in his hand a glittering fairy branch, with nine apples of red gold upon it.† And this was the manner of that branch, that when any one shook it, men wounded and women with child would be lulled to sleep by the sound of the very sweet fairy music which those apples uttered, and no one on earth would bear in mind any want, woe, or weariness of soul when that branch was shaken for him. Cormac exchanged for this branch his wife and son and daughter, overcoming their grief by shaking the branch. But after a year, Cormac went in search of them. And he chanced upon a land where many marvels were wrought before his eyes, and he understood them not. At length he came to a house wherein was a very tall couple, clothed in clothes of many colours, and they bade him stay. And the man of the house brought a log

---

* D'Arbois de Jubainville, p. 326.

† Otto Küpp, Z.f.D. Phil. xvii, i, 68, examining Wolfram's version sees in the branch guarded by Gramoflanz and broken by Parzival a trace of the original myth underlying the story. Gramoflanz is connected with the Magic Castle (one of the inmates of which is his sister), or with the otherworld. Küpp's conjecture derives much force from the importance given to the branch in the Irish tales as part of the gear of the otherworld.

and a wild boar, and if a quarter of the boar was put under a quarter of the log, and a true story was told, the meat would be cooked. At Cormac's request the host told the first story, how that he had seven swine with which he could feed the world, for if the swine were slain, and their bones put in the sty, on the morrow they would be whole again; and the hostess the second, how that the milk of her seven white kine would satisfy the men of the world. Cormac knew them for Manannan and his wife, and then told his story how he had lost and was seeking for wife and children. Manannan brought in the latter, and told Cormac it was he who gave him the branch, that he might bring him to that house. Then they sat down to meat, and the table-cloth was such that no food, however delicate, might be demanded of it, but it should be had without doubt; and the drinking cup was such that if a false story was told before it, it went in four pieces, and if a true one, it came whole again, and therewith was the faith of Cormac's wife made evident. And Manannan gave branch and cloth and goblet to Cormac, and thereafter they went to slumber and sweet sleep. Where they rose upon the morrow was in the pleasant Liathdruim.

The foregoing examples have been akin to the incident of the Maiden Castle. We have seen the race of immortals caring for the sons of men, signalling out and alluring to themselves the brave and wise hero. In the tales we are now about to examine the benefit conferred by the visitor upon the inmates of the Magic Castle is insisted upon. But we must first notice a tale which presents many of the incidents of the Grail romances, without actually belonging to the same story group as they. In Campbell's No. LXXXVI, the Daughter of King Under the Waves, Diarmaid, the fairest and bravest of the Fenian heroes, weds a fay who, as her description indicates, belongs to the same order of beings as the damsels who lure away Connla and Bran, the son of Febal. She comes to him in loathly guise, and the other heroes shrink from her; but Diarmaid, courteous as he is brave, gives her the shelter of tent and bed and has his reward. She builds for him such a castle as the fay mistress of the Knight of the Black Tomb (*supra*, p. 17) builds for her lover. But she warns him that after a threefold reproach as to how he found her she would have to leave him. Through the cunning of Fionn he is led to break the taboo and "it was in a mosshole he awoke on the morrow. There was no castle, or a stone left of it on another." Diarmaid sets forth to seek his wife, he finds her ailing to death, and to be cured she must have three draughts from the cup of the King of the Plain of Wonder. Helped by a little russet man, he gets the talisman, as was prophesied of him; but, advised by the little russet man, he gives the maiden to drink out of a certain well, which changes their love into aversion, and he returns to the light of day.

This last feature should be noted as characteristic. The mortal lover always tires sooner than the fay mistress. Oisin cannot stay in Tír-na n-Og   Perceval gives but one night to the Lady of the Chessboard.

We now come to the " unspelling" stories, and I will cite in the first place one which is the most striking testimony I know of to the influence of this formula upon Celtic mythic lore. There is a widely spread folk-tale of a hero robbed of three magic gifts and getting them back thus ; by chance he eats some fruit or herb which changes him into an ass, causes his nose to grow, sets horns upon his head, or produces some equally unpleasant result. Another herb he finds heals him. Armed with specimens of either, he wins back his talismans. In Grimm it is No. 122, Der Krautesel, and in Vol. III., p. 201, variants are given. In one the hero is one of three soldiers, and he receives the gifts from a little grey man. But neither here nor in the variants given by Dr. R. Köhler (Orient und Occident, II., p. 124) is the opening the same as in Campbell's No. X.—The Three Soldiers.

The three come to a house in the wilderness dwelt in by three girls who keep them company at night, but disappear during the day. In the house is a table, overnight they eat off it, and when they rise the board is covered, and it would not be known that a bit had ever come off it. At the first night's close one soldier gets a purse never empty; at the second, the next one a cloth always filled with meat; and the third, the youngest (the hero), a transporting whistle. But as they leave he must needs ask them who they are, and they burst out crying, " They were under charms till they could find three lads who would spend three nights with them without putting a question—had he refrained they were free."

In one variant the time of probation lasts a year, and the talismans are : a cup that empties not, and a lamp of light, the tablecloth of meat, and a bed for rest. In another the damsels are swanmaids,* and the visitors are bidden " not to think nor order one of us to be with you in lying down or rising up."†

There can, I think, be little doubt that this last variant represents the oldest form of the story, and that the swanmaid damsels belong to the otherworld, as do the daughter of King Under the Waves and the maiden who fetches Connla. There is nothing surprising in swanmaids being the object of a taboo, this is so invariably the case in myth and folk-lore that it is needless to accumulate instances ; what is unique to my knowledge, I speak under correction, is the fact of these damsels being in possession of the talismans, one of which is so obviously connected with the Grail. It may be noted that the obligation laid upon the hero is the direct opposite of that in the Grail romances, in the one case a question must not be asked, in the other it must. In this respect Campbell's tale of course falls into line with all the widely spread and varying versions of the Melusine legend. The supernatural wife always forbids her husband some special act which, as is perhaps natural, he can never refrain from doing.

The next form of the Bespelled Castle legend is one which has attained far greater celebrity than any other on account of its traditional association with historical personages. It pictures the inmate of the castle as a King, with his warriors around him, sunk into magic sleep, and awaiting a signal to come forth and free his folk. To many English readers this legend will be more familiar in connection with Frederick Barbarossa‡ or with Holger

---

* This recalls the fact that Oengus of the Brug fell in love with a swanmaid. See text and translation Revue Celtique, Vol. III., pp. 341, *et. seq.* The story is alluded to in the catalogue of epic tales (dating from the tenth century) found in the Book of Leinster.

† In a variant from Kashmir (Knowles' Folk-tales of Kashmir, London, 1888 p. 75, *et. seq.*), Saiyid and Said, this tale is found embedded in a twin-brethren one.

‡ Frederick (I.) Barbarossa is a mistake, as old as the seventeenth century

the Dane than with any Celtic worthy. Yet the oldest historic instance is that of Arthur.* I have quoted (*supra*, p. 122) Gerald's words relating to the mountain seat of Arthur. A more definite tradition, and one closely resembling the episode in the Grail romances, is the one noted by Gervasius of Tilbury† (c. 1211 A.D.). A groom of the Bishop of Catania, following a runaway horse even to the summit of Mount Etna, found himself in a far reaching plain, full of all things delightful. A marvellous castle rose before him, wherein lay Arthur on a royal bed, suffering from the wound inflicted upon him by Modred his nephew, and Childeric the Saxon, and this wound broke out afresh each year. The King caused the horse to be given to the groom, and made him many rich presents.‡

This tradition of Arthur in Sicily raises some very interesting questions. For one thing it is a fresh example of the tremendous

---

(*cf.* Koch, Sage vom Kaiser Friedrich in Kyffhäuser, Leipzig, 1886), for Frederick II., the first German Emperor of whom the legend was told. The mistake was caused by the fact that Frederick took the place of a German red-bearded god, probably Thor, hence the later identification with the *red-bearded* Frederick, instead of with that great opponent of the Papacy whose death away in Italy the German party refused for many years to credit.

* Unless the passage relating to Carl the Great quoted by Grimm (D.M., III., 286) from Mon. Germ. Hist., Vol. VIII., 215, " inde fabulosum illud confictum de Carolo Magno, quasi de mortuis in id ipsum resuscitato, et alio nescio quo nihilominus redivivo," be older.

† Liebrecht's edition of the Otia Imperialia, Hanover, 1856, p. 12, and note p. 55.

‡ Martin Zur Gralsage, p. 31, arguing from the historical connection of Frederick II. with Sicily, thinks that the localisation of this Arthurian legend in that isle was the reason of its being associated with the Hohenstauffen; in other words, the famous German legend would be an indirect offshot of the Arthurian cycle. I cannot follow Martin here. I see no reason for doubting the genuineness of the traditions collected by Kuhn and Schwartz, or for disbelieving that Teutons had this myth as well as Celts. It is no part of my thesis to exalt Celtic tradition at the expense of German; almost all the parallels I have adduced between the romances and Celtic mythology and folk-lore could be matched from those of Germany. But the romances are historically associated with Celtic tradition, and the parallels found in the latter are closer and more numerous than those which could be recovered from German tradition. It is, therefore, the most simple course to refer the romances to the former instead of to the latter.

and immediate popularity of the Arthurian legend. It also shows with what rapidity a tradition, however remote in its origin from a particular spot, may associate itself with that. Of more immediate interest to us is the question whether this tradition has any direct connection with the Grail romances, whether it has shaped or been shaped by them. Martin refers the Maimed King of the romances to the same myth-root as the wounded Arthur waiting in Etna or in Avalon till his wound be healed and he come forth. It seems to me more likely that in so far as the wound is concerned there is a coincidence merely between the two stories, and that the Wounded King belongs properly to the feud quest. I do not, however, deny that the fact of the Lord of the Bespelled Castle, of the otherworld, being sometimes pictured as suffering from an incurable wound, may have aided that fusion of the two strains of legend which we find in the romances.

It is not my purpose to examine here in detail the innumerable versions of this widely-spread tradition*, the more so as I have been able to trace no exact parallel to that presentment of the story found in Heinrich von dem Türlin and in the Didot-Perceval. No other version of this form of the legend, to my knowledge, pictures the Bespelled King as awaiting the deliverance of death at the hands of his visitor. Before endeavouring to find a reason for the singularity of Heinrich's account, I will first quote one variant of the common form of the legend which has not been printed before save by myself in the Folk-Lore Journal, Vol. I., p. 193.† King Arthur sleeps bespelled in the ruins of (Richmond) Castle. Many have tried to find him but failed. One man only, Potter Thompson by name, wandering one night among the ruins chanced upon the hall wherein sat the King and his men around a table upon which lay a horn and a sword. Terrified, he turned and fled, and as he did so a voice sounded in his ears—

"Potter Thompson, Potter Thompson,
    Had'st thou blown the horn,
    Thou had'st been the greatest man
    That ever was born."

---

* See Grimm, D.M., Ch. XXXII.; Fitzgerald, Rev. Celt., IV., 198 ; and the references in Liebrecht, *op. cit.*

† Personally communicated by the Rev. Mr. Sorby, of Sheffield.

for then he would have freed Arthur from his magic sleep. Never again could he reach that hall.

This version, besides being practically inedited has the merit of exemplifying that association of the sword with the Lord of the Bespelled Castle to which I have already alluded.

The instances of the visit to the otherworld which have thus far been collected from Celtic mythic literature, and which have been used as parallels to the unspelling quest of the romances, are more closely akin to one example of this incident, Perceval's visit to the Castle of Maidens, than to that found in Heinrich and the Didot-Perceval. None, indeed, throw any light upon that death-in-life which is the special feature in these two works. All are of one kind in so far as the disposition of the inmates towards the visitor is concerned; he is received with courtesy when he is not actually allured into the castle, and the trials to which he is subjected are neither painful nor humiliating. But it will not have escaped attention that the Conte du Graal contains another form of the visit, one which I have hitherto left unnoticed, in Gawain's visit to the Magic Castle. A new conception is here introduced : the Lord of the Castle* is an evil being, who holds captive fair dames and damsels ; they it is, and not he, whom the hero must deliver, and the act of deliverance subjects him to trial and peril (*supra*, p. 14, Chr. Inc. 17). Let us see if this form affords any explanation of the mysterious features of Heinrich's version. This incident may, it is easily conceivable, be treated in two ways ; the hero may be a worthy knight and succeed, or a caitiff and fail. A story of this latter kind may throw some light upon Gawain's adventures at the Magic Castle. The story in question (The Son of Bad Counsel) is ascribed by Kennedy, Legendary Fictions, pp.

---

* In Chrestien the part of the Magician Lord is little insisted upon. But in Wolfram he is a very important personage. It may here be noted that the effects which are to follow in Chrestien the doing away with the enchantments of this Castle, answer far more accurately to the description given by the loathly Grail-Maiden of the benefits which would have accrued had Perceval put the question at the Court of the Fisher King than to anything actually described as the effect of that question being put, either by Gautier, Manessier, or Gerbert. This castle seems, too, to be the one in which lodge the Knights, each having his lady love with him, which the loathly maiden announces to be her home.

132, *et seq.*, to an author of the early eighteenth century, Brian Dhu O'Reilly, and traced back to an older Ossianic legend—Conan's delusions in Ceash, of which Kennedy prints a version, pp. 232, *et seq.* The hero of the story comes to the Castle of a Gruagach, named the Giant of the Unfrequented Land, and his wife, daughter to the King of the Lonesome Land. The name of the castle is the Uncertain Castle. Very fair is their daughter, and she is proffered to the hero for his promised aid against other fairy chieftains. After playing at backgammon with the Gruagach, the hero lays himself to bed. He is assailed, as he fancies, by great dangers from which he hastens to flee, and, waking, finds himself in a ridiculous plight with his lady-love, and the other folk of the castle laughing at him. In the morning he awakes, " and his bed was the dry grass of a moat."

The names of the personages in the story at once recall those of the romances—the Waste Land or Forest, the Castle Perillous, and the like—and one of the trials, the being shot at with fairy darts, is the same as that to which Gawain is exposed in the Conte du Graal. But it is interesting chiefly as being a version of a widespread tale of how gods or heroes penetrating to the other world are made mock of by its inmates. In Scandinavian mythology the story is well-known as Thor's visit to Utgarth Loki. It is equally well-known in the Fionn saga, and, considering the many points of contact we have hitherto found between Fionn and the Grail hero, the Fenian form claims our notice. The oldest preserved form of the story, that in the Book of Leinster, has been printed with translation by Mr. Whitley Stokes, Revue Celt., Vol. VII., pp. 289, *et seq.*—Fionn comes at nightfall with Cailte and Oisin to a house he had never heard of in that glen, knowing though he was. A grey giant greets them; within are a hag with three heads on her thin neck, and a headless man with one eye protruding from his breast. Nine bodies rise out of a recess, and the hideous crew sing a strain to the guests; "not melodious was that concert." The giant slays their horses; raw meat is offered them, which they refuse; the inmates of the house attack them ; they had been dead had it not been for Fionn alone. They struggle until the sun lights up the house, then a mist falls into every one's head, so that he was dead upon the spot. The champions rise up whole, and the house is hidden from them, and every one of the household is hidden.—In the later Fenian saga (later that is as far as the form in which it has come down to us is concerned) the story closely resembles Thor's visit. Kennedy (Bardic Stories, pp. 132, et seq.) has a good version.*—Fionn and his comrades follow a giant, on his shoulders an iron fork with a pig screeching between the prongs, behind him a damsel scourging him. They follow them to a house wherein is an aged hoary-headed man and a beautiful maid, a rough giant cooking the hog, and an old man having twelve eyes in his head, a white-haired ram, and a hag clad in dark ash coloured garment. Two fountains are before the house : Fionn drinks of one which at first tastes sweet, but afterwards bitter to death; from the other, and though he never suffered as much as while drinking, when he puts the vessel from his lips he is as whole as ever he was. The hog is then shared; the ram left out of count revenges itself by carrying out the guest's share, and smite it with their swords as they may, they cannot hurt it. The hag then throws her mantle over the guests, and they become four withered drooping-headed old men; on the mantle being removed they resume their first shape. These wonders are explained. The giant is *sloth*, urged on by *energy ;* the twelve-eyed old man is the *world ;* and the ram the *guilt of man ;* the wells are *truth* and *falsehood ;* the hag *old age.* The warriors sleep and in the morning find themselves on the summit of Cairn Feargaill with their hounds and their arms by them.

This tale betrays its semi-literary origin at once; and, though there is no reason to doubt that the Irish Celts had a counterpart to Thor's journey to Giantland, I am inclined to look upon the version just summarised as influenced by the Norse saga. Certain it is that the popular version of Fionn's visit to Giantland is much more like the eleventh century poem, preserved in the Book of Leinster, than it is like the mediæval, "How Fionn fared in the House of Cuana." I have already alluded (*supra*, p. 186)

* Kennedy follows in the main Oss. Soc., Vol. II, pp. 118, *et. seq.*, an eighteenth century version translated by Mr. O'Kearney. This particular episode is found, pp. 147, *et. seq.* I follow the Oss. Soc. version in preference to Kennedy's where they differ.

to one feature of the tale of Fionn's enchantment, but the whole
tale is of interest to us.—As Fionn and his men are sitting round
the fire boasting of their prowess in comes a slender brown hare and
tosses up the ashes, and out she goes.   They follow her, a dozen, to
the house of the Yellow Face, a giant that lived upon the flesh of
men.   A woman greets them, and bids them begone before the Face
returns, but Fionn will not flee.   In comes the Face and smells out
the strangers.   Six of the Fenians he strikes with a magic rod, " and
they are pillars of stone to stop the sleety wind."   He then cooks
and devours a boar, and the bones he throws to the Fenians.   They
play at ball with a golden apple, and the Face puts an end to
Fionn's other comrades.   Hereafter he wrestles with Fionn, and the
griddle is put on the fire till it is red hot, and they all get about
Fionn and set him on the griddle till his legs are burnt to the hips
('twas then he said, " a man is no man alone"), and stick a flesh-
stake through both his hams, so that he could neither rise nor sit,
and cast him into a corner.   But he manages to crawl out and
sound his horn, and Diarmaid hears it and comes to his aid, and
does to the Face as the Face did to Fionn, and with the cup of
balsam which he wins from him makes Fionn whole.—It is not
necessary to dwell on the parallel between Diarmaid healing his
uncle Fionn, wounded with a stake through the two thighs, by
winning the cup of balsam, and Perceval healing his uncle
(mehaignié des II cuisses) by the question as to the Grail.   This,
alone, would be sufficient to show us what rôle the Grail played in
the oldest form of the feud quest before the latter was influenced
by the visit to the Bespelled Castle.

    If we look at the stories we have just summarised, we shall
easily understand the meaning of the Magic Castle vanishing at
dawn.   As sleep is brother to death, so are night and its realm
akin to the otherworld ; many phantoms haunt them and seem
quick and strive with and often terribly oppress the mortal
wanderer through this domain, but with the first gleam of sunlight
they vanish, leaving no trace behind them, and the awakening hero
find himself in his own place.   The conditions of the visit to the
otherworld are thus partly determined by man's nightly experience
in that dreamland which he figures to himself as akin to, if not an

actual portion of the land of shades. This visit, as we have seen, is conceived of in several ways. Its object is almost invariably to win precious talismans ; all we have comes to us from our forefathers, and it is natural to suppose that in the world whence they came, and whither they go back, is to be found all that man seeks here, only in a form as more wonderful than earthly objects as the dwellers in the otherworld are mightier and cleverer than man. At times the talismans are held by beneficent beings, who either gladly yield them to the mortal visitor, or from whom they may be won by the exhibition of valour and magnanimity; at times by evil monsters with whom the mortal must strive. In either case the visitor arrives at nightfall and in the morning awakes to the life of this earth.

The secondary or Gawain form of the myth, as found in the Conte de Graal, may help us to understand Heinrich's version. It is to free imprisoned damsels that Gauvain undergoes the trials of the Magic Castle. Now the effect of his visit in the German poem *is* to free the sister of Gansguoter, who, with her maidens, remains when the other inmates of the castle, released by the question, have utterly vanished.* But what means the death-in-life condition of the King and his men ? Is it merely an expedient to account for their sudden vanishing at daylight ? I rather see here the influence of another form of the unspelling myth, one that mixed with Christian elements has powerfully impressed the popular imagination, and is in many European countries the only one in which this old myth still lives on.†

---

* The story as found in Heinrich may be compared with the folk-tale of the Sleeping Beauty. She is a maiden sunk in a death-in-life sleep together with all her belongings until she be awakened by the kiss of the destined prince. May we not conjecture that in an older form of the story than any we now possess, the court of the princess vanished when the releasing kiss restored her to real life and left her alone with the prince ? The comparison has this further interest, that the folk-tale is a variant of an old myth which figures prominently in the hero-tales of the Teutonic race (Lay of Skirni, Lay of Swipday and Menglad, Saga of Sigurd and Brunhild), and that in its most famous form Siegfried, answering in Teutonic myth to Fionn, is its hero. But Peredur is a Cymric Fionn, so that the parallel between the two heroes, Celtic and Teutonic, is closer than at first appears when Siegfried is compared only to his Gaelic counterpart.

† I have not examined Gawain's visit to the Magic Castle in detail, in the

The inmates of the Magic Castle or house are in this form figured as men doomed for some evil deed to haunt that particular spot, until some mortal is bold enough to win their secret and bring them rest. One would think that under the circumstances they would be as amiable as possible to any visitor. But the older form of the story persists, and they have not terrors or trials enough for the man who is to be their deliverer. I will only quote one version, from Irish sources.*

A youth engages to sleep in a haunted castle. If he is alive in the morning he will get ten guineas and the farmer's daughter to wife. At nightfall he goes thither, and presently three men in old-fashioned dress come down in pieces through a hole in the ceiling, put themselves together, and begin playing at football. Jack joins them, and towards daybreak he judges they wish him to speak, so he asks them how he can give them rest if rest they want. " Them is the wisest words you ever spoke," is answered to him. They had ground the poor and heaped up wealth evilly. They show him their treasure, and tell him how to make restitution. As they finish, " Jack could see the wall through their body, and when he winked to clear his sight the kitchen was as empty as a noggin turned upside down." Of course Jack does as he is told, and has the daughter to wife, and they live comfortably in the old castle.†

---

first place because it only bears indirectly upon the Grail-Quest, and then because I hope before very long to study the personality of Gawain in the romances, and to throw light upon it from Celtic mythic tradition in the same way that I have tried in the foregoing pages to do in the case of Perceval.

* Kennedy, Legendary Fictions, p. 154, et. seq.

† Grimm, Vol. III., p. 9 (note to Märchen von einem der auszog das Fürchten zu lernen), gives a number of variants. It should be noted that in this story there is the same mixture of incidents of the Magic Castle and Haunted Castle forms as in the romances. Moreover, one of the trials to which the hero's courage is subjected is the bringing into the room of a coffin in which lies a dead man, just as in Gawain's visit to the Grail Castle. Again, as Grimm notes, but mistakenly refers to Perceval instead of to Gawain, the hero has to undergo the adventures of the magic bed, which, when he lays himself down in it, dashes violently about through the castle and finally turns topsy turvy. In connection with this story, and with the whole series of mythical conceptions noted in the Grail romances, Chapter XXXII. of the Deutsche Mythologie deserves careful study. Grimm compares Conduiramur's (Blanchefleur's) nightly visit to Percival's chamber

We have here, it seems to me, the last echo of such a story as one of those which enter into the Grail romances. In Heinrich's version, as elsewhere in these romances, different story types can be distinguished, different conceptions are harmonised. Many, indeed, are both the early conceptions and the varying shapes in which they embodied themselves, to be traced in the complex mass of the romances. That a kinsman is bound to avenge a blood feud, and that until he does so his kin may suffer from ailment or enchantment and their land be under a curse ; that the otherworld is a land of feasting and joyousness and all fair things ; that it contains magic treasures which he who is bold may win ; that it is peopled with beings whom he may free by his courage ; that it is fashioned like dreamland—all these ideas find expression.

If the foregoing exposition be accepted we have a valuable criterion for the age of the immediate originals of the romances. That famous version of the legend which pictured the dwellers in the otherworld as Kings, spell bound, awaiting the releasing word to come forth and aid their folk, to which special circumstances gave such wide popularity in the later middle ages, causing it to supplant older tales of gods dwelling in the hollow hills, this version has left no trace upon the romances. These must, therefore, be older than the full-blown Arthurian legend. One or two minor points may be briefly noticed. The ship in which is found the magic sword which wounds all bold enough to handle it save the destined Knight may be thought to have taken the place of an older island. The loathly Grail messenger shows the influence of the two formulas : as coming from the Bespelled Castle,* type of the otherworld, she

to the appearance at the bedside of the delivering hero ot that white maiden, who is so frequently figured as the inmate of the Haunted Castle. As niece of the Lord of the Grail Castle, Blanchefleur is also a denizen of the otherworld, but I hardly think that the episode of Perceval's delivering her from her enemies can be looked upon as a version of the removal of the spells of the Haunted Castle. In a recent number of the Revue des Traditions Populaires (III., p. 103), there is a good Breton version of the Bespelled Castle sunk under the waves. A fair princess is therein held captive ; once a year the waves part and permit access, and he who is bold enough to seize the right moment wins princess and castle, which are restored to earth.

* Whether it be the Castle of the Fisher King, *i.e.*, the Castle of the Perceval Quest ; or the Magic Castle, *i.e.*, the Castle of the Gawain Quest.

should be radiantly fair; as the kinswoman of the destined avenger, under spells until the vengeance be accomplished, she is hideous in the last degree.

But before we take leave of this incident we must examine two features upon which, as yet, no light has been thrown, the meaning of the epithet the *Fisher* King, and the hero's silence upon his first visit to the Castle of Talismans.

CHAPTER VIII.

The Fisher King in the Conte du Graal, in the Queste, and in Borron and the Grand St. Graal—The accounts of latter complete each other—The Fish is the Salmon of Wisdom—Parallel with the Fionn Saga— The nature of the Unspelling Quest—The Mabinogi of Taliesin and its mythological affinities—Brons, Bran, Cernunnos—Perceval's silence : Conte du Graal explanation late ; explanation from the Fionn Saga—Comparison of incident with *geasa* ; nature of latter ; references to it in Celtic folk-tales and in old Irish literature, Book of Rights, Diarmaid, Cuchulainn—*Geasa* and *taboo*.

THE Conte du Graal, as we have seen, offers no satisfactory explanation of the Fisher King. By Chrestien he is represented on Perceval's first meeting with him as angling from a boat steered by his companion (v. 4,187) ; he directs Perceval to his castle. Perceval is afterwards informed that, being wounded and consequently unable to mount on horseback, fishing is his only solace, whence the name applied to him (vv. 4,681, *et seq.*). This is practically all the Conte du Graal has to say about him, as the continuators, whilst repeating the epithet, add no fresh details. Indeed in none of the after-visits of Perceval is the King represented as fishing, or is there the slightest reference to, let alone insistence upon, this favourite occupation of his. It is another proof of the inadequacy of Birch-Hirschfeld's theory of the development of the legend, that it represents Chrestien, who, *ex hypothesi*, divested Borron's poem of its religious character, as retaining this feature due wholly to religious symbolism, whilst the continuators with their obvious fondness for such symbolism entirely neglected it. The Queste, which in so far as the quest portion is concerned is formally connected with the Conte du Graal, says nothing about the Fisher, nor does that section of the Grand St. Graal which presents the same Early History as the Queste. In Borron's poem, on the other hand, and in that later section of the Grand St. Graal which agrees with it, an explanation is given of the epithet. According to Borron, Brons catches a fish at Joseph's bidding; Joseph, having placed the vessel on the table and covered it with a towel, takes the fish and lays it opposite the vessel; the people are then called together, and it is possible to distinguish the sinners from the righteous (vv. 2,500–2,600). Joseph is afterwards told by an angel, that, as Brons was a good man, it was the Lord's will he should catch the fish (vv. 3,310, *et seq.*), and he is to be called the Rich Fisher (v. 3,348). In the Grand St. Graal (Vol. II., pp. 248, *et seq.*) not Brons but his son Alain is bidden by Joseph to fish, and this with a view to providing food for the sinners of the company whom the Holy Vessel leaves unsatisfied. Alain fishes from a boat with a net. He catches but one fish, and there are at first murmurs, but Joseph, by virtue of Alain's prayers, multiplies the fish so that it feeds the host, and thus Alain wins the name of Rich Fisher.

These accounts complete each other. Chrestien dwells upon the continued act of fishing which, for aught to the contrary we learn from him or his continuators, is always fruitless. Borron and the Grand St. Graal dwell upon the one successful haul, and especially upon the miraculous properties of the one fish caught. Reading the two accounts together, we find that the Fisher King passes his life seeking for a fish which, when caught, confers upon him the power of distinguishing good from evil, or enables him to furnish an inexhaustible meal to his men.

The Conte du Graal has been shown to derive more of its substance from the feud quest—the Didot-Perceval from the unspelling quest. Borron's poem, as far as its primitive Celtic elements are concerned, is probably to be ranged with the Didot-Perceval, to which many links unite it. We may, therefore, turn to Celtic stories belonging to either of these formulas for parallel features. The inexhaustible nature of the fish at once recalls the pigs of Manannan Mac Lir (*supra*, p. 194); they, too, can feed a multitude. But it is in stories formally connected with the feud quest that we find what I venture to suggest is an adequate explanation of the nature of the Fisher King and of the fish. The latter is, I think, the Salmon of Wisdom,* which appears so often and so prominently in Irish mythic lore; and the former is that being who passes his life in vain endeavours to catch the wonderful fish, and who, in the moment of success, is robbed of the fruit of all his long toils and watchings. I am prepared to admit that the incident as found in Borron's poem has been recast in the mould of mediæval Christian symbolism, but I think the older myth can still be clearly discerned and is wholly responsible for the incident as found in the Conte du Graal.†

Let us first look at the Irish story. This is found in an account, to which allusion has already been made, of the Boyish Exploits of Finn Mac Cumhail.‡ It is there told how Finn seeks his namesake, Finn-eges, to learn poetry from him, as until then he durst not stay in Ireland for fear of his foes. Now Finn-eges had remained seven years by the Boyne, watching the salmon of Linn-Feic, which it had been foretold Finn (himself as he thought) should catch and know all things afterwards. Finn, who conceals his name, takes service with him and the salmon is caught. Finn is set to watch it while it roasts, but warned not to eat of it. Inadvertently he touches it with his thumb, which he burns, and carries to his mouth to cool. Immediately he becomes possessed of all knowledge, and thereafter he had only to chew his thumb to obtain wisdom. Finn-eges recognises that the prophecy has been fulfilled, and hails his pupil as Finn.

It is needless to dwell upon the archaic features of this tale,

---

* For fuller information about this mysterious fish, see Rhys, Hibbert Lectures, pp. 553–54.

† In an already quoted tale of Campbell's (LVIII., the Rider of Grianaig) allusion is made to the "black fisherman working at his tricks." Campbell remarks that a similar character appears in other tales. Can this wizard fisher be brought into contact with the Rich Fisher of Pseudo-Chrestien (*supra*, p. 8), who knew much of black art, and could change his semblance a hundred times?

‡ Complete text, edited by Kuno Meyer, Revue Celt., Vol. V. Major portion of text with English translation by Dr. J. O'Donovan, Oss. Soc., Vol. IV. The tract as a whole is only known to us from a fifteenth century MS.; but the earlier portion of it appears in the L.n.H., in a strongly euhemerised form, only such incidents being admitted as could be presented historically, and these being divested of all supernatural character. See my paper, "Folk-Lore Record," Vol. IV., for a discussion of the genuine and early character of the tract.

which represents the hero seeking service of a powerful magician, from whom he hopes to learn the spells and charms that may guard him against his foes.   Here, as in many other portions of the Ossianic saga, Fionn is strikingly like a Red Indian medicine man, or the corresponding wizard among other savage tribes.   It is more to our purpose to note that this tale contains the fullest presentment of Fionn as hero of the Expulsion and Return Formula, and that a similar incident is to be found in the lives of other heroes of the formula (notably Siegfried : the Adventure with Mimir.)   Now, as we have already seen that Peredur-Perceval is a formula hero, there is nothing remarkable in finding an analogous incident in his *sage*.   A formal connection is thus at once made out. But we must look into the matter a little closer, as the incident found in the romances is but a faint echo, and that in part distorted by alien conceptions, of the original story.

The unspelling quest in one form resolves itself ultimately into the hero's search for riches, power, or knowledge, in prosecution of which he penetrates to the otherworld.   This is figured in the Grail romances both by Brons' or Alain's (who here answers to Fionn) catching the wonderful fish, and by Peredur-Perceval coming to the house of Brons, the Fisher King (who here answers to Finn-eges), winning from him the mysterious vessel of increase, and learning the secret words which put an end to the enchantments of Britain. In the Grail romances the idea of wisdom is not associated with the Grail, the vessel, at all ; it is either bound up with the fish, as in the Irish tale, or is the possession of the Fisher King as the wonder-working spells are the possession of Finn-eges.

But in the Welsh tradition which corresponds to that of Fionn and the salmon, it is the vessel, the cauldron, or rather the drink which it holds, which communicates the gift of wisdom and knowledge.   I allude, of course, to the story of Gwion, set by Ceridwen to watch the cauldron of inspiration, inadvertently tasting its contents, becoming thereby filled with knowledge, pursued by Ceridwen, who swallows him, and in whom he re-incarnates himself as Taliesin, the Allwise Bard.   Campbell had already (Vol. IV., p. 299) drawn attention to the similarity of the two stories, and equated Fionn, father of Oisin, with Gwion, father of Taliesin ;

and, as Professor Rhys has now (Hibbert Lectures, p. 551) given the equation his sanction, it may be accepted as philologically sound.

I have hitherto refrained in the course of these studies from making any use of the Mabinogi of Taliesin, or of references to the cauldron of Ceridwen of a like nature with those contained in that tale; but it will, I think, be admitted now that the Welsh Mabinogi, however late in form, and however overlaid it may be with pseudo-archaic bardic rubbish, does go back to a primitive stratum of Celtic mythology.

In connection with this myth the name Brons is of high import. This catcher of the fish, this lord of the Grail, at once suggests Bran, who is also a guardian of the magic cauldron. Professor Rhys (pp. 85–95) shows reason for looking upon Bran (as he is presented in the Mabinogi of Branwen) as the representative of an old Celtic god, Cernunnos, that Celtic Dis from whom, as Cæsar reports, the Gauls claimed descent, and who, as god of the other-world and the shades was also god of knowledge and riches. We are thus brought back again to the fundamental conception of the Grail quest.

It is to this tale that I would turn for one of the possible explanations of Perceval's silence at the Court of the Fisher King. That the romance writers did not understand this incident is evident from the explanation they give.

Gonemans' moral advice to his nephew on the evil of curiosity may have its foundation in a possible feature of the original, about which I shall speak presently; or it may simply be an expedient of Chrestien's or of his immediate model. In either case its present form is obviously neither old nor genuine. The silence of Perceval may, perhaps, be referred to the same myth-root as Fionn's concealment of his name whilst in the service of Finn-eges.[*] This prohibition might extend not only to the disclosing of his name by the mortal visitor to the realm of the shades, but to the utterance of any words at all. As he might not eat or drink in the

---

[*] A reason for this concealment may be found in the idea, so frequently met with in a certain stage of human development, that the name is an essential portion of the personality, and must not be mentioned, especially to possible enemies or to beings possessed of magical powers, lest they should make hurtful use of it.

underworld, so he might not speak lest he lose the power to return to the land of the living. One tale we have seen (*supra*, p. 195) does contain this very injunction to say no word whilst in company of the dwellers in the Bespelled Castle. In this case we should have to assume that two varying redactions of the theme have been maladroitly fused into one in the romances—that, namely, which bids the visitor to the otherworld abstain from a certain act, and that which, on the contrary, bids him perform a certain act, failure of compliance with the injunction being punished in either case. The positive injunction of one form of the story is used as an explanation of the hero's failure in another.

An alternative hypothesis is that whilst the hero's unreadiness of speech, the cause of his want of success at his first visit, comes wholly from the unspelling quest, the motive by which the romances seek to account for that unreadiness comes from the feud quest. The latter, as has been shown, is closely akin to many task-stories ; and it is a frequent feature in such stories, especially in the Celtic ones, that the hero has to accomplish his quest in spite of all sorts of odd restrictions which are laid upon him by an enemy, generally by a step-mother or some other evil-disposed relative. In the language of Irish mythic tradition Perceval would be under *geasa* to ask no questions, and Gonemans' advice would be the last faint echo of such an incident. The form which such prohibitions take in Celtic folk-tales is very curious. The *gess* is generally embodied in a magical formula, the language of which is very old and frequently unintelligible to the narrators themselves. As a rule, the hero, by advice of a friendly supernatural being, lays a counterspell upon his enemy. Thus, in " How the Great Tuairsgeul was put to Death " (Scot. Celt. Rev. I., p. 70) the magician "lays it as crosses and charms that water leave not your shoe until you found out how the Great Tuairsgeul was put to death." The hero retorts by laying the same charms that the magician leave not the hillock until he return. In Campbell, No. XLVII., Mac Iain Direach, the stepmother, "sets it as crosses, and as spells, and as the decay of the year upon thee; that thou be not without a pool of water in thy shoe, and that thou be wet, cold, and soiled until, etc.;" and the hero bespells her, "that thou be standing with the one foot on the great house and the other foot on the castle : and that thy face be to the tempest whatever wind blows, until I return back." The formula in Campbell, No. LI , the Fair Gruagach is very archaic. " I lay thee under spells, and under crosses, under holy herdsmen of quiet travelling, wandering woman, the little calf, most feeble and powerless, to take thy head and thine ear and thy wearing of life from off thee if thou takest rest by night or day ; where thou takest thy breakfast that thou take not thy dinner, and where thou takest thy dinner that thou take not thy supper, in whatsoever place thou be, until thou findest out in what place I may be under the four brown quarters of the globe."

These instances will suffice to show the nature of the *gess* in Celtic folk-lore, but some references to older Irish literature are necessary to show its great importance in the social and religious life of the race.   O'Donovan (Book of Rights, p. xlv.) explains the word *geasa* as " any thing or act forbidden because of the ill luck that would result from its doing ;" also " a spell, a charm, a prohibition, an interdiction or hindrance." This explanation occurs in the introduction to a poem on the restrictions (*geasa*) and prerogatives (*buada*) of the Kings of Eire, found in the Book of Ballymote (late fourteenth century) and Book of Lecan (early fifteenth century).   The poem is ascribed to Cuan O'Lochain (A.D. 1024), and, from the historical allusions contained in it, O'Donovan looks upon it as in substance due to that poet, and as embodying much older traditions.   Some of these *geasa* may be quoted.   For the King of Eire, " that the sun should rise upon him on his bed in Magh Teamhrach ;" for the King of Leinster, " to go round Tuath Laighean left hand-wise on Wednesday ;" for the King of Munster, " to remain to enjoy the feast of Loch Lein from one Monday to another ;" for the King of Connaught, " to go in a speckled garment on a grey speckled steed to the heath of Luchaid ;" for the King of Ulster, " to listen to the fluttering of the flocks of birds of Luin Saileach after sunset." * Even these instances do not exhaust the force or adequately connote the

---

* *Cf.* the whole of the Book of Rights for an exemplification of the way in which the pre-Christian Irishman was hedged and bound and fettered by this amazingly complicated system of what he might and what he might not do.

nature of this curious institution. In the Irish hero-tales *geasa* attach themselves to the hero from his birth up, and are the means by which fate compasses the downfall of the otherwise invincible champion; thus it is a *gess* of Diarmaid that he never hunt a swine, and when he is artfully trapped into doing it by Fionn he meets his death; it is a *gess* of Cuchulainn's that he never refuse food offered him by women, and as he goes to his last fight he accepts the poisoned meal of the witches though he full well knows it will be fatal to him.* But, besides this, *geasa* may also be an appeal to the hero's honour as well as a magic charm laid upon him, and it is sometimes difficult to see by which of the two motives the hero is moved. Thus Graine, wife of Fionn, lays *geasa* upon Diarmaid that he carry her off from her husband, and though he is in the last degree unwilling he must comply.†

Enough has been said to show that we have in the *geasa* a cause quite sufficient to explain the mysterious prohibition to ask questions laid upon Perceval, if the first explanation I have offered of this prohibition be thought inadequate.

---

* They offer him dog's-flesh cooked on rowan spits, and it has been conjectured that the *gess* has a totemistic basis, Culann's Hound (Cuchulainn) being forbidden to partake of the flesh of his totem.

† It is only within the last 100 years that our knowledge of savage and semi-savage races has furnished us with a parallel to the "geasa" in the "taboo" of the Polynesian. I am not advancing too much in the statement that this institution, although traces of it exist among all Aryan races, had not the same importance among any as among the Irish Gael. It is another proof of the primitive character of Irish social life, a character which may, perhaps, be ascribed to the assimilation by the invading Celts of the beliefs and practices of much ruder races.

215

CHAPTER IX.

Summing up of the elements of the older portion of the cycle—Parallelism with Celtic tradition—The Christian element in the cycle : the two forms of the Early History ; Brons form older—Brons and Bran— The Bran conversion legend—The Joseph conversion legend : Joseph in apocryphal literature—Glastonbury—The head in the platter and the Veronica portrait—The Bran legend the starting point of the Christian transformation of the legend—Substitution of Joseph for Bran—Objections to this hypothesis—Hypothetical sketch of the growth of the legend.

I HAVE now finished the examination of all those incidents in the Grail Quest romances which are obviously derived from some other sources than Christian legend, and which are, indeed, referred by pronounced adherents of the Christian-origin hypothesis to Celtic tradition. I have also claimed a Celtic origin for features hitherto referred to Christian legend. This examination will, I trust, convince many that nearly all the incidents connected with the Quest of the Grail are Celtic in their origin, and that thus alone can we account for the way in which they appear in the romances. The latter are, as we have seen, in the highest degree inconsistent in their account of the mystic vessel and its fortunes; the most cursory examination shows the legend to be composed of two parts, which have no real connection with each other ; the older of these parts, the Quest, can easily be freed from the traces of Christian symbolism ; this older part is itself no homogeneous or consistent tale, but a complex of incidents diverse in origin and character. These incidents are : the rearing of the hero in ignorance of the world and of men; his visit to the court of the King, his uncle; his slaying of his father's murderer, the trial made of him by means of the broken sword ; his service with the Fisher King ; his quest in search of the sword and of the vessel by means of which he is to avenge the death or wounding of his kinsman; his accomplishment of this task by the aid of a kinsman who is under spells from which he will not be loosed until the quest be ended; the adventure of the stag-hunt, in which the bespelled kinsman tests the hero's skill and courage; the hero's visit to the Castle of Talismans; the prohibition under which he labours; his failure to accomplish certain acts; the effects of his failure; his visit to the Magic Castle, the lord of which is under the enchantment of death-in-life; his visit to the Castle of Maidens; his visit to the Castle Perillous; and his deliverance of the captive damsels by means of the trials which he successfully undergoes. To one and all of these incidents Celtic parallels have been adduced; these have in each case been drawn from stories which present a general similarity of outline with the Grail romances, or share with them similar guiding conceptions, whilst at the same time they are so far disconnected with them that no hypothesis of borrowing can account for the features they have in common. The inconsistencies of the romances have been explained by the fusion into one of two originally distinct groups of stories, and this explanation is confirmed by the fact that traces of this fusion may readily be found in the parallel Celtic tales. These latter, when studied by scholars who never thought of comparing them with the Grail romances, have been found to contain mythical elements which other scholars had detected independently in the romances. Those features of the romances which have perplexed previous students, the Fisher King and the omitted question, have been explained from the same group of Celtic traditions, and in accordance with the same scheme of mythical interpretation which have been used to throw light upon the remainder of the cycle. Finally, the one Celtic version of the Grail Quest, the Mabinogi, which presents no admixture of Christian symbolism, has been shown, when cleared of certain easily distinguishable interpolations, to be genuine in character, and to present the oldest form of one of the stories which enters into the romances.

I have tried not to force these parallels, nor to go one step beyond what the facts warrant. I have also tried to bear in mind that a parallel is of no real value unless it throws light upon the puzzling features in the development of the romances. I thus rest my case, not so much upon the accumulative effect of the similarities which I have pointed out between the romances and Celtic tradition, as upon the fact that this reference of the romances to certain definite cycles of Celtic myth and legend makes us understand, what otherwise we cannot do, how they came by their present shape. It now remains to be seen if this reference, can in any way explain the Christian element in the legend, which I have hitherto left almost entirely out of account. Birch-Hirschfeld's hypothesis is condemned, in my opinion, by its failure to account for the Celtic element; although I do not think an explanation of a late and intruding feature is as incumbent upon me as that of the original Celtic basis of the legend is upon him, I yet feel that an hypothesis which has nothing to say on such a vital point can hardly be considered satisfactory. It is the Christian transformation of the old Celtic myths and folk-tales which gave them their wide vogue in the Middle Ages, which endowed the theme with such fascination for the preachers and philosophers who used it as a vehicle for their teaching, and which has endeared it to all lovers of mystic symbolism. The question how and why the Celtic tales which I have tried, not unsuccessfully I trust, to disentangle from the romances were ever brought into contact with Christ and His disciples, and how the old mystic vessel of healing, increase, and knowledge became at last the sacramental cup, must, therefore, be faced. The hypotheses set forth in the preceding page might be accepted in their entirety, and the merit of this transformation still be claimed, as Birch-Hirschfeld claims it, for the North French poets, to whom we owe the present versions of the romances. On first reading Birch-Hirschfeld's book, I thought this claim one of the flaws in his argument, and, as will be seen by reference to Chapter IV., other investigators, who accept the Christian origin of the larger part of the legend, hold that it has been shaped in these islands, or in accordance with Celtic traditions now lost. I think we can go a step farther. A number of myths and tales have been used to illustrate the romances. In them may be found the personages through whom probably took place the first contact between Celtic mythic tradition and Christian legend.

We must revert for one moment to the results obtained in Chapter III. by an examination of the way in which the Grail and its fortunes are mentioned in the romances. We there distinguished two forms of the distinctively Christian portion of the legend, the Early History. In both Joseph is the first possessor and user of the holy vessel, but in one its farther fortunes are likewise bound up with him or with his seed. He, or his son, it is who leads the Grail host to Britain, who converts the island, and by whom the precious vessel is handed down through a chosen line of kings in anticipation of the promised Knight's coming. In the other form, on the contrary, Joseph has nothing to do with Britain, which is converted by Brons and his son, Alain; Brons is the guardian of the holy vessel, and, in one version, the fisher of the mystic fish, whilst in another his son takes this part. There is repeated insistence upon the connection between the Grail host and Avalon. Finally Brons is the possessor of "secret words," and may not die until he has revealed them to his grandson.

This account is, we saw, later in form than the Joseph one. As we have it, it was written after the greater portion of the Conte du Graal, after that redaction of the Early History made use of by the author of the Queste and of the firs draft of the Grand St. Graal. Its influence only makes itself felt in the later stages of development of the legend. But none the less it clearly represents an older and purer form of the Early History than that of the Queste and of Chrestien's continuators. It has not been doctored into harmony with the full-blown Arthurian legend as the Joseph Early History has. It is still chiefly, if not wholly, a legend, the main purport of which is to recount the conversion of Britain.

Such a legend is surely more likely to have been shaped by Welsh or Breton monks than by North French *trouvères*. And when we notice the Celtic names of the personages, and their connection with the Celtic paradise, Avalon, there can remain little, if any, doubt respecting the first home of the story. We may thus look upon Brons, owner of a mystic vessel, fisher of a mystic fish, as the hero of an early conversion legend. But the name Brons has at once suggested to most students of the cycle that of Bran. The latter is, as we saw in the last Chapter, the representative of an old Celtic god of the otherworld. He is the owner of the cauldron of renovation. He is also the hero in Welsh tradition of a conversion legend, and is commonly known as Bran the Blessed. Unfortunately the only explanation we have of this epithet occurs in a late triad, to which it is not safe to assign an earlier date than the fourteenth century. He is described therein as son of Llyr Llediath, " as one of the three blissful Rulers of the Island of Britain, who first brought the faith of Christ to the nation of the Cymry from Rome, where he was seven years a hostage for his son Caradawc."* But if late in form this triad may well embody an old tradition. It gives the significant descent of Bran from Llyr, and thereby equates him with Mannanan Mac Lir, with whom he presents otherwise so many points of contact. It is quite true that the Bran legend, as is pointed out to me by Professor Rhys, is mentioned neither in the earliest genealogies nor in Geoffrey. But it should be noted that the Grand St. Graal does bring one member of the Brons group, Petrus, into contact with King Luces, the Lucius to whom Geoffrey ascribes the conversion. Again, the epithet " blessed " is applied to Bran in the Mabinogi of Branwen, daughter of Llyr. I have placed this tale as a whole as far back as the eleventh-tenth centuries, and my arguments have met with no opposition, and have won the approval of such authorities as Professor Windisch and Monsieur Gaidoz. But the Mabinogi, as we have it, was written down in the fourteenth century ; the last transcriber abridged it, and at times did not apparently understand what he was transcribing. By his time the full-blown Bran legend of the triad was in existence, and it may be contended that the epithet was due to him and did not figure in his model. On the other hand, Stephens (Lit. of the Cymry, p. 425) quotes a triad of Kynddelw, a poet of the twelfth century, referring to the three blessed families of the Isle of Britain, one of which is declared by a later tradition to be that of Bran.† Again, the triads of Arthur and his

---

* Mr. Elton (Origins, pp. 291, 292) looks upon Bran and Caradoc as original war gods. Caradoc, he thinks, was confounded with Caractacus, Bran with Brennus, and hence the two personages were sent to Rome in imitation of the presumed historical prototypes.

† Kynddelw's triad does not really refer to the "blessed " families at all, but

Warriors, printed by Mr. Skene, Four Ancient Books, Vol. II., p. 457, from MS. Hengwrt, 566, of the beginning of the fourteenth century, and probably at least fifty years older, mentions the " blessed head of Bran."* On the whole, in spite of the silence of older sources, I look upon the epithet and the legend which it presupposes as old, and I see in a confusion between Bran, Lord of the Cauldron, and Bran the Blessed, the first step of the transformation of the Peredur *sage* into the Quest of the Holy Grail. In the first capacity Bran corresponds to the Lord of the Castle of Talismans. From the way in which the fish is dwelt upon in his legend, it may, indeed, be conjectured that he stood to Peredur in some such relation as Finneges to Fionn. As hero of a conversion legend he came into contact with Joseph. We do not know how or at what date the legend of the conversion of Britain by Joseph originated. It is found enjoying wide popularity in the latter half of the twelfth century, the very time in which the romances were assuming their present shape. Wülcker (Das Evangelium Nicodemi in der abendländischen Literatur, Paderborn, 1872) shows that the legend is not met with before William of Malmesbury; and Zarncke, as already stated (*supra*, p. 107), has argued that the passage in William is a late interpolation due to the popularity of the romances.† But to accept Zarncke's contention merely shifts back the difficulty. If William did not first note and give currency to the tradition, the unknown predecessor of Robert de Borron and of the authors of the Queste and Grand St. Graal did so; and the question still remains how did he come by the tradition, and what led him to associate it with Glastonbury. Birch-Hirschfeld, it is true, makes short work of

---

to the "faithful" or "loyal" families. Stephen's mistake arose from the fact of the name Madawc occurring in two sets of triads, one relating to the "lordly" families of Britain in which the family of Llyr Llediath also figures, and one to the faithful families. In both triads the name is probably a mistake for Mabon. (Note communicated by Professor Rhys.)

I let the statement in the text stand, to exhort myself and others to that fear of trusting authorities which in scholarship is the beginning of wisdom.

* Professor Rhys tells me this passage can only mean " Blessed Bran's head."

† Mr. Ward endorses Zarncke's contention. According to him there is no trace of any connection between Joseph and the evangelisation of Britain which can be said to be older than the romances. The statements of the "De ant. eccl. Glast." are, he thinks, no guide to the knowledge or opinions of William of Malmesbury.

this difficulty. The fact that there is no earlier legend in which Joseph figures as the Apostle of Britain is to him proof that Borron evolved the conception of the Grail out of the canonical and apocryphal writings in which Joseph appears, and then devised the passage to Britain in order to incorporate the Arthurian romances with the legend he had invented. It is needless to repeat that this theory, unacceptable on *a priori* grounds, is still more so when tested by facts.

But Joseph under other aspects than that of Apostle of Britain is worthy of notice. The main source whence the legend writers drew their knowledge of him was the Evangelium Nicodemi, the history of which has been investigated by Wülcker. The earliest allusion in western literature to this apocryphal gospel is that of Gregory of Tours (Wülcker, p. 23), but no other trace of its influence is to be met with in France until we come to the Grail romances, and to mystery-plays which relate Christ's Harrowing of Hell. In Provence, Italy, and Germany the thirteenth and twelfth centuries are the earliest to which this gospel can be traced. In England, on the contrary, it was known as far back as the latter quarter of the eighth century; Cynewulf based upon it a poem on the Harrowing of Hell, and alludes to it in the Crist; the ninth century poem, "Christ and Satan," likewise shows knowledge of it, and there is a West-Saxon translation dating from the early eleventh century.

Whence this knowledge and popularity of the gospel in England several centuries before it entered prominently into the literature of any other European people? Wülcker can only point by way of answer to the early spread of Christianity in these Islands, and to the possibility of this gospel having reached England before it did France or Germany. He also insists upon the early development of Anglo-Saxon literature.

Whether the fact that the apocryphal writings which told of Joseph were known here when they were unknown on the Continent be held to warrant or no the existence of a specifically British Joseph legend, they at all events prove that he was a familiar and favourite legendary figure on British soil. It would be rash to go any farther, and to argue from the inadequacy of the reasons by which Wülcker seeks to account for the early knowledge of the Evangelium Nicodemi in England, that Joseph enjoyed particular favour among the British Christians, and that it was from them the tidings of him spread among their Saxon conquerors.

The legendary popularity of Joseph in these islands, though not in any special capacity of Apostle of Britain, is thus attested. Let us admit for argument's sake that the conversion legend did first take shape in the twelfth century, is it not more likely to have done so here, where the apocryphal writings about him were widely spread, than in France, where they were practially unknown? And why if Borron, or any other French poet, wanted to connect the Holy Vessel legend which he had imagined with Arthur, should he go out of his way to invent the personages of Brons and Alain? The story as found in the Queste would surely have been a far more natural one for him. And why the insistence upon Avalon? We have plain proof that Borron did not understand the word, as he explains it by a ridiculous pun (*supra*, p. 78).*

These difficulties are met in a large measure if we look upon

---

* I may here notice a theory to which my attention has only just been called. It is found cited in a work of great research, *Die Fronica*, by Professor Karl Pearson, Strassburg, 1887. The author quotes an opinion of Mr. Jenner, of the British Museum, that the head in the platter of the Mabinogi may be derived from a Veronica portrait. Professor Pearson expresses doubt, because such a procession of the Veronica portrait and the Passion Instruments as the scene in the Mabinogi would, *ex hypothesi*, imply is not known to him before the fourteenth century, whereas the Mabinogi must be attributed, at latest, to the middle of the thirteenth century. Mr. H. L. D. Ward informs me that the suggestion was his. Noting the connection of the Veronica and Grail legends, testified to by Borron, it occurred to him that the whole scene at the Wounded King's might be derived from the former legends. The Wounded King, healed by the Grail, would thus be a counterpart of the leprous Vespasian healed by the Veronica portrait, which some wandering "jongleur" turned boldly into an actual head. But it must be noted that in Borron, our authority for the connection of the two legends, there is no Wounded King at all; in the Conte du Graal the Maimed King is not healed by any special talisman, but by the death of his enemy, the visible sign of which is that enemy's head, whilst in the "procession" (which Mr. Ward thinks to have been intended as a vision), the Grail is certainly a vessel, and has no connection whatever with any head or portrait. The theory thus requires that the version which gives the oldest form of the hypothetical remodelled Veronica legend omitted the very feature which was its sole *raison d'être*.

Bran (Brons) as the starting point of the Christian transformation of the legend. In any case we may say that a conversion legend, whether associated with Joseph or anyone else, would almost inevitably have gravitated towards Glastonbury, but there are special reasons why this should be the case with a Bran legend. Avalon is certainly the Welsh equivalent of the Irish Tír na n-Og, the land of youth, the land beyond the waves, the Celtic paradise. When or how this Cymric myth was localised at Glastonbury we know not.* We only know that Glastonbury was one of the first places in the island to be devoted to Christian worship. Is it too rash a conjecture that the Christian church may have taken the place of some Celtic temple or holy spot specially dedicated to the cult of the dead, and of that Lord of the Shades from which the Celts feigned their descent? The position of Glastonbury, not far from that western sea beyond which lie the happy isles of the dead, would favour such an hypothesis. Although direct proof is wanting, I believe that the localisation is old and genuine: Bran, ruler of the otherworld, of Avalon, would thus come into natural contact with Glastonbury; and if, as I assume, Joseph took his place in the conversion legend the association would extend to him. The after development of the legend would then be almost a matter of course. Bran, the ruler in Avalon, would pass on his magic gear (cauldron, spear, and sword, as in the case of the Tuatha de Dannan) to Bran the Blessed, who would in his turn transfer them to Joseph. And once the latter had entered into the legend, he would not fail to recall tha last scene of the Lord's life with which he was so closely associated, not by any pseudo-gospel but by the canonical

---

* Mr. Ward thinks the localisation a late one, and that practically there is no authority for it of an older date than the romances. He points out in especial that Geoffrey's Vita Merlini, which has so much to say about the "insula pomorum" in no way connects it with Glastonbury. There is considerable doubt as the etymology of Glastonbury, but there is substantial unanimity of opinion among Celtic scholars of the present day in referring it to a Celtic rather than to a Saxon source. Be this as it may, the fact remains that at sometime in the course of the twelfth century the old Christian site of Glastonbury took, as it were, the place of the Celtic paradise, and it seems far more likely that the transformation was effected in virtue of some local tradition than wholly through the medium of foreign romances.

writings themselves, and thus the gear of the old Celtic gods became transformed into such objects as were most prominent in the story of the Passion and of the scene that immediately preceded it. The spear became that one wherewith Christ's side was pierced. As for the vessel, the sacramental nature is the last stage of its Christian development; its original object was merely to explain the sustenance of Joseph in prison, and to provide a miraculous refreshment for the Grail host, as is shown by the Early History portion of the Conte du Graal and by the Queste. In a dim and confused way the circumstances of the Resurrection helped to effect the change of the pagan resuscitation-cauldron into a symbol of the risen Lord. And some now lost feature of the original legend—some insistence upon the *contents* of the vessel, some assimilation of them to blood—may have suggested the use to which the vessel was first put.

This hypothesis assumes many things. It assumes a Bran conversion legend, of which the only evidence of anything like the same date as the romances is a single epithet; it assumes that the hero of this legend was originally an old Celtic divinity; it assumes a Joseph conversion legend, for which there is really no other evidence than that of the romances; it assumes the amalgamation of the two legends, and that Joseph took over in a large measure the *rôle* and characteristics of Brons. And when it is recollected that the primary assumption, the identification of the two Brans, rests in a large measure upon the appearance of the fish in the Brons legend, that this fish is nowhere in Celtic tradition associated with Bran, that it is associated on the other hand with a being, Fionn, whom we have compared with Peredur, but that it is absent from the Peredur-saga, the hypothesis must be admitted to be of a tentative nature. I fully appreciate the force of the objections that can be urged against it; at the same time it has the merit of accounting for many puzzling features in the legend. When in the same story two personages can be distinguished whose *rôle* is more or less of the same nature, when the one personage is subordinated in one version and has disappeared altogether from the other, it is quite legitimate to conclude that two originally independent accounts have become blended, and that one has absorbed the other. The hypothesis is on safe ground so far. It thus explains the presence of Brons in the legend, as well as his absence from some versions of it; it has something to say in explanation of the connection with Glastonbury; it explains in what way the Celtic traditions were started on their path of transformation; and it provides for that transformation taking the very course it did. There is nothing to be urged against it on *a priori* grounds; once admit the premisses, and the rest follows easily and naturally. Its conjectural character (the main objection to it) is shared in an even higher degree by the other hypotheses, which have essayed to account for the growth and origin of the legend, and *they* have the disadvantage of being inherently impossible.

In the light of the foregoing investigations and hypotheses we may now amplify the sketch history of the whole cycle given in Chapter III. The Peredur-saga probably came into existence in much its later form at an early date in the Middle Ages. A number of older mythical tales centered in a, perhaps, historical personage. The circumstances of his life and adventures may have given them not only cohesion, but may also have coloured and distorted them; nevertheless they remained, in the main, mythical tales of the same kind as those found all over the world. One of these tales was undoubtedly a Cymric variant of the Celtic form of the Expulsion and Return formula; another dealt with the hero's journey to the Land of Shades; traces of many others are to be found in the Mabinogi. Another Celtic worthy, Gwalchmai, was early associated with Peredur, and the two stood in some such relation to each other as the twin brethren of a widely spread folk-tale group. Curiously enough, whilst comparatively few incidents in the Peredur-saga were worked up into the version which served as immediate model to the North French romances, that version contained many adventures of Gwalchmai's which have not been preserved in Welsh. We can trace three main crystallizations of the original saga-mass; one represented by the Proto-Mabinogi contained the feud quest, and, probably, some only of the other adventures found in the present Mabinogi; the second, based more on the lines of the Expulsion and Return formula, is represented by the Thornton MS. romance; in the

third the feud quest was mixed up with the hero's visit to the
Bespelled Castle, and those portions of the Gwalchmai-saga which
told of his visit to Castle Perillous as well as to the Bespelled
Castle. Whilst the Proto-Mabinogi was probably in prose, the
Proto-Conte du Graal was probably in verse, a collection of short
lais like those of Marie de France. Meanwhile, one of the chief
personages of the older mythic world which appear in the Peredur-
saga, Bran, the Lord of the Land of Shades, of the Bespelled
Castle, of the cauldron of healing, increase and wisdom, and of
the knowledge-giving salmon, had become the Apostle of Britain,
his pagan attributes thus suffering a Christian change, which was
perfected when Joseph took the place of Brons, bringing with
him his gospel associations and the apocryphal legends that had
clustered round his name. Thus a portion of the saga was
Christianised, whilst the other portion lost its old, fixed popular
character, owing to the fusion of originally distinct elements, and
the consequent unsettling both of the outlines and of the details of
the story. Incidents and features which in the earlier folk-tale
stage were sharply defined and intelligible became vague and
mysterious. In this state, and bearing upon it the peculiarly weird
and fantastic impress of Celtic mythic tradition, the story, or
story-mass rather, lay ready to the hand of courtly poet or of
clerical mystic. At first Christian symbolism was introduced in a
slight and meagre way—the Brons-Joseph legend supplied the
Christian meaning of the talismans, and that was all. But the
Joseph legend was soon vigorously developed by the author of the
work which underlies the Queste and the Grand St. Graal. He
may either not have known or have deliberately discarded Brons,
the old Celtic hero of the conversion, as he certainly deliberately
thrust down from his place of pre-eminence Perceval, the Celtic hero
of the Quest, substituting for him a new hero, Galahad, and for the
adventures of the Conte du Graal, based as they were upon no
guiding conceptions, fresh adventures intended to glorify physical
chastity. With all his mystic fervour he failed to see the full
capacities of the theme, his presentment of the Grail itself being in
especial either over-material or over-spiritual. But his work
exercised a profound influence, as is seen in the case of Chrestien's

continuators. Robert de Borron, on the other hand, if to him the merit must be assigned, if he was not simply transcribing an older, forgotten version, was a more original thinker, if a less gifted writer. Although he was not able to entirely harmonise the conflicting accounts of which he made use, he yet succeeded in keeping close to the old lines of the legend whilst giving a consistent symbolical meaning to all its details. His work came too late, however, to exercise the influence it should have done upon the development of the legend; the writers who knew it were mere heapers together of adventures, and the very man who composed a sequel to it abandoned Robert's main conception.

The history of the Legend of the Holy Grail is, thus, the history of the gradual transformation of old Celtic folk-tales into a poem charged with Christian symbolism and mysticism. This transformation, at first the inevitable outcome of its pre-Christian development, was hastened later by the perception that it was a fitting vehicle for certain moral and spiritual ideas. These have been touched upon incidentally in the course of these studies, but they and their manifestation in modern as well as in mediæval literature deserve fuller notice.

228

CHAPTER X.

Popularity of the Arthurian Romance—Reasons for that Popularity—
Affinities of the Mediæval Romances with early Celtic Literature;
Importance of the Individual Hero; Knighthood; the *rôle* of Woman;
the Celtic Fairy and the Mediæval Lady; the Supernatural—M.
Renan's views — The Quest in English Literature, Malory — The
earliest form of the Legend, Chrestien, his continuators—The Queste
and its Ideal—The Sex-Relations in the Middle Ages—Criticism of
Mr. Furnivall's estimate of the moral import of the Queste—The Merits
of the Queste—The Chastity Ideal in the later versions—Modern
English Treatments : Tennyson, Hawker—Possible Source of the
Chastity Ideal in Popular Tradition—The Perceval Quest in Wolfram;
his Moral Conception ; the Question ; Parzival and Conduiramur—
The Parzival Quest and Faust—Wagner's Parsifal—The Christian
element in the Legend—Ethical Ideas in the folk-tale originals of the
Grail Romances : the Great Fool, the Sleeping Beauty—Conclusion.

FEW legends have attained such wide celebrity, or been accepted
as so thoroughly symbolical of one master conception, as that of
the Holy Grail. Poets and thinkers from mediæval times to our
own days have used it as a type of the loftiest goal of man's effort.
There must be something in the romances which first embodied
this conception to account for the enduring favour it has enjoyed.
Nor is it that we read into the old legend meanings and teachings
undreamt of before our day. At a comparatively early stage in
the legend's existence its capacities were perceived, and the
works which were the outcome of that perception became the
breviary and the exemplar of their age. There are reasons, both
general and special, why the Celtic mythic tales grew as they did,
and had such overwhelming vogue in their new shapes. In no
portion of the vast Arthurian cycle is it more needful or more
instructive to see what these reasons were than in that which
recounts the fortunes of the Grail.

The tales of Peredur and Gwalchmai, bound up with the

Arthurian romance, shared its success, than which nothing in all literary history is more marvellous.   It was in the year 1145 that Geoffrey of Monmouth first made the legendary history of Britain accessible to the lettered class of England and Continent.   He thereby opened up to the world at large a new continent of romantic story, and exercised upon the development of literature an influence comparable in its kind to that of Columbus' achievement upon the course of geographical discovery and political effort. Twenty years had not passed before the British heroes were household names throughout Europe, and by the close of the century nearly every existing literature had assimilated and reproduced the story of Arthur and his Knights.   Charlemagne and Alexander, the sagas of Teutonic tribes, the tale of Imperial Rome itself, though still affording subject matter to the wandering jongleur or monkish annalist, paled before the fame of the British King.   The instinct which led the twelfth and thirteenth centuries thus to place the Arthurian story above all others was a true one. It was charged with the spirit of romance, and they were preeminently the ages of the romantic temper.   The West had turned back towards the East, and, although the intent was hostile, the minds of the western men had been fecundated, their imagination fired by contact with the mother of all religions and all cultures. The achievements of the Crusaders became the standard of attainment to the loftiest and boldest minds of Western Christendom. For these men Alexander himself lacked courage and Roland daring. The fathers had stormed Jerusalem, and the sons' youth had been nourished on tales of Araby the Blest and Ophir the Golden of strife with the Paynim, of the sorceries and devilries of the East.   Nothing seemed impossible to a generation which knew of toils and quests greater than any minstrel had sung, which had beheld in the East sights as wondrous and fearful as any the jongleur could tell of.   Moreover, the age was that of Knight Errantry, and of that phase of love in which every Knight must qualify himself for the reception of his lady's favours by the performance of some feat of skill and daring.   Such an age and such men demanded a special literature, and they found it in adaptations of Celtic tales.

The mythic heroic literature of all races is in many respects alike. The sagas not only of Greek or Persian, of Celt or Hindu, of Slav or Teuton, but also of Algonquin or Japanese, are largely made up of the same incidents set in the same framework. But each race shapes this common material in its own way, sets upon it its own stamp. And no race has done this more unmistakably than the Celtic. Stories which go back to the first century, stories taken down from the lips of living peasants, have a kinship of tone and style, a common ring which no one who has studied this literature can fail to recognise. What stamps the whole of it is the prevailing and abiding spirit of romance. To rightly urge the Celtic character of the Arthurian romances would require the minute analysis of many hundred passages, and it would only be proving a case admitted by everyone who knows all the facts It will be more to the point to dwell briefly upon those outward features which early (*i.e.*, pre-eleventh century) Celtic heroic literature has in common with the North French romances of the twelfth and thirteenth centuries, especially as we thus gain a clue to much that is problematic in the formal and moral growth of the Arthurian cycle in general and of the Grail cycle in particular.

In Celtic tradition, as little as in mediæval romance, do we find a record of race-struggles such as meets us in the Nibelungenlied, in the Dietrich saga, or the Carolingian cycle.* In its place we have a glorification of the individual hero. The reason is not far to seek. The Celtic tribes, whether of Ireland or Britain, were surrounded by men of their own speech, of like institutions and manners. The shock of opposing nations, of rival civilisations,

---

* The pre-Christian Irish annals, which are for the most part euhemerised mythology, contain also a certain amount of race history ; thus the struggle between the powers of light and darkness typified by the antagonism between Tuatha de Danann and Fomori, is doubled by that between the fair invading Celts and the short dark aborigines. But the latter has only left the barest trace of its existence in the national sagas. Not until we come to that secondary stage of the Fenian saga, which must have been shaped in the eleventh and twelfth centuries, and which represents the Fenians as warring against the harrying Northmen, does the foreign element reappear in Irish tradition.

could not enter into their race-tradition. The story-teller had as his chief theme the prowess and skill of the individual " brave," the part he took in the conflicts which clan incessantly waged with clan, or his encounters with those powers of an older mythic world which lived on in the folk-fancy. To borrow Mr. Fitzgerald's convenient terminology, the "constants" of this tradition may be the same as in that of other Aryan races, the "resultants" are not. To give one instance: the conception of a chief surrounded by a picked band of warriors is common to all heroic tradition, but nowhere is it of such marked importance, nowhere does it so mould and shape the story as in the cycles of Conchobor and the Knights of the Red Branch, of Fionn and the Fianna, and of Arthur and his Knights. The careers of any of the early Irish heroes, the single-handed raids of Cét mac Magach or Conall Cearnach, above all the fortunes of Cuchullain, his hero's training in the Amazon-isle, his strife with Curoi mac Daire, his expeditions to fairy-land, his final holding of the ford against all the warriors of Erinn, breathe the same spirit of adventure for its own sake, manifest the same subordination of all else in the story to the one hero, that are such marked characteristics of the Arthurian romance.

Again, in the bands of picked braves who surround Conchobor or Fionn, in the rules by which they are governed, the trials which precede and determine admission into them, the duties and privileges which attach to them, we have, it seems to me, a far closer analogue to the knighthood of mediæval romance than may be found either in the Peers of Carolingian saga or in the chosen warriors who throng the halls of Walhalla.

In the present connection the part played by woman in Celtic tradition is perhaps of most import to us. In no respect is the difference more marked than in this between the twelfth century romances, whether French or German, and the earlier heroic literature of either nation. The absence of feminine interest in the earlier *chansons de geste* has often been noted. The case is different with Teutonic heroic literature, in which woman's *rôle* is always great, sometimes pre-eminently so. But a comparison of the two strains of traditions, Celtic and Teutonic, one with the other, and again with the romances, may help to account for much that is otherwise inexplicable to us in the mediæval presentment of the sex-feelings and sex-relations.

The love of man, and immortal, or, if mortal, semi-divine maid is a "constant" of heroic tradition. Teuton and Celt have handled this theme, however, in a very different spirit. In the legends of the former the man plays the chief part; he woos, sometimes he forces the fairy maiden to become the mistress of his hearth. As a rule, overmastered by the prowess and beauty of the hero, she is nothing loth. But sometimes, as does Brunhild, she feels the change a degradation and resents it. It is otherwise with the fairy mistresses of the Celtic hero; they abide in their own place, and they allure or compel the mortal lover to resort to them. Connla and Bran and Oisin must all leave this earth and sail across ocean or lake before they can rejoin their lady love; even Cuchullain, mightiest of all the heroes, is constrained, struggle as he may, to go and dwell with the fairy queen Fand, who has woed him. Throughout, the immortal mistress retains her superiority; when the mortal tires and returns to earth she remains, ever wise and fair, ready to welcome and enchant a new generation of heroes. She chooses whom she will, and is no man's slave; herself she offers freely, but she abandons neither her liberty nor her divine nature. This type of womanhood, capricious, independent, severed from ordinary domestic life, is assuredly the original of the Vivians, the Orgueilleuses, the Ladies of the Fountain of the romances; it is also one which must have commended itself to the knightly devotees of mediæval romantic love. Their "dame d'amour" was, as a rule, another man's wife; she raised in their minds no thought of home or child. In the tone of their feelings towards her, in the character of their intercourse with her, they were closer akin to Oisin and Neave, to Cuchullain and Fand, than to Siegfried and Brunhild, or to Roland and Aude. Even where the love-story passes wholly among mortals, the woman's rôle is more accentuated than in the Teutonic sagas. She is no mere lay-figure upon a fire-bound rock like Brunhild or Menglad, ready, when the destined hero appears, to fall straightway into his arms. Emer, the one maiden of Erinn whom Cuchullain condescends to woo, is eager to show herself in all things worthy of him; she tests his wit as well as his courage, she makes him accept her conditions.* In the great tragic tale of ancient Ireland, the Fate of the Sons of Usnech, Deirdre—born like Helen or Gudrun, to be a cause of strife among men, of sorrow and ruin to whomsoever she loves—Deirdre takes her fate into her own hands, and woos Noisi with outspoken passionate frankness. The whole story is conceived and told in a far more "romantic" strain than is the case with parallel stories from Norse tradition, the loves of Helgi and Sigrun, or those of Sigurd and Brunhild-Gudrun. And if the lament of Deirdre over her slain love lacks the grandeur and the intensity with which the Norse heroines bewail their dead lords, it has, on the other hand, an intimate, a personal touch we should hardly have looked for in an eleventh century Irish epic.†

Another link between the Celtic sagas and the romances is

---

* The Tochmarc Emer, or the Wooing of Emer by Cuchullain, has been translated by Professor Kuno Meyer in the Archæological Review, Nos. 1–4 (London, 1888). The original text is found partly in the Leabhar na h-Uidhre, partly in later MSS.

† The fate of the Sons of Usnech is known to us in two main redactions, one found in the Book of Leinster (compiled in the middle of the twelfth century from older MS.) printed by Windisch, Irische Texte (first series) pp. 67–82, and translated by M. Poinsignon, Revue des Traditions Populaires, III, pp. 201–207. A text printed and translated by J. O'Flanagan (Transactions of the Gaelic Society of Dublin, 1808, pp. 146–177), agrees substantially with this. The second redaction has only been found in later MSS. Mr. Whitley Stokes has given text and translation from a fifteenth century MS. (Irische Texte, II. 2, pp. 109–178), and O'Flanagan has edited a very similar version (loc. cit. pp. 16–135). This second version is fuller and more romantic; in it alone is to be found Deirdre's lament on leaving Scotland, one of the earliest instances in post-classic literature of personal sympathy with Nature.

But the earlier version, though it bear like so much else in the oldest Irish MS. obvious traces of abridgment and euhemerism, is also full of the most delicate romantic touches. Part of Deirdre's lament over the slain Noisi may be paraphrased thus :—"Fair one, loved one, flower of beauty; beloved, upright and strong; beloved, noble and modest warrior. When we wandered through the woods of Ireland, sweet with thee was the night's sleep! Fair one, blue-eyed, beloved of thy wife, lovely to me at the trysting place came thy clear voice through the woods. I cannot sleep; half the night my spirit wanders far among throngs of men. I cannot eat or smile. Break not to-day my heart; soon enough shall I lie within my grave. Strong are the waves of the sea, but stronger is sorrow, Conchobor."

their treatment of the supernatural. Heroic-traditional literature
is made up of mythical elements, of scenes, incidents, and formulas
which have done service in that account of man's dealings with
and conceptions of the visible world which we call mythology.
All such literature derives ultimately from an early, wholly
animistic stage of culture. Small marvel, then, if in the hero-
tales of every race there figure wonder-working talismans and
bespelled weapons, if almost every great saga has, as part of its
dramatis personæ, objects belonging to what we should now call
the inanimate world. Upon these a species of life is conferred,
most often by power of magic, but at times, it would seem, in
virtue of the older conception which held all things to be endowed
with like life. All heroic literatures do not, however, accentuate
equally and similarly this magic side of their common stock.
Celtic tradition is not only rich and varied beyond all others in
this respect, it often thus secures its chief artistic effects. The
talismans of Celtic romance, the fairy branch of Cormac, the
Ga-bulg of Cuchullain, the sounding-hammer of Fionn, the
treasures of the Boar Trwyth after which Prince Kilhwch sought,
the glaives of light of the living folk-tale, have one and all a
weird, fantastic, half-human existence, which haunts and thrills
the imagination. No Celtic story-teller could have " mulled " the
Nibelung-hoard as the poet of the Nibelungenlied has done.
How different in this respect the twelfth century romances are
from the earlier German or French sagas, how close to the Irish
tales is apparent to whomsoever reads them with attention.*

I do not for one moment imply that the romantic literature of

---

* M. Renan's article " De la Poésie des Races Celtiques " (Revue des Deux
Mondes, 1854, pp. 473–506) only came into my hands after the bulk of this chapter
was printed, or I should hardly have dared to state in my own words those
conclusions in which we agree. It may be useful to indicate those points in
which I think this suggestive essay no longer represents the present state of
knowledge. When M. Renan wrote, the nature of popular tradition had
been little investigated in France—hence a tendency to attribute solely to the
Celtic genius what is common to all popular tradition. Little or nothing was
then known in France of early Irish history or literature—hence the wild,
primitive character of Celtic civilization is ignored. The "bardic" literature
of Wales was still assigned wholesale to the age of its alleged authors—hence

the Middle Ages was what it was, wholly or even mainly in virtue of its Celtic affinities. That literature was the outcome of the age, and something akin to it would have sprung up had Celtic tradition remained unknown to the Continent. The conception of feudal knighthood as a favoured class, in which men of different nations met on a common footing; the conception of knightly love as something altogether dissasociated from domestic life, must in any case have led to the constitution of such a society as we find portrayed in the romances. What is claimed is that the spirit of the age, akin to the Celtic, recognised in Celtic tales the food it was hungering for. It transformed them to suit its own needs and ideas, but it carried out the transformation on the whole in essential agreement with tradition. In some cases a radical change is made; such a one is presented to us in the Grail cycle.

The legend thus started with the advantages of belonging to the popular literature of the time, and of association through Brons with Christian tradition. Its incidents were varied, and owing to the blending of diverse strains of story vague enough to be plastic. The formal development of the cycle has been traced in the earlier chapters of these studies; that of its ideal conceptions will be found to follow similar lines. Various ethical intentions can be distinguished, and there is not more difference between the versions in the conduct of the story than in the ideals they set forth.

To some readers it may have seemed well nigh sacrilegious to trace that

> . . . . . . vanished Vase of Heaven
> That held like Christ's own Heart an Hin of Blood,

to the magic vessels of pagan deities. In England the Grail-

---

a false estimate of the relations between the profane and ecclesiastical writings of the Welsh. Finally the three Mabinogion (The Lady of the Fountain, Geraint, Peredur), which correspond to poems of Chrestien's, are unhesitatingly accepted as their originals. The influence of Welsh fiction in determining the courtly and refined nature of mediæval romance is, in consequence, greatly exaggerated. It is much to be wished that M. Renan would give us another review of Celtic literature based on the work of the last thirty years. His lucid and sympathetic criticism would be most welcome in a department of study which has been rather too exclusively left to the specialist.

legend is hardly known save in that form which it has assumed in the Queste. This French romance was one of those which Malory embodied in his *rifacimento* of the Arthurian cycle, and, thanks to Malory, it has become a portion of English speech and thought.* In our own days our greatest poet has expressed the quintessence of what is best and purest in the old romance in lines of imperishable beauty. As we follow Sir Galahad by secret shrine and lonely mountain mere until

> Ah, blessed vision! Blood of God,
> The spirit beats her mortal bars,
> As down dark tides the glory slides,
> And star-like mingles with the stars.

we are under a spell that may not be resisted. And yet of the two main paths which the legend has trodden that of Galahad is the least fruitful and the least beautiful. Compared with the Perceval Quest in its highest literary embodiment the Galahad Quest is false and antiquated on the ethical side, lifeless on the æsthetic side.

As it first meets us in literature the legend has barely emerged from its pure and simple narrative stage. There is a temptation to exaggerate Chrestien's skill of conception when speculating how he would have finished his work, but we know enough, probably, to correctly gauge his intentions. It has been said he meant to portray the ideal knight in Perceval. As was formerly the wont of authors he presents his hero in a good light, and he may be credited with a perception of the opportunity afforded him by his subject for placing that hero in positions wherein a knight could best distinguish himself. In so far his work may be accepted as his picture of a worthy knight. But I can discover in it no scheme of a quest after the highest good to

---

* Malory is a wonderful example of the power of style. He is a most unintelligent compiler. He frequently chooses out of the many versions of the legend, the longest, most wearisome, and least beautiful; his own contributions to the story are beneath contempt as a rule. But his language is exactly what it ought to be, and his has remained in consequence the classic English version of the Arthur story.

be set forth by means of the incidents at his command. Perceval
. .   matter of course, punctual in obeying the counsels
          r and of his teachers, Gonemans and the hermit-
          ʒtedly repentant when he is convicted of having
           religious duties. But it cannot be said that the
          rtations or the hero's repentance, confession, and
         ɪrk, or are intended to mark, a definite stage in a
         rds spiritual perfection. The explanation of the
        ɪs a consequence of his sin in leaving his mother,
         le real thought has been bestowed upon the subject.
        on, whether wholly Chrestien's, as I am tempted to
         placently reproduced from his model, gives the
         is skill in constructing an allegory. Beyond
        . such points (the hero's docility) as were indicated
        ᵧ ʜis model, or, as in the case of his religious opinions,
were a matter of course in a work of the time, Chrestien gives
Perceval no higher morality, no loftier aims than those of the day.
The ideal of chastity, soon to become of such importance in the
development of the legend, is nowhere set forth. Perceval, like
Gawain, takes full advantage of what *bonnes fortunes* come in
his way. And if the Quest connotes no spiritual ideal, still less
does it one of temporal sovereignty. Had Chrestien finished his
story he would have made Perceval heal the Maimed King and
win his kingdom, but that kingdom would not have been a type
of the highest earthly magnificence. We have seen reason to
hold that Chrestien made one great change in the story as he
found it in his model; he assigns the Fisher-King's illness to a
wound received in battle. This he did, I think, simply with a
view to shortening the story by leaving out the whole of the
Partinal episode. No mystical conception was floating in his
mind. Yet, as we shall see, the shape which he gave to this
incident strongly influenced some of the later versions, and gave
the hint for the most philosophical *motif* to be found in the
whole cycle.

The immediate continuators of Chrestien lift the legend to no
higher level. I incline to think that Gautier, with less skill of
narrative and far greater prolixity, yet trod closely in Chrestien's

footsteps.   In the love episodes he is as full of charm as the more celebrated poet.   The second meeting of Perceval and Blanchefleur is told with that graceful laughing *naïveté* of which French literature of the period has the secret.   But of a plan, an animating conception even such slight traces as Chrestien had introduced into the story are lacking.   Here, as in Chrestien, the mysterious talismans themselves in no way help forward the story. Chrestien certainly had the Christian signification of them in his mind, but makes no use of it.   The Vessel of the Last Supper, the Spear that pierced Christ's side might be any magic spear or vessel as far as he is concerned.   The original Pagan essence is retained ; the name alone is changed.

Thus far had the legend grown when it came into the hands of the author of the Queste.   The subject matter had been partly shaped and trimmed by a master of narrative, the connection with Christian tradition had been somewhat accentuated.   It was open to the author of the Queste to take the story as it stood, and to read into its incidents a deep symbolical meaning based upon the Christian character of the holy talismans.   He preferred to act otherwise.   He broke entirely with the traditional framework, dispossessed the original hero, and left not an incident of his model untouched.   But his method of proceeding may be likened to a shuffle rather than to a transformation.   The incidents reappear in other connection, but do not reveal the author's plan any more than is the case in the Conte du Graal.   The Christian character of the talismans is dwelt upon with almost wearisome iteration, the sacramental act supplies the matter of many and of the finest scenes, and yet the essence of the talismans is unchanged. The Holy Grail, the Cup of the Last Supper, the Sacramental Chalice is still when it appears the magic food-producing vessel of the old Pagan sagas.   What is the author's idea ?   Undoubtedly to show that the attainment of the highest spiritual good is not a thing of this world; only by renouncing every human desire, only by passing into a land intermediary between this earth and heaven, is the Quest achieved.   In the story of the prosecution of that Quest some attempt may be traced at portraying the cardinal virtues and deadly sins by means of the adventures of the questers, and of the innumerable exhortations addressed to them. But no skill is shown in the conduct of this plan, which is carried out chiefly by the introduction of numerous allegorical scenes which are made a peg for lengthy dogmatic and moral expositions. In this respect the author compares unfavourably with Robert de Borron, who shapes his story in full accord with his conception of the Grail itself, a conception deriving directly from the symbolic Christian nature he attributed to it, and who makes even such unpromising incidents as that of the Magic Fisher subserve his guiding idea.*

If the author's way of carrying out his conception cannot be praised, how does it stand with the conception itself? The fact that the Quest is wholly disassociated from this earth at once indicates the standpoint of the romance. The first effect of the Quest's proclamation is to break up the Table Round, that type of the noblest human society of the day, and its final achievement brings cheer or strengthening to no living man. The successful questers alone in their unhuman realm have any joy of the Grail. The spirit in which they prosecute their quest is best exemplified by Sir Bors. When he comes to the magic tower and is tempted of the maidens, who threaten to cast themselves down and be dashed to pieces unless he yield them his love, he is sorry for them, but unmoved, thinking it better "they lose their souls than he his." So little had the Christian writer apprehended the signification of Christ's most profound saying. The character of the principal hero is in consonancy with this aim, wholly remote from the life of man on earth. A shadowy perfection at the outset, he remains a shadowy perfection throughout, a bloodless and unreal creature, as fit when he first appears upon the scene as when he quits it, to accomplish a quest, purposeless, inasmuch as it only removes him from a world in which he has neither part nor share. Such human interest as there is in the

---

* See p. 112 for a brief summary of Borron's conception ; Sin the cause of want among the people ; the separation of the pure from the impure by means of the fish (symbol of Christ) ; punishment of the self-willed false disciple ; reward of Brons by charge of the Grail ; symbolising of the Trinity by the three tables and three Grail Keepers.

story is supplied by Lancelot, who takes over many of the
adventures of Perceval or Gawain in the Conte du Graal. In
him we note contrition for past sin, strivings after a higher
life with which we can sympathise. In fine, such moral teaching
as the Queste affords is given us rather by sinful Lancelot than
by sinless Galahad.

But the aversion to this world takes a stronger form in the
Queste, and one which is the vital conception of the work, in the
insistence upon the need for physical chastity. To rightly understand the author's position we must glance at the state of manners
revealed by the romances, and in especial at the sex-relations as
they were conceived of by the most refined and civilised men and
women of the day. The French romances are, as a rule, too
entirely narrative to enable a clear realisation of what these were.
Wolfram, with his keener and more sympathetic eye for individual
character—Wolfram, who loves to analyse the sentiments and to
depict the outward manifestations of feeling of his personages—is
our best guide here. The manners and customs of the day can be
found in the French romances; the feelings which underlie them
must be sought for in the German poet.

The marked feature of the sex-relations in the days of chivalry
was the institution of *minnedienst* (love-service). The knight
bound himself to serve a particular lady, matron or maid. To
approve himself brave, hardy, daring, patient, and discreet was
his part of the bargain, and when fulfilled the lady must fulfil
hers and pay her servant. The relation must not for one moment
be looked upon as platonic; the last favours were in every case
exacted, or rather were freely granted, as the lady, whether maid
or wedded wife, thought it no wrong thus to reward her knight.
It would have been "bad form" to deny payment when the
service had been rendered, and the offender guilty of such conduct
would have been scouted by her fellow-women as well as by all
men. Nothing is more instructive in this connection than the
delightfully told episode of Gawain and Orgueilleuse. The latter
is unwedded, a great and noble lady, but she has already had
several favoured lovers, as indeed she frankly tells Gawain. He
proffers his service, which she hardly accepts, but heaps upon him

all manner of indignity and insult, which he bears with the patient and resourceful courtesy, his characteristic in mediæval romance. Whilst the time of probation lasts, no harsh word, no impatient gesture, escapes him.   But when he has accomplished the feat of the Ford Perillous he feels that he has done enough, and taking his lady-love to task he lectures her, as a grave middle-aged man might some headstrong girl, upon the duties of a well-bred woman and upon the wrong she has done knighthood in his person.   To point the moral he winds up, at mid-day in the open forest, with a proposition which the repentant scornful one can only parry by the naïve remark, " Seldom she had found it warm in the embrace of a mail-clad arm."   Not only was it the lady's duty to yield after a proper delay, but at times she might even make the first advances and be none the worse thought of.   Blanchefleur comes to Perceval's bed with scarce an apology.*   Orgueilleuse, overcome with admiration at the Red Knight's prowess, offers him her love. True, she has doubts as to the propriety of her conduct, but when she submits them to Gawain, the favoured lover for the time being, he unhesitatingly approves her—Perceval's fame was such that had he accepted her proffered love she could have suffered naught in honour.

Customs such as these, and a state of feelings such as they imply, are so remote from us, that it is difficult to realise them, particularly in view of the many false statements respecting the nature of chivalrous love which have obtained currency.   But we must bear in mind that the age was pre-eminently one of individual prowess.   The warlike virtues were all in all.   That a man should be brave, hardy, and skilful in the use of his weapons was the

---

* The greater delicacy of the Welsh tale has already been noted. " To make him such a offer before I am wooed by him, that, truly, can I not do," says the counterpart of Blanchefleur in the Mabinogi. " Go my sister and sleep," answers Peredur, "nor will I depart from thee until I do that which thou requirest." I cannot help looking upon the prominence which the Welsh story-teller has given to this scene as his protest against the strange and to him repulsive ways of knightly love. The older, mythic nature of Peredur's beloved, who might woo without forfeiting womanly modesty, in virtue of her goddesshood, had died away in the narrator's mind, the new ideal of courtly passion had not won acceptance from him.

essential in a time when the single hero was almost of as much account as in the days of Achilles, Siegfried, or Cuchullain. That *minnedienst* tended to this end, as did other institutions of the day which we find equally blamable, is its historical excuse. Even then many felt its evils and perceived its anti-social character. Some, too, there were who saw how deeply it degraded the ideal of love.

A protest against this morality was indeed desirable. Such a one the Queste does supply. But it is not enough to protest in a matter so profoundly affecting mankind as the moral ideas which govern the sex-relations. Not only must the protest be made in a right spirit, and on the right lines, but a truer and loftier ideal must be set up in place of the one attacked. In how far the Queste fulfils these conditions we shall see. Meanwhile, as a sample of the feelings with which many Englishmen have regarded it, and as an attempt to explain its historical and ethical *raison d'être*, I cannot do better than quote Mr. Furnivall's enthusiastic words : " What is the lesson of it all ? Is the example of Galahad and his unwavering pursuit of the highest spiritual object set before him, nothing to us ? Is that of Perceval, pure and tempted, on the point of yielding, yet saved by the sight of the symbol of his Faith, to be of no avail to us ? Is the tale of Bohors, who has once sinned, but by a faithful life . . . at last tasting spiritual food, and returning to devote his days to God and Good—is this no lesson to us ? . . . On another point, too, this whole Arthur story may teach us. Monkish, to some extent, the exaltation of bodily chastity above almost every other earthly virtue is ; but the feeling is a true one ; it is founded on a deep reverence for woman, which is the most refining and one of the noblest sentiments of man's nature, one which no man can break through without suffering harm to his spiritual life."

It would be hard to find a more striking instance of how the " editorial idol " may override perception and judgment. He who draws such lofty and noble teachings from the Queste del Saint Graal, must first bring them himself. He must read modern religion, modern morality into the mediæval allegory, and on one point he must entirely falsify the mediæval conception.

Whether this is desirable is a question we can have no hesitation in deciding negatively. It is better to find out what the author really meant than to interpret his symbolism in our own fashion.

The author of the Queste places the object and conditions of his mystic quest wholly outside the sphere of human action or interest; in a similar spirit he insists, as an indispensable requirement in the successful quester, upon a qualification necessarily denied to the vast majority of mankind. His work is a glorification of physical chastity. "Blessed are the pure—in body—for they shall inherit the Kingdom of Heaven," is the text upon which he preaches. In such a case everything depends upon the spirit of the preacher, and good intent is not enough to win praise. His conception, says Mr. Furnivall, is founded upon a deep reverence for woman. This is, indeed, such a precious thing that had the mediæval ascetic really felt it we could have forgiven the stupidity which ignores all that constitutes the special dignity and pathos of womanhood. But he felt nothing of the kind. Woman is for him the means whereby sin came into the world, the arch stumbling-block, the tool the devil finds readiest to his hands when he would overcome man. Only in favour of the Virgin Mother, and of those who like her are vowed to mystical maidenhood, does the author pardon woman at all. One single instance will suffice to characterize the mediæval standpoint. When the Quest of the Holy Grail was first proclaimed in Arthur's Court there was great commotion, and the ladies would fain have joined therein, "car cascune dame ou damoiselle (qui) fust espousée ou amie, dist à son chiualer qu'ele yroit od lui en la queste." But a hermit comes forward to forbid this; "No dame or damsel is to accompany her knight lest he fall into deadly sin." Wife or leman, it was all one for the author of the Queste ; woman could not but be an occasion for deadly sin, and the sin, though in the one case less in degree (and even this is uncertain), was the same in kind. Fully one-half of the romance is one long exemplification of the essential vileness of the sex-relation, worked out with the minute and ingenious nastiness of a Jesuit moral theologian. The author was of his time; it was natural he should think and write as he did, and it would be uncritical to blame him for his degrading view of womanhood or for his narrow and sickly view of life. But when we are bidden to seek example of him, it is well to state the facts as they are.*

If his transformation of the story has been rudely effected without regard to its inherent possibilities, if the spirit of his ideal proves to be miserably ascetic and narrow, what then remains to the Queste, and how may we account for its popularity in its own day, and for the abiding influence which its version of the legend has exercised over posterity. Its literary qualities are at times great ; certain scenes, especially such as set forth the sacramental nature of the Grail, are touched with a mystical fervour which haunts the imagination. It has given some of the most picturesque features to this most picturesque of legends. But I see in the idea of the mystic quest proclaimed to and shared in by the whole Table Round the real secret of the writer's success. This has struck the imagination of so many generations and given the Queste an undeserved fame. In truth the conception of Arthur's court, laying aside ordinary cares and joys, given wholly up to one over-mastering spiritual aim, is a noble one. It is, I think, only in a slight degree the outcome of definite thought and intent but was dictated to the writer by the form into which he had recast

---

* The perplexities which beset the modern reader of the Queste are reflected in the Laureate's retelling of the legend. Nowhere else in the Idylls has he departed so widely from his model. Much of the incident is due to him, and replaces with advantage the nauseous disquisitions upon chastity which occupy so large a space in the Queste. The artist's instinct, rather than the scholar's respect for the oldest form of the story, led him to practically restore Perceval to his rightful place as hero of the quest. *His* fortunes we can follow with an interest that passing shadow, Galahad, wholly fails to evoke. Nor, as may easily be seen, is the fundamental conception of the twelfth century romance to the Laureate's taste. Arthur is his ideal of manhood, and Arthur's energies are practical and human in aim and in execution. What the " blameless king " speaks when he first learns of the quest represents, we may guess, the author's real attitude towards the whole fantastic business.

It is much to be regretted by all lovers of English poetry that Hawker's Quest of the Sangraal was never completed. The first and only chant is a magnificent fragment ; with the exception of the Laureate's Sir Galahad, the finest piece of pure literature in the cycle. Hawker, alone, perhaps of moderns, could have kept the mediæval tone and spirit, and yet brought the Quest into contact with the needs and ideas of to-day.

the story. Galahad had supplanted Perceval, but the latter could not be suppressed entirely. The achievement of the quest involved the passing away out of this world of the chief heroes, hence a third less perfect one is joined to them to bring back tidings to earth of the marvels he had witnessed. Lancelot, to whom are assigned so many of Perceval's adventures, cannot be denied a share in the quest ; it is the same with Gawain, whose character in the older romance fits him, moreover, excellently for the *rôle* of "dreadful example." By this time the Arthurian legend was fully grown, and the mention of these Knights called up the names of others with whom they were invariably connected by the romance writers. Well nigh every hero of importance was thus drawn into the magic circle, and the mystic Quest assumed, almost inevitably, the shape it did.

This conception, to which, if I am right, the author of the Queste was led half unconsciously, seems to us the most admirable thing in his work. It was, however, his ideal of virginity which struck the idea of his contemporaries, and which left its mark upon after versions. An age with such a gross ideal of love may have needed an equally gross ideal of purity. Physical chastity plays henceforth the leading part in the moral development of the cycle. With Robert de Borron it is the sin of the flesh which brings down upon the Grail host the wrath of Heaven, and necessitates the display of the Grail's wondrous power. Here may be noted the struggle of the new conception with the older form of the story. Alain, the virgin knight, would rather be flayed than marry, and yet he does marry in obedience to the original model. Robert is consistent in all that relates to the symbolism of the Grail, but in other respects, as we have already seen, he is easily thrown off his guard. In the Didot-Perceval, written as a sequel to Robert's poem, the same struggle between old and new continues, and the reconciling spirit goes to work in naïve and unskilful style. The incidents of the Conte du Graal are kept, although they accord but ill with the hero's ascetic spirit. In the portion of the Conte du Graal itself which goes under Manessier's name, along with adventures taken direct from Chrestien's model, and far less Christianised than in the earlier poet's work, many occur which are simply transferred from the Queste. No attempt is made at reconciling these jarring elements, and the effect of the contrast is at times almost comic. In two of the later romances of the cycle the fusion has been more complete, and the result is, in consequence, more interesting. The prose Perceval le Gallois keeps the original hero of the Quest as far as name and kinship are concerned, but it gives him the aggressive virginity and the proselytising zeal of Galahad. Gerbert's finish to the Conte du Graal is, perhaps, the strangest outcome of the double set of influences to which the later writers were exposed. Without doubt his model differed from the version used by Gautier and Manessier. It is more Celtic in tone, and is curiously akin to the hypothetical lost source of Wolfram von Eschenbach. The hero's absence from his lady-love is insisted upon, and the need of returning to her before he can find peace. The genuineness of this feature admits of little doubt. Many folk-tales tell of the severance of lover and beloved, and of their toilful wanderings until they meet again ; such a tale easily lends itself to the idea that separation is caused by guilt, and that, whilst severed, one or other lover must suffer misfortune. Often, as in the case of Diarmaid and the Daughter of King Under the Waves (*supra*, p. 194), definite mention is made of the guilt, as a rule an infringed taboo. Such an incident could scarcely fail to assume the ethical shape Gerbert has given it. Thus he had only to listen to his model, to take his incidents as he found them, and he had the matter for a moral conception wholly in harmony with them. The chastity ideal has been too strong for him. His lovers do come together, but only to exemplify the virtue of continence in the repulsive story of their bridal night. After Gerbert the cycle lengthens, but does not develop. The Queste retains its supremacy, and through Malory its dominant conception entered deeply into the consciousness of the English race.

How far the author of the Queste must be credited with the new ideal he brought into the legend is worth enquiry. Like so much else therein, it may have its roots in the folk and hero tales which underlie the romances. The Castle of Talismans visited by Perceval is the Land of Shades. In popular tradition the incident takes the form of entry into the hollow hill-side where the fairy king holds his court and hoards untold riches. Poverty and simplicity are the frequent qualifications of the successful quester; oftener still some mystic birthright, the being a Sunday's child for instance, or a seventh son; or again freedom from sin is required, and, perhaps, most frequently maidenhood.* The stress which so many peoples lay upon virginity in the holy prophetic maidens, who can transport themselves into the otherworld and bring thence the commands of the god, may be noted in the same connection. No Celtic tale I have examined with a view to throwing light upon the Grail romances insists upon this idea, but some version, now lost, may possibly have done so. Celtic tradition gave the romance writers of the Middle Ages material and form for the picture of human love; it may also have given them a hint of the opposing ideal of chastity.†

All this time it should be noted that no real progress is made in the symbolical machinery of the legend. The Holy Grail becomes superlatively sacrosanct, but it retains its pristine pagan essence, even in the only version, the Grand St. Graal, which knew of Borron and of his mystical conception.

Such, then, had been the growth of the legend in one direction. The original incidents were either transformed, mutilated, or, where they kept their first shape, underwent no ethical deepening or widening. The talismans themselves had been transferred from Celtic to Christian mythology, but their fate was still bound

---

* *Cf.* Grimm, Deutsche Mythologie, II, 811, and his references.

† The ideas held by many peoples in a primitive stage of culture respecting virginity are worthy careful study. Some physiological basis may be found for them in the phenomena of hysteria, which must necessarily have appeared to such peoples evidences of divine or demoniac possession, and at that stage are hardly likely to have been met with save among unmarried women. In the French witch trials these phenomena are often presented by nuns, in whose case they were probably the outcome of a life at once celibate and inactive. On the other hand the persons accused of witchcraft were as a rule of the most abandoned character, and it is a, morally speaking, degraded class which has furnished Professor Charcot and his pupils with the subjects in whom they have identified all the phenomena that confront the student of witch trials.

up with the otherworld.   He who would seek them must turn his
back upon this earth from which the Palace Spiritual and the
City of Sarras were even more remote than Avalon or Tir-na n-Og.
Was no other course open ?   Could not framework and incidents
of the Celtic tales be retained, and yet, raised to a loftier, wider
level, become a fit vehicle for philosophic thought and moral
exhortation ?   One side of popular tradition figured the hero as
wresting the talismans from the otherworld powers for the benefit
of his fellow men.   Could not this form of the myth be made to
yield a human, practical conception of the Quest and Winning of
the Holy Grail ?

We are luckily not reduced to conjecture in this matter.   A
work largely fulfilling these hypothetical requirements exists in
the Parzival of Wolfram von Eschenbach.   On the whole it is the
most interesting individual work of modern European literature
prior to the Divina Commedia, and its author has a better claim
than any other mediæval poet to be called a man of genius.   He
must, of course, be measured by the standard of his time.   It
would be useless to expect from him that homogeneity of narrative,
that artistic proportion of style first met with 150 years later in
Italy, and which from Italy passed into all European literatures
Compared with the unknown poets who gave their present shape
to the Nibelungenlied or to the Chanson de Roland he is an
individual writer, but he is far from deserving this epithet even in
the sense that Chaucer deserves it.   His subject dominates him.
Even when his philosophic mind is conceiving it under a new
aspect he anxiously holds to the traditional form.   Hence great inconsistencies in his treatment of the theme, hence, too, the frequent
difficulty in interpreting his meaning, the frequent doubt as to how
far the interpretation is correct.   Here, as in the discussion
respecting the *origines* of the Grail legend, resort must often be
had to conjecture, and any solution of the fascinating problems
involved is necessarily and largely subjective.

Wolfram's relation to his predecessors must be taken into
account in estimating the value of the Parzival.   The earlier
portion of his work differs entirely, as we have seen, from any
existing French romance ; so does the finish in so far as it agrees

with the opening. The greater part of the story is closely parallel
to Chrestien; there are points of contact, peculiar to these two
writers, with Gerbert. Little invention, properly so called, of
incident can be traced in the Parzival. The part common to it
and Chrestien is incomparably fuller and more interesting in the
German poet, but the main outlines are the same. Wolfram has,
however, been at some pains to let us know what was his conception of the legend. That much is allowed to remain at variance
therewith is a clear proof of his timidity of invention.

Doubt, he says, is the most potent corrupter of the soul. Whoso
gives himself over to unfaith and unsteadfastness treadeth in
truth the downward path. God Himself is very faithfulness.
Strife against Him, doubt of Him, is the highest sin. But
humility and repentance may expiate it, and he who thus repents
may be chosen by God for the Grail Kingship, the summit of
earthly holiness. Peace of soul and all earthly power are the
chosen one's; alone, unlawful desire and the company of sinners
are denied him by the Grail.

How is this leading conception worked out? The framework
and the march of incidents are the same as in the Conte du Graal.
One capital change at once, however, lifts the story to a higher
level. The Fisher King suffers from a wound received in the
cause of unlawful love, in disobedience to those heavenly commands which govern the Grail community. The healing question
can be put only by one worthy to take up the high office Amfortas
has dishonoured, in virtue of having passed through the strife of
doubt, and become reconciled to God by repentance and humble
trust. If Parzival neglected to put the question on his first
arrival at the Grail Castle, it was that in the conceit of youth
he fancied all wisdom was his. Childish insistence upon his
mother's counsels had brought down reproof upon him; he had
learnt the world's wisdom.from Gurnemanz, he had shown himself
in defence of Conduiramur a valiant knight, worthy of power and
woman's love. When brought into contact with the torturing
sorrow of Amfortas, he is too full of himself, of his teacher's wisdom,
to rightly use the opportunity.

The profound significance of the question which at once releases the sinner, and announces the one way in which the sin may be cancelled, namely, by the coming of a worthier successor, is due, if we may credit Birch-Hirschfeld, to an accident. Wolfram only knew Chrestien. The latter never explains the real nature of the Grail, and the German poet's knowledge of French was too slight to put him on the right track. The question, " Whom serve they with the Grail ? " which he found in Chrestien, was necessarily meaningless to him, and he replaced it by his, " Uncle, what is it tortures thee ? " The change *may* be the result of accident as is so much else in this marvellous legend, but it required a man of genius to turn the accident to such account. It is the insistence upon charity as the herald and token of spiritual perfection that makes the grandeur of Wolfram's poem, and raises it so immeasureably above the Queste.

The same human spirit is visible in the delineation of the Grail Kingship as the type of the highest good. Wolfram's theology is distinctively antinomian—no man may win the Grail in his own strength; it choseth whom it will—and has been claimed on the one hand* as a reflex of orthodox Catholic belief, on the other as a herald of the Lutheran doctrine of grace.† Theological experts may be left to fight out this question among themselves. Apart from this, Wolfram has a practical sense of the value of human effort. With him the Quest is not to be achieved by utter isolation from this earth and its struggles. The chief function of the Grail Kingdom is to supply an abiding type of a divinely ordered Society ; it also trains up leaders for those communities which lack them. It is a civilising power as well as a Palace Spiritual.

In the relation of man to Heaven, Wolfram, whilst fully accepting the doctrines of his age, appeals to the modern spirit with far greater power and directness than the Queste. In the other great question of the legend, the relation of man to woman, he is likewise nearer to us, although it must be confessed that he builds better than he knows. To the love ideal of his day, based wholly upon passion and vanity and severed from all family feeling, he

---

* Domanig, Parzival-Studien, I, II, 1878–80.
† San-Marte, Parzival-Studien, I–III, 1861–63.

opposes the wedded love of Parzival and Conduiramur. The hero's recollection of the mother of his children is the one saving influence throughout the years of doubt and discouragement which follow Kundrie's reproaches. Whilst still staggering under this blow, so cruelly undeserved as it seems to him, he can wish his friend and comrade, Gawain, a woman chaste and good, whom he may love and who shall be his guardian angel. The, thought of Conduiramur holds him aloof from the offered love of Orgeluse. In his last and bitterest fight, with his unknown brother, when it had nigh gone with him to his death, he recalls her and renews the combat with fresh strength. She it is for whom he wins the highest earthly crown, of which her pure, womanly heart makes her worthy. Reunion with her and with his children is Parzival's first taste of the joy that is henceforth to be his.

Passages may easily be multiplied that tally ill with the ideas of the poem as here briefly set forth. But the existence of these ideas is patent to the unprejudiced reader. Despite its many shortcomings, the poem which contains them is the noblest and most human outcome of that mingled strain of Celtic fancy and Christian symbolism whose history we have traced.*

In Wolfram, equally with the majority of the French romance writers, there is little consistency in the formal use of the mystic talismans. Be the reason what it may, Wolfram certainly never thought of associating the Grail with the Last Supper. But its religious character is, at times, as marked with him as with Robert de Borron or the author of the Queste. It is the actual vehicle of the Deity's commands; it restrains from sin; it suffers no unchaste servant; it may be seen of no heathen; the

---

* Some readers may be anxious to read Wolfram's work to whom twelfth-century German would offer great difficulties. A few words on the translation into modern German may, therefore, not be out of place. San-Marte's original translation (1839–41) is full of gross blunders and mistranslations, and, what is worse, of passages foisted into the text to support the translator's own interpretation of the poem as a whole. Simrock's. which followed, is extremely close, but difficult and unpleasing. San Marte's second edition, corrected from Simrock, is a great advance upon the first; but even here the translator has too often allowed his own gloss to replace Wolfram's statement. A thoroughly faithful yet pleasing rendering is a desideratum.

simple beholding of it preserves men from death. This last characteristic would be thought in modern times a sufficient tribute to the original nature of the old pagan cauldron of increase and rejuvenescence. But Wolfram was of his time, and followed his models faithfully. Along with the lofty spiritual attributes of his Grail, he pictures in drastic fashion its food-dispensing powers. The mystic stone, fallen from Heaven itself, renewed each Good Friday by direct action of the Spirit, becomes all at once a mere victual producing machine. We can see how little Wolfram liked this feature of his model, and how he felt the contrast between it and his own more spiritual conception. But here, as elsewhere in the poem, he allowed much to stand against which his better judgment protested. His own share in the development of the legend must be gauged by what is distinctively his, not by what he has in common with others. Judged thus, he must be said to have developed the Christian symbolic side of the legend as much as the human philosophic side. If in Robert de Borron the Grail touches its highest symbolic level through its identification with the body of the dead and risen Lord, we can trace in Wolfram the germ of that approximation of the Grail-Quester to the earthly career of the Saviour which Wagner was to develop more than 600 years later.*

What influence Wolfram's poem, with its practical, human enthusiasm, its true and noble sexual morality, might have had on English literature is an interesting speculation. It would have appealed, one would think, to our race with its utilitarian ethical instinct, with its lofty ideal of wedded love. The true man, Parzival, should, in the fitness of things, be the English hero of the Quest, rather than the visionary ascetic Galahad. Mediæval England was dominated by France and knew nothing of Germany,

---

* J. Van Santen, Zur Beurtheilung Wolfram von Eschenbach, Wesel, 1882, has attacked Wolfram for his acceptance of the morality of the day, and has, on that ground, denied him any ethical or philosophic merit. The pamphlet is useful for its references, but otherwise worthless. The fact that Wolfram does accept *Minnedienst* only gives greater value to his picture of a nobler and purer ideal of love, whilst to refuse recognition of his other qualities on this account is much as who should deny Dante's claim to be regarded as a teacher and thinker because of his acceptance of the hideous mediæval hell.

and when in the late fifteenth and sixteenth centuries we can trace German influence on English thought and writ, taste had changed, and the Parzival was well-nigh forgotten in its own land. It remained so almost until our own days. The Quest after Perfection still haunted the German mind, but it was conceived of on altogether different lines from those of the twelfth century poet. The nation of scholars pictured the quester as a student, not as a knight. When it took shape in the dreary period of Protestant scholasticism the quest is wholly cursed. Faust's pursuit of knowledge is unlawful, a rebellion against God, which dooms him irrevocably. Not until Goethe's day is the full significance of the legend perceived, is the theme widened to embrace the totality of human striving. Thus the last glimpse we have of Faust is of one devoted to the service of man ; the last words of the poem are a recognition of the divine element in the love of man and woman.*

In Germany, as in England, the old legend has appealed afresh to poets and thinkers, and then, as was natural, they turned to Germany's greatest mediæval poet. Wagner's Parsifal would, in any case, be interesting as an expression of one of the strongest dramatic geniuses of the century. Considered purely as a work of literature, apart from the music, it has rare beauty and profound significance. The essentially dramatic bent of Wagner's mind, the stage destination of the poem, must be borne in mind when considering it. Wolfram's conception—youthful folly and inexperience chastised by reproof, followed by doubt and strife, cancelled by the faithful steadfastness of the full-grown man—is obviously unsuited for dramatic purposes. At no one point of Wolfram's poem do we find that clash of motives and of characters which the stage requires. In building up *his* conception Wagner has utilised every hint of his predecessor with wonderful ingenuity. Klinschor, the magician, becomes with him the active opponent of the Grail King, Amfortas, from whom he has wrested the holy

* In the Geheimnisse Goethe shows some slight trace of the Parzival legend, and the words in which the teaching of the poem are summed up: "Von der Gewalt, die alle Wesen bindet, Befreit *der* Mensch sich der sich überwindet," may be looked upon as an eighteenth century rendering of Wolfram's conception.

spear by the aid of Kundry's unholy beauty.   Kundry is Wagner's
great contribution to the legend.   She is the Herodias whom
Christ for her laughter doomed to wander till He come again.
Subject to the powers of evil, she must tempt and lure to
their destruction the Grail warriors.   And yet she would find
release and salvation could a man resist her love spell.*   She
knows this.   The scene between the unwilling temptress, whose
success would but doom her afresh, and the virgin Parsifal thus
becomes tragic in the extreme.   How does this affect Amfortas
and the Grail?   In this way.   Parsifal is the " pure fool,"
knowing nought of sin or suffering.   It had been foretold of him
he should become " wise by fellow-suffering," and so it proves.
The overmastering rush of desire unseals his eyes, clears his
mind.   Heart-wounded by the shaft of passion, he feels Amfortas'
torture thrill through him.   The pain of the physical wound is
his, but far more, the agony of the sinner who has been unworthy
his high trust, and who, soiled by carnal sin, must yet daily come
in contact with the Grail, symbol of the highest purity and
holiness.   The strength which comes of the new-born knowledge
enables him to resist sensual longing, and thereby to release both
Kundry and Amfortas.

In the latest version of the Perceval Quest, as in the Galahad
Quest, the ideal of chastity is thus paramount.   This result is due
to Wagner's dramatic treatment of the theme.   The conception
that knowledge of sin and fellowship in suffering are requisite to
enable man to resist temptation, and that thus alone does he
acquire the needful strength to assist his fellows, however true
and profound, can obviously only be worked out on the stage

---

* We may here note an admirable example of the inevitable, spontaneous
character of the growth of certain conceptions, especially of such as have been
partly shaped by the folk-mind.   There is nothing in Wolfram or in the French
romances to show that the fortunes of the loathly damsel (Wagner's Kundry)
are in any way bound up with the success of the Quest.   But we have seen that
the Celtic folk-tales represent the loathly damsel as the real protagonist of the
story.   She cannot be freed unless the hero do his task.   Precisely the same
situation as in Wagner, who was thus led back to the primitive *donnée*, although
he can only have known intermediary stages in which its signification had been
quite lost.

through the medium of one form of sin and suffering. The long psychological process of Wolfram's poem, the slow growth of the unthinking youth into the steadfast, faithful man, is replaced by a mystic, transcendental conversion. From out a world of human endeavour, human motive, we have stepped into one wholly ascetic and symbolical. The love of man for woman only appears in the guise of forbidden desire; the aims and needs of this world are not even thought of. Every incident has been remoulded in accord with Christian tradition. Wagner fully accepts the sacramental nature of the Grail, and the Grail feast is with him a faithful reproduction of the Last Supper. Holiness and purity are the essence of the Grail, which is cleared from every taint of its pagan origin. And whilst Wagner, following the French models, identifies the Grail with the most sacred object of Christian worship, he also, developing hints of Wolfram's, reshapes the career of his Grail-seeker in accord with that of Christ. Parsifal, the releaser of sin-stricken Kundry, of sin-stricken Amfortas—Parsifal, the restorer of peace and holiness to the Grail Kingdom—becomes a symbol of the Saviour.

In the reasoned, artistic growth of the legend, the plastic, living element is that supplied by Christian tradition. From the moment that the Celtic lord of the underworld is identified with the evangelist of Britain we see the older complex of tales acquire consistency, life, and meaning. Even where the direct influence of the intruding element is slightest, as in the Conte du Graal, we can still perceive that it is responsible for the germs of after development. Sometimes violently and unintelligently, sometimes with a keen feeling for the possibilities of the original romance, sometimes with the boldest introduction of new matter, sometimes with slavish adherence to pre-Christian conceptions, the transformation of the Celtic tales goes on. The cauldron of increase and renovation, the glaive of light, the magic fish, the visit to the otherworld, all are gradually metamorphosed until at last the talisman of the Irish gods becomes the symbol of the risen Lord, its seeker a type of Christ in His divinest attributes.

The ethical teaching of the legend becomes also purely Christian as the Middle Ages conceived Christianity. Renunciation of the world and of the flesh is its key-note. Once only in Wolfram do we find an ideal human in its essence, though dogmatic in form ; the path thus opened is not trodden further, and the legend remains as a whole, on the moral side, a monument of Christian asceticism.

We have seen reason to surmise that the folk-tales which underlie the romances themselves gave the hint for the most characteristic manifestation of this ascetic ideal. It is worth enquiry if these tales have developed themselves independently from the Christianised legend, and if such development shows any trace of ethical conceptions comparable with those of the legend. Can we gather from the tales as fashioned by the folk teaching similar to that of the preachers, philosophers, and artists by whom the legend has been shaped ? Few enquiries can be more interesting than one which traces such a conception as the Quest after the highest good as pictured by the rudest and most primitive members of the race.

Many of the tales which formed a part of the (hypothetical) Welsh original of the earliest Grail romances have been shown to come under the Aryan Expulsion and Return Formula (*supra*, Ch. VI). Among most races this formula has connected itself with the national heroes, and has given rise to hero-tales in which the historical element outweighs the ethical. Sometimes, as in the tale of Perseus, the incidents are so related as to bring out an ethical *motif*; Perseus is certainly thought of as avenging his mother's undeserved wrongs. I cannot trace anything of the kind among the Celts. All the incidents of the formula in Celtic tradition which I know of are purely historical in character. This element of the old Saga-mass thus yields nothing for the present enquiry. Others are more fruitful. Perceval is akin not only to Fionn, but also to the Great Fool. The Lay of the Great Fool was found to tally closely with adventures in the Mabinogi and in the Conte du Graal (*supra*, Ch. VI). It also sets forth a moral conception that admits of profitable comparison with that of the Grail romances.

Ultimately, the Lay is, I have little doubt, one of the many forms in which a mortal's visit to the otherworld was related. Wandering into the Glen of Glamour, the hero and his love encounter a magician; the hero drinks of the proffered cup, despite his love's remonstrances, and forthwith loses his two legs. This is obviously a form of the widely-spread myth which forbids the visitant to the otherworld to partake of aught there under penalty of never returning to earth. But this mythical *motif* has taken an ethical shape in popular fancy. According to Kennedy's version, it is the hero's excess in draining the cup to the dregs which calls for punishment. This change is of the same nature as that noted with regard to a similar incident in the Grail romances. There, the old mythic taboo of sleeping or speaking in the otherworld called at last for an explanation, and found one in Wolfram's philosophic conception. The parallel does not end here. Perceval may retrieve his fault, and so may the Great Fool; Wolfram makes his hero win salvation by steadfast faith, the folk-tale makes its hero in the face of every form of temptation a pattern of stead-fast loyalty to the absent friend and to the pledged word. It may, or may not, be considered to the advantage of the folk-tale that, unlike the mediæval romance, it deals neither in mysticism nor in asceticism. The sin and atonement of the Great Fool are such as the popular mind can grasp; he is an example of human weakness and human strength. The woman he loves is no temptress, no representative of the evil principle—on the contrary, she is ever by his side to counsel and to cheer him.

When it is remembered that the two off-shoots, romantic-legendary and popular, from the one traditional stem have grown up in perfect independence of each other, the kinship of moral idea is startling. The folk-lorist has often cause to wonder at the spontaneous flower-like character of the object of his study; folk-tradition seems to obey fixed laws of growth and to be no product of man's free thought and speech. The few partisans of the theory that folk-tradition is only a later and weakened echo of the higher culture of the race are invited to study the present case. A Celtic tale, after supplying an important element to the Christian-ised Grail legend, has gone on its way entirely unaffected by the new shape which that legend assumed, and yet it has worked out a moral conception of fundamental likeness to one set forth in the legend. It would be difficult to find a more perfect instance of the spontaneous, evolutional character of tradition contended for by what, in default of a better name, must be called the anthropological school of folk-lorists.

We must quit Celtic ground to find another example of an element in the originals of the Grail romances, embodying a popular ethical idea. This instance is such an interesting one that I cannot pass it by in silence. As was shown in Chapter VII, one of the many forms of the hero's visit to the otherworld has for object the release of maidens held captive by an evil power. A formal connection was established between this section of the romance and the folk-tale of the Sleeping Beauty. As a whole, too, this tale admits of comparison with the legend. Its origin is mythic without a doubt. Whether it be regarded as a day or as a year myth, as the rescue of the dawn from night, or of the incarnate spring from the bonds of winter, it equally pictures a victory of the lord of light and heat and life over the powers of darkness, cold, and death. With admirable fidelity folk-tradition has preserved the myth, so that its true nature can be recognised without fail. It would be wrong, though, to conclude that retention of the mythic framework implied any recognition of its mythic character on the part of those who told or listened to the story. Some investigators, indeed, hold it idle to consider it otherwise than as a tale told merely for amusement. But a story, to live, must appeal to moral as well as to æsthetic emotions. In the folk-mind this story sets forth, dimly though it may be, that search for the highest human felicity which is likewise a theme of the Grail romances. What better picture of this quest could be found than the old mythic symbol of the awakening of life and increase beneath the kiss of the sun-god. The hero of the folk-tale makes his way through the briars and tangle of the forest that he may restore to the deserted castle life and plenty; so much has the tale retained of the original mythic signification. As regards the quester himself, the maiden he thus woos is his reward and the noblest prize earth has to offer him. Where the romance writers made power, or riches, or learning, or personal salvation the goal of man's effort, the folk-tale bids him seek happiness in the common human affections.

Such, all too briefly sketched, has been the fate and story of these tales, first shaped in a period of culture wellnigh pre-historic, gifted by reason of their Celtic setting with a charm that commended them to the romantic spirit of the middle ages, and made them fit vehicles for the embodiment of mediæval ideas. Quickened by Christian symbolism they came to express and typify the noblest and the most mystic longings of man. The legend, as the poets and thinkers of the twelfth century fashioned it, has still a lesson and a meaning for us. It may be likened to one of the divine maidens of Irish tradition. She lives across the western sea. Ever and again heroes, filled with mysterious yearning for the truth and beauty of the infinite and undying, make sail to join her if they may. They pass away and others succeed them, but she remains ever young and fair. So long as the thirst of man for the ideal endures, her spell will not be weakened, her charm will not be lessened. But each generation works out this Quest in its own spirit. This much may be predicted with some confidence: henceforth, whosoever would do full justice to the legend must take pattern by Wolfram von Eschenbach rather than by any of his rivals; he must deal with human needs and human longings; his ideal must be the widening of human good and human joy. Above all, he must give reverent yet full expression to all the aspirations, all the energies of man and of woman.

FINIS.

APPENDIX A.

The Relationship of Wolfram von Eschenbach and Chrestien.

The various arguments for and against the use of any other French source than Chrestien by Wolfram have been clearly summed up by G. Bötticher, Die Wolfram Literatur seit Lachmann, Berlin, 1880. The chief representative of the negative opinion is Birch-Hirschfeld, who first gives, Chapter VIII. of his work, a useful collection of passages relating to the Grail, the Castle, and the Quest, from both authors. His chief argument is this :—The Grail in all the romances except in Wolfram is a cup or vessel, but in Wolfram a stone, a peculiarity only to be explained by Wolfram's ignorance of any source than Chrestien, and by the fact that the latter, in accordance with his usual practice of leaving objects and persons in as mysterious an atmosphere as possible, nowhere gives a clear description of the Grail. He undoubtedly would have done so if he had finished his work. Such indications as he gave led Wolfram, who did not understand the word *Graal*, to think it was a stone. It is inconceivable that Kyot, if such a personage existed, should have so far departed from all other versions as not to picture the Grail as a vessel, inconceivable, again, that his account of it should have been just as vague as Chrestien's, that he should have afforded Wolfram no hint of the real nature of the object. In Chrestien Perceval's question refers to the Grail, but Wolfram, missing the significance of the holy vessel owing to the meagreness of the information respecting it given to him by Chrestien, was compelled to transform the whole incident, and to refer it solely to the sufferings of the wounded King. Again, Chrestien meant to utilise the sword, and to bring Gawain to the Grail Castle ; but his unfinished work did not carry out his intention, and in Wolfram Gawain also fails to come to the Grail Castle ; the sword is passed over in silence in the latter part of the poem.—Simrock, jealous for the credit of Wolfram, claimed for him the invention of all that could not be traced to Chrestien, resting the claim chiefly upon consideration of a sentimental patriotic nature.—In opposition to these views, although the fact is not denied that Wolfram followed Chrestien closely for the parts common to both, it is urged to be incredible that he, a German poet, should invent a prologue to Chrestien's unfinished work connecting with an Angevin princely genealogical legend. It was also pointed out, with greatest fulness by Bartsch, Die Eigennamen im Parcival und Titurel, Germanist. Studien, II., 114, *et seq.*, that the German poet gives a vast number of proper names which are not to be found in Chrestien, and that these are nearly all of French, and especially Southern French and Provençal origin.—Simrock endeavoured to meet this argument in the fifth edition of his translation, but with little success.—Bötticher, whilst admitting the weight of Birch-Hirschfeld's arguments, points out the difficulties which his theory involves. If Wolfram simply misunderstood Chrestien and did not differ from him personally, why should he be at the trouble of inventing an elaborately feigned source to justify a simple addition to the original story ? If he only knew of the Grail from Chrestien, what gave him the idea of endowing it, as he did, with mystic properties ? Martin points out in addition (Zs. f. d. A., V. 87) that Wolfram has the same connection of the Grail and Swan Knight story as Gerbert, whom, *ex hypothesi*, he could not have known, and who certainly did not know him.—In his Zur Gralsage, Martin returned to the question of proper names, and showed that a varying redaction of a large part of the romance is vouched for by the different names which Heinrich von dem Türlin applies to personages met with both in Chrestien and in Wolfram. If, then, one French version, that followed by Heinrich, who is obviously a translator, is lost, why not another ?

The first thorough comparison of Chrestien and Wolfram is to be found in Otto Küpp's Unmittelbaren Quellen des Parzival, (Zs. f. d. Ph. XVII., 1). He argues for Kyot's existence. Some of the points he mentions in which the two poems differ, and in which Wolfram's account has a more archaic character, may be cited : The mention of Gurnemanz's sons ; the food producing properties of the Grail on Parzival's first visit; the reproaches of the varlet to Parzival on his leaving the Grail Castle, " You are a goose, had you but moved your lips and asked the host ! Now you have lost great praise ;"* the statement that the broken sword is to be made whole by dipping in the Lake Lac, and the mention of a sword charm by virtue of which Parzival can become lord of the Grail Castle ; the mention that no one seeing the Grail could die within eight days. In addition Küpp finds that many of the names in Wolfram are more archaic than those of Chrestien. On the other hand, Küpp has not noticed that Chrestien has preserved a more archaic feature in the prohibition laid upon Gauvain not to leave for seven days the castle after he had undergone the adventure of the bed.

Küpp has not noticed that some of the special points he singles out in Wolfram are likewise to be found in Chrestien's continuators, *e.g.*, the mention of the sons of Gurnemanz, by Gerbert.

---

* *Cf.* the reproaches addressed to Potter Thompson (*supra*, p. 198). That the visitor to the Bespelled Castle should be reproached, at once, for his failure to do as he ought, seems to be a feature of the earliest forms of the story. *Cf.* Campbell's Three Soldiers (*supra*, p. 196). If Wolfram had another source than Chrestien it was one which partook more of the unspelling than of the feud quest formula. Hence the presence of the feature here.

I believe I have the first pointed out the insistence by both Wolfram and Gerbert upon the hero's love to and duty towards his wife.

The name of Parzival's uncle in Wolfram, Gurnemanz, is nearer to the form in Gerbert, Gornumant, than to that in Chrestien, Gonemant.

The matter may be summed up thus: it is very improbable that Wolfram should have invented those parts of the story found in him alone ; the parts common to him and Chrestien are frequently more archaic in his case ; there are numerous points of contact between him and Gerbert. All this speaks for another French source than Chrestien. On the other hand, it is almost inconceivable that such a source should have presented the Grail as Wolfram presents it.

I cannot affect to consider the question decidedly settled one way or the other, and have, therefore, preferred to make no use of Wolfram. I would only point out that if the contentions of the foregoing studies be admitted, they strongly favour the genuineness of the non-Chrestien section of Wolfram's poem,* though I admit they throw no light upon his special presentment of the Grail itself.

---

* In Wolfram's work there is a much closer connection between the Gawain quest and the remainder of the poem than in Chrestien. Orgueilleuse, to win whose love Gawain accomplishes his feats, is a former love of Amfortas, the Grail King, who won for her a rich treasure and was wounded in her service. Klinschor, too, the lord of the Magic Castle, is brought into contact with Orgueilleuse, whom he helps against Gramoflanz. It is difficult to say whether this testifies to an earlier or later stage of growth of the legend. The winning of Orgueilleuse as the consequence of accomplishing the feat of the Ford Perillous and plucking the branch is strongly insisted upon by Wolfram and not mentioned by Chrestien, though it is possible he might have intended to wed the two had he finished his poem. In this respect, however, and taking these two works as they stand, Wolfram's account seems decidedly the earlier. In another point, too, he seems to have preserved the older form. Besides his Kundrie la Sorcière (the loathly damsel) he has a Kundrie la Belle, whom I take to be the loathly damsel released from the transforming spell.

APPENDIX B.

The Prologue to the Grand St. Graal and the Brandan Legend.

I believe the only parallel to this prologue to be the one furnished by that form of the Brandan legend of which Schröder has printed a German version (Sanct Brandan) at Erlangen, in 1871, from a MS. of the fourteenth century, but the first composition of which he places (p. 15) in the last quarter of the twelfth century. The text in question will be found pp. 51, *et seq.*: Brandan, a servant of God, seeks out marvels in rare books, he finds that two paradises were on earth, that another world was situated under this one, so that when it is here night it is day there, and of a fish so big that forests grew on his back, also that the grace of God allowed some respite every Saturday night to the torments of Judas. Angry at all these things he burnt the book. But the voice of God spake to him, "Dear friend Brandan thou hast done wrong, and through thy wrath I see My wonders lost." The holy Christ bade him fare nine years on the ocean, until he see whether these marvels were real or a lie. Thereafter Brandan makes ready a ship to set forth on his travels.

This version was very popular in Germany. Schröder prints a Low German adaptation, and a chap book one, frequently reprinted during the fifteenth, sixteenth, and seventeenth centuries. But besides this form there was another, now lost, which can be partially recovered from the allusions to it in the Wartburg Krieg, a German poem of the thirteenth and early fourteenth century, and which is as follows:— An angel brings Brandan a book from heaven : Brandan finds so many incredible things in it that he taxes book and angel with lying, and burns the book. For his unfaith he must wander till he find it. God's grace grants him this at last ; an angel gives him the sign of two fires burning, which are the eyes of an ox, upon whose tongue he shall find the book. He hands it to Uranias, who brings it to *Scotland* (*i.e.*, of course Ireland Schröder, p. 9.

The closeness of the parallel cannot be denied, and it raises many interesting questions, which I can here only allude to. The Isle of Brandan has always been recognized as a Christian variant of the Celtic Tír-na n-Og, the Land of the Shades, Avalon. Schröder has some instructive remarks on this subject, p. 11. The voyage of Brandan may thus be compared with that of Bran, the son of Febal (*supra*, p. 232), both being versions of the wide-spread myth of a mortal's visit to the otherworld. It is not a little remarkable that in the Latin legend, which differs from the German form by the absence of the above-cited prologue, there is an account (missing in the German), of a "conopeus" ("cover" or "canopy," *cf.* Ducange and Diez, *sub voce;* the old French version translates it by "Pavillon of the colour of silver but harder than marble, and a column therein of clearest crystal." And on the fourth day they find a window and therein a "calix" of the same nature as the "conopeus" and a "patena" of the colour of the column (Schröder, p. 27, and Note 41).

Thus there is a formal connection between the Brandan legend and the Grail romances in the prologue common to two works of each cycle, and there is a likeness of subject-matter between the Brandan legend and the older Celtic traditions which I have assumed to be the basis of the romances. But German literature likewise supplies evidence of a connection between Brandan and Bran. Professor Karl Pearson has referred me to a passage in the Pfaffe Amis, a thirteenth century South German poem, composed by Der Stricker, the hero of which, a prototype of Eulenspiegel, goes through the world gulling and tricking his contemporaries. In a certain town he persuades the good people to entrust to him their money, by telling them that he has in his possession a very precious relic, the head of St. Brandan, which has commanded him to build a cathedral (Lambl's Edition, Leipzig, 1872, p. 32). The preservation of the head of Bran is a special feature in the Mabinogi. I have instanced parallels from Celtic tradition (Branwen, p. 14), and Professor Rhys has since (Hibb. Lect., p. 94) connected the whole with Celtic mythological beliefs. This chance reference in a German poem is the only trace to my knowledge of an earlier legend in which, it may be, Bran and Brandan, the visitor to and the lord of the otherworld, were one and the same person.

It is highly desirable that every form of or allusion to the Brandan legend should be examined afresh, as, perhaps, able to throw fresh light upon the origin and growth of the Grail legend. In Pseudo-Chrestien Perceval's mother goes on a pilgrimage to the shrine of St. Brandan.

266

INDEX I.

DRAMATIS PERSONÆ.

[This Index is to the Summaries contained in Chapter II, and the references
are not to page and line, but to Version and Incident. The Versions are distinguished by the following abbreviations :—

Conte du Graal **Co**, Pseudo-Chrestien **PC**, Chrestien **C**, Gautier **G**, Manessier
Ma, Gerbert **Ge**, Wolfram **W**, Heinrich von dem Türlin **H**, Mabinogi of
Peredur **M**, Thornton MS. Sir Perceval **T**, Didot-Perceval **D**, Borron's poem **B**,
Queste **Q** (**Q**¹ and **Q**² refer to the different drafts of the romance distinguished
p. 83) Grand St. Graal **GG**. With the less important entries, or when the
entries are confined to one version, a simple number reference is given. But in
the case of the more important personages, notably Perceval, Gawain, and
Galahad, an attempt has been made to show the life history, by grouping
together references to the same incident from different versions; in this case
each incident group is separated from other groups by a long dash——. Any
speciality in the incident presented by a version is bracketed *before* the reference
initial, and, when deemed advisable, reference has been made to allied as well as
to similar incidents. This detail, to save space, is, as a rule, given only once, as
under Perceval, and not duplicated under other headings, the number reference
alone being given in the latter cases. The fullest entry is Perceval, which
practically comprises such entries as Fisher King, Grail, Sword, Lance, etc.]

ABEL Q37, GG24.
ABRIORIS G9.
ACHEFLOUR T1.
ADAM Q37, GG24.
ADDANC OF LAKE M16, 19.
AGARAN Q23.
AGRESTES GG40.
AGUIGRENONS Co, *Kingrun* W, anonymous M, C6, W, M8.
ALAINS, Celidoine's son GG43.
ALAINS or **ALEIN** (li Gros D, Q, GG) B12——Dprol, 1, 6, 12, Q26, GG30,
43, 45, 51, 58, 59.
ALEINE, Gawain's niece, D1.
ALFASEM GG51, 58.
AMANGONS PC1, 2, 4.
AMFORTAS, see Fisher King.
AMINADAP GG 58.
ANGHARAD Law Eurawc, M12, 14.
ANTIKONIE, see Facile Damsel.

ARGASTES——CLAMADEX.

CLARISSE——GALAHAD.

CLARISSE Co Mons MS. or *Clarissant* Montpellier MS., Itonje **W**——C18, **G**1, **W**.

CLAUDIUS GG3.

CLAUDIUS, son of Claudas **Q**²51.

CORBENIC Q, GG, CORBIÈRE Ma23, **Q**13, 43, 48, **GG**51.

CORSAPIAS GG22.

COWARD KNIGHT Ma17, 19.

CRUDEL Q6, 15, **G**e15, **GG**36-38.

DAVID Q37.

DODINEL Ma14.

ELIEZER Q27.

EMPTY SEAT, see Seat Perillous.

ENYGEUS, ENYSGEUS, or **ANYSGEUS B**7, 8, 11, 12.

EREC D2.

ERNOUS Q39.

ESCORANT Q²51.

ESCOS GG47.

ESPINOGRE Ma5.

ESTROIS DE GARILES Q²51.

ETLYM GLEDDYV COCH M16-18.

EVALACH. Evalach li mescouneus **GG**, Eualac **Q** (Anelac 26), Evelac **Ma, Ge.** Overcoming Tholomes **GG**6, 7, 10, 11, 12, 14, **Q**6, 15, 26, **Ma**3, **Ge**15, name changed to *Mordrains*, which see.

EVE Q37, **GG**24.

FACILE DAMSEL, Anonymous **Co, H, M,** *Antikonie* **W,** C14, **W, H, M**21.

FEIREFIZ W.

FELIX GG3, 11.

FISHER KING. Anonymous **Co,** Amfortas **W,** Brons **B, D,** Alain **GG.** Anonymous (?), **Q**¹, Pelles **Q**². In **M** the Fisher corresponds to Gonemans, In all the French works of the cycle the adjective rich is commonly applied to the Fisher. Splendour of court **PC**1——learned in black art **PC**3——old Surname given to Brons **B**12, to Alain **GG**43. and sick **D**prol, First meeting with Perceval **C**7, **W, D**11, *cf.* **PC**3, **M**6—— Vessel given to him **D**1——commanded to go to the West **D**6. **C**8, **W,** *cf.* **D**2, 12——C11. **W,** *cf.* **D**15, **M**21——**G**7, 8, 9, 16, 18, 19, 20—— Second meeting with Perceval **G**22, **Ma**1-7 or **Ge**1-5, **D**16, *cf.* **M**25—— **Ma**10——Third meeting with Perceval **Ma**22, **Ge**22, **W**——Grandfather of Galahad **Q**¹2, 26. See also Maimed King.

FLEGENTYNE GG22, 29, 31, 37, 59.

GAHMURET W.

GALAHAD (Galaad). *Father:* Lancelot **Q GG**——*Mother:* daughter of King Pelles **Q**¹, **GG,** or Fisher King **Q**²——Seat Perillous **Q**2——Sword **Q**3—— Quest proclaimed **Q**5——Evelac's Shield **Q**6, **GG**50——Devil-inhabited tomb **Q**7, *cf.* **Ge**17——Melians' discomforture **Q**8——Castle of Maidens **Q**9 ——overcoming of Lancelot and Perceval **Q**11——destined achiever of Quest **Q**13——rescue of Perceval **Q**16——Genealogy **Q**26, **GG**21, 30, 58——liken-

GALAHAD——GAWAIN.

_ng to a spotless bull **Q**29——overcoming of Gawain **Q**34——stay on ship **Q**35, 36——sword **Q**36——Maimed King **Q**² 36——capture of Castle Carchelois **Q**39——stag and lions **Q**40, *cf.* **GG**45——castle of the evil custom **Q**41——stay with father **Q**42——healing of Mordrains **Q**44, *cf.* **GG**39——cooling of fountain **Q**45——making white the Cross **GG**40——release of Symeu **Q**46, **GG**49——making whole sword **GG**44——release of Moys **GG**46——five years' wanderings **Q**47——arrival at King Peleur's **Q**¹, Maimed King's **Q**², witnessing of Grail and healing of Maimed King **Q**48-50——Sarras, crowning, death **Q**51, 52.

GALAHAD (GALAAD) son of Joseph **GG**8, 31, 34——King of Hocelice and ancestor of Urien **GG**49——founding of abbey for Symeu **GG**49.

GANSGUOTER H.

GANORT GG33, 35.

GARALAS G13.

GAWAIN. Gauvain **Co, Q, GG**, Gwalchmai **M**, Gawan **W**, Gawein **H**, Gawayne or Wawayne **T**——of the seed of Joseph of Arimathea **GG**48, Arthur's nephew **Co, Q**——conquers Blihos Bliheris **PC**2——allusion to his finding the Grail **PC**3——one of the knights met by Perceval in wood **M**1, **T**2——helps Perceval to disarm Red Knight **T**4——meeting with Perceval after blood-drops incident **C**10, **W**, **M**11——vow to release imprisoned maiden **C**11, **M**20——reproached by Guigambresil **C**12, (Kingrimur) **W**, (anonymous)

Joins in search for Grail with remainder of Table Round **D**2, **Q**, betraying knowledge of Maimed King **Q**5.

M20——tournament at Tiebaut's **C**13, (Lippaot) **W**, (Leigamar) **H**, *cf.* **D**15, where Perceval is hero but Gawain best knight after him——adventure with the facile damsel **C**14, (Antikonie) **W**, **H**, **M**21——injunction to seek bleeding lance **C**14, **W**, (Grail) **H**——adventure with Griogoras **C**16, (Urjan) **W**, (Lohenis) **H**——meeting with scornful damsel, Orgueilleuse, arrival at ferryman's **C**16, **W**——Magic Castle **C**17, **W**, *cf.* **GG**51——may not leave castle **C**17——second meeting with Orgueilleuse **C**18, **W**, (Mancipicelle) **H**——Ford Perillous, Guiromelant **C**18, (Gramoflanz) **W**, (Giremelanz) **H**——marriage with Orgueilleuse **W**,. (?) **C**18——arrival of Arthur to witness combat with Guiromelant **C**18 continued by **G**1, **W**, **H**——fight with Perceval **W**, *cf.* **T**7——reconciliation with Guiromelant **G**1, **W**, **H**——departure on Grail Quest and winning various talismans **H**——[first arrival at Grail Castle according to Montpellier MS. of **Co**]——Brun de Branlant, Brandalis **G**1 and 2——slaying of unknown knight and Quest to avenge him **G**3——Chapel of Black Hand **G**3——arrival at Grail Castle (first

Meeting with Ywain, Gheheris and confession to hermit **Q**10.

according to Mons MS. of **Co**), half successful **G**3, wholly successful **H**, *cf.* **M**25 found by Peredur at Castle of Talismans, and reference in **Q**51

Meeting with Hector de Mares **Q**29.

Welsh version——greetings of country folk **G**3, *cf.* **Ge**3——meeting with

Overcoming at Galahad's hand **Q**34.

his son **G**4——Mount Dolorous Quest **G**19——renewed Grail Quest, re-

JOSEPHES——MORDRAINS.

MORDRED——PERCEVAL.

18, Q26——GG19, 20, stay on island 21, *cf.* Q19——GG27, Q36——GG29 Crudel, and blinding by Grail 37, 38, Q15, Ge15——retires to hermitage GG39, Q44——his shield GG50, Q6.

MORDRED GG45.

MORDRET Ge6, 7.

MORGHE LA FÉE G18.

MORONEUS Q²26.

MORS DEL CALAN PC4.

MOUNT DOLOROUS G19, 20, Ge5.

MOYS, MOYSES (B).   Seat Perillous **B**10, 11, 12, **Dprol**, 1, **GG**41, 46.

NASCIENS GG, Q, Natiien **Ma**——Baptism **GG**14, **Q**6, 26, **Ma**3——Blinded by Grail **GG**16——**GG**18, 19, 20, 21, 22, turning isle and Solomon's ship, 23–27, **Q**35–37——**GG**28, 29, 30, 32, 33, Crudel 37, 38, (called Seraphe) **Q**15——**GG**39——his tomb **GG**50——death **GG**59——appears as hermit in Arthur's time **Q**4, 5, 6, 29.

NASCIENS, son of Celidoine, **GG**39.

NASCIENS, grandson of Celidoine **GG**30, 59.

NICODEMUS B3, 4, 5.

NOIRONS, *i.e.*, Nero **GG**3.

ORCANZ GG48.

ORGUEILLEUSE.   Orguellouse **C**, Orgeluse **W** = Mancipicelle **H, C**16—— **G**1, **W, H**.

OWAIN M, EWAYNE T, YONES C4, **YWAIN** "li aoutres" **Q**6, 9, 10, 29, **GG**49——meets Perceval **M**1, **T**2——helps him **M**3, **C**4.

PARTINAL Ma5, 8, 21, 22.

PECORINS PC4.

PELEUR Q¹5, 47, 48.

PELLEANS GG58.

PELLEHEM Q²35.

PELLES Q²1–3, 14, 27, 36, 44, 48, 50, **GG**59.

PERCEVAL Co, D, Q, GG; Parzival **W, H**; Peredur **M**; Percyvelle **T**.—*Father:* Bliocadrans **PC**; anonymous **Co, Q**; Alain **D**; Gahmuret **W**; Evrawc **M**; Percyvelle **T**; Pellehem **Q**². *Mother:* Anonymous **Co, D, Q, M**; Herzeloyde **W**; Acheflour (Arthur's sister) **T**——brought up in wood **C**1, **W, M, T**1——meets knights (5) **C**1, **W**, (3) **M**1, **T**2——leaves mother **C**1, **W, D, M**1, **T**2——first meeting with lady of tent **C**2, (Ieschute) **W, M**2, **T**3—— arrival at Arthur's Court **C**3, **W, D, M**3, **T**4——laughing prophetic damsel

Puts on red armour for love of Aleine, accomplishes the feat of the Seat Perillous, and sets forth on Quest **D**1 and 2.

C3, **W**, dwarves **M**3——slays *red* knight **C**4, (Ither of Gaheviez) **W**, (colour

Slays the red knight, Orgoillous Delandes, **D**3.

not specified) **M**3, **T**4——overcomes 16 Knights **M**4——burns witch **T**5—— arrival at house of first uncle, Gonemans **C**5, Gurnemanz **W**, Anonymous **M**5, and (different adventure partly corresponding to Ge8) **T**6——first arrival at castle of lady love, Blanchefleur **C**5, Conduiramur **W**, Anonymous **M**8, Lufamour **T**7——first arrival at Fisher King's **C**7, **W, D**11, **M**6——is

PERCEVAL—(*continued*).

reproached by wayside damsel, cousin : (Anonymous) **C**8, (Signne) **W**, **D**12, foster sister **M**7——second meeting with lady of tent **C**9, **W**, **M**9—— overcoming of Sorceresses of Gloucester **M**10——blood drops in the snow **C**10, **W**, **M**11——Adventures with Angharad Law Eurawc ; at the castle of the huge grey man ; serpent on the gold ring ; Mound of Mourning ; Addanc of the Lake ; Countess of Achievements **M**12–19——reproaches of the loathly damsel **C**11, (Kundrie) **W**, **M**20——Good Friday incident and confession to uncle **C**15, (Trevrezent) **W**, **D**14, **M**22——the Castle of the Horn **G**6——the Castle of the Chessboard **G**7, **D**4, **M**24——meeting with brother of Red Knight **G**8——Ford *amorous* **G**9, *perillous* **D**9——second meeting with Blanchefleur **G**10——meeting with Rosette and Le Beau Mauvais **G**11, **D**8——meeting with sister and visit to hermit **G**12, **D**5 and 6——the Castle of Maidens **G**12a——meeting with the hound-stealing damsel **G**13, **D**13, **M**24——meeting with the damsel of the white mule **G**14——tournament at Castle Orguellous **G**16 = **D**15 (Melianz de Lis) and **M**19 (?)—— Deliverance of knight in tomb **G**17——second visit to the Castle of the Chessboard **G**18, **D**13——delivery of Bagommedes **G**19——arrival at Mount Dolorous **G**20——the Black Hand in the Chapel **G**21——second arrival at Grail Castle **G**22–**Ma**1–7 and **G**e1, **D**16, (with final overcoming of Sorceresses of Gloucester) **M**25.

Overcomes Black Knight, slays giant and finds mother **T**9.

Perceval and Saigremors **Ma**8—— Second visit to Chapel of the Black Hand **Ma**11——the demon horse **Ma**

Encounter, unknown to either, with Galahad **Q**11. Meeting with recluse aunt **Q**13.

Assistance at the hands of the Red Knight **Q**16· 12, **Q**18——Stay on the island **Q**19,

Adventure of the ship **Q**33, essay to draw sword **Q**35.

and 20, and temptation by damsel 21, **Ma**13——Delivery of Dodinel's lady love **Ma**14——Tribuet **Ma**15 ——third meeting with Blanchefleur **Ma**16 —— meeting with coward knight **Ma**17——combat with Hector **Ma**20——slaying of Partinal **Ma**21

Receives Galahad's sword **Q**41, bears Galahad company for five years **Q**47 ——adjusts the sword at the Court of Pelles **Q**²48.

——third arrival at Grail Castle **Ma**22——learns death of his uncle the Fisher King from loathly damsel **Ma**23, **W**——retires into wilderness **Q**52, **Ma**24——dies **Q**52, goes to Palestine and dies (?) **T**.

Breaking of sword at the Gate of Paradise **G**e2——Blessings of the country folk for putting question **G**e3—— Mending of sword at forge of the serpent **G**e4——Accomplishment of the feat of the Perillous Seat **G**e5 ——adventures at sister's Castle, with Mordret, and at cousin's, Castle of Maidens **G**e6——encounter with Kex, Gauvain, and Tristan **G**e7, *cf.* **T**7——meeting with Gornumant **G**e8 (*cf.* **T**6) and fight with the resuscitating hag——third arrival at Blanchefleur's Castle, marriage **G**e9—— deliverance of maiden, abolition of evil custom, knight on fire **G**e10–12 —— obtains the promised shield **G**13——combat with the Dragon King **G**e14——arrival at abbey and story of Mordrains **G**e15, **Q**15—— the swan-drawn coffin **G**e16—— Devil in tomb **G**e17, *cf.* **Q**7—— deliverance of maiden from fountain **G**e18——punishment of traitress

INDEX II.

[This Index comprises the whole of the work with exception of the Summaries, for which see Index I. The references are to the pages. The entries apply solely to the page number or page group-number which they immediately precede, and not to all the pages between themselves and the next entry. In the majority of cases a simple number reference is given, and the fuller entries are to those points which the author wishes specially to emphasise.]